INFORMATION COMMUNICATION TECHNOLOGIES-APPLICATIONS

MLII-104

For

Master Degree in Library and Information Science (MLIS)

Useful For

IGNOU, Rai Technology University, KSOU (Karnataka), NIILM University, Bihar University (Muzaffarpur), Nalanda University, Jamia Millia Islamia, Vardhman Mahaveer Open University (Kota), Uttarakhand Open University, Kurukshetra University, Himachal Pradesh University, Seva Sadan's College of Education (Maharashtra), Lalit Narayan Mithila University, Andhra University, Pt. Sunderlal Sharma (Open) University (Bilaspur), Annamalai University, Bangalore University, Bharathiar University, Bharathidasan University, Centre for distance and open learning, Kakatiya University (Andhra Pradesh), KOU (Rajasthan), MPBOU (MP), MDU (Haryana), Punjab University, Tamilnadu Open University, Sri Padmavati Mahila Visvavidyalayam (Andhra Pradesh), Sri Venkateswara University (Andhra Pradesh), UCSDE (Kerala), University of Jammu, YCMOU, Rajasthan University, UPRTOU, Kalyani University, Banaras Hindu University (BHU) and all other Indian Universities.

GULLYBABA PUBLISHING HOUSE PVT. LTD.

ISO 9001 & ISO 14001 CERTIFIED CO.

Published by:

GullyBaba Publishing House Pvt. Ltd.

Regd. Office:
2525/193, 1st Floor, Onkar Nagar-A,
Delhi-110035
(From Kanhaiya Nagar Metro Station Towards Old Bus Stand)
Ph. 011-27387998, 27384836, 27385249
+919350849407

Branch Office:
1A/2A, 20, Hari Sadan, Tri Nagar,
Ansari Road, Daryaganj,
New Delhi-110002
Ph. 011-45794768

New Edition

Author: GullyBaba.Com Panel
ISBN: 978-93-90479-98-6

Disclaimer: Although the author and publisher have made every effort to ensure that the information in this book is correct, the author and publisher do not assume and hereby disclaim any liability to any party for any loss, damage, or disruption caused by errors or omissions, whether such errors or omissions result from negligence, accident, or any other cause.
If you find any kind of error, please let us know and get reward and or the new book free of cost.
The book is based on IGNOU syllabus. This is only a sample. The book/author/publisher does not impose any guarantee or claim for full marks or to be passed in exam. You are advised only to understand the contents with the help of this book and answer in your words.
All disputes with respect to this publication shall be subject to the jurisdiction of the Courts, Tribunals and Forums of New Delhi, India only.

PREFACE

The vital activities of libraries comprise collection development, reference services management, document delivery service, access to organised collections held by the library and assist users in information search and retrieval. There is the basic essentiality of information technology to manage the huge collection of library. It is indispensable to use modern technology to make library services faster. Libraries are facing a new generation of online users who are technologically savvy and integrate information access and use in all spheres of their lives to an unprecedented degree. Gradually, generation is changing with the time and the present generation's library users are too passionate with the technology. It is well known that all the success depends upon the satisfaction of the library users. So, in the present scenario the quickest library service is more approachable through the world-wide web and internet. To provide information to the 'right users' at 'any time', from 'anywhere' in the 'right way' is possible using web based technological settings.

The present GPH book ***'Information Communication Technologies –Applications (MLII-104)'*** describes how technology is being used in library services. It covers Database Design and Management, Library Automation, Library and Information Services and Internet Resources and Services.

The book is written especially in question & answer format to provide students the instant gratification of a correct answer. In this book, we have tried to solve all possible questions from the exams' point of view. Solutions of previous years' question papers have also been included to help students to understand the unique examination structure.

We hope that this book would not be only a favourite study material for the students but also can be a nice resource for teaching. An attempt has been carefully made to present this book more useful and meet the requirements and challenges of the course prescribed by Indian Universities. We wish you a successful and rewarding career ahead. Feedback in this regard is solicited.

– GPH Panel of Experts

ACKNOWLEDGEMENTS

Our compliments go to the **GullyBaba Publishing House Pvt. Ltd.,** and its meticulous team who have been enthusiastically working towards the perfection of the book.

Their teamwork, initiative and research have been very encouraging. Had it not been for their unflagging support, this work wouldn't have been possible. The creative freedom provided by them along with their aim of presenting the best to the reader has been a major source of inspiration in this work. Hope that this book would be successful.

– GPH Panel of Experts

PUBLISHER'S NOTE

The present book MLII-104 is targeted for examination purpose as well as enrichment. With the advent of technology and the Internet, there has been no dearth of information available to all; however, finding the relevant and qualitative information, which is focussed, is an uphill task.

We at **GullyBaba Publishing House Pvt. Ltd.,** have taken this step to provide quality material which can accentuate in-depth knowledge about the subject. GPH books are a pioneer in the effort of providing unique and quality material to its readers. With our books, you are sure to attain success by making use of this powerful study material. Provided book is just a reference book based on the syllabus of particular University/Board. For a profound information, see the textbooks recommended by the University/Board.

Our site **gullybaba.com** is a vital resource for your examination. The publisher wishes to acknowledge the significant contribution of the Team Members and our experts in bringing out this publication and highly thankful to Almighty God, without His blessings, this endeavor wouldn't have been successful.

– Publisher

TOPICS COVERED

CONTENTS

QUESTION PAPERS

CHAPTER 1

DATABASE DESIGN AND MANAGEMENT

INTRODUCTION

An organisation must have accurate and reliable data for effective decision-making. To this end, the organisation maintains records on the various facets maintaining relationships among them. Such related data are called a database. A database system is an integrated collection of related files, along with details of the interpretation of the data contained therein. Basically, database system is nothing more than a computer-based record keeping system, i.e. a system whose overall purpose is to record and maintain information/data.

A database management system (DBMS) is a software system that allows access to data contained in a database. The objective of the DBMS is to provide a convenient and effective method of defining, storing and retrieving the information contained in the database. The DBMS interfaces with the application programs, so that the data contained in the database can be used by multiple applications and users. In addition, the DBMS exerts centralised control of the database, prevents fraudulent or unauthorised users from accessing the data, and ensures the privacy of the data. Database searching is used here to mean searches carried out with the objective of retrieving relevant information including Internet/Web searches, online searches, searching of CD-ROM database and searching of OPACs.

Q1. What is database approach? Enumerate the attitudinal factors that contribute to database approach.

Or

Write short note on Approaches to database.

[Dec-2017, Q.No.-5 (a)]

Ans. Data accessed through computers has been stored on different storage media in the form of individual files. Files proved to be quite satisfactory so long as computerisation was limited to a few application areas and use of computers is restricted. However, the actual users grew in number, with the advent of online sharing systems, with the advent of online sharing systems, the file system gave rise to many serious problems. The discipline of database systems evolved in response to these problems.

Database approach was developed to overcome the limitations of the traditional file-oriented approach. In database approach, data is regarded as an important resource that must be managed like other resources such as people, finance, materials, equipment, etc. In a database system, all data are stored in a single repository called the database. An integrated database provides a consistent and compact view of the organisation's data for all user departments. The database concept is rooted in an attitude of sharing valuable data resources, releasing control of those resources to a common responsible authority, and cooperating in the maintenance of those shared data resources. Each user is provided a unique view of the database depending on his/her information needs. The database approach is not dependent on any particular structure of data. Many of these concepts can be applied to files as well. Databases are fundamentally tools to allow people to organise and manipulate large amounts of data using the power of the computer to quickly translate and deliver that information in a human-readable format. They are compact, fast, easy to use, and allow easy sharing of data between multiple users, and are secure. However, it may be emphasised that the database approach is rooted in the attitude of:

- Sharing valued data resources
- Releasing control of those resources to a common responsible authority
- Cooperating in the maintenance of those shared data resources.

Q2. Explain the term 'Database'.

Ans. A database is a collection of related information stored in a computer so that it is available to many users for different purposes. The content of a database is obtained by combining data from different sources in an organisation, so that the relevant data are available to all users and redundant data can be eliminated or at least minimised.

A database holds recorded data. The content may be textual, graphics, images. etc. Therefore, it is an essential component of all information storage and retrieval systems (IRS), and for the generation of information products and services there from. In setting up an IRS, the first task is to design the database. Hence, the importance of learning and practicing the design and development of databases of various types, – their content, organisation and indexing is required for fast and precise retrieval of information. Databases may be created and stored in the hard disk of a personal computer (PC), or if it is small (few records), on a floppy disk, or ported on to a high density disk (e.g. 40 MB, 120 MB. etc.) or onto CD-ROM, or on magnetic tape, or on a mainframe computer (server) which may be located far away. The latter may be accessible via a local area network (LAN), wide area network (WAN), the Internet. etc. More than one user from different locations can use a database simultaneously. Thus, the design of the database and the software used should be such that it can be accessed and/or manipulated by two or more users simultaneously, for example in a networked environment.

Q3. What are the features of Database? Describe different types of database.

Ans. The main purpose of a database is that the data in the database should be used for a variety of different applications. To achieve this it is important for a database to possess the following features:

(1) it must be substantially non-redundant (that is to say that the database should not have duplication of data) because duplication of data leads to difficulty in ensuring data consistency, and results in the wastage of storage space.

(2) it must be program-independent so that the data can be moved or restructured without the need to make alterations to programs. This concept is known as 'data independence'.

(3) it must be capable of being used by all programs.

(4) it must include all necessary data relationships, to support the variety of different uses to which data is put.

(5) it must have common approach to retrieval, additions and deletions and amendments to data.

Types of Database: Databases may be stored in magnetic or optical media such as disks and accessed either locally or remotely. This may include access to an organisations database covering transactions and financial records or other databases that might be accessed remotely.

In one view, databases can be classified according to types of content: bibliographic, fulltext, numeric, and images (Allan Leake, 2000)

The type of databases can be classified by:

(1) Type of Content: Databases that might be available to information users in public areas and which might be accessed remotely via an online host computer, or more locally on CD-ROM can be categorised into:

(i) Reference Databases: The reference databases refer or point the user to another source such as document, an organisation or an individual for additional information, or for the text of document. The Reference databases can be further divided into:

- **(a) Bibliographic databases,** which include citations or bibliographic references, and sometimes abstracts of literature. They tell the user what has been written and in which source (e.g. journal title conference proceedings) it can be located and if they provide abstract, will summarise the original document.
- **(b) Catalogue databases,** which show the stock of a given library or monographs, journal titles and other items the library has in stock, but do not give much information on the content is rather different from that of the other bibliographic databases, they are worth identifying as separate category.
- **(c) Referral databases,** which offer references to information or data such as the names and addresses or originations, and other directory type data.

(ii) Primary Databases: Primary Source databases contain the original source data, and are one type of electronic document. After successful consultation of a source databases the user should have the information that is required and should not to seek information in an original source (as is the case with reference databases). Data are available in machine readable form instead of, or as well as printed form. Primary databases can be further divided as:

- (a) Numeric databases, which contain numerical data of various kinds, including statistics and survey data;
- (b) Full text databases of newspaper items, technical specification and software;
- (c) Text numeric databases, which contain a mixture of textual and numeric data (such as company annual reports) and handbook data (Rowley, 1996)
- (d) Image Database is a collection of digitised images. It is maintained primarily to support research in image processing, image analysis, and machine vision

(2) Type of Organisation: The optimal structure depends on the natural organisation of the application's data, and on the application's requirements, which include transaction rate (speed), reliability, maintainability, scalability, and cost.

By organisation of contents, databases can be categorised into:

(i) **Logical or Conceptual Database:** It is concerned with how the data is logically organised and how the data can be retrieved for information purposes. In case access is required to a series of linked files, it is necessary to have guidelines regarding allocation of data to specific files within the database system, and defining the optimum links between files. Based on the model followed for the structuring of data there are three basic types of databases and the associated DBMS namely: hierarchical, network and relational.

(ii) **Hierarchical Database:** In this kind of databases, data are stored in the form of a hierarchy. Hierarchy database is like a tree structure which has one root and many branches. It uses the concept of parent child relationship. In this type of database a single file may have many relationships with many files.

(iii) **Network Database:** Compared to hierarchical database, network database eliminates unnecessary duplication of data with associated errors and costs. In this database, a parent can have many children and a child can also have many parent records. These records are physically linked through linked lists.

(iv) **Relational Database:** In this type of database, data is stored in two-dimensional table (rows, and columns), this is a relation between two tables exists with something in common or some data which these two tables share. Each column of a table is referred to as an attribute and the values, which it may contain is called domain of values.

Q4. What do you mean by Database in Library and Information Science?

Or

Discuss database from the point of view of library and information science.

Ans. Database in Library and information Science is defined as "an organised and generally unlinked set of machine readable bibliographic or information source records". Taken collectively, these records constitute a growing file of information that can be used to obtain a variety of products for a range of purpose. These information files are defined according to their scope and subject coverage in many ways. The variety of database types has grown over the last two decades and includes specialist database usually limited in scope to particular subject areas.

In order to understand the concept of bibliographic database, it is necessary to have some basic knowledge relating to files and records. A file is a collection of similar records, with relationship defined between the records. A record is the information contained in the database relating to one document or item. For example in a catalogue database, a record may contain all the information pertaining to a book. If it is a source database, a record may contain the contents of a directory entry or an article of a journal. Each record in a file is composed of a number of fields. Generally, there are two types of fields; fixed length fields and variable length fields. A fixed length field is one which contains the same predetermined number of characters in each record. Fixed length fields are easy and quick to code. They are ideal for such data elements as ISBNs and other type of information, which will be same in each record. On the other hand, a variable length field will consist of different lengths in different records. Variable length fields pose a problem for the computer as it cannot recognise where one field ends and other starts. This aspect needs a mechanism to flag the beginnings and ends of the fields. In other words, there should be codes to indicate the start as well as the termination of variable length fields. MARC record format provides such a mechanism. Normally, bibliographic databases use a mixture of fixed and variable length fields in order to accommodate the requirements of varying kinds of data. Also, within fields there can be units of information that could be designated as sub-fields. Sub-fields need to be flagged so that they can easily be identified.

This method of dividing records into fields and sub-fields allows sub-sets of the database to be selected and retrieved as per the query criterion. It will also facilitate partitioning of the database for the purposes of management and add precision for retrieval.

Clearly, what can be retrieved depends mainly on what is contained in it and the way in which information has been structured. The methods available for structuring of data have already been discussed under database features. One point to be added here, relates to inverted files. In the inverted file approach there may be two or three separate files. Generally, the two-file approach is commonly followed. This approach uses two files, namely, the text file and the index file. The text file contains the actual records while the index file provides access to these records. The index file contains a record for each of the indexed terms from all of the records in the database, arranged in an alphabetical order. Each term is accompanied by information on the frequency of its occurrence in the database in which it is to be located, the record in which it is entered. When a new record is added to the database, it is necessary to update the index file. The text file and the index file are together used for database search. This principle is used in software packages like CDS/ISIS.

Another important concept, which needs to be understood in the context of bibliographic database, is record format. In order to facilitate exchange of bibliographic records between different computer systems, attempts have been made to develop standard record formats. Such formats have been found to be exceedingly useful in cataloguing applications. The standard record formats include the ones like MARC, UNIMARC and MARC-21. etc. These standard formats also embody agreements on the elements of a bibliographic record. The MARC format includes nearly 61 data elements, of which 25 are directly searchable. It is compatible with the latest editions of AACR-2 and DDC. The MARC format is hospitable and can be modified to suit the varied needs.

Q5. Discuss in brief the different levels of database architecture.

Or

Write a short note on "different levels of database architecture". [June-2018, Q.No.-5 (a)]

Ans. The architecture of database provides three separate levels. These three levels are the external level, the conceptual level and the internal level:

- **External Level:** This is the one which is concerned with the way the data is seen by individual users. A user can be either an application programmer or an end user. Most of the users of the database are not concerned with all the information contained in the database. Instead, they need only a part of the database relevant to them. For example, even though an institutes database stores a lot of information, the librarian may not be interested in information about the staff and its salary, etc. This level or view is a restricted view of the database and the same database may provide a number of different other views for different users.

  An external view is thus the content of the database as seen by a particular user. For example, a user from the Personnel Department might regard the database as a collection of data concerning departments and employees, and might be unaware of the product supplier data seen by users in the purchasing department. Each external view is defined by means of an external schema, which consists basically of definitions of each of the various external record types in that external view. For example, the employee external record type might be defined as a six-character employee number field plus a five-digit (decimal) salary field, and so on.

- **Conceptual Level:** This level of abstraction describes what data are actually stored in the database. It also describes the relationships existing among data. Thus, conceptual view is a representation of the entire information content of the database. The conceptual view is defined by means of the conceptual schema, which includes definitions of each of the various conceptual record types. A conceptual record is not similar to the external record on the one hand nor to stored record on the other. The conceptual view is a view of the total database content, and the conceptual schema is a definition of that view. The user at this level is just concerned about the information stored in the database and not the way it is stored. For example, at the conceptual level, the database contains information about an entity type employee. Each individual employee has an employee number (say, six characters), a department–number (four characters), a salary (five decimal digits), etc.

- **Internal Level:** This is a low-level representation of the entire database. This level is also sometimes termed as physical level. It describes how the data is actually stored on the storage medium. The internal view is described by means of the internal schema which defines the various record types, how stored fields are represented, what sequence the stored records are in, etc. Thus this level is the one closest to physical storage. For example, at the internal level employees are represented as a stored record type EMP (for employee), twenty bytes long.

Q6. Explain the term 'Data Structure'. Discuss the major types of data structure.

Or

Define data structure and its need. Explain the three major types of data structure.

Ans. Data are represented by data values held temporarily within program's data area or recorded permanently on a file. Often the different data values are related to each other. To enable programs to make use of these relationships, these data values must be in an organised form. The organised collection of data is called a data structure. Thus, an understanding of data structures is important in gaining an understanding of database management system.

There are three major types of data structures:

(1) Linked Lists: The Linked list is a chain of structures in which each structure consists of data as well as pointer, which stores the address (link) of the next logical structure in the list. A linked list is a data structure used to maintain a dynamic series of data. With a linked list, any data element can be stored separately. A pointer is then used to linked to the next data item.

Fig. 1.1 illustrates the basic concept of linked lists. In this example each row of data is stored separately. Then an index is created on the field (key) Last Name. However, each element of the index is stored separately. An index element consists of three parts: the key value, a pointer to the rest of the data of that row, and a pointer to the next index element. To retrieve data sequentially, start at the first element (Chauhan) and follow the link (pointer) to the next element (Dhote). Each element of the index is found by following the link to the next element. The data pointer in each index element provides the entire data row for that key value. The strength of a linked list lies in its ability to easily and rapidly insert and delete data.

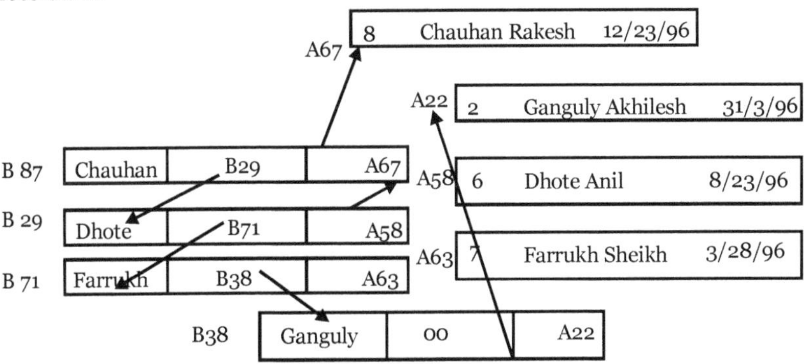

Fig. 1.1: An illustration of linked list

(2) Inverted Lists: Inverted lists may be viewed simply as index tables of pointers stored separately from the data records rather than embedded in pointer fields in the stored records themselves. Distinction should be made between nondense and dense lists. In case of a nondense list only a few of the records in the file are part of the list while a dense list is one with a pointer for most or all of the records in the file. Processing for unique secondary keys (those having 1:1 association with primary keys) is somewhat different than those with 1:M associations with primary keys. In the former case, dense indexes are generated while the later gives nondense indexes. Examples of inverted lists are given below:

List 1

Company	Area	Primary Key
Digital	Computer	1245
Ford	Auto	1175
GM	Auto	1323
Intel	Computer	1231
Lockheed	Aerospace	1152

List 2

Company Symbol	Primary Key
DEC	1245
F	1175
GM	1323
INTL	1231
L	1152

Fig. 1.2: Dense inverted lists

The above lists are dense since there is one-to-one relationship between both company name and primary key and company symbol and primary key.

Fig. 1.3 gives an example of non-dense inverted list for area (relationship between area and primary key is one-to-many).

Area	Primary Key
Aerospace	1152
Auto	1175, 1323
Computer	1231, 1245

Fig. 1.3: Nondense inverted list

The lists are said to be inverted because company names (or area names) have been alphabetised and the corresponding primary keys have been "inverted" or rearranged accordingly.

(3) B-Trees: B-trees are special m–ary balanced trees used in databases because their structure allows records to be inserted, deleted and retrieved with guaranteed worst case performance. A B-Tree is a specialised multiway tree. In a B-Tree each node may contain a large number of keys. The number of sub trees of each node may also be large.

A B-Tree is designed to branch out in this large number of directions and to contain a lot of keys in each node so that height of the tree is relatively small.

This means that only a small number of nodes must be read from disk to retrieve an item.

A B-Tree of order m is multiway search tree of order m such that

(i) All leaves are on the bottom level

(ii) All internal nodes (except root node) have atleast m/2 (non empty) children

(iii) The root node can have as few as 2 children if it is an internal node and can have no children if the root node is a leaf node

(iv) Each leaf node must contain atleast (m/2) – 1 keys.

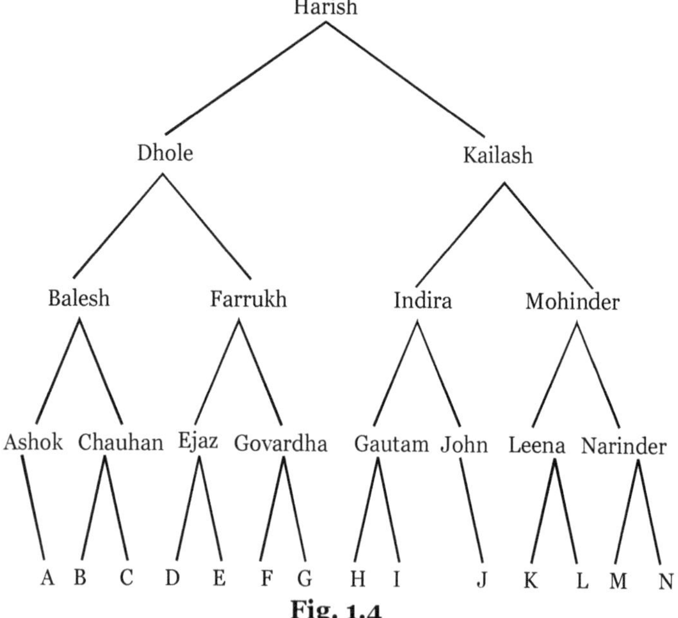

Fig. 1.4

Q7. Write short notes on the followings:

(a) Memory Hierarchy **[Dec-2019, Q.No.-5 (b)]**

Ans. The term Memory Hierarchy refers to a memory system which is partitioned into two or more components which range from high-volume/low speed devices for long-term storage to low- volume/high speed devices for working storage. Computer storage media form a memory hierarchy that includes two main categories of storage:

(1) Primary Memory: This is also known as primary storage, primary memory, main storage, internal storage, main memory, and RAM (Random Access Memory); all these terms are used interchangeably by people in computer circles. Primary Memory is the part of the computer that holds data and instructions for processing. Although closely associated with the central processing unit, primary memory is separate from it. Primary Memory stores program instructions or data for only as long as the program they pertain to is in operation. Keeping these items in primary memory when the program is not running is not feasible for three reasons:

(i) Most types of memory only store items while the computer is turned on; data is destroyed when the machine is turned off.

(ii) If more than one program is running at once (often the case on large computers and sometimes on small computers), a single program can not lay exclusive claim to primary memory.

(iii) There may not be room in memory to hold the processed data.

(2) Secondary Storage: As all of the above categories are volatile memories, there must be some mechanism to 'save' the data and program permanently. Secondary Storage devices facilitate this.

(b) RAID Technology

Ans. RAID (Redundant Array of Inexpensive Disks or Drives, or Redundant Array of Independent Disks) is a data storage virtualisation technology that combines multiple physical disk drive components into one or more logical units for the purposes of data redundancy, performance improvement, or both. A major advance in secondary storage technology is represented by RAID technology. The RAID idea has been developed into an elaborate set of alternative RAID architectures.

The main goal of RAID is to even out the widely different rates of performance improvement of disks against those in memory and microprocessors. While RAM capacities have quadrupled every two to three years, disk access times are improving at less than 10 per cent per year, and disk transfer rates are improving at roughly 20 per cent per year. Though disk capacities are improving at a fast rate, the speed and access time improvements are of much smaller magnitude.

The problem is overcome by using a large array of small independent disks acting as a single high-performance logical disk. A concept called data striping is used. It utilises parallelism to improve disk performance. Data striping distributes data transparently over multiple disks to make them appear as a single large, fast disk. Striping improves overall I/O performance by allowing multiple I/Os to be serviced in parallel, thus providing high overall transfer rates. Data striping also accomplishes load balancing among disks. It should be noted that data can be read or written only one block at a time, so a typical transfer contains 512 bytes (block size = 512 bytes). Data striping can be applied at a finer granularity by breaking up a byte of data into bits and spreading the bits to multiple disks. Using bit-level data striping with 8-bit bytes, eight physical disks may be considered as one logical disk with an eight fold increase in data transfer rate. Each disk participates in each I/O request and the total data read per request is eight times. Data striping may also be done at block level which distributes blocks of a file across disks. In addition to improving performance, RAID is also used to improve reliability by storing redundant information on disks. One technique for introducing redundancy is called mirroring. Data is written redundantly on two identical physical disks that are treated as one logical disk. If a disk fails, the other is used until the first is repaired. Thus RAID technology has contributed significantly to improving the performance and reliability of data storage on disks.

(c) Indexes

Ans. Indexing is a way to optimise the performance of a database by minimising the number of disk accesses required when a query is processed. It is a data structure technique which is used to quickly locate and access the data in a database.

An index (sometimes also referred as a list) can be used in two ways. First, it can be used for sequential access to the indexed file. i.e., access according to the values of the indexed field by imposing an ordering of the indexed file. Second, it can also be used for direct access to individual records in the indexed file on the basis of a given value for that same field. In general, indexing speeds up retrieval but may slow down update.

Address/Pointer

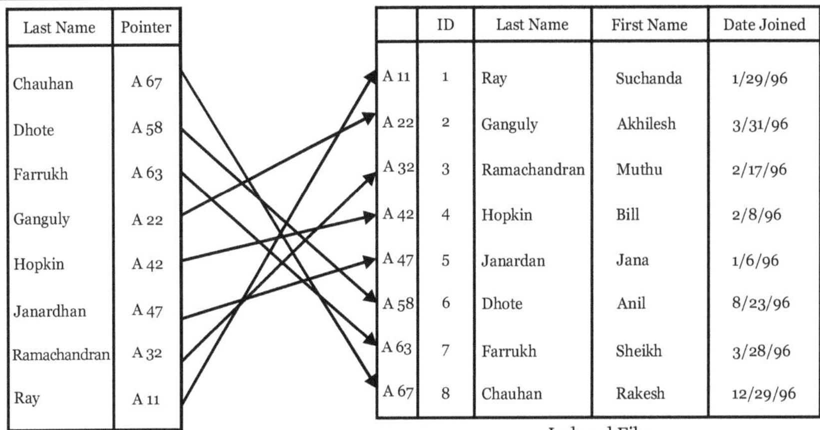

Fig. 1.5: An Illustration of Indexes

(d) Binary Search

Ans. Binary searching is a technique used to substantially lessen the time required to search the indexes of lengthy inverted lists (see 2.3.2). In this technique, the value sought is first compared to the value in the middle of the list. This indicates whether the value sought is in the top or bottom half of the list. The value sought is then compared with the middle entry of the appropriate half. This indicates which fourth the value is in. Then the value is compared to the middle of the fourth, and so on until the desired value is found. Thus the binary search keeps splitting the data set in half until it finds the desired value.

An example of binary search is shown in Fig. To find the entry for Janardan find the middle of the list (Gautam). Janardan is post Gautam so split the second half in half (Kamla). Keep splitting the remainder in half until Janardan is found.

Fig. 1.6: An Example of Binary Search

Q8. What do you mean by Files and their organisations?

Or

Define 'File Organisation' and mention its difference with access method. Explain different access methods.

[Dec-2017, Q.No.- 1.2]

Or

Discuss the meaning of file organisation and the implications of access method on it. Describe different file access methods.

Or

What do you understand by 'File Organisation' and 'Access Methods'? Discuss different access methods applied to file organisation. **[Dec-2019, Q.No.-1]**

Ans. File Organisation refers to the logical relationships among various records that constitute the file, particularly with respect to the means of identification and access to any specific record. In simple terms, storing the files in certain order is called file organisation.

In many cases, all records in a file are of the same record type. If every record in the file has exactly the same size (in bytes), the file is said to be made of fixed-length records. If different records in the file have different sizes, the file is said to be made up variable length records. A file may have variable-length records for several reasons:

- The file records are of the same record type, but one or more fields are of varying sizes (variable-length fields).

- The file records are of the same record type but one or more fields may have multiple values for individual records. Such a field is called repeating field and a group of values for the field is often called a repeating group.
- The file records are of the same record type, but one or more fields are optional.
- The file has records of different record types and hence of varying size (mixed file). This would occur if related records of different types were clustered (placed together) on disk blocks.

The records of a file must be allocated to disk blocks because a block is a unit of data transfer between disk and memory. The division of a track (on storage medium) into equal sized disk blocks is set by the operating system during disk formatting. The hardware address of a block comprises a surface number, track number and block number. Buffer – a contiguous reserved area in main storage that holds one block has also an address. For a read command, the block from disk is copied into the buffer, whereas for a write command the contents of the buffer are copied into the disk block. Sometimes several contiguous blocks, called a cluster, may be transferred as a unit. In such cases buffer size is adjusted to cluster size.

When the block size is larger than the record size each block will contain numerous records, while there can be files with large records that cannot fit in one block. In the latter case the records can span more than one block. Here it is worthwhile to note the difference between the terms File Organisation and Access Method. A file organisation refers to the organisation of the data of a file into records, blocks and access structures; this includes the way the records and blocks are placed on the storage medium and interlinked. An access method on the other hand, provides a group of operations – such as find, read, modify, delete, etc., — that can be applied to a file. In general, it is possible to apply several access methods to a file organisation. Some access methods, though, can be applied only to files organised in certain ways. For example, we cannot apply an indexed access method to a file without an index.

Sequential Access Method: It is the simplest method to store and retrieve data from a file. Sequential organisation simply means storing and sorting in physical on tape or disk. In a sequential organisation a records can be added only at the end of the file. That is in a sequential file, records are stored one after the other without concern for the actual value of the data in the records. It is not possible to insert a record in the middle of the file without re-writing the file. In a sequential file update, transaction records are in the same sequence as in the master file. Records from ' both files are matched, one record at a time, resulting in an updated master file. It is a characteristic of sequential files that all records are stored by position; the first one is at the first position, the second one occupies the second position and third is at third and so on. There are no addresses or location assignments in sequential files.

Indexed Sequential Access Method: The second way of accessing records stored in the system is through an index. The basic form of an index includes a record key and the storage address for a record. To find a record, when the storage address is unknown it is necessary to scan the records. However, if an index is used, the search will be faster since it takes less time to search an index than an entire file of data.

Indexed file offers the simplicity of sequential file while at the same time offering a capability for direct access. The records must be initially stored on the file in sequential order according to a key field. In addition, as the records are being recorded on the file, one or more indexes are established by the system to associate the key field value(s) with the storage location of the record on the fie. These indexes are then used by the system to allow a record to be directly accessed.

To find a specific record when the file is stored under an indexed organisation, the index is searched first to find the key of the record wanted. When it is found, the corresponding storage address is noted and then the program can access the record directly. This method uses a sequential scan of the index, followed by direct access to the appropriate record The index helps to speed up the search compared with a sequential file, but it is slower than the direct addressing.

Direct Access Method: Another method is direct access method also known as relative access method. A filed-length logical record that allows the program to read and write record rapidly. in no particular order. The direct access is based on the disk model of a file since disk allows random access to any file block. For direct access, the file is viewed as a numbered sequence of block or record. There is no restriction on the order of reading and writing for a direct access file.

A block number provided by the user to the operating system is normally a relative block number, the first relative block of the file is 0 and then 1 and so on.

Q9. Describe the concept of Physical Database Design.

Ans. Database design is done before building it to meet needs of end-users within a given application/ information-system that the database is intended to support. The database design defines the needed data and data structures that such a database comprises.

The process of database design process involves the task of converting logical model to working physical model. The objective of physical database design is to fulfil the performance requirements of a set of applications by optimising the use of the DBMS. Key areas include: optimising the index configuration, data placement and storage allocation.

Inputs to Physical Database Design

(1) Logical structure of Database (Normalised relations).

(2) Definition of attributes – data type, integrity control, error handling.

(3) Choice of RDBMS

(i) Hierarchical

(ii) Network

(iii) Relational (DB2, MySQL)

(iv) Object relational (Oracle 8i/9i)

(4) Estimation of database size growth rate and frequency of usage.

(5) Requirements for backup, recovery, response time and retention time.

Guidelines for Database Design: The following are various guidelines for Database Design:

(1) Ensure that the data stored in the files (database tables) are atomic. Data stored in the atomic form can be combined later to generate data in specific form;

(2) Every table must have a primary key which identifies each record in the table distinctly. Descriptive and meaningful name is to be used while naming a field in the table (For example, use product_id instead of ID);

(3) Use single column primary key whenever possible. As most of the join operations are made on primary key and composite primary keys make the operation slower;

(4) Use numeric key whenever possible;

(5) Use primary key name as foreign key for better readability;

(6) Avoid allowing null values to go into the columns that have discrete range of possible values; and

(7) Avoid multiple tables with similar structure when one table is sufficient.

The following aspects influence the physical database design:

(1) Analysing the database queries and transactions: For each query we should specify:

(i) The files that will be accessed by the query.

(ii) The attributes on which any selection conditions for the query are specified.

(iii) The attributes on which any join conditions or conditions to link multiple tables for the query are specified.

(iv) The attributes whose values will be retrieved by the query.

The attributes at (ii) and (iii) are candidates for definition of access structures. For each update transaction we should specify:

(i) The files that will be updated.

(ii) The type of operation on each file (insert, update or delete).

(iii) The attributes on which the selection conditions for a delete or update are specified.

(iv) The attributes whose value will be changed by the update operation.

Here the attributes at (iii) are candidates for access structures and attributes at (iv) are candidates for avoiding an access structure since modifying them will require updating the access structures.

(2) Analysing the expected frequency of queries and transactions: This yields the expected frequency of using each attribute in each file as a selection attribute or a join attribute, over all the queries and transactions.

(3) Analysing the time constraint of queries and transactions: Some queries and transactions may have stringent performance constraints with respect to response time. The selection attributes used by queries and transactions with such time constraints become higher priority candidates for primary access structures.

(4) Analysing the expected frequencies of update operations: A minimum number of access paths should be specified for a file that is updated frequently, because updating the access paths themselves slows the update operations.

Based on the preceding information one can address the physical database design decisions about indexing. The attributes whose values are required in equality or range conditions (selection operation) and those that are keys or that participate in join conditions (join operation) require access paths. The performance of queries largely depends upon what indexes or hashing schemes exist to expedite the processing of selections and joins. On the other hand, during insert, delete, or update operations, existence of indexes adds to the overhead.

The following points may be kept in view while taking decisions for indexing:

(1) The attribute, which is to be indexed, must be a key or there must be some query that uses that attribute either in selection condition (equality or range of values) or in a join.

(2) An index can be made on one or multiple attributes. If multiple attributes from one relation are involved together in several queries, a multi attribute index is warranted.

(3) Clustering index (index created on a non-key field, i.e., if numerous records in a file can have the same value for the field) can be greatly useful in range queries. If several attributes require range queries relative benefits must be evaluated before deciding which attributes to cluster on. At most one index per table can be a primary or clustering index.

(4) RDBMSs generally use B^+ trees for indexing. ISAM and hash indexes are also provided in some systems. B^+ trees support both equality and range queries on the attribute used as the search key. Hash indexes work well with equality conditions, particularly during joins.

Q10. What is Database Management System (DBMS)? Discuss its need and goals.

Ans. A database management system (DBMS) is a software package designed to define, manipulate, retrieve and manage data in a database. A DBMS generally manipulates the data itself, the data format, field names, record structure and file structure. It also defines rules to validate and manipulate this data.

Need of DBMS: File based systems are an early attempt to computerise the manual filing system. For example, a manual file can be set up to hold all the correspondence relating to a particular matter as a project, product, task, client or employee. In an organisation there could be many such files which may be labeled and stored. The same could be done at homes where file relating to bank statements, receipts, tax payments. etc., could be maintained.

What do we do to find information from these files? For retrieval of information, the entries could be searched sequentially. Alternatively, an indexing system could be used to locate the information.

The manual filing system works well when the number of items to be stored is small. It even works quite well when the number of items stored is quite large and they are only needed to be stored and retrieved. However, a manual file system crashes when cross-referencing and processing of information in the files is carried out. For example, in a university a number of students are enrolled who have the options of doing various courses. The university may have separate files for the personal details of students, fees paid by them, the number and details of the courses taught, the number and details of each faculty member in various departments. Consider the effort to answer the following queries.

- Annual fees paid by the students of Computer science department.
- Number of students requiring transport facility from a particular area.
- This year's turnover of students as compared to last year.
- Number of students opting for different courses from different departments.

Goals of DBMS: The database management systems have the following goals:

- To provide retrieval flexibility. It should be relatively easy to link data from different files.
- To facilitate reduction of data duplication and elimination of multiple copies of a master file. Data redundancy control helps in overcoming updating problems and promotes data integrity.
- To ensure high level of data independence. The data is hidden from the programming language, Operating system and

processing environment. It should be up to DBMS to convert the stored data into a form that could be used in whatever language the programmer desires to use.

Q11. Briefly define the following terms:

(a) Data and Information

Ans. Data is the raw material from which information is derived as the end product.

Data represents a set of characters that have no meaning on their own. i.e., it consists of just symbols. On processing, meaning is attached to data, which transforms into information.

To illustrate the difference between these two terms let us consider an example. The digits 050643 as such have no meaning. But if we are told that the first two digits represented a month, the next two digits, a day of the month and the last two, a year, then the set 050643 may represent the date of birth of a person. Processed in another manner the same digits written as 643050 may represent the telephone number of an individual.

(b) Data Hierarchy

Ans. Hierarchy in the organisation of data in descending order of complexity is represented in the fig.

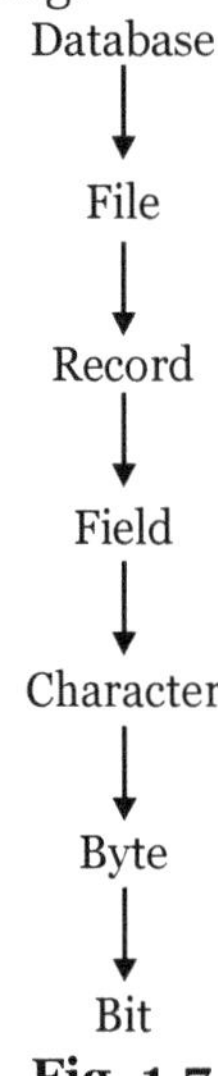

Fig. 1.7

From this hierarchy it is clear that a database is made up of files. Files are composed of records and each record consists of fields or data items. Each field is composed of characters, which are made up of bytes. And lastly, bytes decompose into bits.

(c) Data Integrity

Ans. Data Integrity refers to validity and consistency of data. Data Integrity means that the data should be accurate and consistent. This is done by providing some checks or constraints. These are consistency rules that the database is not permitted to violate. Constraints may apply to data items within a record or relationships between records. For example, the age of an employee can be between 18 and 70 years only. While entering the data for the age of an employee, the database should check this. However, if Grades of any student are entered, the data can be erroneously entered as Grade C for Grade A. In this case DBMS will not be able to provide any check as both A and C are of the same data type and are valid values.

(d) Data Independence

Ans. In the file-based system, the descriptions of data and logic for accessing the data are built into each application program making the program more dependent on data. A change in the structure of data may require alterations to programs. Database Management systems separates data descriptions from data. Hence it is not affected by changes. This is called Data Independence, where details of data are not exposed. DBMS provides an abstract view and hides details. For example, logically we can say that the interface or window to data provided by DBMS to a user may still be the same although the internal structure of the data may be changed.

Q12. Discuss the evolution of DBMS.

Ans. The introduction of the term database coincided with the availability of direct access storage (disks and drums) from the mid-1960s onwards. The term represented a contrast with the tape-based systems of the past, allowing shared interactive use rather than daily batch processing.

In the earliest database systems, efficiency was perhaps the primary concern, but it was already recognised that there were other important objectives. One of the key aims was to make the data independent of the logic of application programmes, so that the same data could be made available to different applications.

The first generation of database systems were navigational and pointers from one record to another. The two main data models at this time were the hierarchic model, epitomised by IBM's IMS system and the Codasyl model (Network model, implemented in a number of products such as IDMS.

The Relational model was first proposed in 1970. Later it was insisted that applications should search for data by content, rather than by following links. This was considered necessary to allow the content of the database to evolve without constant rewriting of applications. Relational systems placed heavy demands on processing resources, and it was not until the mid 1980s that computing hardware became powerful enough to allow them to be widely deployed. By the early 1990s, however, relational systems were dominant for all large-scale data processing applications, and they remain dominant today (2011) except in niche areas. The dominant database language is the standard SQL for the Relational model, which has influenced database languages also for other data models.

As the relational model emphasises search rather than navigation, it does not make relationships between different entities explicit in the form of pointers, but it represents using primary keys and foreign keys. While this is a good basis for a query language, it is less well suited as a modeling language. For this reason a different model, the Entity-relationship model which emerged shortly later (1976), gained popularity for database design.

During 1970s, database technology has kept pace with the increasing resources becoming available from the computing platform: notably the rapid increase in the capacity and speed (and reduction in price) of disk storage, and the increasing capacity of main memory.

Q13. Write down the functions and components of DBMS.

Ans. Functions of DBMS: A database management system is, therefore, a combination of hardware and software that can be used to set up and monitor a database, and can manage the updating and retrieval of data that have been stored in it. Most database management systems have the following functions:

- Creation of a file; addition, deletion, modification of data; creation, addition and deletion of entire files.
- Retrieving data collectively or selectively.
- The data stored can be sorted or indexed according to the user's requirement, discretion and direction.
- Various reports can be produced from the system. These may be either standardised report or may be specifically generated according to specific user definition.
- Mathematical functions can be performed and the data stored in the database can be manipulated with these functions to perform the desired calculations.
- Maintaining data integrity and database use.

Components of DBMS: Components of DBMS are as follows:

- **DML Precompiler (Data Manipulation Language Precompiler):** As its name specifies, this is a compiler that converts DML statements (Statements that allows the users to manipulate the database) in an application program into normal procedure calls in the host language. This precompiler must interact with the query processor in order to generate the appropriate code.
- **DDL Compiler (Data Definition Language Compiler):** The DDL compiler converts the data definition statements (statements that define the tables, database, etc.) into a set of

tables. These tables contain information in the form that can be used by other components of the DBMS.

- **File Manager:** File manager manages the structure and space of the file on disk. This also locates the block in which the required record exists and requests from the disk manager for this block containing the required record and finally provides the required record to the data manager.
- **Disk Manager:** As specified earlier, disk manager provides the block or page that the file manager asks for. The disk manager is a part of Operating System. Disk Manager does all the physical input and output operations.
- **Data Manager/Database Manager:** It is also called database control system. It is a software component of the DBMS or we can say a program module that acts as an interface between the data stored in the database and the queries submitted to the system. Data Manager converts the queries from the user into the file system. It is actually responsible for the storage, retrieval and manipulation of the data in the database. Besides these responsibilities data managers also takes care of maintaining integrity. This means that the appropriate data should be stored in the database. For example, date of joining of an employee should not be less than the current date or the age of an employee for a particular post should lie between 25 and 40. If these constraints are specified in the database, then database manager takes care of them on its own. Database Manager also checks for an unauthorised user accessing the database. Database Manager does not allow any user to access the database without having the permission granted.
- **Query Processor:** The Query Processor takes care of the queries by the database user. The database user when uses the Data Manipulation Language (DML) for retrieving the data, the Query Processor converts it into that form that could be sent to the Data Manager, so that Data Manager can execute it.
- **Data Dictionary:** A data dictionary contains the information/ data about the data. A data dictionary includes all the database descriptions, entity/table descriptions, attributes, etc. Apart from these data dictionary includes the information about the users also, which tables are used by which programs, authorisation of users. A data directory/dictionary is just like a database and its cost depends on how complex it is? More complexity leads to increase in cost. Just like an index helps us to find the chapter easily, data dictionary helps DBA for designing, implementing and maintaining the database and

searching for the desired record in the database. It also helps the managers and end users in their project planning.

Q14. Explain the architecture of DBMS.

Or

Write short note on Architecture of DBMS.

[Dec-2018, Q.No.-5 (a)]

Ans. The logical architecture describes how data in the database is perceived by users. It is not concerned with how the data is handled and processed by the DBMS, but only with how it looks. The method of data storage on the underlying file system is not revealed, and the users can manipulate the data without worrying about where it is located or how it is actually stored. This results in the database having different levels of abstraction.

The majority of commercial Database Management Systems available today are based on the ANSI/SPARC generalised DBMS architecture, as proposed by the ANSI/SPARC Study Group on Data Base Management Systems. Hence this is also called as the ANSI/SPARC model. It divides the system into three levels of abstraction: the internal or physical level, the conceptual level, and the external or view level. The diagram below shows the logical architecture for a typical DBMS.

(1) The External or View Level: The external or view level is the highest level of abstraction of database. It provides a window on the conceptual view, which allows the user to see only the data of interest to them. The user can be either an application program or an end user. There can be many external views as any number of external schema can be defined and they can overlap each other. It consists of the definition of logical records and relationships in the external view. It also contains the methods for deriving the objects such as entities, attributes and relationships in the external view from the Conceptual view.

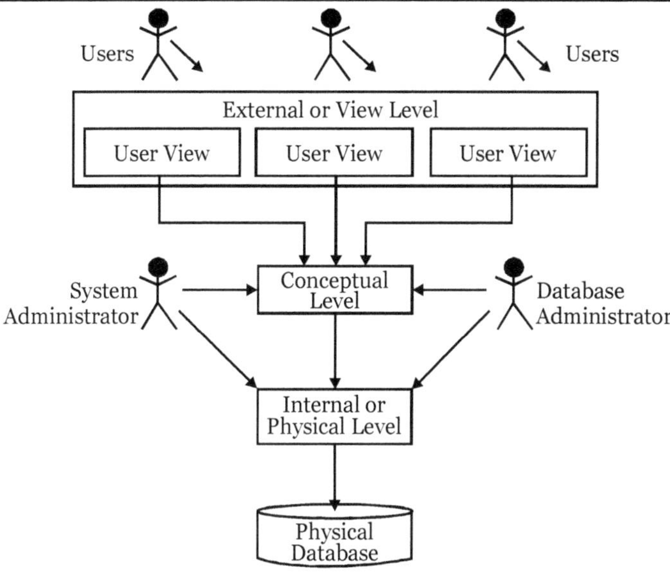

Fig. 1.8

(2) The Conceptual Level or Global level: The conceptual level presents a logical view of the entire database as a unified whole. It allows the user to bring all the data in the database together and see it in a consistent manner. Hence, there is only one conceptual schema per database. The first stage in the design of a database is to define the conceptual view, and a DBMS provides a data definition language for this purpose. It describes all the records and relationships included in the database.

The data definition language used to create the conceptual level must not specify any physical storage considerations that should be handled by the physical level. It does not provide any storage or access details, but defines the information content only

(3) The Internal or Physical Level: The collection of files permanently stored on secondary storage devices is known as the physical database. The physical or internal level is the one closest to physical storage, and it provides a low-level description of the physical database, and an interface between the operating systems file system and the record structures used in higher levels of abstraction. It is at this level that record types and methods of storage are defined, as well as how stored fields are represented, what physical sequence the stored records are in, and what other physical structures exist.

Q15. What do you mean by Data modeling?

Ans. Data modeling is a process by which the data requirements of an organisation or an application area are represented. Conceptual modeling is an important phase in designing a successful database application. The traditional approach is of using the entity-relationship model for this purpose. Enhanced ER or EER model is used for modeling object-oriented databases.

Entity-Relationship Model: The Entity-relationship model, developed by Chen in 1976-77, serves as an excellent tool in the database design process. It provides graphic representation of entities, attributes and relationships. Requirements analysis of the designed database helps in collecting the necessary information in the form of entities and attributes to be included in the database. Based on enterprise rules, the relationships between the entities get identified and the nature of use of the database is determined. The E-R model describes the conceptual schema and is considered as a blueprint of the database under design. After finalisation, an E-R diagram (as the entity-relationship model is generally called) is mapped into one of the selected database models (discussed later in the text) and the system-dependent procedure of database creation is started.

An illustration of the E-R diagram has been given in Fig. It depicts a database on marketing of drugs from medicinal and aromatic plants. The plants or their parts serve as crude drugs which are traded in the market. The standardising agency certifies the quality of drugs while the certifying agency approves the drugs for export. Before supply to the customer, the crude drugs are sometimes processed. In an ER diagram rectangles represent entities, ellipses show attributes, diamonds represent relationships, attributes with underscore show primary keys, attributes with double underscore represent foreign keys and l, n, m show relationship types.

Types of Relationship: A relationship is an association between two or more entities. Entities correspond to record types in a database, which are sets. Thus a relationship represents a correspondence between the elements of n sets. The relationship over two sets is called a binary relationship; the relationship over three sets ternary and over n sets n-ary relationship. Relationships can themselves be treated as entities and assigned attributes (Fig.). Relationships can be grouped into the following types:

- 1:1 (one-to-one)
- 1:n (one-to-many)
- n:1 (many-to-one)
- n:m (many-to-many)

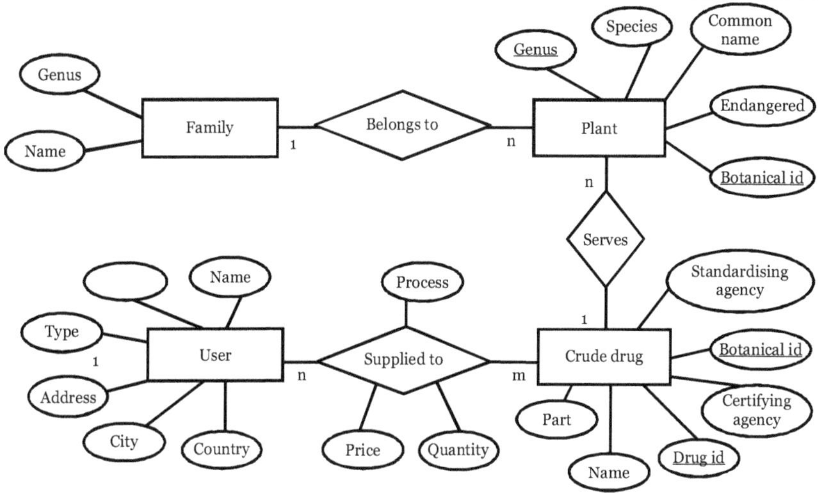

Fig. 1.9

Let us illustrate these relationship types one by one. In a 1:1 relationship, one instance of an entity of a given type is associated with only one member of another type. Let there be a set of country names and a set of city names. Further let us assume that each city in the set is a capital. The relationship between these two sets which can be called "capital" is 1:1 because for each country name there is only one city name and, conversely, each city name corresponds to only one country name.

In a 1:n relationship, one instance of a given type of entity is related to many instances of another type. Let there be a set of departments and a set of faculty members employed in the departments. The department-faculty relationship which can be called 'employed' is of the 1:n type because each department employs several faculty members and each faculty member works only in one department.

The many-to-one (n:1) relationship has the same semantics as 1:n. In the above example, if we change the relationship to faculty-department (in place of department faculty) we will have n:1 relationship type.

Lastly the n:m relationship is one in which many instances of an entity type are associated with many instances of another entity type. Consider a set of faculty members teaching a set of students. The faculty-student relationship ("teaching") is an example of the n:m type relationship because a faculty member can teach `m` students and a student can be taught by 'n' faculty members.

Q16. Describe the concept of 'Data Models'.

Or

What are data models? Explain the three data models referred to as classical models?

Or

What are data model? Enumerate their various types, describing any two of them. [June-2019, Q.No.-1.2]

Ans. Data Models are fundamental entities to introduce abstraction in a DBMS. Data models define how data is connected to each other and how they are processed and stored inside the system. These models provide alternative ways of picturing the relationships and serve as frameworks for mapping the conceptual schema of a database. There are a number of data models in use today but the following three have been most widely implemented:

(1) Hierarchical Model: This database model organises data into a tree-like-structure, with a single root, to which all the other data is linked. The hierarchy starts from the Root data, and expands like a tree, adding child nodes to the parent nodes.

In this model, a child node will only have a single parent node.

This model efficiently describes many real-world relationships like index of a book, recipes. etc.

In hierarchical model, data is organised into tree-like structure with one one-to-many relationship between two different types of data, for example, one department can have many courses, many professors and off-course many students.

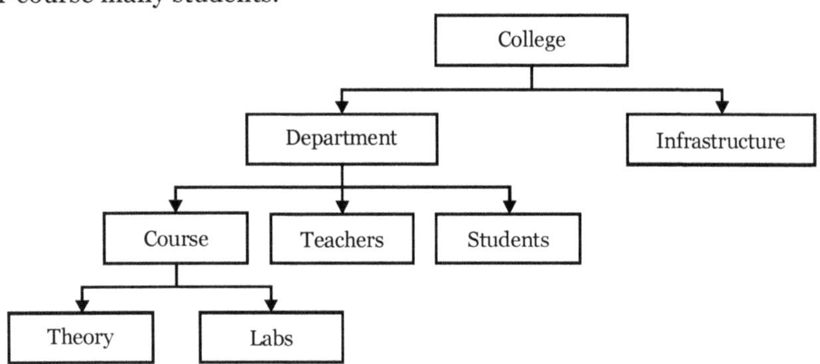

Fig. 1.10

(2) Network Model: This is an extension of the Hierarchical model. In this model data is organised more like a graph, and are allowed to have more than one parent node.

In this database model data is more related as more relationships are established in this database model. Also, as the data is more related, hence accessing the data is also easier and fast. This database model was used to map many-to-many data relationships.

This was the most widely used database model, before Relational Model was introduced.

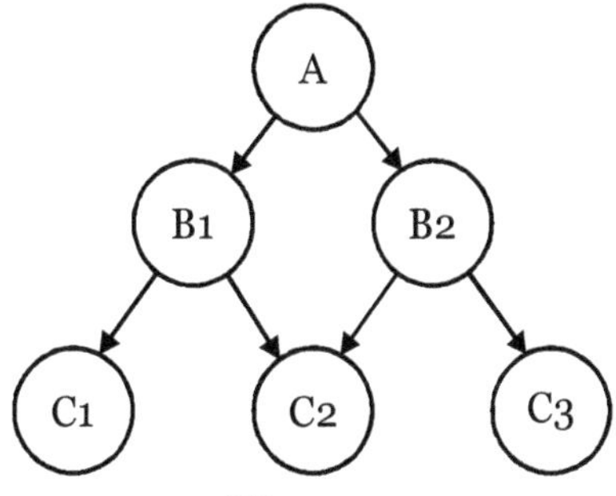

Fig. 1.11

(3) Relational Model: In this model, data is organised in two-dimensional tables and the relationship is maintained by storing a common field.

This model was introduced by E. F Codd in 1970, and since then it has been the most widely used database model, infact, we can say the only database model used around the world.

The basic structure of data in the relational model is tables. All the information related to a particular type is stored in rows of that table.

Hence, tables are also known as relations in relational model.

In the coming tutorials we will learn how to design tables, normalise them to reduce data redundancy and how to use Structured Query language to access data from tables.

student_id	name	age
1	Akon	17
2	Bkon	18
3	Ckon	17
4	Dkon	18

subject_id	name	teacher
1	Java	Mr. J
2	C++	Miss C
3	C#	Mr. C Hash
4	Php	Mr. P H P

student_id	subject_id	marks
1	1	98
2	2	78
3	1	76
4	2	88

Fig. 1.12

(4) Object-oriented Model: The object-oriented data model facilitates handling of objects rather than records. In an object-oriented model an entity is represented as an instance (object) of a class that has a set of properties and operations (methods) applied to the objects. A class represents an abstract data type and is a shell from which one can generate as many copies (called instances) as one wants. In object-oriented approach, the behaviour of an object is a part of its definition. The behaviour is described by a set of methods. The set of methods offered by an object to the others defines the object interface. A class and hence an object may inherit properties and methods from related classes. Objects and classes are dynamic and can be created at any time.

Viewing the data as objects instead of as records provides more flexibility and removes the need to normalise data.

Some of the object building blocks are defined below:

(i) **Objects:** An object is an entity, real or abstract, that has state, behaviour and identity. The state of an object is represented by its attributes and their values. The behaviour of an object is represented by its operations or methods.

(ii) **Messages:** Objects communicate with each other through messages. A message determines what operation is to be performed by an object. A message specifies an operation name and a list of arguments.

(iii) **Classes:** A class is a set of objects that share common attributes and behaviour. Each object is an instance of some class.

The object-oriented approach emphasises incremental software development. The underlying principle of this approach is:

(i) Grow software, don't build it;

(ii) Build components rather than a whole system; and

(iii) Assemble a basic system and then enhance it.

Smalltalk, C++, Java and Object Pascal/Delphi are the object-oriented programming languages used in this approach.

Q17. Explain the concept of 'Relational Database Management System' (RDBMS)? Discuss its keys and their functions.

Or

What is Relational Database Management System (RDBMS)? Describe the criteria for a database management system (DBMS) to be relational (RDBMS). Explain the characteristics of a 'Relation'. [June-2018, Q.No.-1.1]

Ans. A relational database management system (RDBMS) is a program that allows you to create, update, and administer a relational database. RDBMSes store data in the form of tables, with most commercial relational database management systems using Structured Query language (SQL) to access the database.

Characteristics of 'Relation': Relational databases tend to have the following characteristics:

- Values are atomic.
- All of the values in a column have the same data type.
- Each row is unique.
- The sequence of columns is insignificant.
- The sequence of rows is insignificant.
- Each column has a unique name.
- Integrity constraints maintain data consistency across multiple tables.

Keys and Functions of Relational DBMS: Keys play an important role in relational database management systems. Here, are reasons using keys in DBMS system.

- Keys help you to identify any row of data in a table. In a real-world application, a table could contain thousands of records. Moreover, the records could be duplicated. Keys ensure that you can uniquely identify a table record despite these challenges.
- Allows you to establish a relationship between and identify the relation between tables.
- Help you to enforce identity and integrity in the relationship.

A superkey is a set of attributes which taken collectively allows us to identify uniquely an entity in an entity set. If any key is a superkey, a superset of superkey is also a superkey. (If X_1 is a subset of a set X, the X is called superset of X_1).

The smallest superkey, which is also called minimal key, is a key such that no proper subset of it is a superkey. One of the minimal keys is chosen as the primary key. The keys in the set of minimal keys are called candidate or alternate keys. It is up to the database designer to select one of the candidate keys as a primary key.

A primary key is an attribute or a combination of attributes that uniquely identifies a record while a secondary key does not identify a record uniquely. A secondary key identifies all the records corresponding to the key value.

A foreign key is an attribute or a combination of attributes that is used to link tables. In relational database management systems foreign keys are used as linking pins between tables. Foreign keys represent links to the primary keys.

Primary and foreign keys are critical in relational database management systems due to their contribution in defining integrity rules.

A paramount guideline in relational systems is that a primary key or any attribute participating in a composite primary key of a relation cannot have null value. This rule is called entity integrity.

There is another integrity rule, which pertains to foreign keys. According to this rule an attribute that is a foreign key in one table must be a primary key in another table. This rule is known as referential integrity.

Criteria for a DBMS to be Relational: Distinguishing a truly relational DBMS from relational-like systems assumes importance in view of the fact that many new DBMS packages are being labeled as "relational". The minimum conditions for a system to be called relational are:

- The data should be represented in the form of tables.
- Any pointer mechanism should be transparent to the DBMS users.
- The system should support relational algebra operators of SELECT, PROJECT and JOIN. Any system, which fulfils these three criteria, is called minimally relational. A system, which satisfies only the first two conditions, is not a relational system and is called tabular DBMS.

For a DBMS to be fully relational it should additionally support both entity and referential integrity rules and implement all relational algebra operations.

Q18. What is Normalisation of Relations?

Or

Write short note on Normalisation of Relations.

[June-2019, Q.No.-5 (a)] [Dec-2019, Q.No.-5 (a)]

Ans. Normalisation is the process of efficiently organising data in a database. There are two goals of the normalisation process: a) eliminate redundant data (for example, storing the same data in more than one table) and b) ensure data dependencies make sense (only storing related data in a table). Both of these are worthy goals as they reduce the amount of space a database consumes and ensure that data is logically stored.

The normalisation technique is concerned with translating a conceptual design into a set of well designed relational table. The normalisation is a major task in designing a relational database. The process of normalisation ensures that there will be no problem in updating the database and that operations on the various relations will not lead to inconsistent and incorrect data. During the normalisation process, the designer first looks to be sure that the relations are in first normal form, next he or she checks for second normal form and finally for third. The first normal form requires that all occurrences of a record type contain the same number of fields. It may be noted that normalisation is primarily aimed at preventing or reducing data maintenance problems rather than improving retrieval efficiency. Normalisation of relations removes anomalies in the database.

The second and third normal forms require the designer to examine the relationship between key fields and other fields in the record. To conform to second and third normal forms, each non-key field must give us information about the entire key and nothing but the key.

e.g. suppose that one has a relationship as follows:

Order No.	Author	Title	Supplier	Data

If author and title forms a composite key, this relationship is not in second normal form. Note that its author and title would be repeated in each record that stores information about a part in another. If the author changed then every record of a order number would have to be updated. What would happen if there were no order number relating to author or book. Then it is possible that database would like to keep track of the author, since there would be no record having its author. The relations can be made to conform to second normal form by splitting it into two relations.

Order	Author	Title	Supplier	Data
No.	Author	Title	Supplier	Data

Order number and Author could be the combined key for the relation and author can be the key for the second.

Thus, normalisation is a systematic process of transforming initial conceptual design first into a set of relational table in First normal form (1NF) by assigning a unique key to each entity type table and removing repeating group from the tables by splitting each into two or more new entity types or relation tables. The set of relational tables in 1NF may be changed into set of tables in second normal form (2NF) by removing partial functional dependencies within tables. It is accomplished by splitting of these dependencies into new separate tables. The set of tables in 2NF may be converted into a new set of tables in third normal form (3NF) by eliminating transitive dependencies.

First normal form (1NF), Second normal form (2NF), Third normal form (3NF), Fourth normal form (4NF), Fifth normal form (5NF), and the highest normal form is called domain/key normal form (DK/NF). Example of Normalisation Process:

Employee

Employee Name	Place of Work	Child

Employee Name	Place of work	Child		
		Child Name	Date of birth	Sex
Ashok	Varanasi	Suraj	12-7-1985	M
Vinay	New Delhi	Arpita	14-7-1986	F
Surendra	Allahabad	Ashish	15-10-1988	M

Representation of employee

Employee name	Place of work	Child name	Date of birth	Sex
Ashok	Varanasi	Suraj	12-7-1985	M
Vinay	New Delhi	Arpita	14-7-1986	F
Surendra	Allahabad	Ashish	15-10-1988	M

Fig. 1.13: Employee in 2 NF

It can be split into two representation employee and child.

Employee: name, Place of work

Employee Child: Employee name, Child name, Date of birth, Sex

Employee name	Place of work
Ashok	Varanasi
Vinay	New Delhi
Surendra	Allahabad

Employee name	Child name	Date of birth	Sex
Ashok	Suraj	12-7-1985	M
Vinay	Arpita	14-7-1986	F
Surendra	Ashish	15-10-1988	M

Fig. 1.14: Employee in 1NF

Functional Dependencies: Dependency refers to the relationship among attributes. These attributes may belong to the same relation or different relations. Dependencies can be of various types. viz. functional dependencies, transitive dependencies, multi-level dependencies, etc.

Functional dependence is a relationship that exists between any two fields or attributes. We may say that a field A of an n-set O is functionally dependent upon field B of O (written B ® A) if each value of B has precisely one value of A corresponding to it at every instant of time.

It can be represented as:

- $J \rightarrow K$
- $J \rightarrow L$
- $K \rightarrow J$
- $L \rightarrow K$

Transitive dependency is a form of intermediate dependency. For example if we have attributes or groups of attributes A, B and C such that A determines B and B determines C. i.e.

- A→ B
- B→C

In the above example, we can say that there exist transitive dependency between A and O. The multi-valued dependency refers to m:n (many to many) relationships. The multi-valued dependency exist between two data items when one value of the first data item gives a collection of values of the second data item, i.e., it multi-determines the second data items.

Q19. What is designing databases? Write down the procedure for designing a database.

Ans. Designing a database is a highly complex operation. Though it is relatively easy to identify a poorly designed database, there does not exist a unified approach which leads to the best design.

The database design should be flexible enough to meet the requirements of the maximum number of users to the fullest. Besides, the design should also anticipate, to a certain extent, future requirements and make provisions for them. This calls for some intuitiveness on the part of the database designer.

The process of designing a database is an interactive one, which means that initial database structure, changes with usage. However, with time the design tends to get stabilised. Usually, a person designated as database administrator (DBA) controls the design and administration of a database.

A broad step-by-step procedure for designing a database has been summarised below:

(1) First of all data to be represented in the database is determined. For this, the information needs of the users are studied in detail. Based on the information requirements analysis, entities of interest are identified and their attributes examined.

(2) An E-R model of the database representing a conceptual schema is drawn. This is the most important stage in the database design process. The E-R diagram which depicts entitites and their relationships should be as comprehensive as possible.

(3) The E-R model is mapped into a selected database structure (hierarchical, network, relational or any other model). In case a relational model is chosen, tables corresponding to entities and their relations are finalised. The process of normalisation is invoked to check the tables and reshape them if necessary.

(4) An empty database is created using DBMS commands (create TABLE, INDEX. etc.). A data dictionary which defines data item names

and their internal storage format is also created by DBMS. The database design process up to step 3 is system-independent. The process becomes system-dependent after that.

(5) The database is populated. This involves inserting data into the empty database. If data to be inserted is available in machine-readable form, the data loading utility of DBMS can be utilised.

(6) The performance of the database is closely monitored to ascertain whether any tuning is required. Flexibility and speed of access are critically evaluated. The database is also examined for data maintenance problems.

(7) The feedback of the users on the database functionality is analysed and changes in the structure made to optimise the usage.

Q20. What is Distributed Database Systems? Explain the architecture of distributed databases. Describe the justification and options for distributed data.

Or

Write a short note on "distributed database and its advantages". [Dec-2017, Q.No.-5 (b)]

Ans. A distributed database is a single logical database which is fragmented and the fragments spread across computers at different locations that are interlinked by a data communication network to provide integrated access to the data. A distributed database environment requires the data to be shared. A distributed database gives geographical data independence. i.e., a user requesting for data need not know at which site the data is located. This property is often referred to as location transparency and each local site is called a node.

Architecture of Distributed Databases The architecture and schematic representation of a distributed database is shown in Fig.

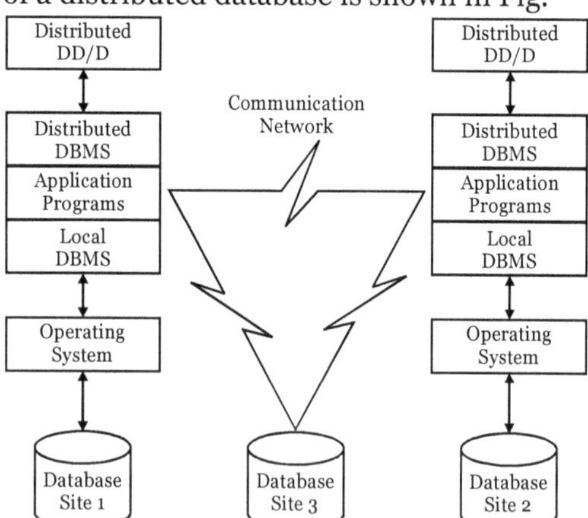

Fig. 1.15: Architecture and schematic representation of a distributed database

As is clear from Fig., each site has a local DBMS as well as a copy of the distributed DBMS. Distributed data dictionary/directory (DD/D) stores information on the location of data in the network as well as data definitions. A request for data is first checked from the distributed data dictionary/directory for location of the required data. In case the data is available at the local site, the distributed DBMS forwards the request to the local DBMS for processing. If the request involves data from other sites, the distributed DBMS routes the request to these sites.

When different nodes in a distributed database have mixed DBMSs (i.e., node 1 may have relational DBMS and node 2 network DBMS) then this distributed DBMS which is capable of handling such an environment is called heterogeneous distributed database management system.

Distributed database management exploits all advantages of centralised and decentralised processing. A decentralised database like a distributed database is also stored on different computers at multiple locations but in this case the computers are not interconnected and hence the data cannot be shared.

Justifications and Options for Distributing Data: The justifications for distributing data can be summed up as follows:

- A distributed database provides increased reliability and availability. Compared to a centralised system, which on failure becomes unavailable to all users, a distributed system will continue to function, though at a reduced level, even when a node fails.
- By encouraging local control of data at different sites, data integrity improves and data administration becomes easier.
- Distribution of data can improve access time if local data is stored locally. By locating data closer to the point of its use, communication cost can be reduced and query response time improved.
- A distributed system facilitates modular growth. New nodes hosting additional database fragments can be added to the system.

There are a number of options available for distributing data in a distributed database. These options include:

- data replication,
- horizontal partitioning,
- vertical partitioning, and
- a combination of the above.

In case of data replication a copy of the database is stored at a few or all sites (full replication). Reliability, saving in telecommunication charges and faster response are the advantages of this option. But additional storage requirements and difficulty in propagating updates are the basic drawbacks. This option is suitable in case updates are infrequent and database interaction is restricted to read-only. CDROM (compact disk read only memory) offers an excellent medium for replicated databases.

Horizontal partitioning of a database involves distributing rows of a relation to multiple sites. New relations (partitions) with the requisite rows are created for this purpose. The original relation can be reconstructed by taking the union of the new relations. Horizontal partitioning can optimise performance by storing fragments of the database at the sites where they are most used.

On vertical partitioning of a database, selected columns of a relation are projected into new relations which are stored at different sites. The main criterion for vertical partitioning is specific data item requirements at individual sites.

A combination of the mentioned options of data distribution may be used depending upon the needs of the distributed system. The basic principle which one must keep in mind is that data should be stored at sites where it will be most frequently used.

Q21. What do you understand by Database systems for management support? Discuss.

Ans. Database systems for management support are broadly referred to as Management Information Systems (MIS). However, for different levels of management, database systems have been categorised based on management functions and expected outputs. Fig. illustrates a hierarchy of information systems corresponding to the three levels of management.

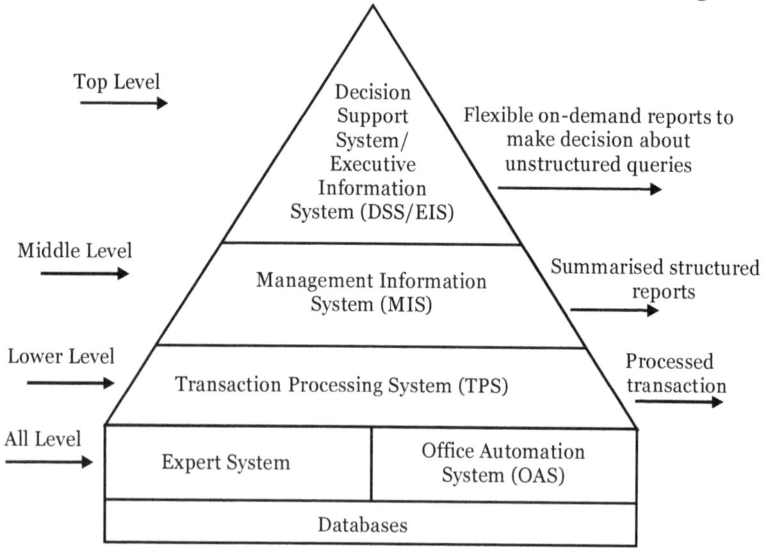

Fig. 1.16: Information systems and management levels

It should be clear from the figure that, for lower level of managers, transaction processing systems (TPS) yielding processed transactions (bills, orders etc) suffice. Middle level managers need management information systems providing summarised structured reports. At the top level, decision support systems (DSS) or executive information systems (EIS) capable of providing brief on-demand reports about unstructured queries are required. Office automation systems and expert systems are used by all levels including non-management.

Q22. What is artificial Intelligence (AI)? List some of the areas of application.

Or

Write a short note on AI and Expert Systems.

[June-2019, Q.No.-5 (b)]

Ans. Artificial intelligence (AI) system is the limb of computer science that deals with making machines that exhibit intelligent behaviour. This is the most sophisticated one that enfolds a number of technologies including expert systems, neural networks, virtual reality, and artificial life. This system works like human brain which has the potentiality of decision-making in some special cases. The system can be used effectively to solve complex problems, recognise patterns, or to make decisions based on complex sets of rules which are often difficult for human being. Neural networks can incorporate new knowledge and improve their own decision-making ability without human intervention.

The main areas of AI are:

- **Robotics:** Robotics is a field that attempts to develop machines that can perform work normally done by people. The machines themselves are called robots. Perception systems are sensing devices that emulate the human capabilities of sight, hearing, touch and smell. Clearly, perception systems are related to robotics, since robots need to have some sensing capabilities. Fuzzy logic is a method of dealing with imprecise data and uncertainty, with problems that have many answers rather than one. Unlike classical logic, fuzzy logic is more like human reasoning. It deals with probability and credibility. That is, instead of being simply true or false, a proposition is mostly true or mostly false or more true or more false.
- **Automated Grammar Checking:** You must have used a word-processor and used its spelling and grammar-checking feature. While spelling checker module works well, there is lot that has to done for the grammar-checking module. The features available in current software are far less than satisfactory. These software fumbles at using proper pronouns, gender or giving proper meaning, etc. For an efficient program

of this kind, it has to be given "intelligence" about knowledge from the real world.

- **Mathematical Theorem Proving:** There had been many attempts of proving mathematical theorems with the help of AI tools. Inference methods are used to prove new theorems.
- **Intelligent Control:** Firstly an expert controller sets a set of rules. The rule whose premise matches the dynamic plant parameter response is selected and implemented. Fuzzy logic is also used in such cases in many industrial plants, e.g. the power control in a nuclear reactor. There are application using fuzzy logic and artificial neural networks for plant estimation, i.e. for designing a process estimator.
- **Expert Systems:** An expert system consists of a knowledge base, database and an inference engine for interpreting the database using the knowledge embedded in the knowledge base. There is sound reasoning process that has to build in order to create an expert system. AI techniques have played significant role in creation of expert systems for weather forecasting; diagnostic systems such as medical diagnosis systems, pathology diagnosis system & customer assistance systems, etc.; financial decision-making systems like fraud detection systems used in credit card companies & systems that expedite financial transactions and classification systems like financial decision-making systems & NASA's galaxy-classification system.
- **Natural Language Understanding:** To understand a natural language like English one has to understand the syntactic (analysis of grammar, compilation) and semantic (meaning of sentences from association of words) interpretation of words. Robots have been designed that understands few instructions, but days are not far when a robot will fully understand a speech in the natural language. There have been examples where full document have been translated in many different languages. Site's http://babelfish.altavista.com/ translation of web pages, is also based on natural language processing.
- **Speech Recognition:** We must have seen the software that types the words as one speaks. These are called phonetic typewriters. Speech understanding has found good commercial value in the recent times, e.g. speech recognition systems are used in reservation through telephone. Dragon Naturally speak, is one such software that needs a mention.

Q23. Define the term 'Information Retrieval'.

Ans. Information retrieval (IR) is the activity of obtaining information system resources that are relevant to an information need from a collection of those resources. Searches can be based on full-text or other content-based indexing. Information retrieval is the science of searching for information in a document, searching for documents themselves, and also searching for the metadata that describes data, and for databases of texts, images or sounds. Automated information retrieval systems are used to reduce what has been called information overload. An IR system is a software system that provides access to books, journals and other documents; stores and manages those documents. Web search engines are the most visible IR applications.

Q24. Write short note on Information retrieval vs. data retrieval.

Ans. In databases, 'data retrieval' is the process of identifying and extracting data from a database, based on a query provided by the user or application. It enables the fetching of data from a database in order to display it on a monitor and/or use within an application. An information retrieval system is designed to analyse, process and store sources of information and retrieve those that match a particular user's requirements. Modern information retrieval systems can either retrieve bibliographic items, or the exact text that matches a user's search criteria from a stored database of full texts of documents. Although information retrieval systems originally meant text retrieval systems since they were dealing with textual documents, modern information retrieval systems deal not only with textual information but also with multimedia information comprising text, audio, images and video. We can therefore characterise data retrieval as deterministic while 'information retrieval' is probabilistic. It is probably for this reason that a separate class of software has been developed for information retrieval system/text retrieval systems. It is therefore useful to have, at this point, a general idea of the principal differences between 'information retrieval' and 'data retrieval'. IRS store documents and/or their surrogates whose components vary considerably in length and character. A 'document' is usually some kind of textual record ranging from the completely unstructured to the more structured. This is a major characteristics that is kept in mind in designing IRS. For example, WINSIS, a software package for text retrieval systems, has been used for many applications that include library collections, hospital records, database of research projects. etc. The search facilities that IRS offer are based on the premise that exact matches between search terms and field values in a record in the database are not adequate.

Q25. Enumerate the parameters for evaluation of search output.

Ans. The two principal parameters that are widely used for evaluating the output of a search in an IRS are:

- **Recall:** A measure of the ability of the IRS to retrieve relevant documents

- **Precision:** A measure of the ability of the IRS to withhold irrelevant documents from being retrieved.

Users' requirements in terms of desired levels of recall and precision vary depending upon a number of factors. The search language of an IRS usually supports modification of the search strategy to regulate the recall and precision output. Three different kinds of searches have been referred to in literature:

- **High Recall Search:** when the user needs to find out all the relevant items on the stated topic. Recall is a parameter used to measure the performance of information retrieval systems; it is measured as the proportion of relevant items retrieved from a collection in a given search session;
- **High Precision Search:** when the user needs only relevant items. i.e., as small a number of non-relevant items as possible. Precision is a parameter used to measure the performance of information retrieval systems; it is measured as the proportion of the retrieved items that are relevant in a given search session.
- **Brief Search:** when the user wants only a few relevant items as opposed to all the relevant items.

Q26. What is search strategy? Write down the stages in database search strategy.

Ans. Search strategy is the action plan which is drawn to conduct a search. It encompasses several steps and levels of work in information retrieval.

The stages in database search may be summarised as follows:

(1) Recognition of an information need: Defining the need for information by the end-user in terms of a specific subject, type of information/document desired. For example, one can specify a bibliographic reference with or without abstract, or how soon the information is needed and other details.

(2) Communication of the information need to the information/database service center: This step is specifically needed when search is not to be done by an end user himself/herself. This step can be done in person, by letter, telephone, e-mail, or through another person.

(3) Recording of the search request: Search request with details is recorded in a Search Record Form (online or printed).

(4) Specification of search request: If necessary and if possible, the reference librarian/information specialist should arrange for a discussion with the end-user and specify the information need as precisely as possible. Aids, such as, a scheme of classification or a thesaurus covering the subject of the query, subject map, known documents or a specialist in the subject of the query can help in the understanding of the topic. The display of these aids can be done online in many cases for the end-user to view.

(5) Select the database resource: Selection of appropriate database(s) likely to yield best results.

(6) Formulate query in search language: Formulation of the query is to be made in the search language of the database and/or the software used in the creation of the database. This implies that the adoption of search strategy and search expressions should be appropriate to the structure, organisation, search language and capabilities of the system. Vocabulary management tools, such as, thesaurus, classification scheme, subject heading lists. etc. associated with the database(s) to be searched assist this step.

(7) Perform the search operation: Perform search on fast access files, Search Strategy involving indexes yields faster result. The end-user can assist in the evaluation of the initial/intermediate search results and provide feedback.

(8) Modification of search: If necessary, modification of search strategy and refinement of the search expression can be done on the basis of the successive end-user feedbacks on the intermediate retrieval results.

(9) Displaying information as per user preference: Selecting the most relevant references/abstracts and arranging the result as desired by end user.

(10) Recording/logging the query: The search procedure adopted and the results obtained can be recorded for future use and analytical studies.

Q27. What do you mean by Compound Queries? Express the Boolean operators using Venn diagrams.

Ans. Compound queries are used when you want to combine the results of two other queries to come up with a new set of results. In a compound query, you can combine the queries by adding their results together, subtracting the results of one query from the other, or intersecting the results to find only the accounts or entries that exist in both queries. Logical AND, OR and NOT are known as Boolean operators. When Boolean operators are used for searching it is known as Boolean search. The operators are used for combining more than one word with certain conditions. These kind of searching also known as combinatorial search. Boolean concepts are often explained with Venn diagrams, which are generally used to explain the set operations. The Venn diagram shows the search area. In Venn diagram, a circle with a word shows the subset of the search area that contains the word written inside it. The overlap of the circles represents the common area of the subsets. For further explanation of our Boolean operators the Venn diagram are used.

Example: INFORMATION OR DATA
INFORMATION AND RETRIEVAL
INFORMATION NOT DATA

The use of OR to link the two terms will result in the retrieval of documents corresponding to both the rectangles; the use of the search expression 'Information NOT Retrieval' will result in retrieving only those documents represented by the area painted green. The OR operator is used when one is searching for documents which have either or both the terms linked this way. The use of OR would be appropriate to link two or more synonyms or near synonyms. The OR operator expands a search and treats the operands as equivalent. AND and NOT on the other hand, limit a search. One and the same search expression may also involve multiple uses of one or more of the Boolean operators. Without exception all search languages accommodate Boolean operators. In actual implementation of these, many search systems use symbols (such as *) to represent the different operators.

Example: (INFORMATION OR DATA) AND RETRIEVAL

There are some major deficiencies with the Boolean operators:

- Boolean operators merely allow retrieval of documents/web pages that contain some term or combination of terms. In practice it is often necessary to specify retrieval requirements more precisely. For example, the search for 'Information Retrieval' has to be expressed either as

  Information AND Retrieval

  or as

  Retrieval AND Information

  to retrieve those documents containing both 'Information' and 'Retrieval' rather than the required set of documents where an occurrence of the word Information immediately precedes the occurrence of the word Retrieval.
- It is tedious to use Boolean operators to include the various morphological variants of a term (e.g., CLASSIFY OR CLASSIFICATION OR CLASSIFYING OR CLASSING)
- Boolean operator AND is often inadequate to express the desired relation between two search terms
- The Boolean model of searching identifies an item as relevant or not on the basis of the presence or not in the document/ record of terms in the query. It attaches equal importance to all the documents thus retrieved and provides no mechanism whatever, for ranking the search output on the basis of some degree of relevance to the query.

One of the methods suggested to overcome this limitation is the 'best match searching', which uses the theory of probability to attach weights to retrieved records. This involves adoption of some quantitative measure of similarity between a query and a document/record in the database and producing a ranked output. Students should note that some of the search engines used for searching the WWW do produce ranked output of 'hits'. How dependable such rankings are is a debatable issue

Q28. Write short note on the following:

(i) Keyword Grouping

Ans. In a complex compound query, which has a number of keywords and/or phrases, and it may be necessary to group or link certain keywords/ phrases with certain other keywords/ phrases.

Example: Consider the following search:

UK AND Football OR USA AND Soccer

In order to avoid retrieving documents that are on Football in U.S.A. which are surely irrelevant here, it is important to be able to group search terms just as in mathematical operations. Parentheses are used to group keywords.

(UK AND Football) OR (USA AND Soccer)

(ii) Truncation Search

Ans. Truncation means concatenation of words. In other words, if the root string of the words is searched it brings all the derivatives derived out of the given root string. Truncation is of three types based on truncation techniques:

- **Left Truncation:** When the root string is concatenated from the left side, it is known as left truncation. For example, if the left truncation is implemented for the root string ISM, it will bring all the words which ends with the string ISM, like

  BRAHAMINISM

  COMMUNISM

  SUPHISM

- **Right Truncation:** When the root string is concatenated from the right side it is known as right truncation. For example, right truncation is used with the root string CLASS, it will bring all the words which starts with the root string CLASS, like

  CLASS

  CLASSIFICATION

  CLASSIFICATIONIST

  CLASSIFIER

(iii) Proximity Operators

Ans. Proximity operators are used to specify the relative location of words in a document. These operators facilitate searching for words that must be in the same phrase, paragraph, or sentence in a record. Proximity operators help us to search for words within a certain distance of one another in databases. For example, a search may require that two concepts be in the same sentence but not necessarily next to each other, as in a phrase. One such operator is NEAR which means that the terms that are entered should be within a certain number of words to each other. Typically, the distance between two concepts can be 10- 25 words. NEAR allows the terms to be in any order. Different search engines may use different proximity operators. The symbols generally used in this type of search are 'w' (with/within) and 'n' (near). For example a search for "library 'near' automation" would retrieve documents containing 'Library automation' and 'Automation of Library'.

Another operator used is 'followed by' which means that one term must follow the other. ADJ (adjacent) serves the same function. A search engine that allows search on phrases essentially uses the same method. i.e., determining adjacency of keywords.

Q29. Write short note on Field-Specific Searches and String Searching.

Ans. Field-Specific Searches: Field-specific searches are a common feature in most systems. This is particularly helpful when the searcher needs to limit the search for a keyword to a particular field. e.g., in the Title or Descriptor field.

A search can be conducted on all the fields in a database, or it may restricted to one or more chosen fields to produce more specific results. Specific fields and codes vary according to the search systems and database. The following examples show some valid DIALOG searches that have been restricted to some specific fields. The general format for using suffix codes is "Syntax: SELECT/ xx,xx ... where xx is a Basic Index field code(s)"

Select computer?/TI	Terms searched in the Title (/TI) field only
S (information OR or Communication) /DE,ID	Terms searched in either the Descriptor (/DE) Identifier(/ID) field.
S S12/TI,AB	Restricts set S12 to either the Title (/TI) or Abstract (/AB) field.

In some cases one can use some prefix codes to restrict a search in a specific field. For example, in DIALOG one can enter the following search expressions to restrict the search in author or corporate source:

Select AU= Chowdhury,G

String Searching: This facility allows users to search for embedded strings of characters within a body of text. The facility is particularly useful in searching for character strings that may not be indexed nor indexed as such. For example, in library catalogues usually the name of the publisher is not indexed. If the need arises for retrieving items in a library published by a specified publisher, string searching can be employed. The search engine will look for the presence of a string of characters (denoting the name of the publisher) in the appropriate field; say the imprint field, in every record in the database.

A major problems in database searching, especially in searching the web is retrieving too many items/web pages. Recognising this problem some search engines provide facilities to sort results in a sequence of decreasing degree of estimated relevance to the query so that the items judged most relevant are listed at the top of the output. Sorting is a very powerful way, which does not actually exclude any matches. However, at present only a few sorting criteria, if any, are supported by some web search engines. In the more conventional IRS the facility is available in some search languages in the form of weighted term searching. Essentially, this facility attaches a 'weight' to every retrieved item based on its calculated degree of relevance to the query and the output is ranked in the decreasing order of relevance. The most relevant documents are at the top of the output list thus saving the time of the end user as s/he will not have to go through a long results list to find some very relevant items at the end of the list.

Q30. Discuss the trends in information retrieval.

Ans. The developments in computer and communication technologies have made the problems of storage and transfer of information easier. This has also made the task of searching and information retrieval more complex. In the last few decades since the advent of large online databases, efforts in IR research have been directed at overcoming some of the problems posed by this increasing complexity. There are two or three major directions in which research in this area is proceeding. While it is difficult to provide a comprehensive overview of all these areas, it is important to have a general idea of the major trends.

Intelligent IR: There have been efforts at making the computer think like a human. The development of some experimental expert systems (e.g., MYCIN) and incorporation of some features of artificial intelligence into IR systems are worth noting here. A few search engines, especially those for searching the web, are attempting to provide the facility of accepting queries in the form of a natural language query;, e.g. 'What is the population of China?'. The search engine then converts the natural language query to an algorithm. There are problems with these tools and they work for some simple and/or common queries but do not work on less common types of queries. Beginning with Belkin's ASK (Anomalous State of Knowledge) hypothesis, there have also been attempts at developing better end-user models and interfaces for IR systems. User interfaces have made many advances especially in terms of elements relating to menus, forms, graphics, hypertext. etc. Natural language processing (NLP) in IR explores how natural language text (texts of documents as well as end users' queries) stored in a computer can be manipulated to transform it into a form suitable for further processing. Research in both the areas, viz,

- Designing NL interfaces that accept queries in the form of a natural language query; and
- On the storage side, NL text processing that supports structuring of large bodies of textual data to automatically derive knowledge structures (e.g., automatic classification) that may be used for accessing and retrieving information from texts is in progress. The developments appear to suggest that IR research is directed at using intelligent information processing technologies such as neural networks to overcome some of the limitations of conventional Boolean IR model. IR research in recent years has established strong links with several related areas such as NLP, Artificial Intelligence, HCI, cognitive sciences. etc. However, it is important to remember that much of this research is still in experimental stages and it will be some time before large structured commercial databases adopt these technologies.

Q31. Discuss the areas of current research in IR Systems.

Ans. Active research efforts are pursued to refine or develop efficient information retrieval systems all over the world. The primary purpose in all these efforts is to get the best results for users. System developers and suppliers are striving to offer a best software package or a service. The information researcher is also equally concerned to develop the best retrieval system. The directions, these research activities are taking, may be summed up as given below:

- **Better Systems Design:** This is primarily to improve methods of matching document descriptors with query descriptors. New methods of searching, other than Boolean search logic has been a major area of further research. Optimum retrieval efficiency, providing a reasonable proportion of relevant hits, and reducing overload of irrelevant hits is another line of research. Speed of retrieval is also implied in this type of research efforts.
- **Improved Retrieval Facilities and Strategies:** Here an attempt is made to improve the efficiency and effectiveness of the system, including the characteristics of the storage requirements, the retrieval speed and the effectiveness of the system. Work in this area seeks to overcome the limitations of inverted file (a term entry system as against an item entry system) by developing fast methods of scanning the contents of database. This involves improving the speed of searching by a set of text scanning algorithms; alternatively to seek hardware-based solutions, most of which are related to speed of text-scanning.

- **Human-Computer Interface:** This is another area of intense research. User-friendly approach is focussed on development of self-explanatory, intermediary computer systems, that would stimulate best-match searching, using knowledge-based techniques taking cue from artificial intelligence.

A very new research trend is surfacing, beginning from 1991, a sort of reawakening of Ranganathan's ideas of postulates and principles for designing of faceted classification systems. Quoting from Parthasarathy [2004]:

"Persons engaging in designing tools and systems are known as Information Architects and their profession as Information Architecture. The contributions of Ranganathan, his Laws, Principles, Categories, Canons, Postulates. etc. are now appearing on the Net freely, with occasional comments or explanations, for the benefit of Information Architects. During the last ten years, papers have started coming on the relevance of Ranganathan's ideas for improving the Net and Webbased services. Classification schemes are used on the Net. They are generally enumerative schemes. It is stated that Colon Classification, which is a faceted scheme with analytico-synthetic approach, will be ideal for improving web-based searches. We should take advantage of this opportunity and develop tools and systems for web-based services on Ranganathan's ideas with the help of software groups in India."

❑❑❑

LIBRARY AUTOMATION

INTRODUCTION

The library plays a critical role in our society it is an important component of any educational institution, which is hub of the teaching, and learning activities where students, researchers and teachers can explore the vast resources of information. In the age of information communication technology, computers are being used for day-to-day housekeeping activity of the library which saves the time of the end users, and library professional also and at the same time avoid duplication of work and make the library service smooth and effective. In the age of ICT library scenario has been drastically changed in terms of collection, organisation and services. Simultaneously, user's demands and attitudes have changed in its kinds. Also the information seeking behaviour of user has dynamically changed. They want relevant, authentic information very quickly within a single place at their hand .This concept has posed challenges for library professionals for quick delivery of library services and information. This development in library field has brought the idea of Library Automation.

Q1. Discuss the basic functions related to housekeeping operations in a library.

Ans. The basic housekeeping functions of a library irrespective of its type or size may be grouped as acquisitions, processing, use and maintenance (Fig.). Their operations follow some definite work flows/ routines and therefore are amenable to computerisation. It means a computer or a group of computers can perform routine clerical chores quickly and cheaply.

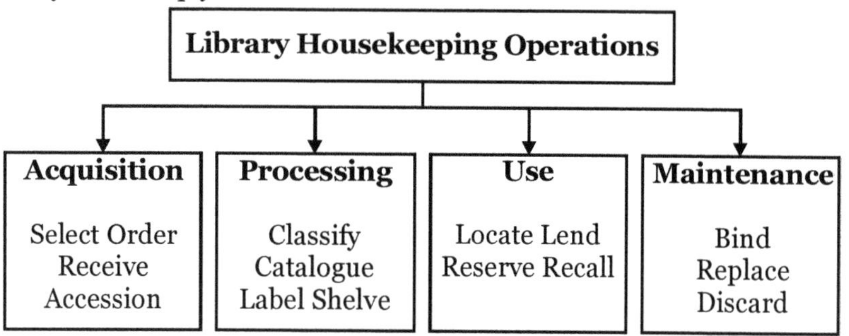

Fig. 2.1

The functions and activities of one division are different from that of the other divisions but are closely related and therefore combined efforts lead towards the better library services.

We may view libraries as complex systems which include subsystems and components. The main two subsystems are operational subsystem and administrative subsystem. Library housekeeping operations form part of the operational subsystem. As per the analytical study of ASLIB (The Association for Information Management, UK), the operational subsystem may be divided into four further subdivisions namely Acquisition, Processing, Use and Maintenance. Within each division there are a number of procedures and within each procedure there are activities. The housekeeping operations as related to the handling of monographic materials in a library system are described in Table 2.1.

Table 2.1: Housekeeping Operations Related to Handling of Monographic Materials in a Library

System	Subsystem	Operational subsystem	Procedures	Activities (Common to all procedures)
Library System	Operational subsystem	Acquisition	Select Order Receive Accession	**Initiate** (To commence a procedure) **Activate** (To implement a procedure through appropriate action) **Record** (To record what action has been taken) **Report** (To notify staff or user about the action taken **Cancel** (To stop a procedure or undoing an action)
		Processing	Classify Catalogue Label Shelve	
		Use	Locate List Lend/Issue Reserve Recall/Return ILL (Inter Library Loan) Photocopy	
		Maintenance	Bind Replace Discard	
	Administrative subsystem			

(1)Acquisition: Acquisition of documents is one of the basic functions associated with any library. A library must acquire and provide all the relevant documents to its users within its budgetary limitations. An acquisition subsystem performs four basic operations. They are selection, ordering, receiving and accessioning of documents. These Procedures are explained below:

(i) Selection: Selection of documents for library users is a very responsible job and should be based on definite principles and accepted norms. For a given library the book budget is limited and it should be spent judiciously to provide services to an optimum number of library users. Therefore, book selection becomes necessary. There are a number of tools (such as bibliographies, publisher's catalogues. etc.) which will be useful to library staff in the selection process. Requests from library users and suggestions from library authority are also considered for selection purposes. Such selections of documents need the approval of the competent authority, before they are ordered for purchase in the library.

(ii) Ordering: This procedure starts with pre-order searching, especially to avoid duplicate orders. In the next stage, purchase orders are generated and placed either directly to the respective publishers or to the list of vendors duly approved by the competent authority. Additionally, generation of reminders for overdue items and cancellation of orders also comes under the purview of ordering procedure.

(iii) Receiving: Documents and invoices or bills usually arrive together. Bills are checked with the order Housekeeping Operations 8 2 list before processing for payment. Newly arrived books are tallied with the bills and the order list to check whether the books received are as per the order and the author, title, edition, imprints and price are correct before accessioning. It is essential to ensure that books are not defective in any way before accessioning.

(iv) Accessioning: A stock register is maintained by libraries in which all the documents purchased or received in exchange or as gift are recorded. Each document is provided with a consecutive serial number. The register is called Accession Register and the serial number to each document is referred to as Accession Number of the document. Accession register is one of the important records of the library. All the above mentioned procedures and related activities of the acquisition subsystem can be mechanised through 'library management software'. In such a system these basic activities are linked with the files of publishers, suppliers, budget and fund accounting, currency. etc. These files are maintained in computer-readable form and are utilised appropriately.

(2) Processing: The processing procedure is the pivot around which all the housekeeping operations revolve in a library. Processing helps in the transformation of a library collection into serviceable resources. The procedures under this subdivision are classification, cataloguing, labeling and shelving.

(i) Classification of Documents: Classification is grouping similar objects together. This principle is used to organise documents in libraries according to their subject content. It forms the foundation of librarianship. The following are the important classification schemes (aka systems), which are used in different libraries of the world: Dewey Decimal Classification (DDC), Universal Decimal Classification (UDC), Library of Congress Classification (LC), Colon Classification (CC) and

Subject Classification (SC). etc. The purposes for classifying of documents are:

(a) To help a user to find a document whose call number (i.e., class number + book number) s/he knows. The class number represents the subject of a book while the book number individualises it among books on the same subject.

(b) To find out all the documents on a given subject.

Classification is a mental process and demands intellectual exercises from a classifier. As a result, automatic synthesis of class numbers requires the application of Artificial Intelligence (AI) techniques in the development of software. In India, some research work on this topic has already been carried out at DRTC, Bangalore for building class numbers (based on Colon Classification) automatically through a software (called Vasya), written in PROLOG (PROgraming in LOGic) – a non-procedural programming language. The electronic version of Dewey (Electronic Dewey) is available on CDROM.

(ii) Cataloguing: A library's first task is to assemble a collection of documents and then it must catalogue that collection. Cataloguing is the prime method of providing access to the collection of a library. The current practices for cataloguing resources in Indian libraries may be tabulated as shown in Table 2.2.

Table 2.2: Current Practices in Cataloguing Resources

Group	Cataloguing Procedure	Product
(1)	Manual cataloguing	Card catalogue
(2)	Computerised cataloguing	Machine readable catalogue OPAC (online Public Access Catalogue)
(3)	Hybrid Model (Use of computer to produce printed catalogue cards and manual filing)	Printed catalogue card Machine readable catalogue OPAC (Online Public Access Catalogue)

All these cataloguing procedures start with technical reading of the document to be catalogued by studying title, sub-title, alternate title, author, editor, edition, reprint, imprint, dedication, preface, table of contents, collation, series, bibliographies. etc. In case of manual cataloguing, the cataloguer makes separate cards for author, title, subject, cross references and analytical entries by following any standard catalogue code (such as AACR-2, CCC. etc.) and file them as per the rules laid down by the library. Computerised cataloguing begins with entering bibliographical data of a book in a predesigned worksheet. The worksheet or datasheet is very similar to a data entry form and is based on any standard bibliographic record format (such as MARC 21, CCF, UNIMARC. etc.). Finally bibliographical data recorded in the worksheets are entered into the computer to produce a machine-readable catalogue file and OPAC. Computer based cataloguing supports importing of bibliographical records for the library resources either from centralised cataloguing service agency or from other libraries. Computer based cataloguing also supports exporting of bibliographical data of its own collection to other library systems. This facility reduces unit cost of cataloguing and ensures standardisation in cataloguing. The recent trend of cataloguing is to utilise Z39.50 protocol to download bibliographical data from other libraries and to provide global access to its own collection through Web OPAC.

(iii) Labeling: It is the work of pasting various labels on different parts of a document. The following labels are generally pasted in books:

(a) Spine label: This is done to make call number (a combination of class number and book number) properly visible to the users when the book is shelved. The size of the label is in the range of 1.25"×1.25".

(b) Ownership slip/mark: These are generally pasted on the inner side of the front cover at left hand top most corner. Ownership marks are put at various parts of a document by rubber stamps. The size of slip is 3"×2.5".

(c) Date slip: It is pasted on the top most portion of the front or back flyleaf of each book. The size of date slip is 5"×3".

(d) Book pocket: On the bottom of the inner right side of the front or back cardboard cover a book pocket is pasted.

(e) Book card: One printed/hand-written book card of size 5"×3" is put in the book pocket of each book.

In a computerised environment, various labels are printed by using library management software. In case of barcode based computerised circulation, accession numbers of documents are converted into barcodes and printouts of barcodes are pasted on the inner back cover of the documents.

(iv) Shelving: Shelving is the arrangement of documents on the shelves to fulfil the fourth law of library science – Save time of the reader. Generally books are arranged on the shelves in a classified order as per the call number. Bound volumes of periodicals are generally shelved alphabetically by title and then by volume numbers.

(3) Circulation: Most libraries lend books and other library materials to be read elsewhere by users. This is convenient for the users; this increases the use made of library collections and reduces the demand on reading space within library building. This function requires some sort of record keeping of what has been lent and to whom. The reasons for keeping loan records are:

(i) To minimise the loss of library materials; and

(ii) To help library staff to answer users' queries about the location of items not on the shelves.

A variety of systems for record keeping of loans have come into being based on needs. These are known as circulation systems. These involve some common jobs for successful implementation such as enrolment of members, issue and return of library documents, reservation of documents, renewal of documents, maintenance of documents and records, maintenance of statistics, inter-library loan, issuing of gate pass. etc.

In a computer based circulation system, the machine-readable file consists of records for all items on loan from the library updated periodically with new records. This file is called "transaction file" and it takes required data from other two files – "document file" and "borrower file".

Modern library management software support barcode based circulation system. In such a system, a barcode reader scans barcode for accession number of a document and the barcode in turn acts as a pointer to the document file. It helps to minimise labour and error in data entry operation. The concept of RFID (Radio Frequency Identification) based circulation system is emerging rapidly in developed countries. It comprises three components: a tag, a reader and an antenna. The tag contains important bibliographical data. The reader decodes the information stored on the chip after receiving it through the antenna and sends data to the central server to communicate library automation system. RFID technology supports patron self-checkout machines and has the ability to conduct inventory counts without removing a single book from the shelves. As a whole, RFID improves library workflow, staff productivity and customer service.

(4) Serials Control: Serials in general and periodicals in particular are essential for research and development (R&D) activities. These are the primary means of communication for the exchange of scientific information. The periodicals or journals subscribed by libraries can be grouped into the following categories:

(i) Indexing/Abstracting periodicals.
(ii) Periodicals containing news items
(iii) Periodicals containing full-text research articles and technical papers

Acquisition of serials/periodicals in a library is different from book ordering system. In contrast to books, the libraries regularly subscribe periodicals against advance payment. The modes of subscription of periodicals in a library are as follows:

(i) Through local vendors/subscription agents
(ii) Through foreign vendors/subscription agents
(iii) Direct from the publishers
(iv) As gift or complementary
(v) Through membership
(vi) In exchange

The fundamental tasks of any serials control system, manual or mechanised, can be listed as below:

(i) Selection of serials
(ii) Selection of subscription mode
(iii) Formulation of terms of procurement
(iv) Selection of vendors
(v) Order
(vi) Advance payment
(vii) Receiving and registration of serials issues in kardex
(viii) Sending reminders in case of issues not received
(ix) Adjustment of advance payment for missing issues
(x) Preparation of list of subscribed journals, new arrivals and serials holdings for consultation by users
(xi) Binding and accessioning of back volumes of serials.

In an automated system all these tasks are performed by library management software efficiently. It reduces workload of library staff. Computer based serials control systems may be predictive or non-predictive.

Predictive systems predict the arrival of individual journal issues and can generate reminders in case of non-receipted issues. Prediction means the ability to inform that a named issue of a named journal will arrive in the library within a stated time interval. Modern library management software supports predictive mode of serials control with the facilities of online acquisition and access of journals through World Wide Web (WWW).

(5) Maintenance: If we don't take proper care to organise and administer the library documents regularly, these documents would become unserviceable resources immediately. The workflow of the maintenance division/section includes following tasks:

Shelf Rectification : It is to shelve misplaced documents in proper locations

Bind : It is to preserve library resources for future and present use

Replace : It is to replace a lost document by the library

Discard/Withdrawn : It is to weed out out-dated and torn and soiled documents from the library for making enough space for usable stock

The integrated library automation environment requires information on lost, damaged, missing and withdrawn documents as well as documents sent for binding. These datasets are to be entered to generate and display appropriate messages for the library users and staff against specific tasks in different modules. This is also required to generate reports on lost books, missing books, books sent for binding. etc. for the library administration.

Q2. Write down the historical perspective of library automation.

Ans. The library automation is well-documented. Early attempts for libraries to employ some semblance of technology to transact business are recorded from the 1930s when punch card equipment was implemented for use in library circulation and acquisitions (Harter 1997). Later in 1945, Vannevar Bush envisioned an automated system that would store information, including books, personal records and articles. Bush (1945) wrote about a hypothetical "memex" system, which he described as a mechanical library that would allow a user to view stored information from several different access points and look at several items simultaneously. His ideas are well-known as the basis for hypertext and computers for their operations. The first appeared at MIT, in 1957, with the development of COMIT, managing linguistic computations, natural language and the ability to search for a particular string of information. Librarians then moved beyond a vision or idea for the use of computers, given the technology, they were able to make great advances in the use of computers for library systems. This leads to an explosion of library automation in the 60's and 70's. Development of low-cost personal computers in 1970s and improved connectivity of 1980s helped establishment of automated library systems mainly in developing blocks of the world. A decade wise analysis of developments in library automation by Mukhopadhyay (2005) is as follows:

- **Pre-computer Era (1950s):** First, there was the pre-computer era of unit record equipment.
- **Stand-alone Era (1960s):** Then came the off-line computerisation in 1960s and early 1970s.

- **On-line System (1970s):** This was followed by the on-line systems of the 1970s.
- **Micro-computer Era (1980s):** The 1980s saw the advent of microcomputers in the form of PCs, emergence of CDROM technology and Local Area Network (LAN).
- **Web Era (1990s):** Internet revolution of 1990s paved the path of web-enabled integrated library systems to support access and operations from anywhere at any time.
- **Open Era (2000s):** Emergence of open library system powered by open source software, open standards and on-the-fly integration with open data and open contents.

The phase of development of library automation. i.e. from 1970 to till date, can be grouped into the following:

- **The First Phase of Library Automation:** In this phase, computerisation of library operations take place by utilising either commercial automation package or software developed in-house. The development of shared copy-cataloguing system (also known as distributed cataloguing) was another significant achievement of this phase that utilised computer and communication technologies for collaboration and co-operation within the library community.
- **The Second Phase of Library Automation:** This phase was characterised by the rise of public access. i.e. the arrival of OPAC as a replacement for the traditional card catalogue. This phase also witnessed major developments in online access to abstracting and indexing databases, union catalogues, resource sharing networks and library consortia.
- **The Third Phase of Library Automation:** This era was characterised by the full text access to electronic documents over high-speed communication channels. Also, in this phase, digital media archiving was an important element of library automation. The advent of internet as a global publishing platform and the largest repository of information bearing objects revolutionised the ways and means of delivering library services. As a result, web-centric library automation was norm of the time.
- **The Fourth Phase of Library Automation:** This phase is also known as 'networked information revolution' phase, which supports a vast constellation of digital contents and services that are accessible through the network at any time and from any place. It can be used and reused, navigated, integrated and tailored to the needs and objectives of each user. Multimedia databases, digital libraries and virtual libraries are major

achievements in this era. Most of the automated library systems in our country are in between the third age and fourth age of library automation.

- **The Fifth Phase of Library Automation:** Library automation of this generation uses interactive, collaborative and participative platform for developing user-oriented library services with the help of Web 2.0 tools and services. This phase also characterised by the capabilities to on-the-fly integration of Linked Open Data (LOD) with local library resources and operations (for example, utilisation of global dataset VIAF (Virtual Internet Authority File) in managing name authority file of local library catalogue and integration social networking tool such as Facebook with OPAC to post like against a library document. The norms of fifth automation age are cloud based library management and web-scale library management.

A timeline for the development of ground-breaking events in library automation are as follows:

- **1936 — 1959:** Introduction of punched card for circulation control in library; Use of IBM 402, 403 and 407 for manipulating, analysis, sorting and retrieval of data; Vannevar Bush introduced the concept of 'Memex' in 1945.
- **1960 — 1969:** Use of general purpose computers that became widely available in the 1960s; H. P. Luhn (1961) used a computer to produce the "Keyword in Context" or KWIC index for articles appearing in Chemical Abstracts; Project "MEDLARS" started in 1961 that applied computer in measuring efficiencies of information retrieval systems; Computerised circulation system first appeared in 1962; Project 'Intrex' started in 1965; Project MARC, initiative by Library of Congress to provide a format for machine readable cataloguing data, started in 1965. etc.
- **1970 — 1979:** Minicomputers were introduced to automate circulation and books were bar-coded; Computer-based acquisition systems were introduced to procure books and serials; ISBDs started appearing from 1971; OCLC established in 1971 to facilitate library co-operation and to reduce costs of processing works; ISO-2709 was developed in 1973 as the standard for data exchange format; OCLC started development of Worldcat in 1975; Library networks started appearing all over the world.
- **1980 — 1989:** Shared copy-cataloguing systems by using computer and communication technologies were established as a norm in 1980s; Remote access to online databases became a

reality; Appearance of CDROM databases on indexing and abstracting journals started in early 1980s; Library automation packages initiated shifting towards relational architecture; Integrated automation packages began appearing in mid-1980s along with decade and made available on campus wide LAN for accessing.

- **1990 — 1999:** Library automation packages started upgrading from client server architecture to web architecture; Large-scale developments took place in the area of resource sharing, union catalogue and computerised interlibrary loan. Release of Z39.50 protocol in 1995 to share bibliographical information and to overcame the problems of database searching with many search languages; Formation of collective purchasing consortia started that can negotiate prices for all members of the consortium; etc.
- **2000 — 2016:** Development of matured and globally competitive open source LMSs; Establishment of open standards like SRW, SRU, MARC-XML and development of standards for different sub-domains of library automation like NCIP (NISO Circulation Interchange Protocol); Applications of Web 2.0 tools and techniques in automated library system; Development of interactive OPAC to support user tagging, rating and comments. etc.

Q3. Discuss the procedural model of library housekeeping operations.

Ans. In considering libraries from the general organisational perspective, the analysis of housekeeping system is useful for planning automation of a library. It is a prerequisite to the design and use of any library management software and to communicate with software vendors and programmers. A close analysis of the operations involved in library housekeeping provides us three hierarchical levels – procedures, activities and tasks.

(1) Procedures and Activities: The eighteen procedures are common to libraries of all types. The design and use of an automated library housekeeping system requires the analysis of all these procedures into their atomic structure. It will help to understand and implement mechanised housekeeping operations in an automated environment. The procedures under each and every operational subsystem have been analyzed by P. A. Thomas (1975) in terms of six possible activities – initiate, authorise, activate, record, report and cancel. All of these activities may not be involved in every procedure. There are one or more of six possible activities against each procedure. The six common activities are defined as:

(i) Initiate: That which makes it apparent that a procedure should be commenced.

(ii) **Authorise:** In some cases, the decision to carry out a certain procedure must be approved before any further action is taken.

(iii) **Activate:** When a procedure is known to be necessary and in some cases approved, it is usually implemented by taking appropriate actions.

(iv) **Record:** The function that states or records what action has been taken.

(v) **Report:** To notify library staff or users that action has been taken.

(vi) **Cancel:** To stop a procedure, in particular the aspect of revoking or undoing an action.

(2) Analysis of Tasks: The third level in the hierarchy is concerned with 'tasks' within an activity under each procedure. Task means a related group of operations carried out to perform a particular kind of job. In an automated library system a task is the collective functions of the elements for the accomplishment of the module at the next higher level. Tasks within each activity, just as the activities themselves, may not all be necessary to each procedure. Most of the works in the operational subsystems of a library include making or using discrete records with bibliographic and administrative information referring to one particular document. In this context, ASLIB defined a set of fifteen tasks for the basic procedures. These are – pass, receive, discard, place, remove, search, duplicate, attach, separate, move, sort. Such tasks are supported by other four element tasks namely read, verify, enter and decide.

The analysis of tasks to perform activities within procedures may be done through a set of five primary questions:

(i) What information is needed for the activity?

(ii) Where from is the information obtained?

(iii) When is it required?

(iv) Who requires it?

(v) How is it used?

These five questions should be asked to carry out possible activities under each procedure. It provides depth to the framework provided by the procedural model. An example of this approach may be shown in the context of five possible activities of book order procedure in acquisition subsystem.

Table 2.3

System	Library system Acquisition				
subsystem	Subsystem				
procedure	Order				
Activities	**Initiate**	**Authorize**	**Activate**	**Record**	**Cancel**
What information?	Author, Title, Sub-title, Edition, Place, Publishers, Date, ISBN etc	Signature of Approval	Library/ Branch Library, Date of Order, Order number, Name of Vendor and Bibliographical details etc.	Administrative data, Biblio-graphic data	Order Number, and Date Vendor, Book details
Where from ?	Bibliographies, Index, Requisition, Suggestions	Competent Authority	Book Selection Tools, MIS	Order form/ order letter	Order File/ Computer Database
When ?	After Select Procedure	Before Activation	After Authorisa-tion	After Activation	After Activation
Who ?	Library Asst./Technical Asst.	Librarian/ Section- on-in-charge	Library Asst./Technical Asst.	Library Asst./ Library clerk	Library Asst.
How ?	Receiving copy of Biblio-graphies, Suggestion slip	Enter Signature	Enter data/ information on Order form/ Computer Database and Generate Order	Filing the Copy of Order form/ Saving in computer	Deletion from Database

Q4. Discuss the computerised acquisition subsystem. Also explain outputs of computerised acquisition jobs.

Ans. Computerised library acquisition systems are designed to handle considerable amount of paper work involved in purchasing library resources. The typical functions of computerised acquisition system are:

- Print purchase order;
- Maintain book fund accounts and print book fund reports;
- Provide information on orders outstanding, and sometimes on works in process – that is, book received but not yet catalogued;

- Payment works such as generation of vouchers or payment orders; and
- Accessioning of received documents.

Apart from these fundamental functions, modern LMSs also support automatic conversion of foreign currencies, checking for possible duplicates, discount calculation, and provision of information for cataloguing or circulation functions, etc. The LMSs also differ from each other in various aspects such as:

- By type of materials handled (most of LMSs handled monographs but some extend supports for serials, electronic resources, etc.);
- By type of orders handled (many LMSs do not support standing, blanket or approval order or gifts and exchanges)
- By type of payment (LMSs differ in dealing advance payment, deposit account or membership)

The ordering and acquisition process involve some basic routine clerical operations, which are applicable to all categories of libraries. As a result, the procedures related to acquisition subsystem have benefited from computerisation. Generally, acquisition subsystem concentrates on monographs and other documents (available in many formats) excluding periodical publications. The basic activities of any computerised ordering or acquisition subsystem can be specified as follows:

- Receive records of items to be acquired
- Check whether items requested are already in the library or on order
- Print orders or dispatch order electronically to suppliers/publisher
- Check when orders are overdue
- Follow up overdue order
- Maintain a file of records of items on order
- Note the arrival of ordered items
- Process for payment
- Maintain book fund statistics and accounts
- Generate printed and electronic listing of various reports
- Control currency conversions
- Maintain vendor performance reports and statistics

The acquisition module of modern library management software should also

- Accommodate a variety of materials, including but not limited to – monographs, monograph in series, annual and cumulative indexes, loose leaf materials, supplements, reports, musical scores;

- Accommodate and identify items in a variety of formats, including but not limited to – print, microform, film, videotape, audio cassette, CD-ROM, magnetic tape, etc.;
- Record, store and display bibliographic information, acquisition type (order, gift, approval, etc.), status (reported, received, etc.), library/branch/copy/ fund information, invoice information, vendor information, accounting information, requestor information, etc.;
- Provide facilities for unlimited number of funds/budget head, vendors, orders, claims and transactions; and
- Accommodate different types of order – regular order, membership, approval, blanket order, deposit account, etc.

Outputs/Reports of Computerised Acquisition Jobs: This step includes the tasks of generating outputs from acquisition module for management operations and user services. Every computer-based system includes only three basic operations – input, processing and output. Computerised acquisition subsystems are no exceptions. Data entering and processing tasks in various pre-acquisition and acquisition works are primarily meant for the generation of various outputs in the form of list, reports, letters and statistics. In summary the outputs from a computerised acquisition subsystem typically are:

- List/Report of item(s) requested
- List/Report of item(s) from supplier/publisher
- Item(s) selected for approval
- Item(s) approved by the authority/library committee
- Item(s) rejected in the approval process
- List of gratis item(s) received by library
- Report on request status
- Printout or soft copy of letters for approval
- Printout or soft copy of order letters and query letters
- Printout or soft copy of reminder letters
- Printout or soft copy of order cancellation letters
- Printout or soft copy of reordering
- Letters for adjustment of advance payments
- Letters to bank for foreign exchange rate
- Report on order status
- List/Report of item(s) selected for order

- List/Report of overdue item
- List/Report of item(s) actually ordered
- Reports of budget commitment
- List/Report of item ordered against advance payment
- List/Report of item(s) received against orders
- Letters of intimation (on arrival of documents)
- Printout of accession register
- Printout of barcode labels
- List of supplier/publishers
- List of currency and exchange rates
- Budget with commitments
- Report of detailed annual budget of library
- Report of amount received in different budget heads
- Report/statistics of vendor performance
- List of recent additions
- Generation of book cards (in case of integrated ordering and cataloguing system)

Q5. What do you mean by computerised cataloguing subsystem? Discuss its basic requirements for catalogue module.

Ans. Development of computerised cataloguing subsystem is one of the most important and intense facets of library automation. In an automated cataloguing system the intellectual work of describing an item or document and analysing its subject content has been done by the library staff, whereas machines have been used to generate a wide variety of products derived from such description and analysis. Automated cataloguing systems are useful to control the clerical and technical processes involved, and to promote the exchange and use of cataloguing data locally, regionally, nationally and globally. Over the last 20 years, databases and online public access cataloguing (OPAC) have gradually replaced the conventional catalogue such as card, sheaf and microform catalogues. The catalogue records have become the central bibliographic record for the library management system. These records are used in the cataloguing subsystem, circulation control and acquisition control. A computerised cataloguing system requires to be standardised for the interchange of cataloguing records. Standardisation and structuring of cataloguing records are based on content designators such as MARC 21 (Machine Readable Cataloguing), CCF (Common Communication Format), UNIMARC (Universal MARC) or other similar standards.

Basic Requirement for Catalogue Module: In view of the recent developments in ICT sector, a modern LMS should provide appropriate facilities on its catalogue module. The basic necessities of module for machine-readable cataloguing may be formulated with the following requirements:

(1) Bibliographic requirements should:

(i) Support different types of classification schemes and vocabulary control devices (e.g. subject heading lists or thesaurus and electronic resources)

(ii) Support standard bibliographic and authority record formats (e.g. MARC, CCF. etc.)

(iii) Enable records to be exported or imported to and from tape, disk or other devices

(iv) Enable a bibliographic record to be retrieved and modified at any time, after entering the data

(v) Support items like monograph, serial, government document or any other type of materials

(vi) Enable catalogue data to be added, validated, updated and removed online via the workstation; and

(vii) Support withdrawal of items, export and import of records

(2) Authority control requirements should:

(i) Be capable to support and incorporate changes in the MARC authority format or other national/international standard formats

(ii) Generate various kinds of references from authority records

(iii) Accommodate:

(a) Personal, corporate and topical name heading in a name authority file

(b) Title, uniform title, and series entries in a title authority file

(c) Subject headings in a subject authority file

(3) OPAC requirements should:

(i) Allow both simple and expert searching

(ii) Support users to enter multiple words or phrases to be searched in one, more than one or all fields

(iii) Support Boolean operators within and across all fields such as:

(a) OR (either one or both terms must be in the record)

(b) XOR (either term, but not both, must be in the record)

(c) AND (both terms must be in the same record)

(d) NOT (following term must not appear in any record)

(iv) Support positional operators

(a) SAME (terms must be in the same field)

(b) WITH (terms must be in the same sentence within a field)

(c) NEAR (terms must be adjacent to one another, but in either order)

(d) ADJ (terms must be immediately adjacent to one another)

(v) Support relational operators (less than, greater than, equal to, etc.)

(vi) Include user self services, features including but not limited to reservation of items, self-renewal, cancellation of reserved items, change of address, phone number, creation of personal profile for CAS and SDI, etc.

(vii) Enable users to limit searches by: publication year, language, item type, item category, location and access

(viii) Support multilingual features

(ix) Enable searchers to specify which fields are to be displayed and to indicate brief or full display of hits

(x) Provide facilities to search global resources in the form of web documents, subject gateways, web-OPAC of other libraries, network resources, bulletin boards, discussion forums, news items, book reviews, tables of contents, best seller lists, etc.

(4) Downloading requirements should:

(i) Be Z39.50 complaint cataloguing system [ANSI/NISO Z39.50 (1995) or ISO 239.50 (1998)]

(ii) Enable to capture bibliographic and authority records from any Z39.50 server through Z39.50 client

(iii) Allow local manipulation of captured data.

(5) Reports and backup requirements should:

(i) Produce a count of all records added, edited by a specific operator or over a specified time period;

(ii) Generate lists, statistics and counts of items added or tabulated by call number, item categories, item location, etc.;

(iii) Produce a list of all citations with authority file violations;

(iv) Support backup of all cataloguing records in suitable media (magnetic, optical, etc.) and easy recovery of records at the time of need.

Q6. Describe computerised cataloguing jobs and basic jobs in cataloguing.

Ans. Computerised Cataloguing Jobs: The objective of any computerised cataloguing procedure is to create appropriate catalogues. To this end records may be drawn from any of the following sources:

(1) Title in Process: This provides the cataloguer with a list of titles, which has been already procured and accessioned by the library staff through acquisition module of the package. These records are then upgraded to the cataloguing standard through necessary addition of new data elements and modification of existing data elements.

(2) Retrospective Conversion: It is the machine-readable cataloguing of old and existing library stock. Here the cataloguing data is first entered on a worksheet or datasheet designed by the library on any standard content designator scheme and then data transferred to the database through manual keying.

(3) Existing Library Catalogue in Machine Readable Form: Development of library OPAC started long back in many libraries of the world and at that time integrated library automation packages were not available. As a result cataloguing data in digital format is available in many libraries which requires to be merged with the catalogue database of newly installed LMS.

(4) Union Catalogue: Union files of the stock of several libraries, or another shared database may be imported, converted into local standard format and finally merged with the catalogue database.

(5) Commercially available Files of MARC Records: In this process records from external databases may be added from tape, or by downloading directly from the files through network. A further option is to acquire records on CD-ROM or DVD-ROM and to download records from them.

Basic Jobs in Cataloguing: The key features of a cataloguing module are:

(1) Authority control;

(2) Data entry:

- (i) for newly acquired document
- (ii) for existing old stock.

(3) Downloading.

These basic works of a cataloguing module should also be supported by regular backup of the catalogue database in suitable media. In the family of magnetic storage devices, Digital Audio Tape (DAT) is the most popular in libraries all over the world. DVD-ROM – an optical storage device with a typical storage capacity of 17 GB is coming a big way to replace all other backup media suitable for the storage of library records.

(1) Authority File Creation and Maintenance: Authority file is essential to control form of index terms or headings, such as author headings, or subject index terms for better retrieval efficiency. Records in this file may be created locally or drawn from externally available files such as the name and subject authority files of the Library of Congress or other agencies. Library automation packages provide facility to create and maintain authority file in the catalogue module. This file is acting as a master database, where entry is to be made once. This gets reflected in various modules of the package. The master file containing authority entries can be consulted during cataloguing, possibly by display in a separate window. The new headings are added immediately to the authority file with an opportunity to review the headings, and the same is authorised for the users to access locally or remotely.

(2) Data Entry for Cataloguing: This facility of the catalogue module of automation packages is utilised for updating and standardisation of bibliographical data elements of newly procured documents and entering bibliographical data of existing stock of the library. Easy and structured data entry form design on the basis of standard content designator scheme is important for local creation of records. An integrated automation package use the same record for cataloguing function as it is used in the acquisition module. In the catalogue module the record is standardised entering additional data elements and rendering of access points with the help of authority file. The transformation of bibliographical data elements of existing stock of any library into machine-readable form is called Retrospective Conversion or simply RECON.

(3) Copy Cataloguing and Downloading: Computerised cataloguing provides a unique advantage of loading and merging of bibliographic and authority records from external databases. This feature of an automated system leads to a reduction in cataloguing effort and a consequent saving in the unit cost of cataloguing. This mode of shared cataloguing is popularly termed as copy cataloguing and implemented in libraries thorough:

(i) Merging of existing machine-readable form of cataloguing data with the catalogue database;

(ii) Relevant and appropriate records from external databases (union catalogues or commercially available catalogue datasets) in magnetic or optical media may be added to the catalogue database, after modification to match local requirements (e.g. indication of added entries, references) and the addition of local data (e.g. call number, accession number, location); and

(iii) Downloading of bibliographical data of relevant records from any Z39.50 server (version 2 or version 3) including but not limited to OCLC, RLG, and Library of Congress, etc. This facility is achieved through the incorporation of Z39.50 copy cataloguing client in the catalogue module of the package.

Q7. Discuss about Computerised Serials Control Subsystem.

Or

What is functional requirement for serials control in ILS? Briefly discuss.

Or

Highlight the workflow of automated serials control.

Ans. In LIS (Library and Information Science) and publishing, the term serials is applied to materials "in any medium issued under the same title in a succession of discrete parts, usually numbered (or dated) and appearing at regular or irregular intervals with no pre-determined conclusion". Serials include periodicals, magazines, journals, yearbooks, annuals, proceedings, transactions. etc. and these are differentiated from monographs by their ongoing or continuing nature.

Serials management subsystem of an ILS has to deal with the features unique in serials control such as:

(1) Periodicals are procured through various subscription modes and by gift or exchange;

(2) Successive issues are received at regular or irregular intervals and it is necessary to ensure that successive issues arrive when they have been published;

(3) Subscriptions to periodicals must be renewed recurrently;

(4) Catalogue data that describe serials must be extensive and should be supported by formats exclusively designed for serials;

(5) Serials change their titles are published under variant titles and may change their frequency of publication, therefore, references must be inserted to link associated periodical titles;

(6) Precise control over the binding of successive issues is very important (alternatively called as back volume management);

(7) Indexes, special issues and supplements must be controlled for effective retrieval; and

(8) Article-indexing is an added advantage for serials control module.

Functional Requirements for Serials Control in ILS: The serials control module of ILS should meet the following functional requirements:

(1) New subscription

(2) Renewal of subscription

(3) Cancellation of subscription

(4) Budget control

- Department/unit-wise budget

(5) Invoice processing

- Invoice for individual issues, or for annual (or other period) subscription

(6) Recording the receipt of journal issues

- Formula for generating expected issues (predictive mode of serials control)

(7) Managing (sending claims for) missing issues

- Sending reminders

(8) Support for domain-specific bibliographic format like MARC 21

(9) Needs to be able to cope with "special editions", supplements and indexes

(10) Should also be able to cope intelligently with name changes (of publication, publisher) and merges or splits (i.e., one journal becomes two, or two join together)

(11) Binding control

(12) Accessioning bound volumes

- Barcoding of accession numbers

(13) Complete holding information for individual title

(14) Report generation

(15) Listing the periodical for browsing

- Hyper linking the e-journals from publisher's sites or consortia sites

(16) Editing and updating of records

(17) Searching in OPAC

- By title
- By publisher
- By distributor
- Sorting by date or volume/issue number

(18) Printing of holdings of periodicals and supporting routing of periodicals

(19) Options for display holdings and receiving of serials in Web-OPAC

(20) Table of contents and other personalised information services

(21) Article indexing (The serials control module should support indexing of journal articles by author, title and subject keywords)

(22) Union list and union catalogue (In union catalogue, the complete holdings information is given along with all its missing issues, discontinuation in subscription, changes in title. etc.).

Workflow of Automated Serials Control: In ILS, the basic workflow of serials control subsystem may grouped into four subdivisions, which are as follows:

Group I: Creation and Maintenance of Master Database: Master databases play important role in serials control module of an ILS. Any number of addition, modification and deletion is possible in the master database and these changes are automatically reflected in all the sub-modules under that module. It reduces data entry work and ensures standardisation. A typical serials control module includes the following:

(1) Title Master: Bibliographical details of new serials are entered (on the basis of standard comprehensive data format like MARC 21 bibliographic format) after the selection and approval process in this file.

(2) Country Master: For entering country of publication data in sub-modules of serials control, this file contains name of countries and their corresponding codes. Country code is generally based on ISO-3166 where each country is represented by two unique characters. e.g. the code of India is **'in'** as per ISO-3166.

(3) Language Master: Now, MARC 21 geographic area code (GAC) has also been used for the purpose in most of the cases. But this file may also contain entries for languages and their three digit codes as per the ISDS manual and CCF manual.

(4) Supplier/Publisher/Binder Master: This master file contains details of all local and foreign subscription agents, publisher of serials and binders along with their corresponding codes. These codes are generally created locally.

The above mentioned master files are essential and the other important master tables are as follows:

(1) Subject Master (holds lists of subject descriptors);

(2) Frequency master (holds codes for serials frequencies);

(3) Budget master (holds financial data necessary for serials acquisition);

(4) Currency master (contains currency description, codes and exchange rate for foreign currencies);

(5) Delivering mode master (contains different modes of delivery of serials by publishers and vendors);

(6) Physical media master (holds forms, formats and media for serials in coded form);

(7) Binding type master (contains different modes of binding (e.g. standard, lather binding, cloth and rexine binding. etc.) and their corresponding codes); and

(8) Letter master (includes formats for every type of letters required for the generation of outputs such as order letter, cancellation of order letter, reminder letters. etc.).

Group II: Subscription and Acquisition: This group's task may be organised by three groups and may be represented as follows:

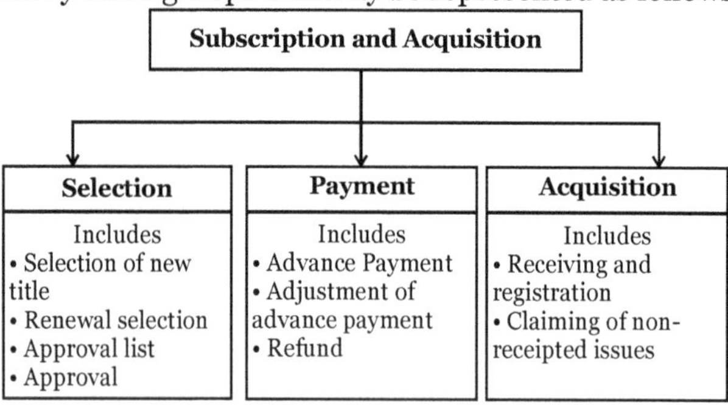

Fig. 2.2: Subscription & Acquisition

As a whole, there are 12 basic works in this group of works related to serials control given in the sequence:

(1) Selection of serials for new subscription;

(2) Renewal or discontinuation of existing journals/serials;
(3) Selection of delivery mode;
(4) Selection of subscription mode;
(5) Formulation of terms of procurement;
(6) Selection of vendors;
(7) Approval from authority;
(8) Ordering and renewal;
(9) Payment;
(10) Receiving and registration;
(11) Reminder generation; and
(12) Adjustment of advance payment for non-receipted issues.

Group III: Cataloguing and Article Indexing: The major jobs of this group are as follows:

(1) Cataloguing: For serials, cataloguing formats are fundamentally similar to those of monographs. But the content and format of serials bibliographic records varies considerably between systems. Some catalogues are based on ISBD(s) and others on ISDS formats. Some cataloguing systems use local formats and some use standard format like MARC 21, CCF/B, UNIMARC. etc.

(2) Article Indexing: Generally, libraries require article indexing option in research institutes. Indexing of articles (also called papers) from journal issues is an optional facility of serials control subsystem. Generally, publishers of primary periodicals produce annual and other sorts of indexes regularly. Apart from such products, libraries also subscribe to number of indexing and abstracting journals related to the areas of their interest. As a result, article indexing is only necessary when available indexing and abstracting services do not cover the core journals on discipline of interest.

Table 2.4: Data elements (minimum) for serials on the basis of MARC 21 bibliographic format (R=Repeatable field and NR=Non-repeatable fields)

Leader	24 character fixed-length field	
00X group		**Control Fields**
005	Date and time of latest transaction (NR)	
006	Serials–(00–17)–Fixed–length field (R)	
008	Fixed–length data elements–General information (NR)	
0X0 group		**Number and Code Fields**
022	ISSN (R)	[##; $a (NR)]
040	Cataloguing Source (NR)	[##; $a (NR)]
041	Language Code (NR)	[0/1_; $a (NR)]
042	Authentication Code (NR)	[##; $a (R)]
043	Geographic Code (NR)	[##; $a (R)]
082	DDC (R)	[0#; $a (R), $b (NR), $2 (NR)]
2XX group		**Title Related Fields**
210	Abbreviated Title (R)	[0#; $a (NR)]
222	Key Title (R)	[#0; $a (NR)]

245 Title Statement (NR)	[00; $a (NR), $c (NR)]
246 Varying Form of Title	[14; $a (NR)]
260 Publication, Distribution etc.	[##; $a (R), $b (R)]
3XX group	**Physical Desription etc. Fields**
300 Physical Description (R)	[##; $a (R), $b (NR), $c (R)]
310 Current Publication Frequency	[##; $a (NR)]
362 Dates of Publication etc.	[1#; $a (NR)]
5XX group	**Note Fields**
500 General Note (R)	[##; $a (NR)]
6XX group	**Subject Access Fileds**
650 Subject Added Entry- Topical Term (R)	[#0; $a (NR), $v (R), $s (R)]
653 Index Term - Uncontrolled	[##; $a (R)]
7XX group	**Added Entry Fields**
710 Added Entry-Corporate Name (R)	[1#; $a (NR), $b (R)]
770 Supplement/Special Issue Entry (R)	[0#; $a (NR), $t (NR),$x (NR), $w (R)]
780 Preceding Entry (R)	[0-0/7; $a (NR), $t (NR), $x (NR), $w (R)]
780 Succeeding Entry (R)	[0-0/8; $a (NR), $t (NR), $x (NR), $w (R)]
841 – 88X group	**Holdings, Location, etc. Fields**
850 Holding Institution (R)	[##; $a (R)]
852 Location/Call Number (R)	[##; $a (NR), $b (R), $c (R)]
856 Electronic Location and Access (R)	[##; $u (NR), $s (R)]

Group IV: Circulation and Binding: Following jobs are included in this group:

(1) Circulation: Circulation pattern of serials differs largely from that of books. But if serials are available for ordinary loan, then the same circulation control system will suffice as for monographs. However, serials are generally reserved for reference use only. In special libraries, the short time loan options for journals are common because of the specific need of users. If the number of transactions per day is large enough, such transaction system may be computerised. Such computerised facility must have a list of serials taken, a list of users and their addresses, and transaction interface with options for the generation of required output.

(2) Binding: Back volume management is a valuable feature of computer based serials control subsystems to inform the library staff of volumes that have been completed and are now ready for binding. After binding of back volume of a journal, accessioning is done for the bounded volume and then holding information for the concerned journal is changed/modified in the bibliographic databases of journals.

Products and Advantages: The output of products of an automated serials control subsystem may be grouped into three basic categories. i.e.

(1) OPAC: It provides search option for journals, journal articles and journal holdings;

(2) Reports and Lists: It provides status reports and MIS reports for decision-making; and

(3) Information Products: Examples include table-of-contents and other altering services including SDI.

OPAC of an ILS allows searching serials by Title (Current title, Complete holdings, Key title, Linked title, Variant title), Subject (Broad subject heading, Subject divisions, descriptors and class number), Publisher, Title history (Title split, Title merge, Title change, Title holdings), ISSN and Free text. Several reports, letters and statistics can be generated by the automated serials control system such as List of suggestions, List of approved titles, List of titles ordered, List of issues received, List of non-receipted issues, List of missing issues. etc.

Serials management has following advantages:

(1) Facilitates creation and maintenance of article indexing database and thereby generates number of user services on demand;

(2) Predicts the arrival of journal issues and generates schedules for receiving journal issues;

(3) Generates various reports in required formats for MIS activities as decision support tool for serials control (requires for addition, deletion and continuation of journals);

(4) Offers easy and simple solutions for fund accounting, payment management and budget control, a critical requirement for serials control;

(5) Facilitates online access to the serials database from anywhere at any time in any format;

(6) Ensures timely reminders generation for missing issues and better binding control for completed volumes; and

(7) It helps library staff in quick production of serials holdings and list of recent arrivals in many forms.

Q8. What is computerised circulation subsystem? Discuss.

Ans. Circulation subsystem of ILSs are effective tool for managing issue, return, renew, reservation and fine calculation easily and quickly. A circulation subsystem in ILS records loan transactions to specify – What material is in the library stock or readily accessible on ILL; Which material is in loan, and from whom or where it can be retrieved and When materials on loan will next be available in library for other users. In ILS, the transaction or loan database is the core of circulation subsystem. This database comprises a series of records, one for each transaction. Each record includes a brief dataset that specifies details of the document (through document number such as accession number), details of the user (through membership code) and transaction details (e.g. date of issue & date of return are extracted from the system date, and due date is calculated automatically). In an integrated setup, the bibliographical details (e.g. author, title edition, place and year of publication) of documents on loan are extracted from the catalogue database and the membership database is utilised for collecting user information. Accession numbers of documents are used as the key data elements in first case, whereas membership codes act as pointer to the member database in the second instance. Data-capturing is generally based on barcodes (to encode/decode both accession number for books and member ID from member card) but the use of RFID technologies in circulation are increasing significantly even in libraries of developing countries.

Q9. What are the various functions of a circulation subsystem?

Ans. By utilising three basic categories of information, a group of functions is generally performed by computerised circulation subsystems. These functions are information about the borrower; information about the resources being borrowed; and information about the loan transaction. An automated circulation system should provide facilities for managing these three categories of information including following support services:

(1) To locate circulating items (on loan, reserved by user, at binding, being reprocessed);

(2) To identify items on loan (to a particular borrower, to a specific class of borrowers);

(3) To record 'personal reserves' for items on loan but desired by another borrower and to issue alerting notice to the library staff on return of the reserved item by a borrower;

(4) To print recall notices (for returning overdue items, for renewing of items);

(5) To arrange renewal of loan;

(6) To notify to the library staff of overdue items and printing of overdue notices;

(7) To calculate fines or overdue charges for generating (printout of fine notices, receipts of fines records, printout of fine receipts);

(8) To generate statistical reports (document related, user related, top ten items by popularity, top ten user by circulation activity. etc.);

(9) To extend provision for handling special categories of borrowers and special types of materials;

(10) To generate and print gate pass and due date slips;

(11) To act as decision support system for better circulation management;

(12) To support various data capturing devices. e.g. barcode readers, smart card and RFID equipments; and

(13) To extend facilities for ILL and maintenance activities.

Q10. What are the various groups of activities for the workflow of automated circulation subsystem? Discuss the output and advantages of computerised circulation subsystem.

Or

Discuss the output and advantages of computerised of circulation subsystem.

Ans. The workflow of automated circulation subsystem begins with defining library circulation rules. Modern ILSs support branch management system in circulation. Circulation rules match patron category with item types by defining number of checkouts, loan days, fine amount, grace period, number of renewals, number of reservations. etc. The various groups of activities for the workflow of automated circulation are as follows:

(1) Membership Management: In a library, this sub-module is basically meant to create and update membership records. The works of this sub-module are:

(i) Master database creation and maintenance facility;
(ii) Member category and privileges management;
(iii) Institute profile and profiles of Departments/Divisions under the institute;
(iv) Calendar to record weekdays and closed days for library;
(v) Member enrollment facility including modification/deletion/ renewal of membership;
(vi) Output generation facility.

(2) Transaction Management: Transaction sub-module includes all the day-to-day activities of circulation section of a library. viz. issue, return, renewal, reservation, reminders for overdue books, searching document availability and listing of items issued to a member.

(3) Reminder Generation: This facility is meant for generating reminders for overdue documents– to a group of members, to individual members, for a particular due date and to all members. By using this facility or by using the master database, the format and text of reminder letter may be modified.

(4) Fiscal Management: An option is provided by fiscal management to manage outstanding dues against a member. It also includes generation of payment receipt. Fine amount may be waiver by authorised staff. This facility should also allow printing of fine statement if a member wants to have a statement of fines.

(5) Inter Library Loan (ILL): It simply means that documents of a library can be issued to the members of other libraries. ILL activities of an ILS are ILL membership management; ILL transactions management and ILL supervision.

(6) Maintenance: It is generally attached with circulation module for recording information about lost documents, documents sent for binding, damaged documents, missing documents and documents withdrawn from library.

Products and Advantages: In an ILS, the products or outputs from automated circulation subsystem are as follows:

(1) List of library members (list of members can be printed either by name or by member code and can be sorted on any required sequence or order);

(2) Items issued over a period (list of documents issued on a particular date or date range);

(3) Items returned over a period (list of documents returned on a particular date or date range);

(4) Items reserved over a period (list of documents reserved on a particular date or date range);

(5) Member ID card (Member ID card with name of the member, membership code, department, institute, category, branch and year may be printed by utilising appropriate facility);

(6) Reminder letters and notifications (preformatted reminder letters for overdue document(s) is a regular task of circulation section);

(7) Item's transaction history (transaction history of any particular document);

(8) Membership expiry list (list of memberships expiring on a particular date or date range);

(9) Member history (list of documents issued and returned by a member during his/her membership period);

(10) Fiscal report (details of the fines collected by the library on a particular date or date range);

(11) Library usage (usage by different categories of library members or by usage of different types of library materials);

(12) Most frequently issued items (list of most frequently issued documents);

(13) Most frequent member (list of most frequent users by circulation activities)

The other important products are as follows:

(1) List of items issued to a member;

(2) 'No dues' certificate;

(3) ILL reports (arrival intimation, reminder, list of items on ILL, overdue charges and payment receipts);

(4) Transaction details undertaken by a staff working at circulation;

(5) List of lost, missing or damaged documents;

(6) List of lost documents for which amount recovered;

(7) List of documents sent to binding;

(8) Order letter for binding;

(9) List of withdrawn items.

Advantages: The ability of library staff in extensive control of stock is the main advantage of automated circulation subsystem. Transaction records can be entered and saved into the main database through a terminal. The central transaction database is updated immediately and subsequent consultation of the database will communicate the current situation.

Issues: Some of the important issues may be enumerated as:

(1) Fines can be calculated on demand;

(2) Reservation and other modification to document records can be made instantly;

(3) Automatic identification of over borrowing and problem borrowers;

(4) Error-free data capturing through barcode, RFID and smart card technology;

(5) Provision of self-checking or self-issue option through web interface; and

(6) Back up provision and exchange of circulation records on the basis of NCIP (NISO Circulation Interchange Protocol) standard.

Q11. Make a comparison between the five generations of ILSs.

Ans. The following table provides a comparative study of five different generations of ILSs in the same line with bit modifications in parameters:

Table 2.5: Five generations of ILSs

Sl. No.	Features	1st Generation	2nd Generation	3rd Generation	4th Generation	5th Generation
(1)	Programming Language	Low level language	COBOL, PASCAL, C	4 GL	OOPS	AJAX
(2)	Operating System	In house	Vendor Speci?c	UNIX, MSDOS	UNIX, Windows and Linux	Mainly Linux distributions
(3)	Data Model	Non-standard	Hierarchical and Network model	Entity-Relation model	Object oriented model	Support for FRBR, FRAD and FRSAD
(4)	Import/Export	None	Limited	Standard	Fully integrated and seamless	Distributed across formats through XML
(5)	Communication	Limited	Some interface	Standard	Full connectivity across Internet	Support for Linked Open Data
(6)	Standards Support	Limited and proprietary	Improved for bibliographic data	Bibliographic and authority data	Standards for all modules	Emphasis on open interoperability

(7)	Portability	Machine dependent and hardware speci?c	Machine independent but Platform dependent	Multi-vendor	Multi-vendor and Platform independent	Complete portability
(8)	Report and statistics	Fixed format, limited ?elds and statistics	Fixed format, unlimited ?elds and moderate statistics	Customised report generation and wide statistical range	Customised report generation with e-mail interface and statistics in different formats	Complete control over report elements and comprehensive statistic generation
(9)	Media	None	None	Available in limited way	Fully available with Multimedia	All formats for digital objects
(10)	Capacity of record holding	Limited	Improved	Unlimited	Unlimited	Unlimited
(11)	Module Integration	None	Bridges	Seamless	Seamless and object-oriented	Seamless with APL for new modules
(12)	Architecture	Standalone	Shared	Client-Server	Web-centric/ Distributed	Cloud and Web-scale
(13)	Interface	Command driven (CUI)	Menu driven (CUI)	Icon Driven (GUI)	Icon driven with Wed and Multimedia (GUI)	Web 2.0 - enabled interfaces
(14)	User Support	Single User	Limited number of users	Unlimited number of Users	Unlimited number of Users	Unlimited concurrent Users
(15)	Multilingual support/ UNICODE	None	Limited (through Hardware support)	Standard	UNICODE based	UNICODE with embedded virtual keyboard for languages
(16)	External resource Integration	None	None	Limited	Improved	Full integration with external datasets
(17)	Discovery and Federated searching	None	None	None	Limited	Support for federated search
(18)	Distribution mode	Close and in-house	Close and proprietary	Close and proprietary	Both close and open source	Mainly open source

Q12. What are the general functions of library automation software?

Ans. LMSs support selection, ordering, acquisition, processing, circulation, serials control, dissemination of information services and also extend help in library administration, planning and decision-making process as a management tool. The individual tasks under each prime function are:

Ordering

•Ordering
•Receiving
•Claiming
•Fund accounting
•Enquiries (order status
•Accessioning
•Bill processing
•Payment
•Reports and statistics

Acquisition Circulation Control

•Setting of user privileges
•Issue, return and renewal
•Reservation
•Fine calculation
•User management receiving status
•Reminders and recalls
•Enquiries (about item, borrower, reservation)
•Reminders and notices
•Reports and statistics and patron sell

Cataloguing

• Standard format support
• Authority control
• Shared cataloguing
• Z39.50 based copy cataloguing
• Output generation
•User services

Serial Control

• Order placement and renewal of subscription
• Receiving and claiming
• Binding control
• Fund accounting
• Cataloguing of serials
• Enquiries (arrival of serials issues)

Access Services

• Reports and statistics
• Public access interface (OPAC)
• Web access and Remote access
• Gateway services

MIS

• Online access
• Reports and statistics
• Analysis of statistics

Q13. Discuss the requirements for library automation software.

Or

Write a short note on OPAC. [June-2018, Q.No.-5 (c)]

Or

Discuss the functional requirements that a library automation software package should satisfy.

[Dec-2019, Q.No.-1]

Ans. A library automation package or LMS should fulfil the expectations of library users, staff and authority in terms of delivery, installation, implementation, maintenance, data conversion, services, utilities, training and other essential requirements for an integrated library management system. Libraries would like to develop or purchase a

LMS that provides the most forward-looking, flexible, extensible and cost efficient solution. The basic requirements for any modern library automation package to satisfy such expectations may be studied under two broad categories – general system requirements and functional requirements.

General System Requirements: These are applicable to all modules of any modern LMS and should include but not limited to the following features:

(1) The LMS must be fully integrated, using a single, common catalogue database for all operations and a common operator interface across all modules.

(2) The LMS should have capability of supporting multiple branches or independent libraries, with one central computer configuration sharing a common database.

(3) The LMS must allow unlimited number of records, users and organisation specific parameters (e.g. loan period rules, fine calculation criteria, hold parameters, etc.).

(4) The package should include following fully developed and operational facilities at multiple customer sites:

- Bibliographic and inventory control
- Authority control
- Public access catalogue
- Web catalogue interface
- Information gateway (telnet, www, z39.50, proxy server, external access, customised web portal)
- Acquisition management
- Serials control
- Electronic data interchange (EDI)
- Reservation and materials booking
- Circulation control
- Customised generation of reports and usage statistics
- One step administrative parameters setting
- Z39.50 server (minimum version 3 and path profile level complaint)
- Z39.50 OPAC and staff client
- Z39.50 copy cataloguing client
- Marc 21 bibliographic and authority record import/export utility
- Outreach services
- Digital media archive system

- Fund accounting
- Inter library loan
- Bills and fines
- Multimedia files
- Interoperability and crosswalk

(5) LMS must provide continuous backup in suitable media (as per the choice of libraries) so that all transactions can be recovered to the point of failure.

(6) LMS must be compliant with the following standards:

- Z39.50 information interchange format
- MARC 21, UNCODE (UTF-8 OR UTF-16)
- Z39.71 holdings statements
- Z39.50 information retrieval service (client and server version 3)
- EDIFACT (EDI standard) IEEE 802.2 and 802.3 Ethernet
- HTTP, TCP/IP, Telnet, FTP, SMTP

(7) The LMS should be based on web-centric architecture and extend support for a range of multi-user and multitasking operating systems and RDBMSs.

(8) The LMS must be compliant with UNICODE standard for multilingual support and RFID for inventory management and self-issue/return facility.

(9) Vendor/Developing group should provide training to enable library staff to familiarise with system functions and operation should provide full and current system documentation in hard copy and in machine-readable form suitable for online distribution, and the LMS should include extensive online help for users and staff.

(10) LMS must support multiple hardware architecture in terms of server, network infrastructure, PC-workstations and peripheral devices.

(11) LMS must be supported with regular maintenance and on-call service, periodical software upgrades, continuous R&D, trouble-shooting of third party software such as database package and the library automation package, distribution of problem fixes/patches and emergency services for system failures and disaster recoveries.

(12) The package must provide security to prevent accidental or unauthorised modification of records through the establishment of access privileges unique to each user on the system and restriction of specific functions to specific users.

(13) LMS should provide graphical user interface, including but not limited to extensive online help, user self-service and personalisation features. The system should be supported with PC-based alternative that

will allow circulation to continue in the event of system failure, communication failure and downtime required for maintenance.

Functional Requirements: These are the minimum essential features to be supported by each functional units or modules of any modern LMS:

(1) Authority Control: The LMS must be capable of incorporating the following features:

- Support for MARC authority format for personal, corporate and topical name headings in a name authority file; title, uniform title and series entries in a title authority file, and subject headings in a subject authority file;
- Provision for generation of SEE, SEE ALSO references and Narrow Term-Broad Term-Related Term relationships network from authority records and link these references to matching access points in OPAC;
- Must allow any bibliographic field to be authority controlled, and include facilities to search, retrieve, and display print and global editing of authority records by authorised operators; and
- Must include provision for multiple thesauri with the ability to produce a list of all citations with authority file violations.

(2) Bibliographic Control: The master bibliographic record of the LMS should extend support for:

- MARC 21 (Machine-Readable Cataloguing) bibliographic and authority record formats;
- MARC record loader that can accept records input from various sources and from various media like tape, diskette or over network;
- Global editing utility that can find and replace data within specified fields; Data format validation during input of bibliographic information;
- MARC 21 format for holding and display of holding on the basis of ANSI Z39.44 serials holdings display format;
- Import and export of bibliographic data through Z39.50 compliant catalogue; Interoperability and crosswalk through incorporation of XML, RDF and metadata schemas (e.g. Dublin Core Metadata).

(3) Online Public Access Catalogue (OPAC): Following are the features of OPAC:

- OPAC must be fully integrated with other modules and accessible through web based client;
- OPAC should provide browse indexes for author, title, and series and browse index combining all four indexes; It should

allow combined, specific and field level searching for all formats along with phrase searching, nested searching and truncated searching;

- It must enable searching by using Boolean operators (OR, XOR, NOT, AND), positional operators (SAME, WITH, NEAR, ADJ) and relational operators ('greater than', 'less than', 'equal to'. etc.) within and across all fields;
- It should provide facility to see processing status (fully catalogued, in process, lost, withdrawn, etc.) and circulation status (in transit, reserve, recalled, on-hold, etc.);
- OPAC should support full, brief, standard and customised display of records including relevancy ranking of search results;
- OPAC should also support bulletin board, information desk and gateway services (to access external databases) along with patron self-service options (e.g. holds, renewals, etc.);
- OPAC must track users' preferences and interests, organised into a list of favourites. These favourites shall be included in a user's personal online account.

(4) Outreach Services: An outreach services module should be available to automate the process required to:

- deliver materials to patrons who cannot physically enter the library;
- create patron interest profiles and reading histories;
- initiate easy selection, delivery and return of items; and
- deliver local history collection and community information services.

(5) Digital Media Archive (DMA) System: The aim of DMA subsystem is to support search, retrieval and viewing of multiple media formats from client machines by using a web browser. It should be able to:

- browse and search (full text and metadata based) contents of text and images in ASCII, HTML, SGML, PDF, TIFF, JPEG, GIF, BMP, PCX, DCX, etc. formats, audio and video clips and streaming audio and video;
- link itself with library OPAC through electronic access field (MARC/UNIMARC 856 field);
- receive and register published documents from an electronic document management system;
- help a user to import one or more files from the user's system and associate them with a metadata schema within the archive;
- support metadata harvesting by using Open Archive Initiative (OAI)/Protocol for Metadata Harvesting (PMH); extend support for various Document Object Identifier (DOI) schemes;

- and accommodate remote document submission system.

(6) System Administration: The administrator or super user should control the overall administration of LMS through a highly secured module for managing the following activities.

- Access control for individual user, for each module and for each function;
- System security to prevent unauthorised access to databases;
- Module should support a standard implementation plan; and
- Module should keep a log of each transaction, which alters the database.

Q14. Describe the concept of implementation of library automation software.

Ans. Library automation is a complex process and should be planned astutely. The entire process of library automation may be divided into the following steps:

- Software selection
- Hardware selection
- Site preparation
- General training
- Customisation
- Defining procedures for
  - Bibliographical data entry
  - Administrative data entry
  - Financial data entry
- Commissioning

It is quite obvious that implementation of these steps requires background study or analysis of the library system. It is a precondition to utilise library automation package for effective results. A library will not be able to take full advantage of automation until and unless its manual functions are streamlined and justified. Therefore, the procedures and tasks followed in different sections should be analysed in terms of the following factors:

- Special features of the library system
- Number of daily transactions (issue/return/reservation)
- Local variations (their validity and (issue/return/reservation) usefulness) and available manpower
- Availability of multilingual documents
- Nature and objective of the library
- Need of information services (CAS/SDI. etc.)
- Annual acquisition and procedures followed for acquisition
- Future plan (in terms of networking and consortia)
- Number of periodicals scrutinised
- Number of users and their categories

Library managers must develop an implementation plan for the library automation project on the basis of above facts, prior to the installation of any equipment and the LMS. The plan shall be incorporated upon written approval of the authority. The plan must include, but is not limited to, the following aspects:

- Identification of all the required tasks
- Timeline for all the required tasks
- An indication of which person/group responsible for completion of each task
- A software installation requirements is checklist
- Expected start and completion dates for each task
- Training courses and course outlines,
- A site preparation requirements
- Description of post-implementation checklist
- Performance testing checklist

Q15. Discuss Library automation software packages available in India.

Or

Enumerate library automation packages of Indian origin. Describe any two of these. [Dec-2018, Q.No.- 2.2]

Or

Write a short note on NewGenLib Software.

[June-2019, Q.No.-5 (c)]

Ans. The automation of library activities in India started in full swing with the introduction of CDS/ISIS. CDS/ISIS is a menu-driven generalised information storage and retrieval system designed by a team of experts under UNESCO/PGI programme. It is specifically meant for the structured non-numerical Introduction databases. In India, erstwhile NISSAT (ceased existence since 2004) with the help of other professional bodies organised a number of training courses on application of CDS/ISIS (DOS and Windows version) in information organisation activities. As a result, a large pool of trained manpower developed all over the country. Some organisations from the experience of use of CDS/ISIS, MINISIS, etc. developed their own LMSs, e.g. DESIDOC developed DLMS (Defence Library Management System), INSDOC (now NISCAIR) came with CATMAN (Catalogue Management) and SANJAY was developed by DESIDOC under NISSAT project by augmenting CDS/ISIS (Version 2.3) for library management activities.

The LMSs presently available in India may be ranked in 2nd, 3rd and in between 3rd and 4th generations on the basis of their features. As far as the origin and application domain is concerned, the LMSs available in India may be grouped into three fundamental groups – LMSs of foreign origin, LMSs developed over LMSs or textual database management systems of foreign origin and LMSs of Indian origin. This grouping may again be sharpened by dividing the packages on the basis of size of library systems, i.e. large library system, medium range library system and small range library system.

(1) Software of Foreign Origin: This group includes library automation packages developed by foreign or multinational vendors and distributed in India either through approved agents or value-added reseller. The discussion covers four most popular packages of foreign origin.

(i) Alice for windows: Alice for windows (AfW), an integrated library automation software package is the product of Softlink, a Brisbane based Australian company. Since its inception in 1983 in Brisbane and as Softlink Asia (New Delhi) in 1996, Softlink has grown steadily and is now considered as one of the leading suppliers of library automation software with over 13000 installations worldwide, including about 150 in India, making it only second to Libsys AfW has the following modules:

(a) Acquisition
(b) Management
(c) Circulation
(d) Periodicals
(e) Journal Indexing
(f) Multimedia
(g) Subject Authority
(h) Web inquiry
(i) Book hire
(j) Multilingual
(k) Patron self checking

Cataloguing in AfW: Apart from the above, the software has a number of function-specific sub-modules such as Union Catalogue, Inter Library Loan, and Library Services. etc. Cataloguing is covered under the Management module.

The information to be recorded for the purpose of Cataloguing of a resource includes- Title, author, edition details, publication details, collation, general material description (GMD), ISBN, keywords, notes (unlimited length), series, subjects, multimedia (images, video, sound, slide shows), topics, suitability levels, country of origin, call number, barcode accession number, loan category, accession date, supplier, price, budget and department.

It is worth mentioning here that out of the above fields, GMD, barcode, accession date and loan category fields are mandatory to be recorded to navigate further. The class number field of a catalogue entry may make use of any of the two classification systems. i.e. Dewey Decimal Classification (DDC) or Library of Congress (LC) classification scheme. Notably, Alice supports USMARC format.

Entering the title of any resource triggers automatic duplicate-checking that brings the closest match, provided the title is not present in the database. AfW caters for cataloguing multiple copies of individual titles which may be shelved at one or multiple locations. A wide variety of materials may be catalogued including video recordings, sound recordings, bits maps, equipment, World Wide Web sites, electronic documents. etc.

AfW facilitates automatic generation of keywords for every significant word in the title and edition fields, if desired. The facility for creation of keywords manually also exists which can be used particularly when title is misleading or ambiguous.

Authority files are maintained for all the authors, publishers, subject headings, series, suppliers, departments, GMD and location. System facilitates to append full name from the appropriate authority files with simply typing the first few letters. There are no limits on the number of subjects, keywords, series that may be added in a record. Significantly, a fast track input approach is also provided for a skeleton entry to be registered in the library.

(ii) BASISPLUS and TECHLIBPLUS: Techlibplus comprehensive package based on BASIS plus, one of the world's leading Document DBMS and Text Retrieval Systems. It is designed to streamline and facilitate all day to day operations of a fully electronic library.

The package provides facilities for patron access, catalogue maintenance, circulation, serials management, acquisitions processing and MARC cataloguing. One of the most significant features of this package is that image references can be stored directly on the databases created through TECHLIB Plus. In other words, users can access images and information stored In databases developed using BASIS Plus DBMS and Text Retrieval System. The package also provides direct access to information contained in Current Contents. TECHLIB Plus is flexible and is simple to customise. It conforms to your library's unique profile and then maintains that profile in new releases of the software. It is built to accommodate continued growth and diversion both in document collection and computing requirements.

TECHLIB Plus is a proprietary item of Information Dimensions Inc., USA and is marketed in India by the National Informatics Centre, New Delhi. Further information relating to this package can be obtained from NIC.

(iii) **KOHA:** There are now almost fourteen open source ILS in the domain of library automation. But Koha is the first open source ILS (released in 2000 as open source) and possibly it is now the most feature rich open source ILS. Koha changed the rule of game in the ILS market and set trends in many ongoing changes in the area of library automation. Koha was originated in public library system of New Zealand. In Maori language Koha means an unconditional gift. The first version (1.0) of Koha made available for downloading as open source software in July 2000. The current stable version is 3.14.06 (released in April 30, 2014). The Koha ILS community is very active and in every month the developer community provides a bugfix release. Koha versions with new features are released in every six months (for example the next stable version 3.16 is expected to be released in June 2014). Koha is an integrated library management system that was originally developed by Katipo Communications Limited of Wellington, New Zealand for the Horowhenua Library Trust (HLT), a regional library system located in Levin near Wellington. In 1999, Katipo proposed developing a new system for HLT using open source tools (PERL, MySQL, and Apache) that would run under Linux and use Telnet to communicate with the branches. The software was in production on 3rd January 2000, and released under the GPL for other people to use in July 2000. Koha 1.01 was released on August 9, 2000. Koha is essentially based on LAMP architecture. Here L is Unix-like OS (different flavours of Linux); A is Apache Web server; M is MySQL RDBMS and P is PERL programming environment. Koha is pioneer in a number of technological achievements such as use of Web 2.0 tools, integration of authority format and bibliographic data format, availability of OPAC interface in 25 different languages, implementation of Z39.50 server and OAI/PMH compatibility, in built support for social networking tools, independent branch management, Web-based self issue, use of open standards for different modules and granular system administration facilities.

Koha is considered as the first and the best ILS from open source domain. It is a global The Koha developer team explored many emerging possibilities to redefine the scope of ILS such as OAI/PMH server, Z39.50 server, OPAC in 25 languages (the list is growing everyday), options for two text retrieval engines (Sebra and Apache-Solr), and options for two cataloguing interfaces (default cataloguing template and Biblios template). However, the major features are as follows:

(a) System administration (global parameters settings for each module, basic parameters settings for library, enhanced contents for integrating cataloguing data with global resources through information mashup, comprehensive report generation, granular access control, independent branch management option, log records supervision, fine tuning of privilege control MARC bibliographic framework set, Z39.50 client settings, etc.)

(b) Acquisitions (basic parameters for acquisition, budget head and fund allocation, real time fund accounting, vendor management, different types of order handling, order through Z39.50 searching, exclusive data entry framework in acquisition module, provision for item related information, etc.)

(c) Cataloguing (comprehensive MARC editor, inclusion and integration of MARC 21 bibliographic and authority framework, integration of thesaurus and authority lists, multilingual data entry, sub module for authority data management, Z39.50 client search for both bibliographic and authority data, implementation of FRBR model in providing item related information, integration of catalogue data with global related resources through titleISBN matching rule, help to manage leader, control (00X) and number and code fields (0XX) in MARC 21, etc.);

(d) Circulation (all required activities support, off-line circulation, granular circulation rules, fine calculation through cron job, RFID integration facility, member photo management, fast cataloguing in circulation module, renew, holds management, user-driven reservation, etc.)

(e) Serials control (predictive mode of serials control, easy management of Kardex of loose issues of journals, holdings management, separate display for back volumes and current issues, provision for routing, easy renewals, creation of frequency master and numbering patterns, vendor-wise claim management, links with cataloguing module and budget head under acquisition module, etc.)

(f) Report generation (predefined reports, custom report format, provision for pick-and-choose fields, auto scheduling of reports, sorting and filtering provision, statistical reports, top lists, format exchange provision); and

(g) OPAC (searching and browsing, enhanced content integration through information mashup, simple and advanced search interfaces, OPAC language change option, user login for personal information environment, authority searching, tag cloud, subject cloud, purchase suggestion, filter by language, item types and library, different sorting options – title, author, relevance, dates, popularity, call number, range search and sophisticated search operators, cart for listing favourite documents, private and public lists, filtering by subtype – by audience, by content type, by format, and by content type, by availability, purchase suggestions, etc.).

(iv) VIRTUA ILS: The Virtua ILS is a comprehensive library automation system that embraces innovative technology and a global perspective. Virtua offers multifaceted solutions to meet a multitude of needs. The hallmarks of the system are ease of use by patrons and staff, skins-based technology, flexibility through configurability and profiling, unique multimedia capabilities and software that adheres to industry standards and best practices. Virtua is a full-function library management system, providing control over workflows for circulation, cataloguing, serials, acquisitions, course reserves and more. It's scalable to support everything from small libraries to some of the world's largest institutions and consortia. And our Software as a Service option provides easy implementation without hardware procurement or technical staff.

Key Features

(a) System administration of Virtua ILS is fully parameterised software. i.e. libraries can configure the setting to achieve maximum flexibility. Its basic system includes modules for OPAC, circulation, reserves, cataloguing, acquisition, serials control and reporting which provides:

- support for excellent security options at different levels of access;
- comprehensive customisation parameters (over 1000) for global settings and each subsystem; and
- extensive and precise control over user activities and helps creation of rich and customised web interface for various collection components for each patron class.

(b) Virtua ILS software ensures management of multiple libraries or branches across a library.

(c) Cataloguing supports national and international standards for data interchange; full support for FRBR, FRAD and RDA. Its basic system may be supplemented by companion products like RFID, MARC data processing suite, ILL manager and patron self-check system; supports multilingual authority control, and networked multimedia database management and seamless access to multiple databases through Z39.50 client. It supports UNICODE and thereby enables the input and display of different languages in their native scripts. In fact, Virtua ILS ensures true multi-lingual catalogue database.

(d) It has comprehensive support for all acquisition activities, integration with institutional financial system and EDI support.

(e) Additional utilities of Virtua ILS include syndetics content enrichment and Over Drive e-books. It comprises PC reservation and print management, iTiva automated telephone notification as well as most self-check and RFID circulation solutions. It allows data exchange with the student information system or financial management system.

(f) User interface helps designing web-enabled digital media achieving and supports development of digital library database. It also provides 'security bit' enabled RFID solution to serve both inventory and theft deterrence functions.

(2) Software Developed over Foreign Packages

(i) LAMP: Library Automation and Management Package (LAMP) is a freeware and available for downloading from Internet at no cost. The package, developed jointly by Netherlands Library Association, Pakistan-Library Association and UNESCO, is based on CDS/ISIS (version 3.07). This MS-DOS-based package is well suited for small libraries like school and college libraries. The package contains five main modules with sub-modules under each. Facilities are grouped under each sub-module. The features of LAMP include the following:

(a) Supports creation of authority files for books and serials (supplier authority, name authority, subject authority. etc.)

(b) Supports use of LCSH subject headings in subject authority file.

(c) The Acquisition module supports all the major tasks related to books and serials acquisition like - creation of budget, purchase order authority file and purchase order data entry; Generation of purchase order; receiving of books and serials; display of order status; reminders to suppliers; Payment and reordering.

(d) Cataloguing module supports data entry for monographs and serials, catalogue card generation, creation of bibliographies, Binding and write off functions

(e) Circulation Indu has the facilities like creation of member database, edit/updating of member database, Issue and return of books and serials, renewal and reservation, checking of availability of documents and checking of outstanding documents, generation of statistics on issued items and library members

(f) Supports a number of other utilities like a generation of gate pass, shelf-card, accession registers, production of various statistical reports, global editing and replacement. etc.

(ii) NG-TLMS.net: NG-TLMS.net is state of the art library automation software based on TLMS (Total Library Management Service). TLMS has developed in Germany by TRANCE group. The route of development for this LMS is TLMS -> NGTLMS -> NGTLMS.net. NG-TLMS.net is designed on the top of TLMS by WebOPAC Applications Pvt. Ltd. It is SQL-backed client-server system, based on Microsoft's .NET platform. It supports CCF, USMARC, Indian UNIMARC (as recommended by Central Secretariat Library, New Delhi) and Z39.50. The NG-TLMS.net supports the following activities and facilities:

(a) Printing of accession register; AACR II card generation; article scan management; authority files creation; auto cataloguing from web sites; auto export & import; Auto keyword generation; automatic barcode generation; letterhead creation; dropdown matching. etc.

(b) Barcode based issue & return and serials control; auto status generation for progress of processing of documents; bulletin board facility; Kardex generation for serials control; complete Intranet support; automatic claim generation for overdue and missing journal issues.

(c) RTF, Dial-up networking, e mail and printing of gate pass; ID card generation; arrival list generation; multi-lingual support, web access of OPAC; power search facility; Fine calculation and receipt generation;

reservation of books; retrospective data conversion; SDI service; search refining; security enhancement; statistics & graphs; stock verification.

(d) UNIMARC input sheet generation; UNIMARC cataloguing; virtual library creation; Z39.50 client & server; UNICODE support (all languages of the world are supported).

(e) Web centric architecture i,e, requires only installation on server. Client uses browser to access all information.

(f) No restrictions on the number of records; acquisition module includes accounting software and is optional; basic software covers all areas, e.g., OPAC, cataloguing and circulation; all Indian Languages supported.

(g) Includes facilities for - WebOPAC, Internet and Intranet via browser, union cataloguing supported in distributed and replication environments, US MARC 21, UNIMARC, CCF and Z39.50 and can be installed by relatively less experienced computer users.

(iii) WINSANJAY: This LMS has been originated from SANJAY, a package based on CDS/ISIS (Version 2.3). It was developed by DESIDOC under a NISSAT project to meet the requirements of library management activities. It includes a set of 35 Pascal programs and 25 special menus. The features of WINSANJAY are as follows:

(a) Windows based and more user friendly than WINISIS and CDS/ISIS for library housekeeping operations. Suitable for medium range libraries.

(b) Effective interlinking of databases (it is a great achievement because WINISIS or CDS/ISIS does not support relational database design model). Interlinks book databases, member databases, vendor databases and budget databases.

(c) Maintenance module restricts the access right to a limited set of users and thereby provides security measures. User module helps library staff to carryout daily routine in circulation, acquisition and online catalogue.

(3) Softwares of Indian Origin: This group includes packages designed and developed by Indian vendors and software agents. The features of the following automation packages are discussed here. Packages are selected for discussion on the basis of their customer base and popularity.

(i) AUTOLIB*:* Autolib is fully integrated multi-user software on Windows Environment, designed to automate various activities of University Libraries, College Libraries, R&D Libraries, Public Libraries and Special Libraries. The software is developed by Auto Lib Software Systems, Chennai and the product range includes:

MS-Access with Visual Basic Version

MS-Access with Visual Basic & WEB Edition

MS-SQL server with Visual Basic Version

MS-SQL server with Visual Basic & WEB Edition

MS-SQL server with Visual Basic

The LMS is module based system, designed and developed by a team of library and information specialists, system analysts, software professionals, network specialists and database designers. The features of Autolib may be listed as: General features: Module based, User Friendly, GUI Environment, Based on client server architecture, Uses Visual Basic 6.0 as front end and MS-SQL V.7.0 RDBMS as back end, Uses TSQL Query Language, Module level Security, Z39.50 Protocol Support, Export/Import of data in ISO 2709 format, Cataloguing of digital resources, Implementation of AACR, CCF, Dublin Core, TCP/IP and Dial-up Network support, Web based reports, Menu based operations, Incorporated Mandatory Fields of CCF, Powerful Search Facility/Query Builder, Printing various reports in several formats, Simple data entry, User ID and password protection, Online help/ documentation, Continuous product up gradation, Customer support and maintenance.

Minimum hardware and software requirements: Server configuration – Pentium II/III 64 MB RAM/4.2 GB HD, 32x CD-Drive/1.44 FDD, Network accessories, SVGA Monitor, Windows NT Server 4.0 and SQL Server 7.0. Client Configuration – Pentium II with 32 MB RAM/4.2 GB HD Windows NT workstation/Windows 9x.

The functional features of this LMS are as follows:

(a) Database Management–data entry/updating of database for user, author, publisher, supplier, member, book, journal issues and back volumes, article report, thesis, standard, non-book materials, budget, subject, department etc

(b) OPAC–powerful and versatile search facility, Simple search for beginners, Query builders for advanced users, query windows for complicated search, boolean search, field level search (single field/multiple fields, author/ title/ keyword/ subject, accession no/ classification, journal name/article name, etc.)

(c) Circulation–transaction, issue, return, renewal of books, journals, back volumes, recall, reservation, cancellation, reminders, reports

(d) Serials Control–subscription of new journals, renewal of journals, receipts of new issues, reminders for missing issues, invoice processing, payments, browsing issues, reports generation

(e) Acquisition Control–duplicate checking, indent processing for new books, book ordering, reminders, receipts of books, invoice processing, payment, budget management

(f) System Administration Module–user ID and encrypted password protection, module level security, budget management, stock verification, global updating, fixing due dates, overdue charges, etc., holiday maintenance, reports, new additions, catalogue (main/author/title), accession register/bibliography, list of books by author/title/publisher/year, subject/call number (by any order), books by unique titles, frequently issued books, frequently accessed books, books issued/returned/reserved, receipt for fine amount/deposit/loss of book. etc., list of users/publishers/suppliers/departments, no-due certificates, stock verification report, budget details, orders, journal list, journal subscription/order report/missing issues.

(g) Article Indexing–allows to create journal article database, allows to create author index and keyword index, allows to search and retrieve journal articles, allows to create index and abstracts, allows to publish CAS bulletin, allows to generate contents pages

(h) Digital Library Module– allows to catalogue multimedia digital resources such as text, images, audio file, video clippings. etc. Allows to catalogue based on Dublin Core standard, Allows to handle various file formats such as .bmp, .jpeg, pdf, .doc, .avi. etc.

(ii) E-Granthalaya: This LMS is developed by National Informatics Centre (NIC), Bangalore centre to suit the requirements of small and medium sized libraries. It is an easy-to-use software package and supports all the routine library operations. The General and Special features of the LMS are as follows:

(a) The package includes functional modules for administration, serials control, acquisition, circulation, OPAC, reports and index;

(b) Generates customised reports and statistics of library usage;

(c) OPAC allows simple and advance search options, supports web-enabled searching;

(d) The package has bilingual capabilities and can be customised to suit all Indian languages supported by ISM 2000 developed by C-DAC, provides options to control access through login id and password and supports quit-in privileges for users and staff;

(e) Supports both standalone and networked operation mode. Recommended server configuration is Pentium III processor, 128 MB RAM and 4.3 GB Hard disc;

(f) Requires Windows NT/Windows 2000 for server and Windows 98/XP/2000 for client machines and uses MS SQL server as backend database;

(g) Requires ISM2000/Leap office 2000 as bilingual tool.

(iii) Granthalaya: This CUI based (DOS & UNIX) modular LMS is developed on FoxPro by INSDOC (now NISCAIR) for medium range libraries. It includes all the modules required for day-to-day library operations. The package is made of seven modules – library administration; query; circulation; acquisition; serials control; technical processing and data administration. The salient features of the LMS are:

(a) Based on object oriented design;

(b) Supports CCF and ISO 2709 for import and export of data;

(c) Supports Boolean operators and range searching;

(d) Provides online help through screen messages;

(e) Generates a dictionary for various data elements for easy searching.

(iv) LIBSUITE: This GUI or CUI LMS, developed by SOFT-AID Computer Ltd., Pune, is based on web-centric architecture and designed to work with different media. LIBSUITE is based on three-tire web centric architecture in which server machine uses Windows NT/2000 and Internet Information Server (IIS) – as web server. The database server relies on Oracle 8i and clients use web interface for accessing server through Internet or Intranet. LIBSUITE extensively uses latest technologies like Active Server Pages (ASP) and Component Object Modeling (COM).

The web-centric architecture ensures that any machine with a web browser can be a client. It also ensures working independent of operating systems in client machines.

The following are the significant features of LIBSUITE:

(a) It provides all the standard modules and supports customised report generation and standard protocols Z39.50
(b) The package bundles follow fully featured modules – acquisition, cataloguing, circulation, queries, serials control, set up and maintenance
(c) Cataloguing module, apart from supporting regular activities manages multi-format materials, generates entire status, i.e. total number of books, number of books issued and number of books available on stack
(d) Circulation module supports all the required operations including ILL and generation of photograph of the member in circulation panel
(e) System administration module supports controls over the access, creation of authority entries and setting of parameters for cataloguing, circulation. etc.
(f) Supports stock verification and global addition and deletion; Acquisition module supports all media and production of accession register
(g) Web-centric architecture ensures use of any machine as client as it does not require the installation of client-side software
(h) Provides easy user interface and ensures seamless navigation through Intranet, and login and password based access as security measure
(i) Includes various utilities like calculator and calendar.

(v) LIBSYS: LIBSYS is the most popular library software in India having more than 1000 installations in different types of libraries.

LIBSYS is an integrated library management software developed in C and C++. Although the software is based on its own bibliographic database, it is available for systems using ORACLE and SQL Server as back-end RDBMS.

Presently, LIBSYS is available in six different editions/versions to suite requirements of different types of libraries. These are as follows:

(a) ***LIBSYS7:*** A true realisation of Lib 2.0, LIBSYS7 delivers unparallel satisfaction for both patrons and library staff. It gives end-to-end manageability of the library operations through its comprehensive modules. As a web-based solution, it provides platform independence. The interactive features in the industry's most advanced OPAC makes LIBSYS7 most rewarding choice for all the Librarians. LIBSYS7 is a product aiming most convenient and pleasing library experience through its value added features.

(b) ***LSEase:*** It has all the strengths required to manage a library with basic needs. It is a package bundled with basic library management modules giving our prospects a low cost – high value proposition. Based on the client-server architecture, it gives users a blend of technology advantage and ease of use. LSEase requires minimal data entry and facilitates easy data back-up. The web-based search facility for bibliographic searches is fast even for large databases.

(c) ***LSAcademia:*** It is a complete ERP Solution to manage an Academic Campus be it a school, college or an institute. It seamlessly integrates different administrative departments and ensures a smooth flow of information among them. On the technological front, LSAcademia is empowered with the latest tools that facilitate process streamlining and efficient working environment for each department and provide seamless information sharing among related entities.

(d) ***LSmart:*** LIBSYS offers LSmart solutions based on RFID and EM technologies, taking automation and security in libraries to a new level. LSmart integrates RFID and EM hardware from world-renowned manufacturers with LIBSYS using its more than two decades of experience in library automation. LSmart has proved to be strong on reliability, flexibility and ease-of-operations and combined with robust and quality hardware equipments.

(e) ***LSNet:*** LSNet makes available a web portal for individual subscribers giving them a common platform for sharing their personal collection among themselves in a seamless manner. LSNet revolves around a virtual library that includes the collection of participating specialised libraries and enables all individual subscribers to maintain and share their collection of books, CD/DVDs, reference material. etc.

(f) ***LSDigital:*** LSDigital is a document digitisation software used by libraries for the purpose of easy management, multi-access, reduction of storage space of the document and the preservation against spoilage of rare books, research papers, important documents and archived newspapers, maps. etc. The software has been designed to facilitate easy searching of text in the document. LSDigital is a complete Digital Resource Management System (DRMS) which can be integrated with any twain compliant scanner.

(vi) NEWGENLIB: NewGenLib is a fully web-based integrated library management software that runs on distributed computers through a network or server. It can also run on local area networks without access to the internet, although some of the advantages of using it via the web will be lost. It uses a number of well-supported and widely-used, reliable and well tested open source components like PostgreSQL, Apache Tomcat and Solr Lucene. NewGenLib is entirely Java-based, platform neutral and uses the following related software technologies in its presentation, web server and database layers. Some advanced functional features of NewGenLib are as follows:

(a) Android mobile and tablet capable;

(b) Integration with Twitter helping send messages of transactions directly to users' Twitter accounts;

(c) Flexibility of defining own search field in OPAC;

(d) Enhanced contents and interactive OPAC like availability of book jackets, google preview, comments/book review, tagging, favourite reading list. etc.;

(e) Zotero compliant OPAC;

(f) RSS Feeds in OPAC;

(g) Faceted Browsing (Refining search results);

(h) Suggestion for other books in the rack;

(i) RFID supports;

(j) Provision for frequently used predefined templates along with freedom of defining own customised data entry templates in cataloguing;

(k) Configurable SMS system – a proof of transaction;

(l) Integration with g-mail or paid mailbox account, which enables automatic sending of e-mail to patrons during issue/return;

(m) Enhanced Report Module for generating in .csv format with a provision for wide customisation;

(n) Provision for integrating with Vufind SOPAC (Ex: OPAC of the Library of Bangalore University);

(o) Catalogue can be harvested through Google site map and thus the visibility of the library can be further improved.

(vii)NEXLIB: This window based LMS was designed and developed by NexEvolve Logic Solutions Pvt. Ltd. It provides a simple point-and-click navigation interface backed by a powerful database engine capable of maintaining millions of records. Nexlib provides all the basic utilities required for the management of libraries, namely, Acquisition, Cataloguing, Circulation, Serials Control and OPAC. The important features of NexLib are as follows:

(a) Acquisition module is fully integrated with the cataloguing module. It can manage a variety of library materials and also fund accounting

(b) Cataloguing module helps to define location of items by floor, shelf number, etc.

(c) The entire circulation task can be carried out from one screen

(d) Provides facility to create unlimited number of user types and member data can be transferred from any existing user information system

(e) OPAC can be accessed through any standard web browser

(f) Generates over 50 pre-defined reports related to library MIS

(g) Ensures easy-to-use library staff interfaces

(h) Full-featured serials control with the support for variety of formats and advanced search option for OPAC

(i) Digital Media Archive (DMA) module for the management of full text articles, newspaper reports, images. etc.

(k) DMA allows incorporation of standard metadata schemas and metadata-based retrieval.

(l) NexLib is a platform-specific LMS and depends on Microsoft products. The hardware and third party software requirements are as follows: Sever should be Pentium III or higher with minimum of 256 MB RAM and preinstalled with windows 2000 sever. Client machine should be Pentium II or higher with 128 MB RAM and preinstalled with windows 98/NT/2000/XP.

(m) Follows client/server architecture and security of library database access is based on Windows NT model

(n) Supports MS Access, MSSQL or Oracle 8i as backend RDBMS and uses Visual Basic (VB) as scripting language.

(viii)SLIM

(a) **SLIM 21:** The greatest advantage of SLIM21 is that we can make data entries in any language we want since it supports Unicode. SLIM 21 version has three levels. i.e. Basic Level (Acquisition Cataloguing, Serials control,

Circulation and OPAC); Enterprise Level (Basic Level integrated with Web-based OPAC, Selective Dissemination Information (SDI), Inter Library Loan (ILL), Current Awareness Service (CAS), Web Proposals, Statistical Analysis); and L2L Level (Basic level + Enterprise level integrated with Z39.50 client, Z39.50 server, MARC-XML). All of these three levels are supported by additional utilities like Colon classification shelving order, Touch Chip Interface (Biometrics), Newspaper monthly billing, Smart Card/RFID interface, Library Map and Newsclipping publishing, Multilingual data processing and retrieval, Support for standards like NCIP, SIP2, ISO-2709. etc.

(b) ***SLIM ++:*** It is a stripped down version of SLIM 21. It supports exports/import through MARC/CCF/ISO-2709 standards and downloading of bibliographic data from online databases through DB Bridge module and Z39.50, generates customised reports on screen/printers/RTF or as text/PDF/HTML files with auto e-mailing facility, supports Unicode based LMS that supports multi-script sequencing for Indian scripts, generates shelving order for documents as per colon classification, supports smart card/RFID based circulation and touch chip (biometric) interface for user authenticity, creates library map for easy location of items and provides user-friendly online help and reference manual.

(ix) SOUL: Software for University Libraries (SOUL) is a state-of-the-art integrated library management software designed and developed by the INFLIBNET Centre based on requirements of college and university libraries. It is a user-friendly software developed to work under client-server environment. The software is compliant to international standards for bibliographic formats, networking and circulation protocols. After a comprehensive study, discussions and deliberations with the senior professionals of the country, the software was designed to automate all housekeeping operations in library. The software is suitable not only for the academic libraries, but also for all types and sizes of libraries, even school libraries. The first version of software. i.e. SOUL 1.0 was released during CALIBER 2000.

The latest version of the software. i.e. SOUL 2.0 was released in January 2009. The database for new version of SOUL is designed for latest versions of MS-SQL and MySQL (or any other popular RDBMS). SOUL 2.0 is compliant to international standards such as MARC 21 bibliographic format, Unicode based Universal Character Sets for multilingual bibliographic records and NCIP 2.0 and SIP 2 based protocols for electronic surveillance and control.

Q16. Write down the evaluation of library automation software.

Or

Explain the criteria for evaluation of a library automation software. [June-2019, Q.No.-2.2]

Ans. The selection of library management software is a complex and time-consuming one. Apart from thorough knowledge of the library system, sub-systems, procedures, activities and tasks, it requires the knowledge of LMSs features and trends in the development of ICT. The selection process should be based on seven basic steps – Evaluation, Comparison, Demonstration of package, Feedback from authority, staff & users, Preliminary selection, Modification and Customisation and Final selection. The process of evaluation should be based on some predefined criteria. After evaluation against checklist, the LMS should be compared with other packages on the basis of services, utilities and features.

Criteria for Evaluation of Library Automation Software: The following factors should be taken into consideration at the time of evaluation of any library automation package:

(1) Vendor Validity: The reputation of software development group or the vendor is extremely valuable. The following questions should be raised to judge the validity:

- (i) Is the vendor also the software developer, or is the vendor a distributor or agent for the software developer?
- (ii) Is there an international presence or is the company localised?
- (iii) How long has the software developer been in the library systems industry?
- (iv) How long has the library software you are interested in been in the market?
- (v) Who uses this software? (Look for someone in close proximity and contact him or her with questions. If possible, make an on-site visit to see the product in action.)

(2) Services Availability Checklist: The services and utilities of any LMS should be checked for the availability of following core, enhanced and value-added services:

- **(i) Core Services:** Acquisition, Cataloguing, Circulation, OPAC, Serials control, Bibliographic format support, Data exchange format support, Article indexing, Retro -conversion, Standard reports and System administration
- **(ii) Enhanced Services:** Customised report generation, GUI-based user interface, Reservation facility, Interlibrary loan

module, Multi-lingual support, Union catalogue, Authority file support and controlled vocabulary, Online help, Online tutorial, Power search facility, Internet support, Intranet support, Web access OPAC, Multimedia interface, Barcode support and Backup utility

(iii) Value-added Services: Patron self service through RFID and Smart card (self circulation, self reservation. etc.), Online user training/orientation, Stock verification facility, Members photo ID card generation, Barcode generation, Fine calculation & receipt generation, Gate pass generation, Bulletin board services & e-mail reports, Electronic SDI, CAS support, Digital media archiving support.

(3) Functional Checklist: The following general features are part of software module testing, and each should be tested or conducted during the evaluation process:

- Searching Capabilities (All modules)
- Data Entry and Editing (All modules)
- Bibliographic/item File and Maintenance
- Bibliographic Interface Software
- Authority Control
- Inventory (Circulation)
- Check-out (Circulation)
- Renewal (Circulation)
- Circulation/Management Reports (Circulation)
- Check-in (Circulation)
- Fines and Fees (Circulation)
- Notice Production (Circulation)
- Holds (Circulation)
- Recalls (Circulation)
- Patron File (Circulation)
- Reserves (Circulation)
- Portable Back-up Units
- Report Writer
- Acquisitions
- Serials
- Electronic Databases
- Gateways
- Network Operations
- Z39.50 Server

- Inter-library Loan

(4) Data Conversion and Backup Utility: The ability of the package in terms of support for data conversion from other library systems and adherence to the international bibliographic data standards and protocols should be checked extensively. In this age of shared cataloguing systems and web integration, the LMS should also support metadata schemas and interoperability issues like XML, RDF and OAI/PMH. Backup facility in suitable media is also to be checked in view of data recovery at the time of need.

(5) Training, Documentation and Customer Support: The vendor must provide:

(i) adequate training facilities without fees for supervisor and operators to:

  (a) manage and operate the system on a day-to-day basis;

  (b) run file backup operations, software utilities and cataloguing utilities;

  (c) troubleshoot and solve simple problems and load software enhancement received from the vendor.

(ii) complete documentation (in hard copy and machine-readable form) must be available with the package along with regular documentation updates and release notes available for local printing or downloading via web; and

(iii) the package must have support from the software vendor for hardware and software maintenance, data conversion, emergency and on-call support and disaster management.

(6) Hardware and Third Party Software Requirements: The vendor should provide a complete list of hardware requirements (processor type and RAM) for server and client machines, operating system requirements and back end RDBMS (with version) requirements. Evaluation should be based on total cost for minimum hardware and third party software requirements of the package.

(7) Performance Testing: Any LMS should be evaluated by checking some performance testing like transaction throughput capacity and response time, hardware functionality, module functionality, conversion testing, database loading, index building. etc.

Comparison of Automation Packages: A comparative study of LMSs selected on the basis of abovementioned checkpoints may be done by taking into account five aspects – hardware requirements, intrinsic features of packages, available services and facilities, customer support services and price.

Hardware and backend software requirement for LMSs: Any LMS is application software, which requires some system software and hardware support for proper functioning. Thus, the selection of LMS should be done on the basis of careful analysis of the basic hardware and software requirements for the package.

Intrinsic features of LMSs: The factors like data storage techniques, programming language(s) used in the development of software, database structure, file organisation, etc., must also be taken into consideration for the comparative study because these factors will determine very important issues of maintenance, upgradation and customisation in future.

Services and facilities available with LMSs: The suitability and superiority of any LMS depends on the available services, facilities and coverage of library/information activities in various modules. The whole range of services available in selected LMSs may be divided into three groups – Core services, Enhanced services and Value added services:

(1) Core Services: These are the basic services necessary for day-to-day library activities and must be available with LMSs. These services may be tabulated for the comparative study as follows:

Table 2.6: Core Services in a Library

SL. No.	Core Services	Score (1 presence of service, 0 absence of service)
(1)	Acquisition	
(2)	Cataloguing	
(3)	Circulation	
(4)	OPAC	
(5)	Serials Control	
(6)	Bibliographic Format Support	
(7)	Data Exchange Format Support	
(8)	Article Indexing	
(9)	Retroconversion	
(10)	Standard Reports/ Administration	
	Total Score	

(2) Enhanced Services: These are the additional set of services, which will make the work of a librarian easy, smooth and seamless, and at the same time these will help users in efficient information retrieval, cross-domain searching and easy navigation.

Table 2.7: Enhanced Services in a Library

SL. No.	Enhanced Services	Score (1 presence of service, 0 absence of service)
(1)	Customised Report Generation	
(2)	GUI-based User Interface and Colour	
(3)	Reservation Facility	
(4)	Interlibrary Loan Module	
(5)	Multilingual Support	
(6)	Union Catalogue	
(7)	Authority File Support and Controlled Vocabulary	
(8)	Online Help	
(9)	Online Tutorial	
(10)	Power Serach Facility	
(11)	Internet Support	
(12)	Intranet Support	
(13)	Web Access OPAC	
(14)	Multimedia Interface	
(15)	Barcode Support / RFID Support	
(16)	Backup in suitable media	
(17)	Z 39.50 Client and Server (Target)	
	Total Score	

(3) Value Added Services: These are the essential work and services of library management and generally not included within the scope of a LMS. But with the development in hardware, software and connectivity, LMSs are presently trying to provide software solution for this type of work and services.

Table 2.8: Value-added services in a Library

SL. No.	Value Added Services	Score (1 presence of service, 0 absence of service)
(1)	Patron Self-Service (Self-Circulation, Self Reservation, etc.)	
(2)	Online User Training/Orientation	
(3)	Stock Verification Facility (RFID)	
(4)	Members Photo ID Card Generation	
(5)	Barcode Generation	
(6)	Fine Calculation & Receipt Generation	
(7)	Gate Pass Generation	
(8)	Bulletin Board Service & E Mail Reports	
(9)	Electronic SDI, CAS & CAL Support	
(10)	Digital Camera Support	
	Total Score	

(4) Customer Support Services: The support services from the software developers/agent at the right time and at the right place is a critical factor to be kept in mind at the time of selection of any LMS.

Table 2.9: Customer Support Services in a Library

SL. No.	Customer Support Services	Score (1 presence of service, 0 absence of service)
(1)	On Call & On Site Support	
(2)	Continued R & D and Software Updating	
(3)	Live Internet Support And Updates	
(4)	Training	
(5)	User Group and Newsletter Services	
	Total Score	

(5) Price: Last but not least, we have to take the price of the packages also into consideration for cost-benefit analysis of available services in the short-listed LMSs. This factor plays an important role in our country because financial crunch is a regular feature in Indian libraries and information centres. As a general trend, commercial LMSs are costlier than the packages developed by government organisations. The price of the software rises with the number of value-added services and enhanced services incorporated in the software. In general, the pricing model of commercial LMSs may be divided into three options – Basic version (Price range: ₹10,000/- to 1,00,000/-), Standard version (Price range: ₹1,00,000/- to 5,00,000/-) and Full version (Price range: ₹5,00,000 onwards). The basic version supports limited collection size and does not have networking features. The standard version supports unlimited collection size and limited number of network users. The full version supports unlimited collection size and unlimited users. Moreover, commercial LMS developers also claim additional charges for customisation, onsite training, data conversion (from other DBMS), software updates (after warranty period) and post warranty annual maintenance charges.

Q17. What do you mean by Trends and Future Directions?

Ans. The rapid developments of ICT have changed the libraries over the last few decades. The library systems all over the world are going through a process of transformation to address the effects and implications of technological change. In response to the needs of the hour, library automation packages are gradually being upgraded to satisfy diversified demands of library authority, staff and users by incorporating various epoch-making features. Some of these features are selected for discussion here on the basis of their importance and utilities in library management.

(1) Unicode: Unicode enables the input and display of different languages of the world in their native scripts. Unicode complaint LMSs are able to dynamically change language at any point without affecting other system users.

Example: A librarian could catalogue a record in English, and then change languages to enter record in Hindi, Bengali, Tamil, Marathi. etc.

Unicode is a character representation standard like ASCII. ASCII is one byte (8 bits) code and can represent only 28, i.e. 256 characters, whereas Unicode is two byte code (16 bits) and can represent 216, i.e. around 65,000 characters. As a result Unicode standard can represent all the scripts of the world including some obsolete scripts such as Bramhi and Kharosti. Unicode provides two encoding formats – UTF-16 (default) and UTF-8 and the present standard (Unicode 4.0) can represent 50,000 characters. The fully functional multilingual system requires the Unicode support by operating system, programming languages, application software and word processors. Unicode support for LMSs is essential in multilingual countries like India.

(2) Z39.50: The growth of shared cataloguing and cooperative cataloguing initiatives allow capturing bibliographic data from remote library servers over the Internet. It reduces unit cost of cataloguing and saves a lot of time for individual libraries. However, the major problem is of variation in software and hardware. Library professionals have to learn the specific features of each system. More the electronic resources grow more will be the confusion on how to access the information from diverse databases. ANSI/NISO Z39.50 standard was developed to share the bibliographical information electronically and to overcome the problems of database searching with different search languages. Z39.50 is a session oriented program-to-program open communication protocol based on client-server computing model. LMS incorporated with Z39.50 copy-cataloguing client (called origin in the standard) submits a search request to any Z39.50 server (called target), which then process the request and returns the result in desired standard. LMS will then place the captured record in the catalogue editor for manipulation.

(3) Web-centric Architecture: Web-centric LMSs allow web based staff and user access and thereby ensures searching, browsing, data entry and system Introduction administration from anywhere at any time against user authentication. In such a system, there is no requirement to install client-side software in client computers. Any machine with standard web browser may be used as client for accessing library database. This architecture applied Common Gateway Interface (CGI) and Hypertext Transfer Protocol (HTTP) to ensure platform independent access to library services. It also helps to overcome space and time Barrier.

(4) Integrated Access Interface: Integrated access interface refers to the ability of LMSs to combine multitude of resources and media type in a single and seamless search mechanism. Such interface should support hypermedia environment to include:

(i) Library catalogue
(ii) Collection acquired in digital form
(iii) Collection digitised in-house
(iv) E-journals and e-books
(v) Purchase datasets on CD ROMs
(vi) Subject gateways
(vii) Other library's OPAC
(viii) Bulletin board, Listserv and Discussion forum
(ix) Information desk
(x) Community information

(5) FRBR based Bibliographic Data Model: FRBR stands for Functional Requirements for Bibliographic Records. It is a conceptual model, proposed and designed by IFLA (International Federation of Library Associations), for the management of bibliographic databases. The model uses entity-analysis techniques to identify entity, attributes and relationships in the bibliographic universe. It also identifies the relevance of each attribute and relationship to the generic tasks performed by users of bibliographic data. Packages are incorporating FRBR model for the design of central catalogue database. Interoperability and Crosswalk: Interoperability means the ability of multiple systems (with different hardware and software platform and data structure interface) to exchange data with minimal loss of content functionality. A crosswalk is a mapping of the elements, semantics and syntax from one metadata schema to those of another. It allows metadata created by one community to be used by another group that employs a different metadata standard. Interoperability and crosswalk ensures exchange of bibliographic data among heterogeneous systems across the globe. LMSs are now supporting various standards and protocols like Z39.50, AI/PMH, METS (Metadata Encoding and Transmission Standard) and MARC-XML to achieve interoperability

(6) RFID and Smart Card Based Inventory Control: Radio Frequency Identification (RFID) is the technology that is slated to replace barcodes in library applications. The RFID tags are placed in books and generally covered with the sticker. RFID reader and antenna are often integrated into patron self-checkout machines or inventory readers. The reader powers the antenna to generate RF field to decode information stored on the chip. Reader sent information to the central server, which in turn communicates with the library automation software. LMSs are incorporating RFID technology for performing self-issue and return, stock verification, theft detection, identification of misplaced books and inventory counts.

RFID compliant LMS increases staff productivity and ensures full-proof security.

Smart card technology is used in libraries to manage public access resources. It makes the process user friendly for librarians as well as for patrons. It supports self-checkout, payment of fees and fines and use of public access resources through using one smart card by patrons. The system also provides excellent privacy, security options and personalisation of services for library users.

(7) Open Source Software: Open Source Software (OSS) is software for which the source code is freely available. It means that anyone can access the source code and make changes.

Such facilities are not available with proprietary or closed source programs. Some examples of open source software are – Linux operating system, Mozila web browser, MySQL RDBMS, Apache web server and PERL. The open source movement has its roots in the 1970s, and is continuing to grow in popularity. Number of integrated library automation packages is available as OSS for downloading and use in libraries all over the world, such as KOHA, MyLibrary, Avantika, etc. Generally, these packages are based on LAMP architecture, i.e. Linux operating system, Apache web server MySQL RDBMS and PERL/PHP as scripting language. Many libraries, faced with budgetary crunches and the resultant lack of technological resources, have opted for open source solutions. The advantages of using OSS for library management are:

(i) Open source systems, when licenced in the typical "general licence" manner, cost nothing (or next to nothing) to use – whether they have one or one thousand users. Thus use of OSS offers substantial cost savings for libraries.

(ii) Open source product support is not locked into a single vendor. The community of developers for a particular open source product tends to be a powerful support structure because of the pride in ownership. Also, anyone can go into business to provide support for software for which the very source code is freely available. Thus even if a library buys an open source system from one vendor, it might choose to get technical support from another company – or to arrange for technical support from a third party at the time of purchase. On top of this flexibility, any library with technical staff capable of understanding source code might find that its own staff might provide better internal support because the staff could have a better understanding of how the systems work.

Q18. Write down the basic concept of "Digitisation". Discuss need for digitisation.

Ans. Digitisation may be defined as the process of converting information into a digital format. In this format, information is organised into discrete units of data (called bits) that can be separately addressed (usually in multiple-bit groups called bytes). This is the binary data that computers and many devices with computing capacity (such as digital cameras and digital hearing aids) can process. Also referred to as image capture, is the process of creating a digital representation or image of an original through scanning or digital photography. Digitisation is a precondition for electronic storage, such as magnetic storage, storage on optical disk, and character recognition (e.g., ICR, OCR).

Need for Digitisation: Digitising a document in print or other physical media (e.g., sound recordings) makes the document more useful as well as more accessible. It is possible for a user to conduct a full-text search on a document that is digitised and OCRed. It is possible to create hyperlinks to lead a reader to related items within the text itself as well as to external resources. Ultimately, digitisation does not mean replacing the traditional library collections and services; rather, it serves to enhance them.

A document can be converted into digital format depending on the objective of digitisation, end user, availability of finances. etc. While the objectives of digitisation initiatives differ from organisation to organisation, the primary objective is to improve the access. Other objectives include cost savings, preservation, keeping pace with technology and information sharing. The most significant challenges in planning and execution of a digitisation project relate to technical limitations, budgetary constraints, copyright considerations, lack of policy guidelines and lastly, the selection of materials for digitisation.

While new and emerging technologies allow digital information to be presented in innovative ways, the majority of potential users are unlikely to have access to sophisticated hardware and software. Sharing of information among various institutions is often restricted by the use of incompatible software.

One of the main benefits of digitisation is to preserve rare and fragile objects by enhancing their access to multiple users simultaneously. Very often, when an object is rare and precious, access is only allowed for a certain category of people. Going digital could allow more users to enjoy the benefit of access. Although, digitisation offers great advantages for access like, allowing users to find, retrieve, study and manipulate material, it cannot be considered as a good alternative for preservation because of ever changing formats, protocols and software used for creating digital objects.

There are several reasons for libraries to go for digitisation and there are as many ways to create the digitised images, depending on the needs and uses. The prime reason for digitisation is the need of the user for convenient access to high quality information. Other important considerations are:

- **Quality Preservation:** The digital information has potential for qualitative preservation of information. The preservation-quality images can be scanned at high resolution and bit depth for best possible quality. The quality remains the same inspite of multiple usages by several users. However, caution needs to be exercised while choosing digitisation for preservation of information.
- **Multiple Referencing:** Digital information can be used simultaneously by several users at a time.
- **Wide Area Usage:** Digital information can be made accessible to distant users through the computer networks over the Internet.
- **Archival Storage:** Digitisation is used for restoration of rare material. The rare books, images or archival material are kept in digitised format as a common practice.
- **Security Measure:** Valuable documents and records are scanned and kept in digital format for safety and security.

Q19. What are the various factors that should be kept in mind while selecting materials for digitisation? Briefly discuss.

Ans. Factors that may be considered for selecting appropriate media for digitisation include the following:

- **Audio:** The sound quality has to be checked and required corrections made together by the subject expert and computer sound editor.
- **Video:** The video clippings are normally edited on Beta max tapes, which can be used for transferring on to digital format. While editing colour tone, resolution is checked and corrected.
- **Photographs:** The selection of photographs is very crucial process. High resolution is required for photographic images and slides. Also, the quality and future needs are to be checked and the copyright aspects are to be taken care of.
- **Documents:** Documents which are much in demand, too fragile to handle, and rare in availability are reviewed and selected for the process. If the correction of literary value demands much input, then documents are considered for publication rather than digitisation. Moreover, the purpose of all digitisation is related to increased access to digitised materials and value addition. The first consideration for digitisation of documents should be intellectual significance of contents in terms of quality, authority, uniqueness, timeliness, and demand. The intellectual contents, physical nature of the source materials, number of current and potential users are therefore, major considerations.

Q20. What are the steps involved in the process of digitisation?

Ans. The following four steps are involved in the process of digitisation. Software, variably called document image processing (DIP), Electronic Filing System (EFS) and Document Management Systems (DMS) provides all or most of these functions:

(1) Scanning: Electronic scanners are used for acquisition of an electronic image into a computer through its original that may be a photograph, text, manuscript. etc. An image is “read” or scanned at a predefined resolution and dynamic range. The resulting file, called “bit map page image” is formatted and tagged for storage and subsequent retrieval by the software package used for scanning. Acquisition of image through fax card, electronic camera or other imaging devices is also feasible. However, image scanners are most important and most commonly used component of an imaging system for transfer of normal paper-based documents.

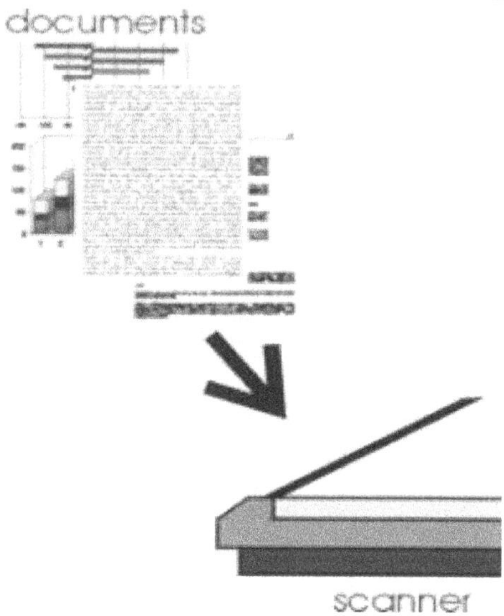

Fig. 2.3: Scanning a document using Flatbed Scanner

Step 1 Place picture on the scanner's glass

Step 2 Start scanner software

Step 3 Select the area to be scanned

Step 4 Choose the image type

Step 5 Sharpen the image

Step 6 Set the image size

Step 7 Save the scanned image using a desirable format (GIF or JPEG)

(2) Indexing: If converting a document into an image or text file is considered as the first step in the process of imaging, indexing these files comprises the second step. The process of indexing scanned images involves linking of the database of scanned images to a text database. Scanned images are just like a set of pictures that need to be related to a text database describing them and their contents. An imaging system typically stores a large amount of unstructured data in a two file system for storing and retrieving scanned images. The first is traditional file that has a text description of the image (keywords or descriptors) along with a key to a second file. The second file contains the document location. The user selects a record from the first file using a search algorithm. Once the user selects a record, the application program keys into the location index, finds the document and displays it.

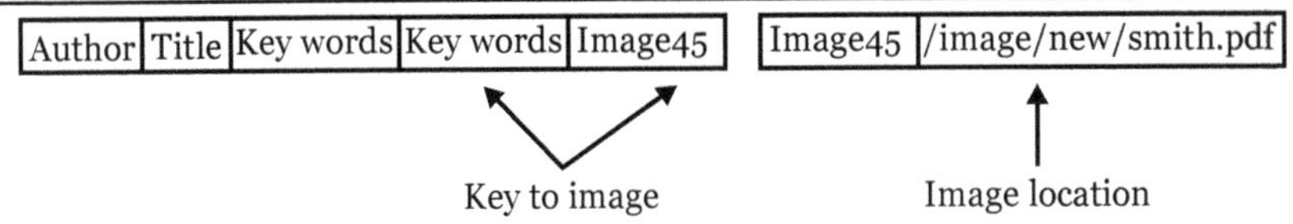

Fig. 2.4: Two File System in an Image Retrieval System

Most of the document imaging software packages, through their menu driven or command driven interface facilitate elaborate indexing of documents. While some document management system facilitates selection of indexing terms from the image file, others allow only manual keying in of indexing terms. Further, many DMS packages provide OCRed capabilities for transforming the images into standard ASCII files. The OCRed text then serves as a database for full-text search of the stored images.

(3) Storing: The most tenacious problem of a document image relates to its file size and, therefore, to its storage. Every part of an electronic page image is saved regardless of present or absence of ink. The file size varies directly with scanning resolution, the size of the area being digitized and the style of graphic file format used to save the image. The scanned images, therefore, need to be transferred from the hard disc of scanning workstation to an external large capacity storage devices such as an optical disc, CD-ROM/ DVD-ROM disc, snap servers. etc. While the smaller document imaging system may use offline media, which need to be reloaded when required, or fixed hard disc drives allocated for image storage, larger document management systems use autochangers such as optical jukeboxes and tape library systems. The storage required by the scanned image varies and depends upon factors such as scanning resolution, page size, compression ratio and page content. Further, the image storage device may be either remote or local to the retrieval workstation depending upon the imaging systems and document management systems used.

(4) Retrieving: Once scanned images and OCRed text documents have been saved as a file, a database is needed for selective retrieval of data contained in one or more fields within each record in the database. Typically, a document imaging system uses at least two files to store and retrieve documents. The first is traditional file that has a text description of the image along with a key to the second file. The second file contains the document location. The user selects a record from the first-file using a search algorithm. Once the user selects a record, the application keys into the location index, finds the document and displays it. Most of the document management system provides elaborate search possibilities including use of Boolean and proximity operators (AND, OR, NOT) and wild cards. Users are also allowed to refine their search strategy. Once the required images have been identified their associated document image can quickly be retrieved from the image storage device for display or printed output.

Q21. Explain the concept of "Input and Output Options of digitisation".

Ans. A document can be converted into digital format depending on the objective of digitisation, end users, availability of finances. etc. There are four basic approaches that can be adapted to transform from print to digital:

(1) Scanning as Image Only: 'Image only' is the lowest cost option in which each page is an exact replica of the original source document. Several digital library projects are concerned with providing digital access to materials that already exists in printed media in traditional libraries. Scanned page images are practically the only reasonable solution for institutions such as libraries for converting existing paper collection (legacy documents) without having access to the original data in computer processible formats convertible into HTML/SGML or in any other structured or unstructured text. Scanned page images are natural choice for large-scale conversions for major digital library initiatives. Printed text, pictures and figures are transformed into computer-accessible forms using a digital scanner or a digital camera in a process called document imaging or scanning. The digitally scanned images are stored in a file as bit-mapped page images, irrespective of the fact that a scanned page contains a photograph, a line drawing or text. A bit-mapped page image is a type of computer graphic, literally an electronic picture of the page which can most easily be equated to a facsimile image of the page and as such they can be read by humans, but not by the computers, understably "text" in a page image is not searchable on a computer using the present-day technology. An image-based implementation requires a large space for data storage and transmission.

Capturing page image format is comparatively easy and inexpensive, therefore, it is a faithful reproduction of its original maintaining page integrity and originality. The scanned textual images, however, are not searchable unless it is OCRed, which in itself, is highly error prone process specially when it involves scientific texts. Options of technology for converting print to digital are given separately.

If OCR is not carried out, the document is not searchable. Most scanning softwares generate TIFF format by default, which, can be converted into PDF using a number of software tools. Scanning to TIFF/PDF format is recommended only when the requirement of project is to make documents portable and accessible from any computing platform. The image can be browsed through a table of contents file composed in HTML that provides link to scanned image objects.

(2) Optical Character Recognition (OCR) and Retaining Page Layout: The latest versions of both Xerox's TextBridge and Caere's Omnipage incorporate technology that allow the option of maintaining text and graphics in their original layout as well as plain ASCII and word-processing formats. Output can also include HTML with attributes like bold, underline, and italic which are retained.

Retaining Layout after OCR: A scanned document is nothing more than a picture of a printed page. It cannot be edited or manipulated or managed based on their contents. In other words, scanned documents have to be referred to by their labels rather than characters in the documents. OCR (Optical Character Recognition) programs are software tools used to transform scanned textual page images into word processing file. OCR or text recognition is the process of electronically identifying text in a bit-mapped page image or set of images and generate a file containing that text in ASCII code or in a specified word processing format leaving the image intact in the process.

(3) Retaining Page Layout using Acrobat Capture: The Acrobat Capture 2.0 provides several options for retaining not only the page layout but also the fonts, and to fit text into the exact space occupied in the original, so that the scanned and OCRed copy never over- or under-shoots the page. Accordingly, it treats unrecognisable text as images that are pasted in its place. Such images are perfectly readable by anyone by looking at the PDF file, but will be absent from the editable and searchable text file. In contrast, ordinary OCR programs treat unrecognised text as wild or some other special character in the ASCII output. Acrobat Capture can be used to scan pages as images, image +text and as normal PDF, all the three options retain page layout.

(i) **Image Only:** 'Image only' is the lowest cost option in which each page is an exact replica of the original source document.

(ii) **Image + Text:** In image+text solutions, OCRed text is generated for each image where each page is an exact replica of the original and left untouched, however, the OCRed text sits behind the image and is used for searching. The OCRed text is generally not corrected for errors since; it is used only for searching. The cost involved is much less than PDF Normal. However, the entire page is a bitmap and neither fonts nor line drawings are vectorised, so the file size of Image + Text PDFs is considerably larger than the corresponding PDF Normal files and pages will not display as quickly or cleanly on screen.

(iii) **PDF Normal:** PDF normal gives the clear view on-screen display. It is searchable, with significantly smaller file size than Image+Text. The result is not, however, an exact replica of the scanned page. While all graphics and formatting are preserved, substitute fonts may be used where direct matches are not possible. It is a good choice when files need to be posted on to the web or otherwise delivered online. If during the Capture and OCR process, a word cannot be recognised to the specified confidence level, Capture, by default, substitutes a small portion of the original bitmap image. Capture "best guess" of the suspect word lies behind the bitmap so that searching and indexing are still possible. However, one cannot guarantee that these bitmapped words are correctly guessed. In addition, the bitmap is somewhat obtrusive and detracting from the 'look' of the page. Further, Capture provides option to correct suspected errors left as bit-mapped image or leave them untouched.

(4) Re-keying: A classic solution of this kind would comprise of keying-in the data and its verification. This involves a complete keying of the text, followed by a full re-keying by a different operator, the two keying-in operations might take place simultaneously. The two keyed files are compared and any errors or inconsistencies are corrected. This would guarantee at least 99.9 per cent accuracy, but to reach 99.955 per cent accuracy level, it would normally require full proof-reading of the keyed files, plus table lookups and dictionary spell checks.

Q22. Discuss the technology of digitisation. Also briefly explain Bit depth or dynamic range, resolution and threshold.

Ans. Digital images, also called "bit-mapped page image" are "electronic photographs" composed or set of bits or pixels (picture elements) represented by "0" and "1". A bit mapped page image is a true representation of its original in terms of typefaces, illustrations, layout and presentation of scanned documents.

As such information contents of "bit-mapped page image" cannot be searched or manipulated unlike text file documents (or ASCII). However, an ASCII file can be generated from a bit-mapped page image using an optical character recognition (OCR) software such as Xerox's TextBridge and Caere's OmniPage. The quality of digital image can be monitored at the time of capture by the following factors:

(1) Bit Depth or Dynamic Range: The number of bits used to define each pixel determines the bit depth. The greater the bit depth, the greater the number of gray scale or colour tones that can be represented. Dynamic range is the term used to express the full range of total variations, as measured by a densitometer between the lightest and the darkest of a document. Digital images can be captured at varied density or bits per pixel depending upon (i) the nature of source material or document to be scanned; (ii) target audience or users; and (iii) capabilities of the display and print subsystem that are to be used. Bitonal or black & white or binary scanning is generally employed in libraries to scan pages containing text or the drawings. Bitonal or binary scanning represents one bit per pixel (either "0" (black) or "1" (white). Gray scale scanning is used for reliable reproduction of intermediate or continuous tones found in black & white photographs to represent shades of grey. Multiple numbers of bits ranging from 2-8 are assigned to each pixel to represent shades of grey in this process. Although each bit is either black or white, as in the case of bitonal images, but bits are combined to produce a level of grey in the pixel that is, black, white or somewhere in between.

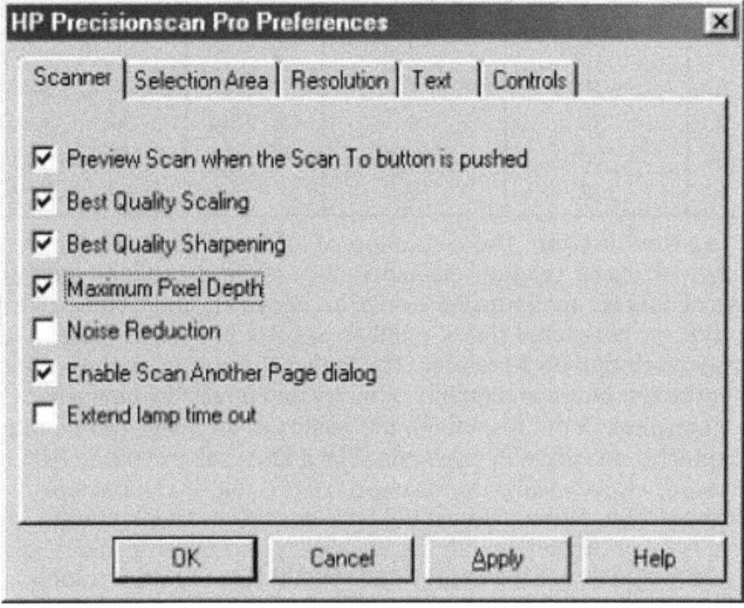

Fig. 2.5: Setting Bit Depth in Precision scan Pro Scanning Software

Lastly, colour scanning can be employed to scan colour photographs. As in the case of grey-scale scanning, multiple bits per pixels typically 2 (lowest quality) to 8 (highest quality) per primary colour are used for representing colour. Colour images are evidently more complex than grey scale images, because it involves encoding of shades of each of the three primary colours. i.e., red, green and blue (RGB). If a coloured image is captured at 2 bits per primary colour, each primary colour can have 22 or 4 shades and each pixel can have 43 shades for each of the three primary colours. Evidently, increase in bit depth increases the quality of image captured and the space required to store the resultant image. Generally speaking, 12 bits per pixel (4 bits per primary colour) is considered minimum pixel depth for good quality colour image. Most of today's colour scanners can scan at 24-bit colour (8 bit per primary colour).

Table 2.10: No. of Bits Used for Representing Shades in Colour and Gray-scale Scanning

Sl. No	No. of Bits	No. of bits/ shades	No. of shades	No. of Shades/pixel
1	2	2	$2^2 = 4$	$4^3 = 64$
2	4	3	$2^3 = 8$	$8^3 = 512$
3	8	4	$2^4 = 16$	$16^3 = 4096$
4	16	5	$2^5 = 32$	$32^3 = 32768$
4	32	6	$2^6 = 64$	$64^3 = 262144$
5	64	7	$2^7 = 128$	$128^3 = 2097152$
6	128	8	$2^8 = 256$	$256^3 = 16777216$

(2) Resolution: The resolution of an image is defined in terms of number of pixels (picture elements) in a given area. It is measured in terms of dots per inch (dpi) in case of an image file and as ratio of number of pixels on horizontal line x number of pixel in vertical lines in case of display resolution on a monitor. The higher the dpi set on the scanner, the better the resolution and quality of image and larger the image file.

Regardless of the resolution, the quality of an image can be improved by capturing an image in grayscale. The additional gray-scale data can be processed electronically to sharpen edges, file-in characters, remove extraneous dirt, remove unwanted page strains or discolouration, so as to create a much higher quality image than possible with binary scanning alone. A major drawback in gray scale is that there is large amount of data capture. It may be noted that continuing increase in resolution will not result in any appreciable gain in image quality after some time, except for increase in file size. It is thus important to determine the point where sufficient resolution has been used to capture all the significant details present in the source document. The black and white or bitonal images (textual) are scanned most commonly at 300 dpi that preserve 99.9 per cent of the information content of a page and can be considered as adequate access resolution. Some preservation projects scan at 600 dpi for better quality. A standard SVGA/VGA monitor has a resolution of 640 × 480 lines while the ultra-high monitors have a resolution of about 2048 × 1664 (about 150 dpi).

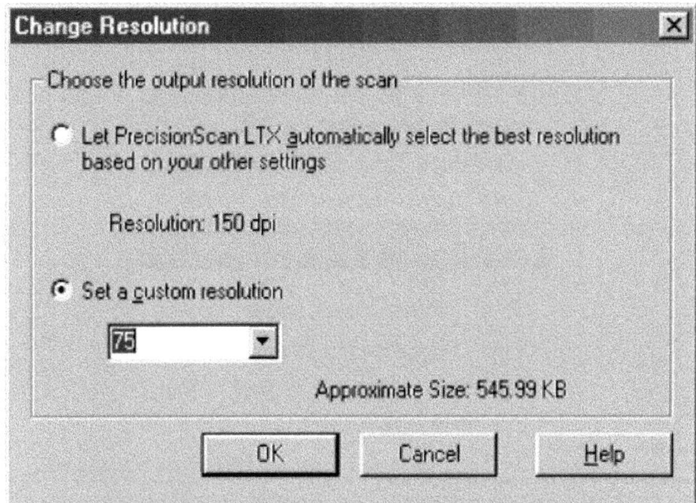

Fig. 2.6: Setting-up Resolution Manually

(3) Threshold: The threshold setting in bitonal scanning defines the point on a scale, usually ranging from 0 - 255, at which gray values will be interpreted as black or white pixels. In bitonal scanning, resolution and threshold are the key determinants of image quality. Bitonal scanning is best suited to high-contrast documents, such as text and line drawings. Gray scale or colour scanning is required for continuous tone or low contrast for documents such as photographs. In gray scale/colour scanning both resolution and bit depth combine to play significant role in image quality.

In line art mode, every pixel has only two possible values. Every pixel will either be black or white. The Line art Threshold control determines the decision point about brightness determining if the sampled value will be a black dot or a white dot. The normal threshold default is 128 (the midrange of the 8-bit 0 - 255 range). Image intensity values above the threshold are white pixels, and values below the threshold are black pixels. Adjusting threshold is like a brightness setting to determine what is black and what is white. Threshold for text printed on a coloured background or cheap-quality paper like newsprint has to be kept at lower range. Reducing threshold from 128 to about 85 would greatly improve the quality of scan. Such adjustments would also improve the performance of OCR software.

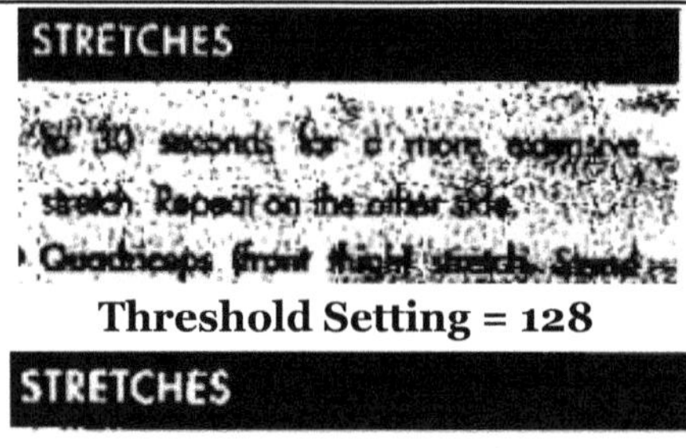

Threshold Setting = 128

Threshold Setting = 85

Fig. 2.7: Threshold Setting in Bitonal Scanning

(4) Image Enhancement: Image enhancement process can be used to improve scanned images at a cost of image authenticity and fidelity. The process of image enhancement is, however, time consuming; it requires special skills and would invariably increase the cost of conversion. Typical image enhancement features available in a scanning or image editing software include filters, tonal reproduction, curves and colour management, touch, crop, image sharpening, contrast, transparent background. etc. In a page scanned in gray-scale, the text/line art and half tone areas can be decomposed and each area of the page can be filtered separately to maximise its quality. The text area on page can be treated with edge sharpening filters, so as to clearly define the character edges, a second filter could be used to remove the high-frequency noise and finally another filter could fill-in broken characters. Gray-scale area of the page could be processed with different filters to maximise the quality of the halftone.

Fig. 2.8: Sharpening Image using HP Precision scan Pro

Q23. What is image compression? Describe the types of image compression.

Ans. Image compression is a type of data compression applied to digital images, to reduce their cost for storage or transmission. Algorithms may take advantage of visual perception and the statistical properties of image data to provide superior results compared with generic data compression methods which are used for other digital data. The image compression algorithms may be grouped into the following types:

(1) Lossless Compression: Lossless compression is preferred for archival purposes and often for medical imaging, technical drawings, clip art, or comics. No information is "lost" or "sacrificed" in the process of compression. Lossless compression is primarily used in bitonal images.

(2) Lossy Compression: Lossy compression methods, especially when used at low bit rates, introduce compression artifacts. Lossy methods are especially suitable for natural images such as photographs in applications where minor (sometimes-imperceptible) loss of fidelity is acceptable to achieve a substantial reduction in bit rate. Lossy compression that produces negligible differences may be called visually lossless.

Methods for lossless compression:

(i) Run-length encoding – used in default method in PCX and as one of possible in BMP, TGA, TIFF

(ii) Area image compression

(iii) Predictive coding – used in DPCM

(iv) Entropy encoding – the two most common entropy encoding techniques are arithmetic coding and Huffman coding

(v) Adaptive dictionary algorithms such as LZW – used in GIF and TIFF

(vi) DEFLATE – used in PNG, MNG, and TIFF

(vii) Chain codes

Q24. Which protocols used for compression?

Or

What is OCR? Why is it important to OCR a digitised image?

Ans. The following protocols are commonly used for bitonal, gray scale or colour compression:

(1) TIFF-G4- International Telecommunication Union (ITU Group 4) is considered as de facto standard compression scheme for black and white or bitonal images. An image created as a TIFF and compressed using ITU-G4 compression technique is called a Group-4 TIFF or TIFFG4 and is considered as defacto standard for storing bitonal images. TIFF- G-4 is a lossless compression scheme. Joint Bi-level Image Group (JBIG)

(ISO-11544) is another standard compression technique for bitonal images.

(2) JPEG: JPEG stands for "Joint Photographic Experts Group". It's a standard image format for containing lossy and compressed image data. Despite the huge reduction in file size JPEG images maintain reasonable image quality. This unique compression feature allows JPEG files to be used widely on the Internet, Computers, and Mobile Devices. The sharing of JPEG images is quick and efficient. Also, a large number of JPEG image files can be stored in minimum storage space. JPEG files can also contain high-quality image data with a lossless compression. In PaintShop Pro JPEG is a commonly used format for storing the edited images.

(3) LZW (Lenpel-Ziv Welch): LZW compression technique uses a table-based lookup algorithm invented by Abraham Lempel, Jacob Ziv, and Terry Welch. Two commonly-used file formats in which LZW compression is used are the Graphics Interchange Format (GIF) and Tag Image File Format (TIFF). LZW compression is also suitable for compressing text files. A particular LZW compression algorithm takes each input sequence of binary digit of a given length (for example, 12 bits) and creates an entry in a table (sometimes called a "dictionary" or "codebook") for that particular bit pattern, consisting of the pattern itself and a shorter code. As input is read, any pattern that has been read before the results in the substitution of the shorter code effectively compresses the total amount of input to something smaller. The decoding program that uncompressed the file is able to build the table itself by using the algorithm as it processes the encoded input.

(4) OCR (Optical Character Recognition): OCR Stands for "Optical Character Recognition." OCR is a technology that recognises text within a digital image. It is commonly used to recognise text in scanned documents, but it serves many other purposes as well. OCR software processes a digital image by locating and recognising characters, such as letters, numbers, and symbols. Some OCR software will simply export the text, while other programs can convert the characters to editable text directly in the image. Advanced OCR software can export the size and formatting of the text as well as the layout of the text found on a page. OCR technology can be used to convert a hard copy of a document into an electronic version (or soft copy. While OCR technology was originally designed to recognise printed text, it can be used to recognise and verify handwritten text as well. There are four types of OCR technology that are prevailing in the market. These technologies are:

- **(i) Matrix/Template Matching:** Matrix matching is simpler than Feature extraction. Matrix Matching compares each character with a library of character matrices. When an image matches one of the matrices of pixels, it labels that image as the corresponding character.

(ii) Feature Extraction: Feature Extraction uses artificial intelligence to analyse features such as closed shapes, diagonal lines, line intersections. etc. This method is flexible and it is employed in both type-written and hand-written documents.

(iii) Structural Analysis: Determines characters on the basis of density gradations or character darkness.

(iv) Neural Networking: Recently, the use of neural networks to recognise characters (and other types of patterns) has resurfaced. Considering a back-propagation network, this network is composed of several layers of interconnected elements. A feature vector enters the network at the input layer. Each element of the layer computes a weighted sum of its input and transforms it into an output by a nonlinear function. During training, the weights at each connection are adjusted until a desired output is obtained. A problem of neural networks in OCR may be their limited predictability and generality, while an advantage is their adaptive nature.

Scanners and image-capturing devices were introduced with one goal in mind: to turn paper documents into electronic file formats that can be stored electronically.

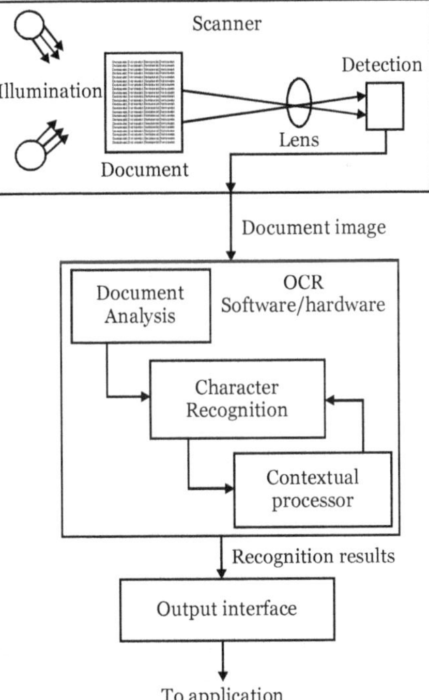

Fig. 2.9: OCR Technology

If we want to convert a document into an editable digital format, using OCR software is the best choice. It provides a fast and reliable alternative to typing manually. The Optical Character Recognition process can save both time and effort when developing a digital replica of the document. Software with integrated OCR technology can convert a document into many different electronic formats, like Microsoft Word, Text (and Rich Text), Excel, and of course, it can also convert scanned PDF files. All documents created through an OCR program are editable and allow us to modify the content as you see fit. If you compare the cost of OCR with the cost of manual data entry, OCR is a lot cheaper. It is already an indispensable part of most large companies' office equipment and is valuable in industries that are heavily scanning documentation, such as legal departments and law offices, financial and insurance companies, government agencies, healthcare institutions, human resources departments, law and real estate firms. etc. OCR has improved upon every aspect of the paperless concept, making documents searchable, editable, accessible, translatable... Document workflows have become less time and resource consuming, resulting in improved office productivity and decreased operating costs for companies.

Q25. Discuss file formats ad media types.

Or

What do you understand by Page Description Language?

Ans. As large amount of document are being digitised and made available online through digital libraries throughout the world, it is pertinent that while archiving documents, physical survival, interpretability, and usability of the data is given importance. For this it is important to give due consideration to encoding standards, file formats and also ensure that the formats are usable and accessible in future. An ideal format for the purpose of archiving would be the one that is a representation rather than a presentation. The most common formats for text archiving are native formats (mostly MS Word), pdf, pdf-a, tex/latex, and xml applications. Other formats that are also prevalent are html, sgml, xhtml. Document formats may be broadly grouped into three types: text based formats, image formats, audio and video formats. Names of file formats applicable in digital library and their file extension are given in Table.

Formats and Encoding used for Text: Text and image-based contents of a digital library can be stored and presented as:

(1) Simple Text or ASCII (American Standard Code for Information Interchange): Simple text or ASCII (American Standard Code for Information Exchange) is the most commonly used encoding scheme used for facilitating exchange of data from one software to another or from one platform to another. "Full-text" I of articles from many journals has been available electronically through online I vendors like DIALOG and STN in this format for over two decades. Typically what is stored in the text of each article, broken into paragraphs, along with bibliographic information is a simple tagged information.

Simple text or ASCII is compact, economic to capture and store, searchable, inter-operable and is malleable with other text-based services. On the other hand, the simple text or ASCII cannot be used for displaying complex tables or i mathematical formulas. Photographs, diagrams, graphics, special characters cannot be displayed in ASCII. ASCII format does not Store text formatting information. i.e. italics, bold, font type, font size or paragraph justification information. Simple text or ASCII in many ways is inadequate to represent many journal articles because of the reasons mentioned above. Although simple text or ASCII is extremely useful for searching and selection. its inability to capture the richness of the original makes it an interim step to structured text formats.

(2) Structured Text (SGML or HTML or XML): Structured text is a very simple and straightforward set of rules how to format a plain text document. The formatting allows to mark the logical structure of sections, paragraphs, bullet lists, etc. Structured text formats have provision for imbed images, graphics and other multimedia formats in the text. SGML (Standard Generalised Markup Language) is one of the most important and popular structured text format. ODA (Office Document Architecture) is a similar and competing standard. SGML is an international standard (ISO, 1986) around which several related standards are built. SGML is a flexible language that gave birth to HTML (Hyper-Text Markup Language), de facto markup language of the World Wide Web, to control the display format of documents and even the appearance of the user interface for interacting with the documents. Like simple text or ASCII, structured text can be searched or manipulated. It is highly flexible and suitable both for electronic and paper production. Well-formatted text increases visual presentation volume of textual, graphical and pictorial information. Structured formats can easily display complex tables and equations. Moreover, structured text is compact in comparison to the image based formats, even after including imbedded graphics and pictures.

Creation of structured text is generally integrated with the production of printed artifacts. SGML is in fact, a format generated as a by-product of printed artifacts generated electronically.

(3) Page Description Language: Page Description Languages (PDLs), such as Adobe's PostScript and PDF (Portable Document Format) are similar to image but the formatted pages displayed to the user are text-based rather than image-based. Post Script and PDF formats can easily be captured during the typesetting process. PostScript is especially easy to capture since most of the systems automatically generate it and conversion program, called Acrobat Distiller, can be used to convert

PostScript file into PDF files. The documents stored as PDF require Acrobat Reader at the user's end to read or print the document. The Acrobat Reader can be downloaded free of cost from the Adobe's Web Site.

Acrobat's Portable Document Format (PDF) is a by-product of PostScript. Adobe's page description language had become the standard way to describe pages electronically in the graphics world. While PostScript is a programming language, PDF is a page-description format.

PDF can have two formats: (i) Text-based PDF that uses outline font technology of PostScript PDL (Page Description Language) from Adobe to describe format of a page; (ii) raster-scanned image PDF without the text output of OCR (Optical Character Recognition). The image PDF is essentially equivalent to TIFF or CCITT G4 formats or to a photograph where text characters cannot be manipulated by the computer. Besides, an image-based PDF may be converted into text-based PDF once it goes through the process of OCR. In this process, scanned image is replaced by the text with fonts and layout matching with the scanned document.

(4) Page Image Format: The digitally scanned images are stored in a file as a bit-mapped page image, irrespective of the fact that a scanned page contains a photograph, a line drawing or text. The bitmapped page image can be created in dozens of different formats depending upon the scanner and its software. National and international standards for image-file formats and compression methods exist to ensure that data will be interchangeable amongst systems. An image file stores discrete sets of data and information allowing a computing system to display, interpret and print the image in a pre-defined fashion. An image file format consists of three distinct components. i.e., header which stores information on file identifier and image specifications; Image data consisting of look-up table and image raster and lastly, footer that signals file termination information. While bit-mapped portion of a raster image is standardised, it is the file header that differentiates one format from another.

TIFF has been developed as the common format for image scanners and DTP software. Since TIFF uses loss-less compression, it preserves the original exactly, retaining layout features, graphics and any character form. Being the bitmap of the original, it has to be passed through OCR software before the text, if any, in the original can be made editable. GIF has been developed for use on the Internet.

Table 2.11: File Formats Used in a Digital Library

Abbreviation	Format	File Extension
ASCII	**File Format for Unstructured Text** American Standard Code for Information Interchange	.txt
SGML	**File Format for Structured Text** Standard Generalised Markup Language	.sgml

HTML	Hypertext Markup Language	.html
XML	Extended Markup Language	.xml
PDF	Portable Document Format (Adobe)	.pdf
Post Script	Post Script (Adobe)	.ps
TEX	Texture Format	.txt
	File Format for Images	
PDF	Portable Document Format	.pdf
BMP	Bit Map Page (Windows)	.bmp
IMG	Ventura Publisher	.img
JPEG	Joint Photographic Expert Group	.mpg
JFIF	JPEG File Format	.jfif
PCP	PC Paint (B & W Mode)	.pcp
PCX	PC Paint Brush (Colour & B & W)	.pcx
PSD	Photoshop	.psd
TGA	True Vision Targa	.tga
PNG	Portable Network Graphic	.png
TIFF	Taged Image File Format	.tif
TIFF-G4	Taged Image File Format with Group 4 Fax Compression	.tif
SPIFF	Still Picture Interchange File Format	.spf
PCD	Photo CD (Kodak)	.pcd
	Audio and Video File Format	
WAVE	Waveform Audio (Microsoft)	.wav
AIFF	Audio Interchange Format	.aif
VoC	Creative Voice	.voc
MIDI	Musical Instrument Digital Interface	.midi
SND	Sound	.snd
AU	Audio (Sun Microsystems)	.au
RAF	Real Audio Format (Progressive Networks)	.ra
AVI	Audio Visual Interleave	.avi
FLA	Macromedia Flash Movie	.fla
FLC	Auto Desk FLIC Animation	.flc
MOV	Quicktime for Windows Movie	.mov
MPEG	Motion Picture Expert Group	.mpg
MP2	MPEG Audio Layer 2	.mp2
MP3	MPEG Audio Layer 3	.mp3

Q26. What are the tools of digitisation? Briefly discuss.

Ans. Digital imaging is an inter-linked system of hardware, software, image database and access sub-system with each having their own components. Tools used for digitisation include several core and peripheral systems. An image scanning system may consist of a stand-alone workstation where most or all the work is done on the same workstation or as a part of a network of workstations with imaging work distributed and shared amongst various workstations. The network usually includes a scanning station, a server and one or more editing, retrieval stations. A typical scanning workstation for a small, production level project could consist of the following:

- Hardware (Scanners, computers, data storage and data output peripherals)
- Software (image capturing and image editing)
- Network (data transmission)
- Display and Printing technologies

Scanners and scanning software are important components of the scanning system.

(1) Scanners: A scanner is an electronic device which can capture images from physical items and convert them into digital formats, which in turn can be stored in a computer, and viewed or modified using software applications. Digital scanners can use laser light to scan an image. These scanners, while offering superb quality, are so expensive as to be beyond most budgets. The scanners that use conventional visible light are more affordable and, hence, far more popular. There are two types of image scanners: vector scanner and raster scanners. The vector scanners scan an image as a complex set of x, y coordinates. Vector images are generally used in Geographical Information Systems (GIS). The display software for the vector image interprets the image as function of coordinates and other included information to produce an electronic replica of the original drawing or photograph. Vector images can be zoomed in portion to display minute details of a drawing or a map. Maps, engineering drawings, and architectural blueprints are often scanned as vector images. Raster images are captured by raster scanners by passing lights (laser in some cases) down the page and digitally encoding it row by row. Multiple passes of lights may be required to capture basic (as a set of bits known as bit map) colours in a coloured image. Raster scanners are used in libraries to convert printed publications into electronic forms. Majority of electronic imaging systems generate raster images. The scanners used for digitising analogue images into digital images come in a variety of shapes and sizes.

Working of Scanner: Scanners operate by shining light at the object or document being digitised and directing the reflected light (usually through a series of mirrors and lenses) onto a photosensitive element. In most scanners, the sensing medium is an electronic, light-sensing integrated circuit known as a charged coupled device (CCD). Light-sensitive photosites arrayed along the CCD convert levels of brightness into electronic signals that are then processed into a digital image. CCD is by far the most common light-sensing technology used in modern scanners.

While selecting a scanner, one should consider resolution, sharpness, and rate of image transfer. The resolution is measured in dots per inch (dpi). The average scanner has at least 300x300 dpi. The number of sensors in a row of the CCD array determines a scanner's dpi. Sharpness depends on how bright the lamp is and the quality of the lens. Image transfer depends on the connection used to connect the scanner to the computer. The slowest is the parallel port. Universal Serial Bus or USB scanners are affordable, easy to use, and have good speed.

The hardware required for a scanner is a connector such as a USB. The software required is a driver. The driver is needed to communicate with the scanner. TWAIN is the language spoken by scanners. Any program that supports TWAIN can acquire a scanned image.

There are following types of Scanners:

(i) **Flatbed Scanners**: Flatbed document scanner is popularly used in a library for carrying out day-to-day scanning activities. Flatbed scanner consists of a glass platen, bright light source and moving panel of optical sensors. Flatbed scanner scans a document in face-down mode. Flatbed scanner is physically connected to computer through a USB connector. Flatbed scanner comes in various models like right-angle, prism and planetary/overhead to handle bound volumes and books. Flatbed scanner can scan usually a document at 600dpi. Many flatbed scanners however, offer higher resolution.

Fig. 2.10: Flatbed Scanner

(ii) **Sheet Feed Scanners:** Sheet feed scanners are similar to flatbed scanners except the document is moved and the scan head is immobile. A sheet-fed scanner looks a lot like a small portable printer.

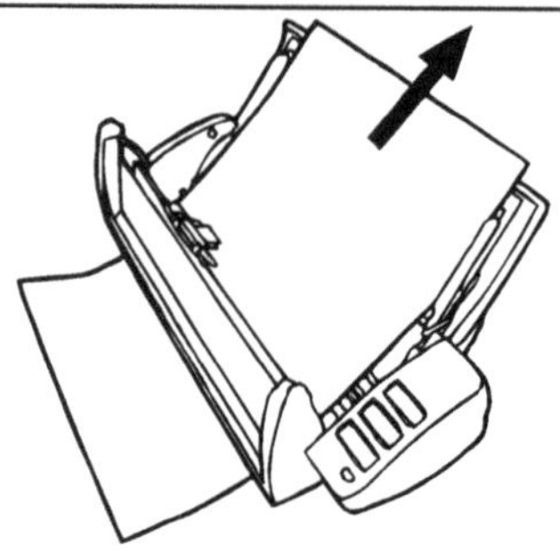

Fig. 2.11: Sheet feed Scanners

(iii) **Drum Scanners:** Drum scanners are used by the publishing industry to capture incredibly detailed images. They use a technology called a **photomultiplier tube** (PMT). In PMT, the document to be scanned is mounted on a glass cylinder. At the center of the cylinder is a sensor that splits light bounced from the document into three beams. Each beam is sent through a colour filter into a photomultiplier tube where the light is changed into an electrical signal.

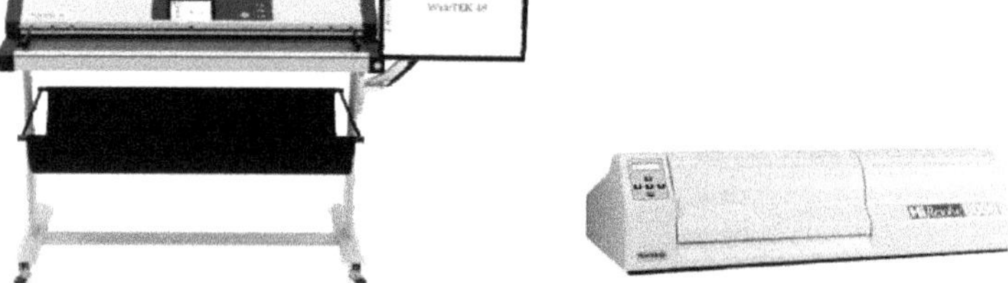

Fig. 2.12: Drum Scanners

(iv) **Digital Cameras:** Digital cameras mounted on copy cradle resemble microfilming stand. Source material is placed on the stand and the camera is cranked up or down in order to focus the material within the field of view. Digital cameras are most promising scanner development for library and archival applications.

(v) **Slide Scanner:** Slide scanners have a slot in the side to accommodate a 35mm slide. Inside the box, the light passes through the slide to hit a CCD array behind the slide. Slide scanners can generally scan only 35mm transparent source materials.

(vi) **Microfilm Scanner:** Specially targeted to library/archival application, microfilm scanners have adapters to convert roll film, fiche, and aperture cards into the same model.

- Saving production time and expenses of distribution and printing
- Fast, easy updating of information
- Access library catalogues and other documents
- Accessible 24 hours a day, 365 days of year to all members of the community via the campus-wide network
- Cost-effective means to reach a world-wide audience
- Easy to use

(i) STM: As an example, the homepage of Harvard University-Campus wide Information System (http://www.harvard.edu) is reproduced below:

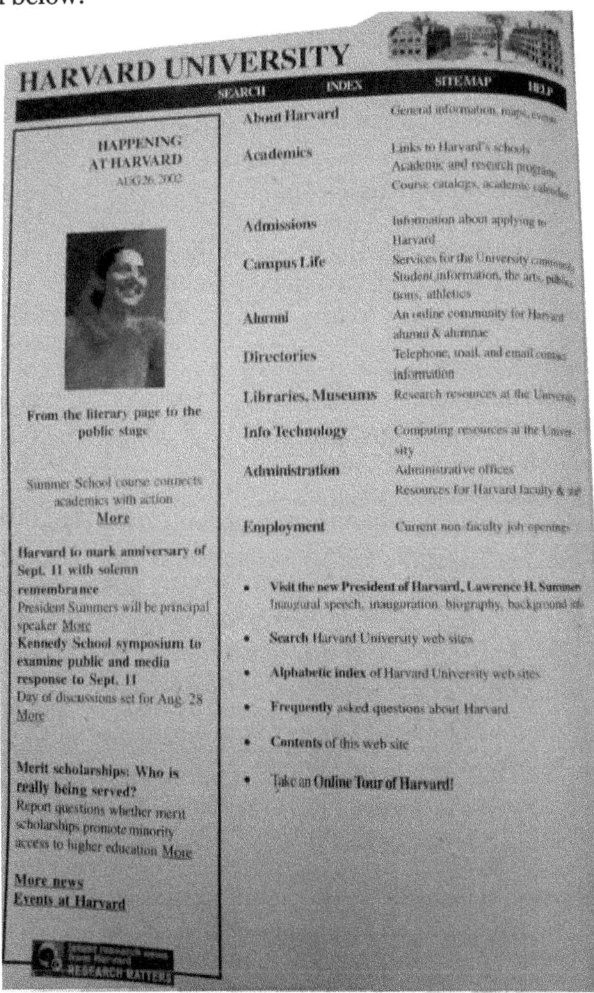

Fig. 15.18: Screen Snapshot of Website of Harvard University

Like audio, video capture also requires a video capture card with input from video cassette player (VCP/VCR), TV antenna, cable or movie camera. The digitised files can be saved as mov, avi, mpg file formats.

Q28. Explain the concept of "Organising digital images".

Or

Write short note on "Organising digital images".

[Dec-2018, Q.No.- 5(b)]

Ans. A disc full of digital images without any organisation, browse and search options may have no meaning except for one who created it. Scanned images need to be organised in order to be useful. Moreover, images need to be linked to the associated metadata to facilitate their browsing and searching. The following three steps describe the process of organising the digital images:

(1) Organise the scanned image files into disc hierarchy that logically maps the physical organisation of the document. For example, in a project on scanning of journals, create a folder for each journal, which, in turn, may have folder for each volume scanned. Each volume, in turn, may have a subfolder for each issue. The folder for each issue, in turn, may contain scanned articles that appeared in the issue along with a content page, composed in HTML providing links to articles in that issue.

(2) Name the scanned image files in a strictly controlled manner that reflects their logical relationship. For example, each article may be named after the surname of first author followed by a volume number and an issue number. For example, file name "smithrkv5n1.pdf" conveys that the article is by "R.K. Smith" that appeared in volume 5 and issue no.1. The file name for each article would, therefore, convey a logical and hierarchical organisation of the journal.

(3) Describe the scanned images file internally using image header and externally using linked descriptive metadata files. The following three types of metadata are associated with the digital objects:

(i) Descriptive Metadata: Include content or bibliographic description consisting of keywords and subject descriptors.

(ii) Administrative or technical Metadata: Incorporates details on original source, date of creation, version of digital object, file format used, compression technology used, object relationship. etc. Administrative data may reside within or outside the digital object and is required for long-term collection management to ensure longevity of digital collection.

(iii) Structural Metadata: Elements within digital objects facilitate navigation. e.g., table of contents, index at issue level or volume level, page turning in an electronic book. etc.

The simplest and least effective method for providing access is through a table of contents and linking each item to its respective object/ image. Content pages of issues of journals done in HTML would offer browsing facility. Full-text search to HTML pages or OCRed pages can be achieved by installing one of the free Internet search engines like Oingo Free Search (http://www.oingo.com/oingo_free_search/products.html); Swish-E (http:// www.berkeley.edu/SWISH-E/);WhatyoUseek (http://intra.whatuseek.com/); Excite (http://excite.com/) and Google (http://www.google.com).

Large scanning projects would, however, require a back-end database storing images or links to the images and metadata (descriptive/ administrative). Back-end database used by most document management systems holds the functionality required by most web applications. Important management systems like File Net have now integrated their database with HTML conversion tools. Further, some of the document management systems have also signed up with Adobe to incorporate Acrobat and Acrobat Capture into their web-based document management systems. These databases entertain queries from users through "HTML forms" and generate search results on the fly. Several digital library packages are now available as "open source" or "free-ware" that can be used not only for organsing the digital objects but also for their search and retrieval.

Q29. Briefly describe Digital Library Software.

Or

Write short note on E-Print archives. [Dec-2017, Q.No.-5(d)]

Ans. DSpace, Eprints, Fedora and Greenstone Digital Library Software are some major application being used by libraries world over to organising digital collection and building digital libraries which are available freely for download on the internet. We will provide here a brief account of digital library softwares available in public domain. The description is an outline of the features of the respective softwares.

(1) DSpcae: DSpace (www.dspace.org) is an open source digital library software developed jointly by MIT (Massachusetts Institute of Technology) libraries and HP (Hewlett Packard) labs. DSpace provides tools for management of digital assets, and is commonly used for building institutional repositories. . It was basically designed to manage, host, preserve and enable distribution of the scholarly output of MIT's faculty.

DSpace helps to create, index and retrieve various types of digital contents which include research articles, grey literature, theses, cultural materials, 3D digital scans of objects, photographs, films, audio/videos, scientific datasets, institutional records, educational materials and other forms of content.

The first version of DSpace was released during November 2002. For the present study installation of 1.4.2 version was carried out and selected for evaluation study. This version was released on 11th May 2007. The latest version of DSpace is 1.5.2 which was released during March 2008.

The following sections lists different observations after having installation of version 1.4.2.

DSpace was established to capture, preserve and communicate the intellectual output of an institution's faculty and researchers through central place.

The collection in DSpace is organised into communities, collections and items. The communities in DSpace include a high-level organisational structure whose only purpose is to divide collections into related groups. Each community contains one or more collections, which are containers for related items. An item is a deposited object of any type: a published article, an image, audio, or video file, notes, a presentation. etc. DSpace is specially designed for digital preservation support for all the documents that are added into the repository in a simple fashion.

Prerequisites: DSpace depends upon the Java programming language and the PostgreSQL open source database system. It also requires a number of additional Java- based elements to be installed: Tomcat, which is a Java based server; a number of Jave code libraries; and the Ant, a Java compiler. It is recommended that Dspace be installed on a Linux or a Unix machine. It requires an experienced system administrator to do the prerequisite installation.

(2) E-prints: GNU Eprints 2.x is a free software which creates online archives (http://software.eprints.org/). The default configuration creates a research paper archive. With its origin in the scholarly communication movement, e-print default configuration is geared to research papers but it can be adapted to other purposes and content. It was developed in the Intelligent Agents, Multimedia Group at the Electronics and Computer Science Department of the University of Southampton.

GNU Eprints is freely distributed to the GNU General Public Licence. The latest version is 2.3 and is available for download at http://software.eprints.org/download.php

Prerequisites

(i) Any computer capable of running GNU/Linux or similar operating system. The faster, the better, but any Intel Pentium II processor will give good performance.

(ii) A GNU operating system. GNU/Linux (a very advanced and free UNIX- like operating system) works just fine, and is in fact the development platform

(iii) Apache WWW server

(iv) Perl programming language, also a number of additional modules

(v) mod_perl module for Apache, which significantly increases the performance of Perl scripts

(vi) My SQL Databes

(3) Greenstone Digital Library (http://greenstone.org): Greenstone is a suite of software for building and distributing digital library collections. It provides a way of organising information and publishing it on the web or on removable media such as DVD and USB flash drives. Greenstone is produced by the New Zealand Digital Library Project at the University of Waikato, and developed and distributed in co-operation with UNESCO and the Human Info NGO. It is *open-source*, multilingual software, issued under the terms of the GNU General Public Licence. Read the Greenstone Factsheet for more information.

The aim of the Greenstone software is to empower users, particularly in universities, libraries, and other public service institutions, to build their own digital libraries. Digital libraries are radically reforming how information is disseminated and acquired in UNESCO's partner communities and institutions in the fields of education, science and culture around the world, and particularly in developing countries. We hope that this software will encourage the effective deployment of digital libraries to share information and place it in the public domain. Further information can be found in the book How to build a digital library, authored by three of the group's members.

(4) Ganesh Digital Library: Ganesha Digital Library version 3.1 (GDL) (http://gdl.itb.ac.id/) is another open source software developed under Indonesian Digital Library Network (IndonesiaDLN). Ganesha Digital Library enables institutions or individuals to share their knowledge and also access and utilise available knowledge in the Indonesian 'giant memory' through the network of IndonesiaDLN digital libraries. The software is available in three publisher editions: Personal, Internet Cafe, and Institution. Released under the terms of the GNU GPL, (GNU General Public Licence).

Q30. Write down the steps of planning and implementation of digital library.

Ans. A digital library is a library in which collections are stored in digital formats (as opposed to print, microform, or other media) and accessible by computers. The content may be stored locally, or accessed remotely. Digitisation is the first step towards building a digital library. It is highly specialised and cost-intensive that requires inputs from diverse branches of knowledge. It is important that objectives, needs and the purpose of digitisation are established clearly. The digitisation proposal should therefore define its goals (objectives) scope, feasiblity, benefits, costs, time required for the developmental phase, implementation issues, deliverables and target users. Careful planning of digital library would bring clarity to the project, save cost, time and human expertise. Planning digital library may include the following steps:

(1) Feasibility: It is important to conduct a feasibility study of the digital library project. The feasibility should be established not only in terms of existence of tools, expertise, volume I number of documents involved in the process of digitisation, but also in terms of target audience, demand for material being digitised and user's requirement. The feasibility study should also reflect whether the library can take-up the project in-house or should it be out-sources.

(2) Planning the Project: The planning of the project needs to cover the following areas:

(i) **Managerial Planning:** Managerial planning would essentially involve the progress of sequencing various tasks their time management and project monitoring. Activities that need managerial planning may include conducting feasibility study, procurement of equipment, recruitment of manpower, digitisation (whether out-sources or done in-house), IPR and rights management issues, integration and organisation of content, finding market, launching and marketing of services. Flow diagrams, PERT, CPM and SWOT analysis and other management techniques may be deployed at this stage.

(ii) **Hardware and Software Planning:** Requirement of creating and hosting digital library in terms of server-side hardware and network components and server-side software components may be planned with their financial implications. Connectivity and bandwidth required for hosting digital library need to be planned.

(iii) **Human Resources Planning:** Human resources need to be planned in terms of staff time involved, training of existing staff and recruitment of new staff with desired skills. Human resources planning would depend on whether the Library is going for in-house digitisation or for outsourcing the process of digitisation. Project management continues to be an important issue even if the digitisation work is being out-sourced. The' Management of the project may be divided in groups with their responsibilities defined. Communication between groups and a reporting structure may be laid down to facilitate open channels of communication and form the basis for sound formative evaluation of the project.

(iv) **Financial Planning:** Financial planning is crucial: Cost of migration from one media to other and from one computer to other may be built-in. Cost of hosting the services and their maintenance should also be planned besides other aspects.

(3) Purchase of Hardware and Software: Choice of technology and the equipment required may be made. These include storage and back up devices, network equipment regained, software for search and access and other related items. The software may be acquired or developed in house. The following steps may be followed in this regard:

(i) Acquire and install hardware and software;

(ii) Acquire and install the network required for hosting the digitised collection. Consider bandwidth requirements that depend upon the media offered by the digital library. While simple text requires relatively low bandwidth to deliver content, images and video require large bandwidth; and

(iii) Acquire and install other components

(4) Selection of Material for Digitisation and 'Born Digital': In the process of execution of the project, the first task is to identify, select, and to prioritise the documents that are to be digitised. If the organisation is itself creating contents, strategies are to be laid down to capture 'born digital' data. If documents are available in digital form, they can be easily converted to other formats. If the selected material is from external sources, IPR issues need to be resolved. It is necessary to obtain permission from the publishers and data suppliers for digitisation, if material being digitised is not available in public domain. Moreover, decision may be taken whether to OCR the digitised images. Documents selected for digitisation may already be available in digital format. It is always economical to buy e-media, if available than their conversion. Moreover, oversised material, deteriorating collections, bound volumes of journals, manuscripts. etc., would require highly specialised equipment and highly specialised manpower.

(5) Placement and Training of Manpower: Since the entire job of developing and or maintaining a digital library is a highly skilled one, there should be no compromise or slackening in the quality of intake or selection of manpower for the job. Also, even if good quality manpower is positioned, they usually need training to upgrade and sharpen their skills for this job. So, necessary training, should form a component of the execution of the project.

(6) Content Creation: The steps involved in content creation include the following:

(i) Conversion of datasets that are 'born digital', for example, convert MS Word file into PDF;

(ii) Conversion of the existing printed sections into digital format (digitisation); and

(iii) Identification of vendors if the digitisation work is to be outsourced.

(7) Execution of the Project: Once the equipment and software and other infrastructure facilities' are installed or positioned, and the priorities of the documents for digitisation laid down, the execution of the project starts. The library may use digital library software like greenstone Digital library, or Dspace. etc.

Feedback is the breakfast of Champions.

Ken Blanchard

You can Help other students.
"Inform any error or mistake in this book."

We and Universe
will reward you for Your Kind act.

Email at : feedback@gullybaba.com
or
WhatsApp on 9350849407

Library and Information Services

Introduction

Today's human society is undergoing a sea change due to phenomenal growth of information. At every moment of our personal and professional life, we are information dependent. Researchers or information seekers are busy in conducting experiments, attending meetings, seminars, symposia. etc. They have little lime left for scanning of documents and making themselves up-to-date in their areas of research. To save their users time and efforts, which they can apply to give pace in their research, work. Keeping these points in view, library and information science professionals have designed various kinds of services known as alerting services to help the researchers and other information seekers. Some of the important alerting services, i.e. current awareness service, selective dissemination of information services, etc.

The term 'bibliographic databases' has traditionally referred to the 'abstracting and indexing services' for the scholarly literature. These services focussed on collecting the citation information and abstracts of research articles and making them searchable. Abstracts have been the focus for the creation of bibliographic databases because they summarize the full research article, are small enough to re-key (the only way to capture the information before electronic publishing), store, and search. The prime objective of any library is to meet the information requirements of its clients most effectively. To meet this objective, the library builds the collection in a planned manner and offers a variety of information services to inform the users what is available and whatever latest has been published in their areas of interest.

Q1. What do you mean by Current Awareness Service? Discuss its characteristics and types.

Ans. Dissemination of information that will keep it users well-informed and up-to-date in their fields of basic interest as well as in related subjects is called Current Awareness Service. It is a system of getting knowledge on recent development, and especially those developments which relate to the special interest of the individual.

CAS is a device of the information system through which the users of information can be informed promptly, as soon as possible after publications but before absorption into the comprehensive secondary sources of current literature on a broad subject field or on an area in which a group of persons are interested, and presented in a manner, volume and rhythm intended to facilitate or cultivate current approach to information.

S.R. Ranganathan defines CAS as "Documentation periodical...listing the documents appearing during the period covered, and without being selected to suit the requirements of a particular reader or of a specific topic under investigation. It endeavours to keep the clientele informed promptly of all the nascent thought created in their fields of work and related fields."

The service is usually in the form of a publication, and attempts to bring information that is current or of recent origin to the attention of its users.

Characteristics of Current Awareness Service: A current awareness service has the following characteristics:

(1) The service does not seek to answer any specific questions that the user may have.

(2) The service is usually confined to a well defined subject area or topic. However, topics from related areas are also covered in the service.

(3) The service may sometimes confine itself to a given type of literature. e.g., patents; or may cover different types of literature.

(4) The service could be bibliographical in nature. e.g., a list of references with or without abstracts. The service could also be discursive. e.g., a newsletter. In this type of current awareness service usually there are short contributions from professionals with the objective of highlighting recent developments or exchanging information and ideas.

(5) The service endeavors to alert its users of the recent development as quickly as possible.

(6) The service attempts to make browsing convenient and easy for the user.

Although published current awareness service is the predominant form, more recently, the service has also been using electronic means. This usually takes the form of an electronic Bulletin' Board which is computer-based, and accessible to users through their terminals. The user browses through items in the electronic board just as he would do in a publication.

Types of CAS: Having understood the need for current awareness services and main characteristics of such service, we may now proceed to examine the different types of such services.

(1) Contents-by Journal Service: In this type of service, the library or documentation centre, or a commercial publisher distribute, a publication which contains copies of contents pages of journals in a broad area. e.g., life sciences. A very good example of a Contents-by-Journal service is the publication called Current Contents published by the Institute of Scientific Information (ISI) in the USA. If a library provides the service, it normally restricts it to the journals received in the library. The rationale behind this type of service is that the journals are the predominant medium for communicating new information. If users can be regularly informed of journal articles appearing; in current journals in broad or narrow areas, they would come to know of recent articles or papers in their areas of interest. The simplest way in which this can be done is to duplicate the contents pages of journal issues and circulate them individually or in a compiled form to users.

Another rationale for this type of service is the fact that users tend to value certain journals very high and look forward to browsing through the issues of these journals as soon as they are received in their library. The contents page service enables them to quickly know the titles of articles published in journals of their interest. Once they identify interesting or useful papers, they can then go to the library and read the papers. Alternatively, they could write to the authors of those papers and obtain a reprint or a copy of the paper. This way the user builds up his personal collection of useful information. The Contents-by-Journal service is perhaps the cheapest and quickest way of providing a degree of current awareness. This is because very little intellectual effort is expended in providing this service. However, this service also suffers from disadvantages. Some of these are:

(i) A lot of effort is called for on the part of the user to locate information that is useful to him.

(ii) Since this type of service provides only titles of papers, it is difficult to determine the usefulness of paper, in many cases, without actually examining the full papers.

(2) Documentation Bulletins or Current Awareness Lists: This is by far the most predominant form of current awareness service provided by libraries. In this kind of service the library or documentation centre scans primary journals and other sources of current information received in the library to identify potentially useful articles of interest to their users The bibliographical details of such articles are collected, and classified or grouped into broad or narrow subject groups. At periodic intervals (fortnightly, monthly. etc.) the collected bibliographic entries are listed under the different subject headings, class numbers, or groups. The list is then duplicated and circulated to users.

It is usual for documentation bulletins to feature the entries in the list in a manner that facilitates browsing. The subject headings or classification numbers and/or subheadings under which entries are listed make it easy for the user to browse through the list. A documentation list could have an author and a subject index, and a contents page. These devices enable a user to locate sections of the bulletin which he should browse in order to get items of information that may be useful to him.

A documentation bulletin may sometimes include abstracts of papers listed in the bulletin. The provision of abstracts greatly enhances the usefulness of the documentation bulletin since the abstract provides additional information about papers. If abstracts are well prepared they can often be substituted for the original paper. Of course, more time will then be needed to produce this service.

Current awareness lists are published or issued by the library of an organisation for use within the organisation, as well as by professional or learned bodies, international agencies and commercial organisations for use by anyone interested in the subject areas covered by the list. Examples of current awareness lists produced by professional bodies are Chemical Titles of the Chemical Abstracts Service, and Current Chemical Papers of the Chemical Society, U.K.

A local current awareness list. i.e., one published or issued by the library can be tailored to suit the need of the users within the organisation. Firstly, the selection of items can be made keeping in mind the subject interest, research projects, product profile. etc. of the organisation and its personnel. Secondly, it is possible to slant the abstract to highlight the usefulness of documents to the organisation. Thirdly, the list can be featured to reflect the areas of interest or product profile of the organisation. Fourthly, the list can include information from more than one type of information source. For instance, the documentation bulletin for an industrial organisation could have references to patent or report literature in addition to journal articles. Usually, current awareness lists produced by professional bodies are more comprehensive in their coverage than locally produced lists.

(3) Research-in-Progress Bulletins: This is another type of current awareness service and, as the name suggests, it alerts users of new research projects and the progress made in the research projects in hand. Such current awareness services usually require the joint effort of more than one organisation working in similar or closely related research areas. A parent body which funds or controls a group of research organisations (e.g., CSIR, ICAR in India) could also bring out Research-in-Progress bulletins with the input to these bulletins being provided by the different laboratories or research centres under that body. As example of this type of service is the United States Department of Agriculture's Current Research information System (CRIS). All USDA laboratories and research stations contribute their input to CRIS. It is a computer-based service and it can be searched to retrieve information on research projects. It is used also for current awareness purposes. Another example of a research-in-progress service that is international in scope is the CARIS (Current Agricultural Research information System) of the Food and Agriculture Organisation (FAO).

A research-in-progress bulletin usually contains information about the laboratory at which the project is being done, names of principal and associate researchers, funds and sources of funds, duration of the project, and special equipment in use, if any. In addition, it includes a narrative description of the research project and/or progress achieved till date.

Now a days, the trend is for the creation and maintenance of research-in-progress databases in computer-readable form similar to the USDA's CRIS system. Such a database can then be used both for retrospective search before a new project is formulated as well as for current awareness services. Such a database can be used also for other purposes. e.g., to produce an inventory of specialised equipment, centres of specialisation. etc.

(4) Newspaper Clipping Service: News papers are current awareness media, since they publish news of recent happening on the political, social, and economic front of a nation or region. News papers carry useful information to everyone from housewives to top management of companies and ministers. Again news papers are of different kinds. Some of them are local or regional in their orientation and coverage, others are national or international. Further, some news papers specialise in economic or financial news and contain in depth analysis of industry, trade, banking, commerce. etc.

Given the above characteristics of news papers, it is not surprising that they are consideration as valuable sources of information. Libraries and documentation centres, therefore, provide information services based on news papers. One such service is the News paper Clipping Service.

In the news paper clipping service, a library subscribes to one or more daily or weekly news papers, carefully chosen for their coverage of areas of interest to the organisation. Each of these news papers is scanned and any items of interest to the user group are clipped (i.e., cut) and pasted on a sheet of thicker paper or card. The clipping is then assigned one or more subject headings or group/class codes. At periodic intervals, (i.e. daily, weekly) the clippings are arranged by subject headings or group code and disseminated to users.

In a small organisation, batches of clippings themselves in one or more groups may be circulated to users. In larger organisations, or where the circulation is wide, a bulletin containing the news item with or without an annotation may be circulated. The clippings themselves are filed in vertical or suspension file folders for possible use at a later date. Those clippings which are considered ephemeral are discarded. News paper clipping services are quite common in libraries of government departments, banks and financial organisations, and industrial development agencies.

Q2. What do you mean by news filtering service? Discuss different sources of news-based services.

Or

News Filtering Service is an important category of CAS. Discuss the different sources of such services.

[Dec-2018, Q.No.-3.1]

Or

Explain the importance of news alerting service for different user groups. Describe different sources for news-based services in Internet Environment. [Dec-2019, Q.No.-3]

Ans. A lot of news is generated in printed newspapers, newsletters, electronic news wires, magazines, trade journals. etc. Some companies called News Aggregators routinely gather and scan all news and supply only what the end-user needs – highly selected and filtered. Such services are called Filtered News Services. Reuters, Desktop Data, PointCast, Dow Jones are some examples of such companies. In India, we have http://www.securities.com. Vans Communications (Now bought over by Friday Corporation) that offer news-based services.

One of the ways of offering tailor-made News filtering services is to do it yourself. However, this is a formidable task considering the vastness of news sources, and resources available to libraries. Therefore, libraries subscribing to news filtering services and outsourcing is the norm. In a way the approach is also outsourcing the work of providing news filtering service

One might think of five different sources of news-based services. These sources are discussed below:

(1) Individual Newspaper Websites: Individual newspaper websites often have a search facility, some going back just a few years and some more than a century. Almost all national and local newspapers are involved in some way in digital archiving, although some will charge for access to images of original archives. To identify titles, websites and history of newspapers worldwide, visit www.onlinenewspapers.com. This is a fabulous, free facility, with the newspapers arranged by continent, country and then alphabetically by title, linking to thousands of newspaper websites from around the world.

Using RSS Feeds: The approach of scanning newspapers websites, though simple, has a number of drawbacks. One has to open several websites, locate specific news items, download and read them. This is highly time-consuming and frustrating. This becomes a real problem as many newspaper Home pages contain lots of images, short movie clips, etc, and this takes time to download. Same news may be repeated in many sites. Poor Internet connection poses its own problems.

Recently, a technology called RSS Feed has become available to overcome the abovementioned shortcomings. Many websites offering news items also provide what is called an RSS feed. New Indian Express is one such Indian newspaper providing RSS Feeds. RSS Feed is an xml file. This file has an URL (address of the page on the website). At the end-user's PC, he has to install a small program generally called RSS Aggregator. Many RSS readers (aggregators) are available for free download and Amphetadesk is one of them. After installing Amphetadesk and invoking it, one has to enter the URL of the XML page in this program. Thereafter, Amphetadesk automatically downloads frequently the XML page (RSS Feed). We will then get on our desktop the latest news brought to us regularly every three hours. If we have entered five news channels then we would have five sets of news items. All of them have the URL of the actual news item plus a short abstract. In this way, one can get himself updated easily with latest news from newspapers of his interest. Several sites give directories of available RSS Feeds. www.feedster.com is an directory example of the site www.disobey.com that provides Amphetadesk also gives its own long list of several thousand RSS feeds. RSS Feeds are also called Channels. There is a provision to display constantly updated news pages on your website using this technology.

(2) Popular Portals Offering News Free: Many websites like Yahoo, Rediff, Sify, Lycos. etc., provide news on their Home Pages. Usually, there is a provision to select subjects of personal interest like politics, entertainment, health, astrology. etc. to provide for such selection, the home page is suitably modified to match users needs. However, these services are too generic in nature and do not meet the technical or work related needs.

(3) Google News Alerting Service: The Search Engine Google provides a news alerting service free of charge. In Feb 2004, it was in Beta testing Stage. The website address is: news.google.com One of the four major component databases in Google is News. News items are gathered automatically from all over the world from news generating sites – newspapers, newsletters, news wires. etc. Without human intervention, they are classified and categorised into appropriate subject groups. Updating of news is continuous throughout. News as captured is made available immediately, showing when it was added (e.g.,"30 minutes ago"). You may use all facilities of Google regular search including Boolean operators, field based searching, limiting by language. etc. To begin with, you have to register yourself for News Alert service; the process is simple – just enter your name and email address and confirm to Google when you are asked to do so via an introductory mail from Google. Thereafter conduct a search in News. When the results are satisfactory, that search query has to be entered in Google alert. We may specify whether you need the alerting once a day by email or as and when the news is added to Google database. You can specify the source (journal/ newspaper). Thereafter fresh updates meeting your query come to your mailbox regularly.

It is worthwhile to remember that Google allows search facilities like:

(i) Limiting by language, country
(ii) Term truncation l Search for synonyms
(iii) Use of Boolean operators, parenthesis, phrase search
(iv) Searching in title, text portions. etc.
(v) Limiting by source of the news.

As an example of use of this facility the experience of the Virtual Information Centre at ICICI Knowledge Park, Hyderabad may be mentioned. Here, the library tracks all news on "ICICI Knowledge Park" if it appears in the title of a news item in any Indian news source. Google searches 90 Indian news sources and sends a daily mail giving the link plus a short abstract, whenever there is a hit/match. It is impossible to subscribe to 90 newspapers; thus it saves cost. The service is extremely fast - the alert is available within minutes of release on the Net. And the service is free.

(4) News Aggregators providing Services for a Fee: A number of companies provide fee-based news filtering services. PointCast, Dow Jones, Desktop Data, Reuters are some examples. These are enterprise-based systems. They are very costly. Only big companies can afford and provide it for their several branches upon proper licensing. Knight-Ridder and Scoop are services that allow filtering based on end-user-controlled searches. Others like Clarinet, Netscape provide for selection categories from pre-sorted set of news categories.

All the fee-based filtering agencies claim to "deliver filtered news directly to the end user". Here delivery may be through fax, email, or on a specially supplied computer terminal directly connected to the vendors computer system by a leased connection. Filtering may be achieved via broad selection of pre-ordered categories or through user driven search, queries formulated using sophisticated Boolean logic. The end-user is usually an institution like a corporate body, university and not an individual.

The librarian evaluates the news filtering services available from several competing agencies and selects the agency to order on India. www.securities.com provides similar news filtering services. One can choose as many categories as needed (countries, industry segments, corporate entities to be watched) and pay accordingly. In the case of Bloomberg and Reuters special terminals and leased line connectivity are needed. The librarian procures the service, installs software and hardware, monitors the users and their usage, and attends to problems, if any. He also attends to terminal/monitor connectivity problems, data updating routines. etc. This is more of a liaison work. An example of a fee based news aggregator – Moreover Technologies.

Moreover Technologies: Moreover Technologies launched in September 2003 is the first real-time weblog search tool for the enterprise. The product harvests information from over 75,000 hand selected, business-critical weblogs in real-time and enables corporate users to gain access to the high value news, commentary and consumer opinion that resides within weblogs. Moreover Technologies assigns each blog a ranking that corresponds to the reliability, integrity and caliber of the blog. Products of Moreover include ci-builder, ci-watch and Alerts.

ci-builder offers an easy and affordable way to provide the organisation with highly targeted real-time news and information by providing the tools to create and customise multiple, tailored news needs. This is for companies needing the ultimate news management tool. The service is delivered to corporate portals, Intranets.

'ci-watch' provides live headline links on any company, topic, or industry, delivered continuously and automatically to your portal, intranet or website. This is for companies who wish to receive high quality, real-time targeted news and information.

(5) Traditional Database Vendors Offering News as a Part of their Services: Several traditional database vendors like Dialog, Nexis, Dow Jones, Reuters and others offer news databases as a part of their service. Their query language and search procedures provide for perfected search strategies to be saved. Such saved search strategies (queries) may be executed on small sets of updated records in a database or a set of database files. In such instances, they become tailor-made SDI service. Nowadays, they are called Electronic Clipping Services.

Q3. Write short note on the following:

(i) Modes of CAS production

Ans. Current Awareness Service products and services may be generated either in-house or outsourced to external agencies.

(1) In-house Generation: In-house generation of CAS is based on manual scanning of documents such as newspapers, journals, patents. etc. and other published information sources. This service is usually based on the local scanning and entry of records of items received in the library. In India, most of the CAS provided by library professionals are manual and in bibliographic form.

In-house generation of CAS involves performing all tasks relating to the CAS by the library staff themselves using internal resources and machinery. When these are produced using computers, apart from computer systems, LAN connectivity, software, training, high-end data storage systems are all needed. In-house generation puts a lot of responsibility on the library. But it makes the library self-reliant; staff gains first hand experience and expertise. Special local requirements can be taken care of easily and quickly. Requests for changes in specifications can be met and the production can be made dynamically effective. List of Additions and Content Pages reproduction are easy to manage locally. In CAS, selection and location of literature items of relevance to user groups is a specialist's job and library staff is better at it.

Most of the CAS products require a central master database of bibliographic records to be established. This has to be constantly updated. Indexing using a thesaurus involves technical competency of the Library Staff. This part of the job is difficult for outside agency to handle. Some software packages for CAS are listed in Table.

Table 3.1: List of Some Software Packages for CAS Applications

S. No.	Package	Vendor/Supplier
(1)	Basis	Information Dimension Inc
(2)	BRS/Search	BRS Software Products
(3)	CAIRS	Leatherhead Food Research Association
(4)	ORBIT	Maxwell Online Inc
(5)	STATUS	Harwell Computer Power
(6)	TINLIB	Information Made Easy Limited
(7)	Book Shelf	Logical Choice
(8)	Datfkex	Dataflex
(9)	Extract	Software Solution
(10)	Procite	Personal Bibliographic Software Inc

(2) Outsourcing CAS Activity: There are two distinct situations where CAS may be done better by external agency:

(i) Where outside agency produces or partly produces a CAS product

(ii) Where, instead of (or in addition to) using in-house database, an external database (either online, CD-ROM or onsite) is used

In the case of (i) above, an external agency is used when library has inadequate staff, or they do not have sufficient knowledge; or when the work involved is so huge, that outsourcing would be beneficial. In the case of (ii), several ready-made databases are available with database vendors like Dialog, STN, and BRS, etc. Some advantages using online databases for CAS work are:

(i) Comprehensive collection of data

(ii) Automatic updating by vendor

(iii) Easy and quick searching facilities
(iv) Duplication avoidance when multiple files are used
(v) Ability to download data records and incorporate them into local database
(vi) Ability to handle graphics, formulas, trademarks. etc.

(ii) Evaluation of CAS

Ans. In order to find out whether the money spent on CAS activity is worth the expenditure, some kind of evaluation of the usage, usefulness and effectiveness is required. Usage refers to how many people use the service and how frequently, Usefulness means whether users find contents of relevance to their work as indicated by their coming back to library for further reference. Effectiveness denotes whether as a result of CAS products, saving of users time is seen whether their productivity enhances, and other relevant aspects.

Some questions that may be asked while evaluating computer-based CAS services are given below:

- Is the coverage comprehensive?
- Is the database updated regularly and frequently?
- Is the cost of the whole service reasonable?
- Is the user-interface user friendly, easy to use, easy to learn, etc?
- Can one handle non-text (graphics) matter easily?
- Can the output be formatted in different ways?

Besides these general questions, individual services call for specific questions as well. For example, if there is a CAS on Forthcoming Events, then following questions become relevant:

- Are the entries relevant?
- Is the bulletin released with enough time to benefit by it?
- Are the contact addresses and phone numbers reliable and correct?
- Does it give info on cancelled or postponed events?
- Does it provide indexes to location (venue), subject, sponsor. etc.

Q4. What is Selective Dissemination of Information? Explain the components and operational features of SDI.

Ans. Selective Dissemination of Information was a concept first described by H.P. Luhn for the scientist/engineers of IBM. According to him, "The Selected Dissemination of Information is the service within an organisation which concerns itself with the channelling of new items of information, from whatever sources, to those points within the organisation where the probability of usefulness in connection with current work or interest in high. On the other hand, the service endeavours to withhold such information from the points where the probability is low."

An SDI system may be said to comprise of the following components:

- **A Document Database:** A file containing document description and terms representing the subject content of the documents being described. Since SDI is a computer-based service, the document database is in computer-readable form. The document database used in SDI is for recent or current literature. The terms chosen to describe document content are usually drawn with the help of a thesaurus.
- **A Set of User Profiles**: A file describing users or recipients of the SDI service and their subject interests. The user profiles file is again a computer-readable file. The building of - user profiles is an important activity and is described in greater detail below. The terms to describe user interests are also drawn from the same indexing vocabulary (thesaurus) used to index the items going into the document database. The use of the same terminology to describe document content and user interests ensures good matching of user interests with document content.
- **Mechanism to Match Document Descriptions with user Descriptions**: The mechanism used to match documents with users is the computer. In fact, a computer program running inside the computer does the matching of user interests with documents.
- **A User-SDI System Interface:** An interface is a common boundary that permits useful interaction or communication. The SDI service interface may be said to comprise of the following : The users of the SDI service. SDI notifications of recent literature that match given users' interests. . Request to users to provide feedback on the notifications sent to them. The feedback provided by the user is about the usefulness or otherwise of the notifications sent to him. intermediaries in the SDI system operation, These are the information scientists within the organisation who interact with the user and are knowledgeable about the document database and its c characteristics, and in the creation of user profiles.

Workflow in SDI Operation: The four functional operation (major activity areas) of an SDI system may be said to be:

- **Selection:** in the selection phase, the subject and other characteristics of new documents are matched with the interests of users expressed in terms of subject and other characteristics.

- **Notification:** The selection phase matches document characteristics (content) with user profiles. Only those documents that satisfy a given user's profile (search expression) are selected for dissemination.
- The items selected for dissemination have to be notified. i.e., listed, and sent to the user. The notification usually takes the form of a list of references with or without abstracts. Since the SDI service is for current information, it is important that the notifications should contain adequate information about the documents being notified. Providing detailed abstracts of documents is the best way of informing the user about the contents of documents.
- **Feedback:** The user is expected to provide feedback to the SDI personnel in the feedback from sent along with the SDI on the relevance of each of the items listed in the SDl service provided to him. Once the feedback from the user is received, it 1s analysed to examine whether the items being disseminated are in fact useful to him. If a majority of the items are found useful, then it can be concluded that the User Profile has been properly prepared. On the contrary, if many items are not found useful, it may be concluded that the User Profile does not truly represent the user's interest and must be modified.
- **Modification:** Meaningful interaction between the user and the SDI system for profile refinement begins after he has been provided SDI notifications., i.e. citations and abstracts of documents that match his profile. The provision of feedback on the usefulness of the documents disseminated enables a better understanding of the user's needs. When a user indicates through his feedback that the output was not useful, the SDI system operators begin to modify his profile. The SDI system personnel analyse the reasons for the dissemination of the items that were not found useful. This could result in the revision or modification of the user's profile or search expression for the user. The modified profile's performance is again monitored to ensure that it is better than the earlier profile.

Sometimes, however, modification of the user's profile may be initiated by the user telling the SDI personnel about a change in his interests. For instance, if the user takes up a new, research project, then his interests may change and he may inform the SDI system personnel to modify his profile suitably.

The functional aspects of an SDI System. viz. Selection. Notification, Feedback, and Modification are shown in Fig.

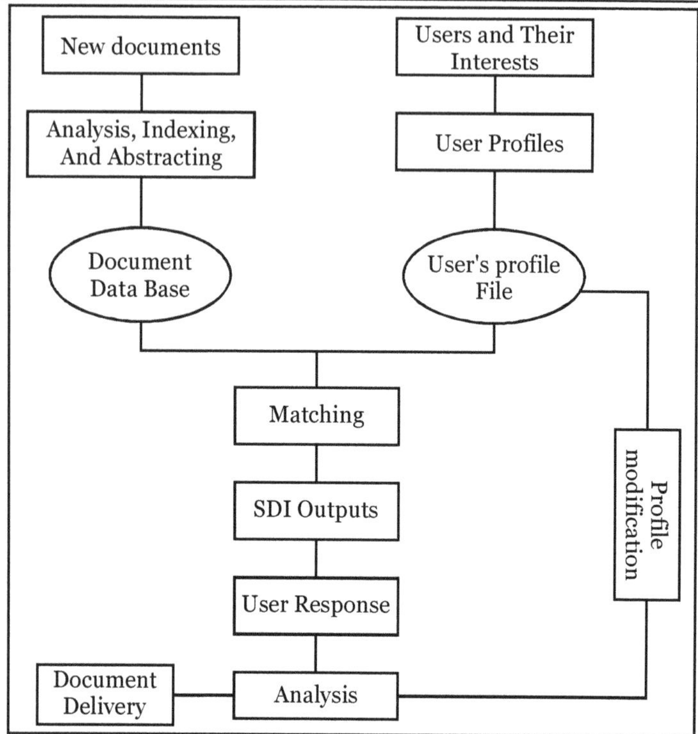

Fig. 3.1: Selective Dissemination of Information (SDI) Functional Flowchart

Q5. Write short note on the following.

(i) SDI services: some example

Ans. SDI can be offered at the institutional level by an institution or by some national level organisation at the national level. It may be free of charges or commercial (fee-based). It may be using local databases or external databases.

Some years ago, obtaining computerised bibliographic databases for SDI work was very costly and computer facilities were very scarce. At that time, INSDOC, Delhi, and BARC, Bombay used to obtain database magnetic tapes on a periodical basis, mount them on their computer facilities and run SDI service. The output was sent in paper format once a month via post. Scientists all over India were served for a nominal fee. Subsequently, with the availability of better telecommunication facilities in the country for online accessing of international databases, a number of organisations started providing SDI services to their research/academic/technical staff. Such organisations include DESIDOC, Delhi; BARC, Mumbai; ICRISAT, Hyderabad, NCL, Pune, etc. INSDOC (now NISCAIR) provides SDI service to any individual or organisation on payment. The National Centre for Science Information (NCSI), located in the Indian Institute of Science Campus, Bangalore provides such a service to the users in the Institute.

(ii) SDI using CD-ROM databases

Ans. With the advent of databases in CD-ROM format, several libraries started offering SDI using internally available (acquired) CD-ROM databases. This involves using the latest updates of the databases. Database vendors like OVID, Silver Platter, etc give their own SDI facilities as a part of search facility. Here, multiple databases may be searched. In this case, necessity to avoid duplicate record arises. The SDI queries may be 'scheduled' to be run at periodic intervals. The results are dispatched by email or by post. In many cases, the search software is so simple that the user himself can form queries and set up individualised profiles. Quite a bit of disintermediation has come about in the SDI arena.

Q6. Enumerate the comparison of CAS and SDI.

Ans. CAS and SDI are both alerting services. There are certain commonalities and a few differences.

Table 3.2

No.	Current Awareness Service	Selective Dissemination of Information
1	CAS is awareness service directed towards all the users who need it.	SDI is a personalised service and is directed towards the individuals or homogenous group.
2	Subject coverage may be board.	Highly specific subject- searches based on user's query.
3	Output includes mostly bibliographic data.	Often tends to includes abstract as well.
4	CAS is provided by circulating the current list of periodicals among all the users.	SDI service is based on matching the user's profile with the document profile
5	No profile matching is involved	User profile is matched using sophisticated query algorithms.
6	CAS all the information is circulated to the user on the given topic.	SDI is a selective service based on the exact information need of the user.
7.	Feedback is not important in CAS service.	Feedback is an important step is providing SDI service.
8.	Continuous omnibus type of service.	Service may change as far as individual user is concerned, as soon as his interests change.

Q7. Explain the concept of Electronic Clipping Services (ECS). Discuss its few international database agencies and their services.

Or

What do you understand by Electronic Clipping Service (ECS)? Is it a form of SDI service Describe the operation of ECS with particular reference to the services provided by DIALOG: Alert services and ISI: Alert Services. [June-2018, Q.No.-3.1]

Ans. One of the major problems faced by the information professionals is to monitor the news, both in real-time and with periodic updates, appearing in over thousands channels of televisions and daily news papers published world over. It may not be possible to collect, select, store and disseminate news/information from all sources within a very short interval of time. However, some information providers created electronic clipping services and disseminating selected news/ information to their users. Most of them are foreign-based, whereas, big organisations and institutions in India like DESIDOC, NIC are offering this service to their users on limited basis. In this service, user's can set up profiles on electronic clipping service providers to monitor current events news relevant to their areas of interest and evolving issues.

Generalities of ECS: It is often possible to select multiple files in one go for searching. In many cases, the database vendor himself offers several groups or clusters of subject related files. As far as display is concerned, some vendors provide various options: only title, abstract also, keyword, full text of the original article, inclusion of graphics. etc.

The periodical output is delivered to the user in many ways as follows:

- Fax
- Personal email box
- Email box allotted by vendor (example: Dial mail of Dialog) on his computer system – (this usually involves being connected to the vendor's machine for longer time leading to extra charges)
- On special terminals supplied by the vendor that can be used with leased lines
- Printed on paper using remote printer and dispatched through courier or postal system (preferred mode for full text)

When multiple files are searched, there could be duplicate records. Duplication identification and elimination is a facility with some systems. How fast does the database file get updated is another aspect be to looked into. This could be real time, or vary from file, to file from a daily to weekly to monthly. These services are generally aimed at corporate customers. Such customers may internally distribute the results to different departments or user groups. In such cases, corporate clients may want some facility to identify the output or invoice by the sub-accounts so to say. If a central library is receiving a large number of printouts from different vendors for different users, then some identification of local client or the user to whom the printout is meant, will be useful.

Here it may be difficult to elaborate all national and international agencies offering electronic clipping service but some of the important ones are narrated below:

(1) P.A.S.S. PORT (Data Times): It offers several electronic clipping services, all packaged under the name P.A.S.S. Port (Personalised Automated Search Service). This service analyses the user's need, tries several search strategies to see which worlts best, then establishes a profile for daily delivery to the user's account. The standard electronic clipping service searches about 300 databases on Data Times and runs the search daily. One of the more unusual P.A.S.S. Port features is its same day coverage of about 100 newspapers. The someday news alert service searches a subset of articles focussing on regionally significant topics, chosen by the editor of the selected newspapers. This service delivers articles matching the user's interest profile to the user's fax machine or mail account by 7:00 A.M. Eastern time. It includes articles within seven days of the date of their publications. This service is primarily a clipping service for daily newspapers, broadcast transcripts and wire services. P.A.S.S. Port searches transmitted by fax are formatted in two columns of text, containing an article full-text, or the articles citation, document ID number and first few paragraphs. The cost of on-demand full-text article delivery is US $5 per article. One of the major problems in electronic clipping service from- multiple newspapers is retrieval of duplicate or near-duplicate articles, with several papers picking up the same wire story. Data Times thus provides the option to remove duplicate articles, although some users in anay want to see all coverage of a particular topic. Duplicate detection is performed by comparing text rather than headings, and multiple copies of stories, in which 70 per cent of the text is the same, as eliminated. Profile can be set to run once a day, alternate day, weekly or any periodicity opted by the user.

(2) Alert Service (DIALOG): DIALOG offers alert service by permitting its user to create, edit and review their user's profiles through menu-driven system. It permits delivery or search results to a fax or ally electronic mail system accessible through Internet. Information delivered through alert service call be presented in any standard or user-defined formats. Each alert file includes the file(s) searched, the search statement(s) used and each record in a standard DIALOG output style. It also includes duplicate detection features.

(3) Dow Jone's CLIP Service: This service identifies news as soon as it is added to the database. Since CLIP service includes newswires, this helps the users to monitor late breaking news automatically. The user is prompted to indicate the files to be monitored, the search strategies to be used and the name of resulting 'folder'. Each folder can have up to five search statements. User is asked to specify the delivery options for the clippings. The user has the option to review the headlines of the clipped articles before viewing the full-text. Clippings are kept in a folder for 30 days if not deleted by the user before then. Clippings call be delivered by fax, AT&?' Mail, Easy Link, MCI Mail, or Sprint mail.

(4) News Flash (News Net): News Net began as a service offering electronic versions of industry newsletters. It has since expanded to include newswii.es, directories and source books and gateway access to company information. Its primary use is electronic clipping service and to monitor industry trends or to track late-breaking stories on the newswires. Retrieved information can be stored by date, keywords, phrase, or database code. This service is menu-driven with the following options:

(i) ability to specific both activation and expiry dates.
(ii) sorting of results by issue date, title of publication, or alphabetically by keywords.
(iii) ability to undelete search phrases deleted within the past two weeks and return them to active monitoring.
(iv) ability to copy existing folder setting to create new folder.
(v) The news is delivered online or through fax.

(5) ECLIPSE (NEXIS): Besides current awareness service, ECLIPSE offers retrospective search facility. The user has option to view search results partially or in full. An ECLIPSE search is established by running a search, reviewing the results and then saving. User can select an update interval, i.e. daily, weekly, monthly, etc. and select delivery option, i.e. online or to a standalone NEXIS printer. Delivery to commercial electronic mail system accessible through the Internet such as MCI Mail, Compu Serve and AT&T Mail, and by fax. Unfortunately, it does not permit editing of stored searches.

(6) ISI: Alerting Services: ISI Profile-based Alerting Services: These unique web-based alerting services may be used for individuals, as well as for the needs of an entire organisation. Profiles are filtered against a database of 9,000 journals. 'Personal Alert' is a highly customised profile based alerting service covering nearly 16000 high impact STM journals, books, and conference proceedings. 'Research Alert' is a print-based service delivering complete bibliographic information on personalised profiles of individual users.

Table-of-contents Alerting Services: 'Journal Tracker', 'Corporate Alert', 'ISI Chemistry Alert', 'Current Chemical Reactions' and "Current Contents Service" come under this category. Print version of the Current Contents is the most popular and widely used by STM community and it is issued in 7 sections:

(i) Life Sciences

(ii) Physical Chemical and Earth Science
(iii) Engineering, Computing & Technology
(iv) Arts and Humanities
(v) Social and Behavioural Sciences
(vi) Agriculture, Biology and Environment Sciences
(vii) Clinical Medicine

Current Contents Search is available through several agencies like: OVID Technologies, Silver Platter Information, Gale Group, Dialog, Data Star. etc.

(7) Evaluation of Electronic News Clipping Services: These evaluation criteria are especially meaningful in the case of web-based News Clipping services. These have been adopted from Competitive Edge website: (http:// www.clipresearch.com/comparison.pdf).

Q8. Explain the term "New Directions for Alerting Services".

Ans. Over the decades information needs of the users have not been changed although users may have become more sophisticated with the quality of internal printed documents that are expected and in the use of information technology to support information dissemination, storage and retrieval. Following are some of the major changes that have been observed in recent years:

- Information seekers working in ail organisation have become more aware of fie need of current information.
- Organisations involved in research and development activities have realised that current awareness of information is the major factor in competitive intelligence.
- More emphasis should be given on the needs of individuals rather than organisation as a whole. Thus the demand for tailored current awareness service has increased as compared to generalised one.
- Machine-readable current awareness services overcome all problems of speed, time and currency of information and now information seekers prefer network 'version of CAS than the conventional printed mode of dissemination of information.

As the demand for tailored current awareness services have increased during the recent past, librarians and information scientists may need to play effective roles as a part of a team of a research project in the organisation and not to offer current awareness service from a distance.

Q9. What is Bibliographic fulltext service? Write down the need for bibliographic fulltext service.

Ans. The term 'bibliographic databases' has traditionally referred to the 'abstracting and indexing services' for the scholarly literature. These services focussed on collecting the citation information and abstracts of research articles and making them searchable. Abstracts have been the focus for the creation of bibliographic databases because they summarise the full research article, are small enough to re-key (the only way to capture the information before electronic publishing), store, and search.

Nowadays, the scenario is fast changing. More and more journals are available in fulltext as well as in print. Many publishers, content aggregators, and intermediaries are offering fulltext of the original to be downloaded instantly, immediately upon bibliographic search/retrieval is done on the computer system. It is no more the case of difficult work involving many steps: find what you want in one step, locate the original in some library in another step, order a photocopy or the original document via interlibrary loan as next step, pay if necessary and get it in the last step.

Now in one single step, searching, retrieving, ordering, getting Fulltext are all carried out. Providing access to fulltext bibliographic databases, allowing library patrons to download fulltext directly, providing training to users in database searching and facilitating all these is called Fulltext Bibliographic Service.

Need for Bibliographic fulltext Service: A library for a variety of reasons provides fulltext bibliographic services. Convenience, saving in time due to quick and almost immediate delivery, greater customer satisfaction, higher levels of affordability are some reasons why libraries offer fulltext services. Patrons are no more satisfied with abstracts. They demand immediate response for originals and are not prepared to wait for several days. They are prepared to bear the extra cost involved in quick fulfilment of their requirements. Greater availability of fulltext has led to the reader psychology: "Let us look at the original anyway". The fulltext is available in digital form right at the desktop of the reader—the reader need not go to the library but can use the facility of the library's subscription even sitting in his home or office. Advances in technology have rendered storing of large volumes of information files on personal computers very cheap. This again has spurred fulltext bibliographic usage.

Q10. Write down the players in bibliographic fulltext service.

Ans. Supply Chain Management (SCM) is a field of growing academic interest, as reflected in the increase in related literature. The Council of Supply Chain Management Professionals not only defines SCM as the "planning and management of all activities involved in sourcing and procurement, conversion, and all logistics management activities," but also emphasises its role in the integration between players involved in the entire supply chain. SCM interest lies in its contribution to a competitive advantage, in terms of differentiation and the reduction of operating costs, especially in the current context of intense competition, globalisation, and active consumer participation. It is argued that better SCM results in superior performance, through the adoption of exemplary practices. A wide range of publications support the existence of significant relationships between SCM practices and organisational performance, especially from the economic perspective.

Traditional database vendors like Dialog, Lexis-Nexis, Dow Jones. etc., get content from journal publishers and add indexes on their own and make them searchable on computer. Learned societies may own database-vending agencies—for example American Chemical Society that publishes the famous Chemical Abstracts(CA), owns STN—a database company. STN has many fulltext sources. Besides making Chemical Abstracts available via STN, ACS also licences out content of CA to database vendors like Dialog, Data Star. etc.

Content aggregators are those that gather content from several small publishers and make the content accessible via web. Emerald, EBSCO and Ingenta are some content aggregators. EBSCO for instance buys content from hundreds of journal producers and makes it available in fulltext format through EBSCO gateways. Most often, linking to the publishers' original archive or mirror sites provides the access to fulltext.

Between the content aggregators and the library (and its patrons), there could be a third party: access facilitators. For example, Athens provides a facility for the library to manage user accounts for all its patrons on several database producers or content aggregators using a single interface.

Another recent trend that is gaining ground is the 'eprint' archives. The author or the institution where he works, creates a repository of his/their own publications in their private servers and make them accessible free of charge. Archives generally contain fulltext of the articles as it was prior to peer review stage. Eprint archives are reliable and are free sources for fulltext.

Close to the librarian are some artificially formed groups or entities called library consortia. Libraries subscribing to several titles in common (duplicates) get together, form a consortium and strike a deal with publisher(s) for lower prices. Such consortia have special licensing agreements for usage of full text among their patrons.

Thus, we see that authors, journal publishers, learned societies, content aggregators, database vendors, access facilitators, library consortia, eprint archives managers are some players in the supply/usage chain of full text resources.

Q11. Write down the directory of full text sources of Journal Publishers, online vendors and database producers.

Ans. There are some directory of full text sources are as follows:

(1) Full text Sources Online (FSO) (http;//www.infotoday.com/): Full text Sources Online (FSO) is a directory of periodicals accessible online in full text through 23 aggregators and content providers. Published annually in January, FSO lists over 59,000 newspapers, journals, magazines, newsletter, newswires and transcript.

Each title entry comprises the aggregators and databases that provide the publication online in full text. Coverage dates, frequencies, and lag times of titles appearing online, as well as ISSNs and document types, are included. Also provided are more than 45,000 publisher's URLs indicating free archives, selected coverage, and Open Access Journals. Subject, geographic, and language indexes are supplied as well.

FSO is also available in digital format as **FSO Online** and for licence as FSOe. FSO Online provides the same complete information from FSO, and is updated weekly online. FSOe is the licenced text version of the FSO database for network or intranet use, with quarterly updates. Contact Lauri Rimler at 908-219-0088 or **lwrimler@infotoday.com** for pricing information.

(2) Journals List of EBSCO Fulltext Databases: It would be a good idea to look into publishers' journal's list relating to fulltext databases to find out the coverage and scope. Each journal title has a unique ID within the EBSCO system. Publisher's name differentiates it from similar titles from different publishers. A journal may have separate ISSN allotted - one for paper version, another for online versionif this is the case both the ISSNs are shown. Whether the vendor provides Pay Per View service or not is indicated. [Pay-per-view: you need not be a regular subscriber - for a small fee you can download the fulltext of an article, making payment using your credit card]. Besides subject of the journal, the period (in terms of volumes/years) for which fulltext is available in EBSCO is indicated in last two columns. The actual catalogue is a large file. It is in itself highly useful to check bibliographical details, ISSN, publishers name. etc. From an examination of the journal list of databases, we discern the coverage, strengths, scope, subject. etc.

(3) INGENTA as a Fulltext Source: Ingenta is another fulltext source. Examine the contents of Table 9.2. It gives some a sample listing of journal titles available with Ingenta. Whether the online version is available to print subscribers free of charge, whether pay-per-view facility is provided (for those non-subscribers) and if yes, the charges per article including copyright fees are all shown. The last column is particularly interesting as it tells wide variety of fulltext access provisions adopted by different publishers.

Table 3.3: Ingenta-Sample Listing of Fulltext Journals

Publisher	Free to print subscribers	Pay-per-view access	Publisher royalty fee	Notes
Association of Applied Biologists	Yes	Yes	£7.00	Free access also available for

				subscribing members of the Association
Association for Laboratory Automation	Yes	N/A		Articles currently available free of charge
Association of Learned and Professional Society Publishers	Yes	Yes	$20.00	Free access to ALPSP members via ALPSP website
Association of Schools of Allied Health Professions	Yes	Yes	$15.00	
Australian Academic Press	Yes	Yes	$6.00	
Australian Nursing Federation	Yes	Yes	$15.50	Volumes and Issues of the Australian Journal of Nursing are also available online to individuals. Issue: $24.00, Volume: 565.00
Beech Tree Publishing	Yes	Yes	$6.81	
Begell House. Inc.	Yes	No		
Bentham Science Publishers	No	Yes	$30	2001/2001 issues available free of charge
BIOS Scientific Publishers	Yes	Yes	$20.00	
British Editorial Society for	Yes	Yes		

Bone and Joint Surgery				
Blackwell Publishing	Yes	Yes	£13.00 ($28.00 for Periodon-tology 2000 Immunological Reviews)	Formerly Blackwells Publishers, Blackwell Science and Munksgaard. Online premium for former BSC titles
British Institute of Radiology	Yes	Yes	$15 for 24 hours	Made available via High Wire

Q12. What do you understand by Library Consortia? Briefly discuss.

Ans. Consortium is ubiquitous because of digital form of information published across the world through Internet. It refers to co-operation, co-ordination and collaboration among the libraries for the purpose of sharing information resources. In India, the real drive for co-operation was seen during 1980s due to the developments in Information and Communication Technology. Some of the academic libraries in India have formed consortia. A few of the major consortia in India are given below:

(1) CSIR- Science Direct Consortia: The Council of Scientific and Industrial Research (CSIR) in India has 40 scientific laboratories involved in basic and applied research in various disciplines. Many of the laboratories have well equipped libraries, and some of them act as the main information centers in different subjects functioning as consultant libraries at the national level. Access to electronic journals through the use of state-of-the art technology is possible in many of the libraries belonging to these laboratories. Each of the laboratories have a well established library or documentation centre that is also backed up with strategic information support from the National Institute of Science Communication and Information Resource (NISCAIR), a constituent establishment of CSIR formed with the merger of INSDOC and (NISCOM).

To augment CSIR research and development activities, NISCAIR implemented agency for the process of providing access to globally available Electronic Journals to entire S & T staff of CSIR and its constituent units through a consortia approach. As a first step, in recent past NISCAIR on behalf of CSIR has entered into an agreement with M/s. Elsevier Science to access its odd 1,500 e-journals and further intends to strengthen its information resource base by subscribing e-access of more and more journals published globally. CSIR consortium extended its access by creating appropriate agreements on consortium basis with the other providers of E-journals.

(2) Fulltext Access via JCCC: J-Gate is a Journal Gateway technology developed by Informatics India, Bangalore. J-Gate provides a bibliographic database of over 13,000 STM journals. Besides bibliographic data and index words, abstracts are also included.

Three important components are:

(i) A directory of journals covered,

(ii) A database of articles contained in these 13,000 journals,

(iii) A powerful search mechanism for locating desired articles via author, title, publication, subject. etc.

When J-Gate contents are customised for a specific library (say NIMHANS in Bangalore) then, we have JCC- J-Gate Custom Content. If several libraries get together forming a consortium and a J-Gate is developed for them, the JCCC- J-Gate Custom Content for Consortium emerges. Here the content for print and electronic versions of all journals in the consortium libraries are indexed to form a single database for easy access of all concerned. In addition, details of availability of a specific issue in member libraries are indicated. There is a provision for the users in any participating library to ask for a photocopy or softcopy via e-mail as an attachment. For each journal title, although more than one library may be holding it, one of the libraries is designated as document delivery library for that title. The utility of JCCC lies in the assured availability of articles and easy procurement via online ordering methods.

For instance, Virtual Information Centre of ICICI Knowledge Park, Hyderabad has set up a consortium called JCCC@VIC. Its members are:

(i) Indian Institute of Chemical Technology,

(ii) Hyderabad Centre for Cellular Molecular Biology, Hyderabad

(iii) ICRISAT, Hyderabad

(iv) National Institute of Nutrition, Hyderabad

(v) National Chemical Laboratory,

(vi) Pune University of Hyderabad, Hyderabad

(vii) Virtual Information Centre, Hyderabad

In this consortium, the emphasis is not on joint procurement of journals. It is on increasing the utilisation of journals subscribed by many institutions by providing access to digital contents and assured formalised way of inter-library loan or document delivery mechanism. Nearly 500 journals of member libraries are selectively covered. The database of articles for 2002 and 2003 contains 2.3 lakh records. This gateway provides a unique facility called 'My TOC'.

Here the end-user can select journal titles of his choice- he would get regular e-mail alerts telling when TOC from his select journals are added (updated) into JCCC database.

While JCCC@VIC is the first one to be established in January 2002, within a short span of two years several such efforts have come up. Some are:

(i) JCCC@INDEST for INDEST Consortium

(ii) JCCC@HELINET for Health Information Network in Bangalore

(iii) JCCC@TB-CEAR for National Tuberculosis Institute, Bangalore

(iv) JCCC@GAU for Gujarat Agricultural University

(3) INDEST Consortium: The "Indian National Digital Library in Engineering Sciences and Technology (INDEST) Consortium" was set up in 2003 by the Ministry of Human Resource Development (MHRD) on the recommendation of an Expert Group appointed by the Ministry. The IIT Delhi has been designated as the Consortium Headquarters to coordinate its activities. The Consortium was re-named as INDEST-AICTE Consortium in December 2005 with the AICTE playing a pivotal role in enrolling its approved engineering colleges and institutions as members of the Consortium for selected e-resources at much lower rates of subscription. The Consortium enrolls engineering and technological institutions as its members and subscribe to electronic resources for them at discounted rates of subscription and favourable terms and conditions. The Ministry provides funds required for subscription to electronic resources for 62 centrally-funded Government institutions including IITs, IISc Bangalore, NITs, ISM, IIITs, IIMs, NITTTR's and few other institutions that are considered as core members of the Consortium. The benefit of consortia-based subscription to electronic resources is not confined to its core members but is also extended to all educational institutions under its open-ended proposition. 60 Govt./Govt.-aided engineering colleges are provided access to selected electronic resources with financial support from the AICTE and 102 universities/institutions have joined the Consortium under its self-supported category in 2012. The total number of members in the Consortium has now grown to 1235.

The INDEST-AICTE Consortium is the most ambitious initiative taken so far in the country. It is the biggest Consortium in terms of number of member institutions in Asia. The Consortium attracts the best possible price and terms of agreement from the publishers on the basis of strength of its present and prospective member institutions. The Consortium subscribes to over 12,000 electronic journals from a number of publishers and aggregators. The consortium website at http://paniit.iitd.ac.in/indest hosts searchable databases of journals and member institutions to locate journals subscribed by the Consortium, their URLs and details of member institutions.

Q13. What are Eprint Archives and why are they important sources for fulltext articles?

Ans. An **eprint** or **e-print** is a digital version of a research document (usually a journal article, but could also be a thesis, conference paper, book chapter, or a book) that is accessible online, usually as green open access, whether from a local institutional or a central digital repository.

A draft of a paper, before it is sent to the publisher is called pre-print. The publisher sends the draft to 'peers' in the field and obtains their comments for review, modification or validation of the technical content of the paper. Thereafter, he edits it for language, style, standardisation of format; he also adds meta- data for index preparation. The copy of the paper after peer-review is called post-print. The electronic versions of both pre-prints and post-prints together are called eprints. Eprints are important sources for fulltext.

If a fellow scientist wants a copy of a journal article, he may order on a document delivery centre such as INSDOC (now called NISCAIR), or the British Library (BLLD). etc. Or, he may to get it through inter-library loan from his library. He may even order a copy via 'pay-per-view' sites from the publisher's website or from some content aggregator's website.

The last option (pay-per-view) is costly but immediate deliveries may be expected. Each download under this method might include heavy copyright clearance fees raging from $5 to $40 depending upon the publisher. Scientists in developing countries cannot afford to pay hefty copyright fees but also cannot afford to be without current research literature.

According to one study, (mentioned in the Self-Archiving FAQ): For every one of the 2,500,000 articles published annually in the 24,000 research journals it is a fact that it is not accessible to most of its potential users because of unaffordable toll-barriers. And (this too is critical) this would remain true even if all 24,000 journals were sold at cost.

To overcome this problem, OAI—Open Access Initiative—has been started. OAI mandates the standardisation of meta-data used for indexing the literature in archive collection. The software for archiving, retrieving the contents are all easily available as open source software free of charge. All the servers distributed across the globe following OAI standards can easily be treated a vast single virtual collection.

Authors can self-archive their preprints. They can obtain permission from the publishers for archiving post-prints too. In the absence of such permission forthcoming, he can add a 'corrigendum' indicating the differences between the pre-print and the post-print. This would help users to know exactly how the publisher modified the pre-print through peerreview process. Eprint archives increase the availability of fulltext version of scientific papers and they are almost always free. Out of the 24,000 peer-reviewed journals, nearly 1,000 are now available in open access archives around the world. A comprehensive listing of eprint archives is available at http://archives.eprints.org/. How to go about establishing an archive is explained in the handbook that may be downloaded from: http://software.eprints.org/handbook/. All apprehensions of authors who may hesitate to start self-archiving are cleared through an FAQ called "Self-Archiving FAQ" which is also available at the same address.

Eprint archives are useful in this way: Authors increase the impact of their research output, as multiple sources are available for procurement of copies. Archival sources are cheap.

Greater readership results in faster dissemination of information and further creation of new innovative ideas. Eventually, the society benefits in the long-run.

Before concluding this section, let us remember that self-archiving should not be confused with self-publishing. Self-publishing deals with the author keeping copies of his own papers in his own website or in his institution website. It could be in Blogs too. No peer review is involved. Contents of such papers may be commercial, self-promoting, challengeable and so on. Some might amount to vanity-publishing too where the author pays money to publisher to publish and distribute copies of his work. Generally, scientific community does not consider such publications as 'noteworthy'. However, as sources of a scientist's works, they may serve as useful sources for fulltext.

In India, maintaining an extensive collection of pre-prints procured from authors and peers in the field of mathematics, in paper form, was practiced very successfully by the Institute of Mathematical sciences (Matscience), Chennai till as along ago as late seventies. Now, IISc has established an e-print archive of all papers published by scientists, researchers, and engineers.

Q14. Discuss fulltext article sources available on the Internet.

Ans. Fulltext article sources available on the Internet are as follows:

(1) Northern Light Business Research Library (www.northernlight.com): Northern Light Business Research Library is designed to meet the needs of self-research supporting business professionals and enterprise information centers wanting to support this kind of end-user. It is an easily usable, effective, and affordable research tool based on content, which includes:

(i) The Business Web: millions of pages of web content editorially selected to be of high quality for business research

(ii) Thousands of trade journals and a comprehensive array other periodicals selected for their deep repositories of industry expertise and insight

(iii) Business wires for up-to-date breaking information

(iv) Local and regional newspapers to provide the regional business perspective

Northern Lights is available at an annual flat fee of USD 19,500/-. Unlimited downloading of fulltext articles is permitted.

(2) Questia (www.questia.com): The Questia library includes more than 94,000 academic books and more than 174 million journal, magazine, and newspaper articles from more than a thousand of the world's leading publishers, Questia offers quality sources selected by librarians and approved by professors, and many of the resources are peer-reviewed.

(3) Xanedu (www.xanedu.com): This is another fulltext source on the net, useful for MBA, Education and other students. Articles from newspapers magazines are covered. Annual fees range from USD 20 to USD 70. Searching is simple and easy.

(4) Findarticles.com (www.findarticles.com): This is a sister website of the search engine 'looksmart'. Nearly 3.5 million fulltext articles from 700 publications (many of them scholarly) are available for free searching and downloading. However, the percentage of latest articles is low.

Q15. What are the Non-Bibliographic Fulltext Resources?

Ans. Online searching in bibliographic databases has for many years been a standard feature in many technological libraries and information services. Now that the database vendors are including more and more nonbibliographic databases in their systems, the occasional searching seems to be shifting into regular use of them. To a technical university library heavily into online searching the increase in number and variety of the nonbibliographic databases gives reason to both enthusiasm and concern. It offers more possibilities for direct retrieval of source data rather than just references, and thus, one hopes, improved information access and retrieval. On the other hand the effective utilisation of the source databases to the greatest benefit of the end user, whose information needs we want to satisfy, sets us demands which go beyond those encountered in bibliographic database searching. We shall take a look at a few of such non-bibliographic resources.

(1) Legal Resources: There are databases that offer Fulltexts of bare acts, rules framed under various acts, regulations, notifications, forms, bye-laws, and so on. Another series of fulltext documents are the judgements pronounced by various courts of justice. These documents are almost always in public domain and are copyright free. Law enforcement authorities, law firms, researchers in social sciences need this information.

Besides the Government of India website managed by National Informatics Centre, GOI Delhi, private companies like Sohonet India,

Manupatra, Juriix and others provide online as well CD- based database products that offer Fulltexts of the above documents.

(2) Standards: Similarly standards issued by various standardisation bodies in different countries are important sources of information. Some standards bodies are ISO, BIS BSI, UMIL, ASTM, and the like. Standards are used in industrial and research libraries but they are not so much in demand in academic libraries. Provision of access to fulltext of standards is imperative for the prior types of libraries. Standards get updated or revised frequently - therefore regular annual subscriptions become essential. For example, a complete set of Indian Standards (some 18000 titles) is available as a set of CDs for use on corporate Intranet.

(3) Government Notifications: State and Central Governments issue several notifications and public documents called Government Orders (GOs for short). Public as well as other government departments need such GOs. Complete set of Fulltext of government documents is available in AP Government website. Most of government documents are free of charge or are priced very low.

(4) Conference Proceedings: Papers presented in conferences, seminars, workshops. etc. offer recent and nascent information. They in fact form a part of Grey Literature, not easily procurable.

Access to conference proceedings and fulltexts of papers presented is indispensable in special libraries. Nowadays the seminar volumes are released in CD format as well as on websites. Fulltext is a specialty of such sources.

For example, Indegene (www.indegene.com) specialises in offering fulltext access to a number of medical-related annual seminars held in India. During the past two years they have published more than 120 Fulltext seminar volumes in CD on subjects such as cardiology, Diabetology, ENT, Nephrology, Neurology, Obstetrics and Gynecology, Ophthalmology, Plastic Surgery, Urology, Radiology. etc.

Q16. Enumerate the examples of Fulltext Databases.

Ans. There are some examples of fulltext databases are as follows:

(1) Database Covered by INDEST: The INDEST subscribes to 16 electronic resources that include 9 full-text resources and 7 bibliographic databases. Most bibliographic databases are accessible to IITs and IISc. The bibliographic databases include: Compendex Plus; INSPEC; SciFinder Scholar; MathSciNet; Web of Science; JGATE and JCCC.

(2) Indmed: A bibliographic database covering prominent peer reviewed Indian biomedical journals. Database designed to provide medical professionals/researchers/students and the medical library professional quick and easy access to Indian literature. This database covers 75 prominent Indian journals. These have been selected from more than 200 journals. Fulltext of more than 20 journals is included. The website address is: http://indmed.nic.in. The list of journals follows. Access is free.

List of Journals covered by Indmed:

(i) Endodontology
(ii) Health Administrator
(iii) Indian Journal of Aerospace Medicine
(iv) Indian Journal of Allergy Asthma and Immunology
(v) Indian Journal of Anaesthesia
(vi) Indian Journal of Chest Diseases and Allied Sciences
(vii) Indian Journal of Clinical Biochemistry
(viii)Indian Journal of Community Medicine
(ix) Indian Journal of Medical Microbiology
(x) Indian Journal of Occupational and Environmental medicine
(xi) Indian Journal of Occupational Therapy
(xii) Indian Journal of Otolaryngology and Head and Neck Surgery
(xiii)Indian Journal of Pharmacology
(xiv)Indian Journal of Thoracic and Cardiovascular Surgery
(xv) Indian Journal of Tuberculosis
(xvi)J.K. Practitioner
(xvii)Journal, Indian Academy of Clinical Medicine
(xviii)Journal of The Anatomical Society of India
(xix)Journal of Indian Association of Paediatrics Surgeons
(xx) Journal of Indian Society of Pedodontics and Preventive Dentistry
(xxi) Medical Journal Armed Forces India
(xxii) NTI Bulletin

(3) Vidyanidhi: Database of Theses: Vidyanidhi ("Treasure of Knowledge" in Sanskrit) began as a pilot project to demonstrate the feasibility of Electronic Theses and Dissertations in the Indian context This project got underway in the year 2000 at the Department of Library and Information Science, University of Mysore, Manasagangotri, Mysore, sponsored by the National Information System for Science and Technology, Department of Scientific and Industrial Research, Ministry of Science and Technology, Government of India. Vidyanidhi, in many ways, is an attempt to implement the directives of content development outlined by the Action Plan of the National Task Force on Information Technology and Software Development, of the Government of India as far as the university theses are concerned. The policy initiatives identified in the Plan make it mandatory for all universities or deemed universities across the country to host every thesis/dissertation on a designated website. This national policy has provided a policy framework for initiating a digital library of ETDs in India.

Currently Vidyanidhi is evolving into an Information Infrastructure and portal for strengthening and augmenting the doctoral research capacities of Indian Universities. This Initiative is supported and funded by:

(i) The Ford Foundation
(ii) Microsoft Corporation

The Vidyanidhi also has the strategic support from the University Grants Commission.

Vidyanidhi Project's vision is to build and strengthen the research capacities and enhance the quality of doctoral research research in India and the mission is to prepare the future generation of scientists to be better equipped to harness the power of ICTs to work and play a more effective role in the creation, accessing and use of knowledge. The vision is to help usher in the E-paradigm of academic life and work culture, there by exploiting the immense possibilities of digital libraries. Digital library technologies offer enormous advantages over traditional print world. The digital library is not just a storehouse of knowledge and information but a dynamic landscape for the creation and use of knowledge.

(4) Indiastat.com: Indiastat.com provides an in-depth statistics of India-specific socio-economic facts and figures culled from various secondary level authentic sources. Over half-a-million pages of statistical data have been qualitatively analysed, condensed and presented in a user-friendly format. The data can be downloaded in MS-Excel/HTML formats.

Academicians, researchers and professionals in marketing, finance, socio-economic studies and a host of other disciplines, will find Indiastat.com an extremely useful resource for their India-centric information needs. It is a paid site accessible only to registered members.

Table 3.4: Subjects Covered by Indiastat.com

Agriculture	**Banks and Financial Institutions**	**Civil Supplies and Distribution**
Consumer Affairs	Companies	Cooperatives
Crime and Law	Demographics	Economy
Education	Electoral Data	Environment and Pollution
Foreign Trade	Forest and Wildlife	Geographical Data
Health	Housing	Industries
Insurance	Labour and Workforce	Market Forecast
Media	Meteorological Data	Mines and Minerals
Per Capita Availability	Petroleum	Power

Social and Welfare	Schemes	Sports
States and U.Territories	Telecommunication	Tourism
Transport	Urban Areas	Villages

Q17. Discuss some typical software tools facilitating online access via institutional network.

Ans. When a librarian performs duties related to digital resources such as procurement, providing access, promoting institutional archiving. etc. he becomes a digital librarian. Some of the IT related tasks he can or has to perform in connection with online databases are discussed now. Here, a few typical software tools facilitating online access via institutional network are as follows:

(1) Providing Access to External Databases: Automating the Process: A librarian may subscribe to a number of online bibliographic databases. These are accessible by connecting to the websites of publishers of the databases. The publishers generally provide access using IP number restriction or the UserID & Password Authentication or both.

In the case of IP number access, all users from different PCs connected to the LAN of the institution go through a single Proxy Server. Proxy server authenticates the user then permits further access to the online vendor. In the case of UserID and Password combination, this pair of data has to be entered every time access is desired. The librarian cannot reveal the password to all and has to keep it a secret. It is not possible to enter the password by himself all the time. There are many methods available to tackle this problem. One simple method is described below.

There is public domain software called Roboform, which works in conjunction with the web browser. Hundreds of sites on the Internet require you to register yourself so that you can view contents of those sites. Registration may be mostly free. However, you may be forced to enter the same data again and again (name, email, address, etc). Roboform automates the process of filling up forms on the web. It asks and stores most commonly used (asked for) data just once. Later, whenever a form is encountered the fields are filled up automatically; it allows you to verify and edit some fields if need be. Then, Roboform sends (submits) form data to the party.

Roboform has a facility to fill the form and submit the form without user's confirmation also. Passwords may be preserved in a protected encrypted file. You may use this facility to enter UserID/Password info about a number of sites including online database vendors. Thus, you can permit your readers to use the online databases without their having to know the password.

(i) **Athens (http://www.athensams.net/):** Athens, a product of EduServ in the United Kingdom, is a service that manages access to web-based licenced resources by students and other off campus users. "Athens is, fundamentally, a central repository of organisations, usernames and passwords with associated rights. It has extensive account management facilities for organisations to create and manage usernames and passwords, and to allocate rights to individual usernames". Athens is not a proxy-based solution, but rather relies on its centralised system to grant or deny access to a particular resource requested by a user. Athens allows the library to have granular control over who has access to which electronic resources. The library may desire to permit access to certain specified online collections to select set of its users from different remote locations, say from campus network, from homes.

Athens has been available for about seven years, but there are still publishers who do not participate and, thus, libraries using Athens must still have some additional remote authentication procedure for those vendor resources that are not Athens-enabled. Athens ties up with several online web-based information providers like database producers, aggregators, publishers. etc. Elsevier Science Direct, Wiley Inter Science, Dialog's DataStar and others provide access via Athens. More than 260 resource providers work with Athens. About 850 organisations like National Health and Safety, UK's Higher Education department, etc., add up to 2.3 million individual end-users.

(ii) **Ariel software for Providing Full text service via Fax:** The Ariel software is loaded on an Internet-enabled computer, can receive and send electronic information to other libraries which have installed Ariel. Availability of most of the peer reviewed research journals in electronic format, inexpensive technology to scan articles and improved electronic delivery mechanisms are some of the enabling factors that have contributed to well-established electronic document delivery system now available commercially. More recently most of the secondary services that were available on CD ROM or through online search services are now available on the Internet where the bibliographic references are linked to their full- text on the publisher's site.

The technology has now been perfected and there are several electronic document delivery services that allow a user to download and article in full-text from their site or deliver them electronically as attachment to e-mail. Most electronic publishers and aggregators like OCLC, OVID, etc., are offering full-text of articles through their websites. Ariel enables academic and research libraries to electronically convey and share scanned or digitised documents such as articles published in scholarly and professional journals vital to academic and scholarly research- between and within institutions, in high-resolution TIF or PDF formats across the Internet. Introduced in 1991, Ariel now has more than 10,000 installations.

(2) Remote Access to Fulltext Databases: Example of British Library Network: The British Library Network in India offers remote access to certain databases to individual members. Databases currently offered at the desktop of individual users are:

(i) EBSCO—Academic Premier and Business Premier
(ii) Infotrac: Same facilities are available
(iii) Encyclopaedia Britannica online
(iv) Ashridge virtual learning site

Each member is given a UserID and Password at the time of his joining. Service started in September 2003.

Each and every member has to login to the British Council site (www.britishcouncil.org/ library) with his/her user id and password. This will authenticate the member; once it is done, they have the access to all above- listed products without using further authentication. This means, EBSCO or other sites recognise only British Council Library authentication (IP) not the members. If any library wants to develop such facility, they must have authentication software like Athens. etc. British Library has developed its own version of 'Athens' software for this purpose. The software provides for all supplementary activities like 'forgetting password', 'lost card'. etc.

Statistics: At any point of time, the administrator can find out how many members are using the system (logged on to various hosts) and how long each member has been using the system. EBSCO provides periodical statistics on usage like: How many people logged in during a particular period; how many articles were downloaded/printed; which are most used journals or least used.

(3) Role of the Digital Librarian in Consortium Access to Fulltext Resources: Apart from taking part in procurement of journals (paying subscription, signing the contract. etc.), librarians in each of the member institutions of a consortium have to perform certain administrative tasks like:

Entering details of IP address of the Proxy server of the LAN through which his members would reach out to the websites of publishers. This has to be done for each title in the appropriate web server of the publisher directly using Administrator Access.

Entering UserID & Password for the online subscription in the front-end search software used for access. If there is a common password, this may have to be protected and maintained secret.

If there are several sites from which fulltext access is possible for an institution, then he has to prioritise them. (Some may be free as a part of consortium access; some may be on special licensing basis, etc).

He has to ensure that the usage within the institution is as per stipulated conditions. Number of simultaneous accesses, number of fulltext articles downloaded, etc to be monitored to be within limits.

If remote-access from off-campus locations is provided, then tasks relating to this have to be carried out-for instance, a complete list of eligible users along with names, UserId passwords. etc. will have to be passed on to intermediary parties like Athens or others.

(4) Role of the Digital Librarian in Promoting or using Eprint Archives: A digital librarian, a type of specialist information professional who manages and organises the digital library, combines the functionality for information, elicitation, planning, data mining, knowledge mining, digital reference services, electronic information services, representation of information, extraction, and distribution of information, co-ordination, searching notably CD-ROMs, online, Internet-based WWW, multimedia access and retrieval.

As far as the Digital Librarian and eprints are concerned, his involvement may be described as follows:

(i) Realising the importance of a relatively low-cost source for fulltext articles, he should fully exploit this segment of resource. That is, maintain a complete list of archives (URLs) and use them frequently.

(ii) He can co-operate with the institutional authorities in setting up the server, install software, obtain training for himself and his staff, build the local collection, publicise the importance of self-archiving and so on.

(iii) He can help the author of his institution in self-archiving of their documents into institutional or public archives.

(iv) He can take part in adding suitable meta-data for indexing purposes.

Q18. What do you understand by Copyright and Licensing issues?

Or

Write a short note on "copyright and licensing issues in Bibliographic full text services". [Dec-2018, Q.No.-5 (c)]

Or

Write a short note on Copyright issues in DDS.

[Dec-2019, Q.No.-5 (d)]

Ans. Copyright is a right given by the law to creators of literary, dramatic, musical and artistic works and producers of cinematograph films and sound recordings. In the case of printed publications, copyright issues are fairly well- known and accepted. Under the 'Fair Use' clause, librarians can provide a single complete fulltext copy of an article to a patron meant for his personal study and research. Copyright law permits this. Moreover, if the original version of the printed book is not easily procurable in India, the library may make upto three copies of a book for circulation in the library. However, when it comes to downloading fulltext articles from bibliographic databases, publishers are not that liberal. As copyright laws are silent with respect to digital content, the usage is heavily bound by specific licensing terms and conditions entered into between the copyright owner (usually usurped by publisher from the author) and the user. Access to and subsequent usage (copying, forwarding, storing) are all severely restricted. Institutional customer oriented access methods using IP address, UserID and Password pair. etc. has been discussed already. Number of downloads allowed per year may be specified. Number of persons simultaneously accessing the database may be limited. Forwarding fulltext as an attachment to mail may be prohibited. Usage of CD-ROM databases beyond the period of subscription may be disallowed—but this aspect of usage is being liberalised nowadays. In the case of e-books (monographs), if the library licences for 2 copies of a certain title, then the software would not permit downloading more than 2 copies at one time. Unless one of the copies is 'returned' to the library (the user may have the softcopy on his e-book reader or his computer but he cannot read it once the book is returned), the librarian cannot 'issue' it to others.

When the library provides fulltext access by remote dial-up or off-campus access then he has to ensure that only authorised users access the -contents as per specified conditions.

Copyright residing in the copyright law (or agreement) not only prevents others from mere copying but also confers other rights—rights of translation, rights of abridgement, summarisation, adaptations, etc. Therefore, the librarian needs to be aware of further activities connected with the e-content he is allowing access to his users. For instance, if a researcher downloads a fulltext article in German and gets it translated into English on his own, without obtaining copyright clearance from the owner for carrying out translation, then he (the library patron) and the librarian may both be pulled up for copyright violations! The librarian will be unknowingly abetting copyright violations. When the librarian procures a fulltext version of a journal article, after paying copyright fees, say from INGENTA or similar sources (pay per view sites), the copyright fee paid may be only for copying and not for other (say translation) rights.

Q19. Discuss some likely trends in the near future with respect to fulltext sources and their usage.

Ans. "Fulltext searching" implies searching complete texts. Since September 2003, Amazon.com—popular Internet bookseller—has been providing "Search Inside the Book" feature. Using this facility, more than 1,20,000 books can be searched fulltext. That is, every word in the complete books is indexed. The buyer can see relevant pages of his interest before deciding to buy. This trend is likely to make fulltext resources more easily searchable and usable.

Similar to Amazon, Google—the famous Search Engine—is experimenting with indexing and retrieving fulltext academic scholarly articles. An experimental project with the collaboration of MIT and twenty other institutions to make eprint archives searchable via Google is under way. This would make searching easy and popular.

SCOPUS of Elsevier: SCOPUS is a Science-only fulltext service offered by Elsevier. It provides a very comprehensive access point for 13,000 titles taken from 4,000 STM publishers. About 100 Open Access titles are also included (rest are peer-reviewed ones). In addition to journal articles in STM, web- based sources are searched using SCIRUS— a science search engine of Elsevier. The system is hassle free, easy to use and enables the researcher to locate the fulltext in much fewer clicks than other such facilities.

SCOPUS provides complete "forward and backward linking" — it provides links to articles citing the article you are viewing and as well links to articles cited in the article you are viewing. Web of Science, popularly called WOS, (of ISI, USA) is well known for citation linking and fulltext search facility. Compared to that Scopus, WOS is based on 8500 titles only and all of them are not just science - many social science titles are also included. Therefore, Scopus as a unique fulltext source for STM scores better. Scopus takes its data from several databases like EMBASE, Compendex, Medline, and PsychInfo. etc. The Search Front End has been developed after studying how scientists search and what librarians are looking for.

Looking at the above developments, we may safely say that more and more fulltext sources will become accessible and usable in STM area soon.

Q20. What do you mean by 'Document Delivery Service'? Write down the various modes of Document Delivery Service.

Or

Write note on modes of Document Delivery Service.

[June-2018, Q.No.-5(d)]

Ans. Document delivery services (DDS) is concerned with the supply of document to the user on demand either in original or its photocopies irrespective of the location and form of original document. The Document Delivery Centre (DDC) on demand, deliver the copies of papers from learned journals, conference proceedings and other material available in their collection. Every DDC will also make the required effort to procure and supply the paper from other institution.

Various modes of document delivery service are as follows:

Libraries endeavour to meet the demand for documents through different methods. These include the following:

- Supply from the library collection itself;
- By obtaining documents from other libraries on inter-library loan;
- By joining library consortia for subscription to journals and databases (particularly full-text databases) and sharing the resources;
- By procuring copies of documents from other libraries, documentation centers and commercial document supply agencies like publishers, etc; and
- By accessing and downloading web-based documents.

These modes are discussed below:

- **Document Delivery from Library Collection:** This involves providing a document requested by the user by picking it up from the library itself, if it is available. This is usually the easiest or quickest way of document delivery. But, at times, it is not fast enough if the document is already issued to another user.
- **Document Delivery through ILL:** In this method, the library contacts another library, which has the required document and obtains it through inter-library loan and delivers to the user who is a bonafide member of the borrowing library. In this process the user usually gets the original document but this borrowing would be strictly as per the terms and conditions of issue, of the lending library. Also, if the requested book is issued to another user of the lending library, it cannot be quickly borrowed on ILL.
- **Document Delivery by Joining Library Consortia:** Library consortia are usually formed to achieve sharing of the journal resources savings in subscription costs. In addition, the journal supplier through the consortium approach, who is usually a large publisher, provides online access to full texts to several additional journals over and above the journals subscribed by the consortium. Using this access facility, libraries can meet a member of demands for delivery of journal articles and other documents transacted by the consortium. In India, the consortium being operated by IITs, IISC, NITs,IIMs. etc., titled INDSET is a such consortium.
- **Document Delivery by Processing Copies from Suppliers:** This is a common method of obtaining documents demanded by the user if they are not held by the library, nor by

the libraries covered by ILL arrangement. However, since procuring documents involves expenditure, this approach for document delivery is used only for bonofide members of the library and when such procurement is approved by the competent authority.

- **Document Delivery by Collecting it from Websites:** A number of websites of publishers and other document generating agencies usually make fulltexts of their open (not classified) documents available on their websites. Such documents are permitted to be downloaded by those who require them either free or against payment. If a document requested from the library is not held by the library, and if it is available on the web, often the user may himself download the document instead of placing the demand on the library. In spite of this, libraries often have to meet such demands by providing a downloaded document copy.

Q21. Explain the term 'Electronic Document Delivery Service' with their advantages.

Or

Write note on Electronic Document Delivery Service.

[June-2019, Q.No.-5(e)].

Ans. Electronic Document Delivery Service as "The transfer of information traditionally recorded in a physical medium (print, videotape, sound recording. etc.) to the user electronically via e-mail or World Wide Web. The libraries employ digital technology to deliver the information contained in the documents and files placed on reserve and requested via inter-library loan."

This mode of document delivery refers to supplying documents or their copies to the users by electronic or digital transfer. For this, the library may obtain a document available in the full text database of another library, a publisher or a database producer by any of the following methods:

- Online searching and downloading the required document
- Downloading the document from relevant CD-ROM database and transferring it electronically to the user's computer. Necessary payment for such downloading is done by the library and also the document delivery is made within the provisions of copyright law.

Advantages of Electronic Document Delivery: Libraries find it highly advantageous to deliver documents requested by the users, electronically. The advantages are as follows:

- **Increase in Efficiency:** Electronic documents are usually made available on the web or other networks, by the concerned publishers or database produces (of course, some are free and some others are chargeable). So, libraries can search online, the availability of the requested document and instantly downloaded it and pass on to the users. Thus, the service can be operated at a great speed.

- **Cost-effectiveness:** Electronic transfer of documents would not involve the charges of packing, postage. etc., as is the case with printed or paper-based documents. Since many libraries would have access to the web via a dedicated telecommunication link, it would hardly cost anything to download; such cost is negligible even if the downloading takes place in dial-up mode.
- **Simultaneous Availability of the Document to Several Users:** If a document is stored in electronic/digital form, several eligible users can simultaneously access it and download the required portions. Thus, the original remains in the library, even if the document is sent to another library (electronically). Such a facility is obviously not available with the printed versions of documents. If a lending library has only a printed version of a document, it would normally prefer to scan the document (or the required pages) and transmit electronically to the borrowing library, as an email attachment, instead of sending the hard copy by mail.
- **Increased Demands can be Effectively Met:** When a library provides efficient/speedy document delivery service, demand for the service is likely to go up substantially. Even then, efficiency of the service can be maintained by using electronic document delivery method, without increase in staff.

Q22. Explain the various steps in document delivery service.

Ans. The steps usually involved in document delivery service are the following:

(1) Identification of Bibliographic Details of the Document: Often, the bibliographic details of the document given by the user are either incomplete or wrong. So, it would save time and effort for the library staff first to check these details. Proper reference tools are to be used for getting the correct details – for books it could be 'Book in-Print', publishers' catalogues or library OPACs' for journal articles, it could be abstracting and indexing journals or international bibliographic databases. etc. The library may create a directory of such reference sources or database producers in relevant subject disciplines.

(2) Identification of the Supplier of the Document: When the bibliographical details of the required information is identified, it needs to locate the source of supply for the same. The most automated method to locate the source of supply is linked with the searching process. A command is made on the machine on which the search is being carried out and the article is ordered automatically. The system checks the local holdings and automatically places orders for those items which are not held locally.

(3) Making a Formal Request or Placing Order for Supply: When the required information and the source of supply is identified, it needs to send an order for the specified item to the supplier. The request call be placed through several ways. The simplest way to place the request is through post. However, in the era of information technology this way is relatively outdated. Now there are many automated systems for tile transmission of requests to document suppliers which include fax, e-mail, telephone. etc. Besides these, many database hosts also offer documents ordering modules and many document suppliers have their own systems.

(4) Processing of the Request and Supply of the Document by the Supplier: When orders are received at the supplier and by whatever means, the request has to be processed. Ideally, it should be done as quickly as possible. In the traditional document delivery, when the request has been received and validated, the required I item is retrieved from the shelf and either dispatched on loan or a photocopy is, produced and is dispatched. In an automated processing system, the request is scanned if it is in printed form or downloaded if it is by email and the details of the requested document get matched with the relevant OPAC of the library and if the matching is positive, then the concerned section in the library is intimated electronically for retrieving the document. If the fulltext of the document is available in an electronic /digital form, the document is transmitted to the requester after the request of the payment is verified by the software. Such an electronic matching of the request with the OPAC and dispatching the document is operated by BLDSC by a system called AUTOMATCH.

(5) Receipt of the Document and Delivery to the User: The user concerned is now intimated about the availability of the document, and the document, in original, or photocopies of the required pages, as the case may be, are handed over to him/her and cost of acquiring/ photocopying is realised, as per library rules. Document may be delivered through other modes also, as indicated below, such as by post/courier, through messenger, through intranet, as email attachment, through fax.

Q23. Discuss about some document supplying agencies.

Or

Write a short note on document delivery service of NISCAIR. [Dec-2017, Q.No.-5 (e)]

Ans. Libraries in general, also provide document supply services. They provide documents or their copies, as the case may be subject to copyright regulations, from their own collections if the requested documents are available. Otherwise, they procure the documents (or their copies) from external sources for their member-users and this extra service is usually not extended to others. However, document delivery centers whose objective is to provide documents to any bonafide readers on request, usually against payment, extend this service to any such user. Similarly, document delivery agencies that operate on commercial lines also provide the service by collecting the documents (or their copes) from other sources and they usually do not maintain large collections.

Another important point to be noted in this connection is that certain agencies specialise in document delivery in certain subject disciplines. And some database producers supply copies of documents only from their databases. Some of such agencies are briefly presented below:

(1) ISI Document Solutions (IDS):

(http://www.isinet.com/products/dosdelivery/ids)

ISI Document Solution (SM) is a document delivery service of The Institute for Scientific Information (ISI). ISI assigns a unique journal title accession number, which is listed in the ISI Document Solution Number (GA) field, to each journal issue. You can use ISI Document Solution Numbers to order individual journal articles from ISI. IDS provides full text articles from over 16,000 titles covered in the ISI database which covers scholarly journals in the disciplines of science and technology, social sciences, art and humanities. Articles can be ordered via OCLC ILL, DataStar, OVID, Dialog, through the basic indexes of ISI and the ISI websites as well as through email, fax, telephone and by mail. The charges include a standard processing fee; a variable copyright fee and the copies are copyright cleared. These are delivered to users via fax, mail, or courier.

(2) Canadian Institute for Scientific and Technical Information (CISTI)

(http://cisti-icist.nrc-cnrc.gc.ca/dosdel/delivery)

CISTI is one of the world's major sources of information in all areas of science, technology, engineering and medicine. One can access CISTI collection as well as the collection of the Canadian Agriculture Library (CAL). Articles, conference proceedings, books. etc. can be ordered from CISTI via OCLC ILL, DOCLINE, OVID Web Gateway, email, fax, telephone or mail. Articles are delivered via fax, Ariel, or courier. Books are delivered via courier only.

(3) British Library Document Supply Centre (BLDSC)

(http://www.bl.uk/services/document/articles.html)

British Library On Demand is the improved document supply service from the British Library. The British Library Document Supply Centre (BLDSC) is the world's foremost document supply service. It receives over 4 million requests each year (including over 1 million from other than UK) for all categories of literature. BLDSC is one of the well-known Centres in the field of document supply. It provides a rapid and comprehensive document delivery and interlibrary loan service to researchers and scholars in all kinds of libraries and organisations. It is regarded as the central organisation for interlibrary loans in UK. Though, particularly strong in sciences and technology and medicine, the BLDSC collects materials in all subject areas of human knowledge in many languages. The Centre holds journals, books, conference proceedings, reports, theses, official publications, gray literature of all kinds, music, patents. etc. It supplies documents from its own collection held at Boston Spa and other parts of the British Library. Documents of any length and data can be ordered from BLDSC via OCLC/ILL, Dialog Data Star, ARTTel, ARTEmail, British Library Automated Information Service (BLAISE)/ LINE, telephone, fax and mail. Documents supplied are copyright cleared because it has direct agreement with publishers and copyright clearing agencies in United Kingdom. Articles are delivered via fax, Ariel or mail. Books are delievered via airmail. Billing can be through the NELINET monthly statement and/or the Interlibrary loan Fee Management (IFM) option. BLDSC provides two ways for passing the requests. Organisations or libraries can request document on loan or they can order documents through the Article Direct Service of BLDSC. Each user organisation must register with the BLDSC and establish an account before using the Library Privilege Photocopy Service (formerly known as International Photocopy Service). Individual user also needs to open his customer account with BLDSC with minimum deposit of Pound 100 or US$160. Payment can also be made through credit card or through the Web Order Form or a performa invoice can be sent through fax or email. One article, regardless of length, airmail delivery cost comes to Pound 7.25 or US$11.50. If document is taken on loan, the present charges for airmail delivery is Pound 13.25 or US $21.25.

(4) National Library of Australia (http://www.nla.gov.au/webpac/)

The National Library of Australia (NLA) is the largest reference library in Australia, responsible under the terms of the National Library Act for "maintaining and developing a national collection of library material, including a comprehensive collection of library material relating to Australia and the Australian people. The catalogue of NLA provides information on its holdings. The majority of materials held at the library are available for loan. Some of the materials, however, are part of a special collection and is not available for loan. Individuals who wish to use library materials need to contact their institution library or local public library to arrange for them to borrow the materials on their behalf. Since June 1, 2000 NLADSS has ceased accepting vouchers as payment for inter library loans and document supply. In place of this, libraries, using the NLADSS, can choose the following methods of payment:

(i) Kinetic Document Delivery (KDD) payment service.

(ii) Monthly account (payable by cheque or credit card)

(5) Inforetrieve - The Article Store

(http://www.ingenta.com/)

Inforetrieve has assembled one of the world's largest libraries of articles and journal contents, through ongoing partnerships and alliances with publishers and content producers. It provides copies of published documents, in accordance with copyright law. It uses a network of libraries, electronic resources, publishers and other primary document suppliers to deliver the documents. This service claims to fulfil 95 per cent of the users documents demand. Articles can be ordered from Info retrieve via OCLC ILL, Web, e-mail, fax, and telephone. Articles are copyright cleared and delivered to the user via Ariel, fax, mail, or courier. Ariel is a commercial software package, produced by the Inforetrieve, which sends and receives documents as TIFF or PDF files over the Internet. It must be installed on the requester's workstation in order to use this delivery method.

(6) Ingenta Journals

(http://www.ingenta.com/)

Ingenta Journals was launched in May 1998 and now it offers a single point of free access to the abstracts of over 9,00,000 full text articles from over 2800 academic and professional journals from over 35 leading publishers. It provides documents to more than 3 million users annually. It allows anyone anywhere in the world to browse and search database of articles free of charge and to view titles of contents, bibliographic information and abstracts. More than 8000 academic, research and corporate libraries, institutions and consortia from all over the world are currently using this service. Subscribers can view full text articles free of cost whereas non-subscribers have to pay for that. Users can order documents for immediate electronic delivery and payment can be made through credit cards on the screen.

(7) AskIEEE

(http://www.ieee.org/services/askieee/)

The AskIEEE service is the Document Delivery Service of the Institute of Electrical and Electronics Engineers, Inc which provides photocopies of articles published by the IEEE. It has different levels of delivery options, i.e. first class mail, facsimile. etc. All requests are fulfilled from its own collections.

(8) Chemical Abstracts Service/Document Delivery Service (CASDDS)

(http://www.cas.org/support/dds.html)

The CASDDS supplies most of the documents cited in Chemical Abstracts. It provides photocopies for non-copyrighted publications, publications registered with Copyright Clearance Centre, American Chemical Society publications, and publications from organisations with whom CAS has right-to-copy agreements. It also provides loan service to international customers for a period of 28 days. Documents are supplied through normal post, airmail, fax, and courier. It does not supply multiple copies of a single document.

(9) OCLC Full Text Option Program

Using the OCLC/ILL Full Text Option, libraries can request ASCII text documents using OCLC/ILL procedures and workflows. The documents are delivered within minutes of the receipt of the request in the body of e-mail messages. Requesters can use the OCLC/ ILL Fee Management service to pay for the supplied documents.

(10) PEAK: Pricing Electronic Access to Knowledge

(http://www.umdl.umich.edu/peak)

PEAK is a research project of University of Michigan in which Elsevier Science and the University of Michigan are working together to create and manage a host service for all 1110 journals published by the Elsevier, including North Holland, Butterworth and Pergamon Press. In this service, user can have unlimited access to a specific article for a fixed price. User can also select and purchase a fixed number of articles for use.

(11) Science Direct

(http://www.sciencedirect.com)

Science Direct is an online host facility for scientific and technical information. It offers libraries and their users desk top access to remotely stored full text of journals published by the Elsevier Science and other participating publishers. Users can have single user or multi-user licence for one or more year subscriptions. This service is very popular in science and technology libraries all over the world.

(12) Uncover Desktop Image Delivery

(http://www.uncweb.carl.org/uncover/imgfaq.html)

Uncover offers full text articles from its database from over 2500 journals. Nearly 300 scholarly, universities and trade publishers have granted permission to deliver articles from their publications. It allows users to order articles and to download including images, graphics, photographs. etc. Articles can be delivered by the Uncover after charging handling charges and copyright fee.

(13) National Technical Information Service (NTIS)

(http://supprot.dialog.com/publications/docdelivery)

The NTIS is the largest single resource for the government- funded scientific, technical, engineering and business related information available today.

It provides access to over 2 million publications covering over 35 subject areas brought out during the past 50 years. Users can make their payment through credit cards or they can open their deposit accounts with NTIS. Documents are delivered by the NTIS through airmail or surface mail.

(14) University Microfilms International (UMI) Dissertations Services

(http://www.umi.com)

University Microfilms International offers comprehensive full text document delivery service of dissertations and masters theses in a variety of formats. Documents can be ordered through credit cards or users can open deposit account with UMI. Copies can be had in microfilm, microfiche, soft cover paper or hard cover paper. UMI charges different costs for different countries and different types of users, i.e. academics, non-academics, etc

(15) United States Patent and Trademark Office (USPTO)

(http://www.uspto.gov/patft/)

United States Patents Full Text and Full Image Database contains two parts:

(i) Patents Grant Database which includes full text of patents granted since 1976 and full images since 1790

(ii) Patent Application Database.

Users can search a particular patent document using Quick Search option, Advance Search option and Application Number Search option. They can display the search result on computer monitor or download it or place an order for printed copies to the USPTO.

(16) Chicago Public Library

The Chicago Public Library is one of the Patents and Trademarks Depository Libraries in the United States. The library provides copies of U.S. patents as well as foreign patents. The library holds an almost complete collection of British patents from 1617 to mid-1994 in German patents from 1912 to 1938. The copies can be obtained through the Xerox Copy Centre.

(17) DERWENT Publications Ltd.

The Patents Supply Division of Derwent Publications Ltd offers a comprehensive patent delivery service with very rapid turnaround at low prices. Patents published anywhere in the world and cited in the World Patent Index may be ordered from Derwent. Delivery options available are: normal service, express service, fax service or translated documents from other languages. Order can be placed through any mode and user can open deposit account with the Derwent.

(18) Patent Information System (PIS)

To provide technological information contained in patents or patent related literature through publication service, search service and patent copy supply service, the Government of India established Patent Information System (PIS) at Nagpur in 1980. PIS operates subscriber advance payment scheme. Under this scheme, user interested in availing regular service by way of procurement of patent document, may remit an amount of not less than ₹1000/- or in multiples of thereof and open an account in his name. On receipt of payment, the user is allotted a Subscriber Account Number (SAN) by the office of PIS. The charges for the information or service provided are debited to the account and debit credit statements are sent.

(19) National Institute of Science Communication and Information Resources (NISCAIR)

The Indian National Scientific Documentation Centre (INSDOC) now NISCAIR has been offering document delivery service at national level since 1952. The service is provided utilising the entire country's resources including those of National Science Library and the Pilot Electronic Library of NISCAIR. The requests are received by mail, fax, telex and e-mail. The location of required document is identified using the computerised National Union Catalogue of Scientific Serials in India (NUCSSI). Requests from scientific and technical libraries located in the country are received for document delivery. These are sorted out on the basis of availability of source documents. NISCAIR supplies copies of documents from its own library collection of about 8000 periodicals including over 2100 journals in electronic form. Using the local resources, on an average 73 per cent requests are met within 2 weeks, and 85 per cent within 4 weeks. Procurement of copy of document from other Indian or foreign libraries usually takes about 8-12 weeks time. Another form of document delivery service offered by NISCAIR is Contents, Abstracts and Photocopies Service (CAPS) and Full Text Journal Service (FTJS).

(20) Other Document Delivery Agencies: Besides these agencies, there are some other national and international document delivery services, which are providing documents in various disciplines. Some of these are:

(i) ChemWeb: The World Wide Club for the Chemical Community (http://www.chemweb.com/)
(ii) News Library (http://www.newslibrary.infi.net/noframe2.htm)
(iii) Docdeliver (http://www.docdeliver.com/)
(iv) The Electric Library (http://www.elibrary.com/)
(v) Information Quest (http://www.eiq.com/)
(vi) ACM Digital Library (http://www.acm.org/dl/)
(vii) Articles in Physics (http://www.ojps.aip.org/)
(viii) Bioline Publications (http://www.bioline.org.br/)
(ix) BioMedNet: Internet Community for Biological and Medical Researchers (http://www.biomednet.com/)
(x) ChemPort (http://www.chemport.org/html/english/about.html)

Q24. Write short note on Copyright facilitators.

Ans. A document, not in public domain and coming under the purview of copyright, needs to be copyright cleared from the copyright holder before supply to the user. The supply can be made after getting permission from the copyright owner. To overcome the problems of getting permission from the owner, granting licence to the user or documents supplier, to collect copyright fees from the end user and to distribute royalty to the actual owner of the copyright. etc. a need was felt to establish copyright facilitating agencies. These agencies could work as switching system among users, documents suppliers and copyright owners. Some of the western countries have already established copyright licensing agencies in this regard. In India, it is still on experimental stage. The functions of these agencies are to negotiate fees with the copyright holders, i.e. publishers, authors. etc. and charge the copyright fees from the users either directly or through clearing house and pay the agreed dues to the copyright holder.

Q25. List some of the major copyright licensing agencies and copyright clearing houses facilitating document delivery.

Ans. Copyright Licensing Agencies: Various copyright licensing agencies are discussed below:

(1) Copyright Clearance Centre (CCC), USA: At the suggestion of the US Congress, a non-profit organisation namely, Copyright Clearance Centre (CCC) was founded in 1978. During the past two and a half decade, it has distributed million dollars royalties to authors of books and contributors to professional journals in the form of articles. The CCC charges a nominal service fee for each work. The copyright holders are required to fill in a Rights Holder Authorisation Agreement with CCC. The CCC offers the following four types of services to its users:

(i) **Academic Permissions Service (APS):** Academic Permissions Service (APS) is a convenient and cost-effective way to obtain permissions to make photocopies of copyrighted materials for course packs and classroom handouts. On behalf of the copyrights holders, CCC grants permission to academic institutions, academicians and bookshops for photocopies of copyrighted materials for their use in the courses or classroom handouts and royalty, as set by the rights holders, is collected from the users.

(ii) **Electronic Course Content Service (ECCS):** Permission is granted by the CCC to the users for the digital use of copyrighted materials for storage in electronic form, electronic course materials through a protected password. This password is issued for a limited period of time.

(iii) **Transactional Reporting Service (TRS):** The CCC grants instant permission to libraries, information centers, document delivery centers, document suppliers, photocopying shops, information providers, individuals or organisations involved in information dissemination and documents supply activities. It collects royalty fees as set by the copyrights holders.

(iv) Foreign Authorisation Service (FAS): Royalties collected for the photocopying of US works in foreign countries is distributed by the CCC under this service.

(2) Copyright Licensing Agency (CLA), UK: The Copyright Licensing Agency (CLA) offers a range of licences to copy onto and from paper and also electronic copying. It does not store and deliver documents to the end users. It also acts as an agent of the CCC.

(3) Canadian Copyright Licensing Agency (CANCOPY), Canada: The Canadian Copyright Licensing Agency (CANCOPY) receives royalties from the Government of Canada for the copies made within the Canadian Government. The CANCOPY distributes royalties to the "Copyright Collective in the Province of Quebec" (COPIBEC) or CCC or other agencies, which further pay the royalties to the rights holders. Its functions are almost similar to the functions of the CCC.

Copyright Clearing Agency of India: Indian Reprographic Rights Organisation (IRRO) is a copyright society established under Section 33 of the Copyright Act, 1957. The IRRO has been collectively formed by the Federation of Indian Publishers (FIP), Authors Guild of India (AGI) and some professional associations and individuals. To minimise the activities of infringement of copyright, at present, unfortunately, we have no licensing agency as established in USA, UK and Canada. On the pattern of licensing agencies like CCC, CLA and CANCOPY, there is a need to have a mechanism of licensing agency in India for granting licences of copyrights. Similarly, we should also establish a national agency/clearing house for supply of documents to the end users. The copyright clearing house should be well equipped with the latest information and communication technologies and skilled and professional manpower to facilitate users of copyrighted materials. This should work as a facilitator between users and copyrights holders and collect fees from users and distribute royalties to the owners after charging a nominal service charge. Publishers, authors, librarians, academic institutions, government and all those associated with these activities may join hands in this regard. Some efforts have already been made to constitute a Copyright Clearing Agency of India (CCAI), which will grant licence to the users on behalf of the rights holders. This can minimise the problem of infringement of copyrights up to some extent.

Q26. Define the term 'Reference Service' and how it is needed in a library and information centre?

Ans. The term "**reference service**" is defined simply as personal assistance provided to library users seeking information. Ranganathan has defined reference service as a personal service to each reader in helping her/him to find the document, answering the particular query, pinpointedly, exhaustively and expeditiously. Ranganathan has also emphasised that the reference service aims at providing the right book to the right reader at the right time.

W. Bishop has defined reference service as, "the service rendered by a librarian in aid of some sort of study. It is an organised effort on the part of libraries in aid of the most expeditious and fruitful use of their books."

Margaret Hutchins has defined reference service as direct personal aid within a library, to persons in search of information for whatever purpose and also various activities specially aimed at making information as easily available as possible.

William Katz opines that reference service is behind the scene activities of the reference library in the selection, acquisition and maintenance of the library stock and its careful and administration.

The essence of reference service as revealed in the definitions given above, is Providing assistance to the users/readers in the use of libraries and their collections Organising collection and services to ensure their maximum usage Saving precious time of the readers Acquiring and maintaining appropriate reference collection.

Need of Reference Service in Library and information Centre: Reference service is the vital function of any library. Though the ever-expanding availability of electronic resources tends to influence the nature of reference service, the essential component of "service" remains the same. The availability of electronic resources-subscription based and free Internet resources make the reference service more essential. The users have a wide range of information sources, which need to be evaluated for authenticity and currency. The users experience a phenomenon of information explosion, information deluge. They feel lost, adrift in the vast ocean of information. Reference service, which is also personalised service, helps the users in getting exactly what they want. Libraries, by providing, intensive need based reference service reaffirm their importance and centrality as service institutions for excellence. There has been a lot of emphasis on providing reference service. It is considered indispensable in libraries because of the following reasons:

- Rising readers' expectations and needs
- Information deluge or information overload
- Variety of documents
- Availability of information and communication technologies.

Q27. Describe the various steps in the 'Reference Service Process'.

Ans. Reference process is the process of answering questions to satisfy the information requirements of the user. In other words it is a process of satisfying, specific, recurrent information needs.

Performing reference work requires more than learning a limited number of reference sources. No reference librarian can remember all the reference sources, that could satisfy a specific query, nor keep up with the constant flow of new materials. But with tlie aid of systematic approach for satisfying information requests the reference person can apply certain basic principles to locate an answer, regardless of the nature of the query asked. This approach involves interaction between the library user, library resources and the reference librarian. With an understanding of the reference process a reference librarian is not restricted to a limited number of reference sources but can apply general principles when answering unique or difficult requests. Time is also a vital factor in providing reference service. Providing correct information is of 110 use to the user until it is given in time. This helps in achieving the very basic objectives of reference service, i.e. providing right information in the right time. The complete reference process i,e. from the receipt of all information request to communication of an answer to the user can be broken down into a series of decision-making steps:

(1) Query Analysis: The first step in the reference process is the identification of the essential information in the request of a library user. At this initial stage, the reference librarian analysis the query to determine the subject of the request and to identify the type of information needed. The query may be for exhaustive search or only a fact finding type.

(2) Reference Interview: The next step is to determine whether any clarification or amplification of the query is required. This process is called reference interview. Reference interview is the most important step of the whole reference process, which requires discussion with the user about the request in order to gain a more complete understanding of the actual information need. The basic purpose of the reference interview, no matter how brief or how long, is to:

(i) Ascertain what information the user wants for his particular question or problem. Depth of knowledge on the subject of query requested.

(ii) Clarify the question in terms of itself (i.e., what it really means, rather than how it is expressed), and. in terms of translating it into query statement words or phrases.

(iii) Ascertain the amount, level and difficulty of the materials which will answer that question.

(iv) Ascertain the time and resources required to answer the query.

This technique demands the highest communication and articulation skills to elicit the exact nature of the user's need for assistance and research support. If the librarian begins the search with an inaccurate understanding of what is really wanted, the information generated will be of no use to the user. This wastes time for both, and may discourage the user from seeking reference service again.

To have a better understanding of the actual information need, reference librarian designs search request forms. To get maximum information from user in relation to a particular query, apart from verbal discussions, the users are requested to fill these search request forms which helps a lot to ascertain the actual information need of the user.

(3) Refining User Statement: Once the actual information need has been clarified, the next step is to refine the statement of the user and transform the query statement of the user into subject descriptors/keywords, i.e. translating query words into language of answer providing tools, Transforming the query statement into search terms is not merely a translation of query words into search terms but it is much more than this. The step involves the selection of search terms from various sources and standardising these selected search terms with the help of thesauri, such as, Spine Thesaurus, INSPEC Thesaurus, Thesaurus of Engineering and Scientific Terms, etc.

(4) Formulation of Search Strategy: The fourth step is to formulate a search strategy. Search strategy is the line of action formulated for searching the information. This step is very important as formulation of search statement involves the grouping of selected search terms into search subsets using Boolean logic, For example, all synonyms, related terms from a search subset using 'OR' and final answer is the result of combining the different subsets with 'AND' operator. The terms which should not make the part of searched information may be excluded using 'NOT' operator.

(5) Searching: Once the line of action for searching information is chalked out, the reference librarian can mentally identify categories of reference tools likely to contain the type of information needed. Any reference query, no matter how basic, needs to have access to a variety of information resources. The amazing developments in information technology have revolutionised the process of information storage and retrieval. Apart from conventional paper media and traditional on-line searching, a large number of reference sources are now available in the form of CD-ROM databases. Further, internet-based services are playing a vital role in providing ready reference as well as exhaustive literature search services in today's scenario. It is in this step that the reference librarian determines whether to search the answer from the conventional or electronic resources including internet.

(6) Notification to the User: After search process is over, the reference librarian should inform the user and disseminate information in appropriate form as quickly as possible as speed of supply is critically important. Also, the result of the search should be appropriately formatted because presentation and delivery of the result reflects the efficiency and involvement of reference librarian in answering the query. It may be given in printed, audio-visual or any other form acceptable to the user. Supplied information must fulfil the requirements of the user. It must have relevance for him.

(7) Feedback Analysis and Evaluation: No improvement can be made in any system, including reference service, unless it is properly evaluated. A main component of such evaluation is obtaining feedback from the user on the relevance of the information provided. The reference librarian should therefore seek invariably feedback on the relevance of the information supplied and try to improve the service for further requests so that he can satisfy the users better. It is important to design a feedback mechanism, say, using a performa, and seek feedback against every supply of information. The search methodology or process is to be improved continually based on such feedback. Other components of the evaluation are the speed of supply, the courtesy extended, initiative taken to continue to supply information like the requirement is met, and so on. He should make sure that information provided to the user has been well accepted by him. He should politely ask the user to provide feedback about the relevance of the information, satisfactory level of the service rendered to him. etc. User may make certain comments/suggestions, which may be taken in a positive way for the improvement of the reference service.

(8) Unanswered Questions: The final step is selection of an answer. This step is crucial because the information identified in this step must be accurate, complete and useful to the user.

The process is completed only if that information proves to be satisfactory to the user. Otherwise the query is re-negotiated, and the individual steps in the decision-making process are repeated. Providing complete and correct answer to an information request is dependent on the decisions made in each of the steps of the reference process. Errors at any of the decision-making stage would result in an incorrect or inadequate answer. If the reference librarian misunderstands the message of the query, he or she will end up searching for the wrong information. Correctness and timeliness are the two basic components of a satisfactory answer.

Q28. What do you understand by Digital Reference Service? Discuss its types with examples.

Or

What is a digital reference service? Enumerate their categories depending upon the mode of receiving question and delivering information. Explain their advantages and disadvantages. [Dec-2017, Q.No.-3.2]

Or

Discuss the modes of providing digital reference service. [June-2019, Q.No.-3.1]

Or

Write a short note on Digital reference service. [Dec-2019, Q.No.-5 (c)]

Ans. The Library of Congress launched the collaborative Digital Reference Service in June 2000. Today more than 100 libraries from various countries are participating in this collaborative venture. This is a worldwide network of libraries in which OCLC builds and maintains a database of profiles of participating institutions, maintains a question - and-answer database system that enables participants to catalogue answers and store them in a searchable/browsable database and provides help in marketing, registration, training and user support. Currently this is a free service. It is an international web-based cooperative network of librarians. This collaborative Digital Reference Service delivers reference assistance to researchers any time, any place. It supports reference efforts by combining the power of resources and manpower with the diversity and availability of libraries and librarians everywhere. Using advance technology that directs questions to the appropriate library based on the subject profiles, this digital notebook pools librarians, expertise to bring quality and professionalism in on-line reference service. The following are some of the advantages of this service.

- One library is linked to the other libraries for subjects, languages and collections outside its scope and coverage.
- Libraries and information scientists can add value to reference interactions by obtaining answers to difficult questions from expert librarians at other institutions.
- Librarian can improve his library's ability to respond more quickly and accurately on a broader spectrum of research.
- This service offers reference service beyond working hours of library.
- Reference transactions are stored in a question and answer knowledge database that can be accessed for ready reference.
- Reference questions can be answered from books, journals, magazines, citations from oil-line catalogues and licenced databases and references to web sites. The requesting library notified by e-mail to retrieve the answer from the server.

Based on the mode of receiving question and delivering information, the digital reference service can be broadly categorised into two groups:

(1) E-Mail Reference Service: The e-Mail reference transaction involves back-and-forth exchange of information, users would not get any immediate answer. But users can ask a question when they think of it, at any time of the day or night. And they do not have to take time to make a special trip to the library. In other words, the users send e-mail to the library with a reference question, asking whatever information they feel necessary. The library sends reply by e-mail, fax, phone or letter as it finds convenient. In such a case, the controller of all questions initially receives and examines and then routes them to appropriate staff. Technical questions are forwarded to technical staff, circulation related questions to the circulation staff, reference questions to the reference librarian, and so on.

Advantages

- Who feel shy and uneasy about asking questions in person, face-to-face or by telephone.
- Who are poor in oral communication.
- Who may not be able to visit library due to certain difficulties in physical movement, living at a long distance from the library, and so on.

Disadvantages

- Reference librarian cannot establish eye contact or conduct face-to-face reference interview to seek any clarification with the user.
- It is difficult to judge the urgency of the requirement of information.
- To know the degree of the user's satisfaction for further modification of search strategy for providing more relevant answer.
- Speed of asking a question and getting an answer depends upon the volume of email traffic and communication link over the Internet.
- Reference librarian needs to make more efforts in understanding the meaning of the asked question. Sometimes, he misses the focus of the asked question because users often do not clearly express the question.

E-mail Reference Service Advantages for the Reference Librarian

- Reference librarian finds more time to think, plan, chalk out search strategy and finally search the answer.
- Simple or easy questions can also be answered by other staff.
- Reference librarian can devote more time on questions of complex nature.
- This way the workload of reference process can be distributed among other staff.
- Question can also be diverted to the experts, if required.
- There is no restriction on working time. Question can be answered any time after working hours.
- This mode of receiving and answering questions is very cost-effective

(2) Real Time Digital Reference Service: In real time digital reference service, the exchange of information is live (it takes place in real time) between user and reference librarian. This service is still on experimental stage in developing countries because it requires advanced computer technology, faster and better communication connectivity, interactive audio and video capacity and availability of computers at home and work place. This service is not a replacement of conventional or e-mail reference service but a supplement to these services.

Advantages

- This is a synchronous service in which reference librarian responds immediately in real time.
- Reference interview is conducted at a faster pace than e-mail.
- Clarification can be sought online. Reference librarian can demonstrate to the user about how to use reference sources,
- Web sites, expert or whom the user should contact. This allows user to walk through
- The reference source to find answer. In addition to this, Voice Over Internet Protocol
- (VOIP) allows reference librarian to talk to users and hear them while connected and while locating the sources.
- This service can be offered at any time, any day (24/7 basis).
- Reference librarian can chat with several persons simultaneously.

Disadvantages

- The technology is still at premature stage.
- It is a labour-intensive service.
- It makes reference librarian busy in answering the questions because it involves
- Several back-and-forth message transactions. He may not find time to answer the urgently needed questions.
- It is stressful for reference librarian as well as user because one is waiting for other's message.
- For every inquiry, user needs to type questions every time and reference librarian also need to answer in typed form.
- Typing speed and errors occurring during typing in the text cause, both reference librarian and user, difficulties in communicating their messages because real time chating demands fast and accurate typing speed.

Real Time Digital Reference Technologies:

- 24/7 Reference

- Anexa.com
- AOL Instant Messenger
- Conference Room
- Desktop Streaming
- DigiChat
- e-Gain Live
- e- Gain Voice
- Group Board
- Human Click
- Live Assistance
- Live helper
- Live Person
- Net Meeting
- Reference Services
- 273
- Netscape IRC
- On Demand
- Question Point
- Rakim
- Right Now Live
- Virtual Reference Software

Q29. Write down the evaluation of digital reference service.

Ans. Evaluation is an important component of any activity which is being undertaken in the library. It helps in finding out and assessing if the service is helping the users, for whom it is intended. Evaluation can be done by collecting the users' feedback on the services, which are being offered to them. The services can be modified, extended or changed in the light of the feedback received from the users. The feedback can be collected through the questionnaire or interview method or both.

Lankes has laid down the following measures/components for assessing the quality of digital reference services rendered by any library or information centre or organisation.

- **Outcome Measures (Quality of Answers):** Accuracy of response, appropriateness to user audience, opportunities for interactivity, instructiveness, and impacts resulting from the digital reference process.
- **Process Measures (Effectiveness and Efficiency of Process):** Service accessibility, timeliness of response, clarity of service procedures, service extensiveness (percentage of

questions answered), staff training and review, service review and evaluation, privacy of user information, user awareness (publicity)

- **Economic Measures (Costing and Cost-effectiveness):** Cost to conduct a digital reference session, infrastructure needed to support quality digital reference service, and impact of these costs on other library expenditures.
- **User Satisfaction (Degree of Satisfaction):** Satisfaction indicators. i.e., accuracy, behaviour of staff, facilities. etc.

Q30. What are the major digital reference service projects?

Ans. Some of the prominent digital reference services projects are as follows:

(1) Collaborative Digital Reference Service (CDRS): The Collaborative Digital Reference Service (CDRS), currently being launched by the Library of Congress and its partner libraries, provides just such an opportunity to connect users with accurate, timely, and credible information anytime anywhere. Today more than 100 libraries from various countries are participating in this collaborative venture. This is a worldwide network of libraries in which OCLC builds and maintains a database of profiles of participating institutions, maintains a question -and-answer database system that enables participants to catalogue answers and store them in a searchable/browsable database and provides help in marketing, registration, training and user support. Currently this is a free service. It is an international web-based cooperative network of librarians. This collaborative Digital Reference Service delivers reference assistance to researchers any time, any place. It supports reference efforts by combining the power of resources and manpower with the diversity and availability of libraries and librarians everywhere. Using advance technology that directs questions to the appropriate library based on the subject profiles, this digital notebook pools librarians, expertise to bring quality and professionalism in on-line reference service. The following are some of the advantages of this service:

(i) One library is linked to the other libraries for subjects, languages and collections outside its scope and coverage.

(ii) Libraries and information scientists can add value to reference interactions by obtaining answers to difficult questions from expert librarians at other institutions.

(iii) Librarian can improve his library's ability to respond more quickly and accurately on a broader spectrum of research.

(iv) This service offers reference service beyond working hours of library.

(v) Reference transactions are stored in a question and answer knowledge database that can be accessed for ready reference.

(vi) Reference questions can be answered from books, journals, magazines, citations from oil-line catalogues and licenced databases and references to web sites. The requesting library notified by e-mail to retrieve the answer from the server.

There are three main components of CDRS:

(i) Members Profiles (MP), which contain information on strengths and features of the members. It include addresses (including e-mail), hours of services, collection strengths, staff strengths, what is out of scope, geographical locations of the users served, any special service, average number of questions received. etc.

(ii) Request Manager (RM), software for entering, routing and answering reference questions. It receives, sorts out routes and tracks down the incoming questions and delivers the credible answers to the end user.

(iii) Knowledge Base (KB), a searchable database for questions and answers sets. It is an archive of questions and answers for future use.

(2) Automatic Reference Librarians for the World Wide Web: This project was initiated by the University of Washington to create software agents that posses reference intelligence – a limited understanding of complex technical topics, but a very sophisticated understanding of how and where to find high quality information on the World Wide Web. It works on the basis of wrapper technology. Wrapper technology is a data that precedes or frames the main data or a program that sets up another program so that it can run successfully. This service involves the following steps:

(i) The user asks a question.

(ii) The Query Router assigns a topic to the query.

(iii) The topic maps to a number of relevant wrappers.

(iv) The parallel web search module sends request via wrappers to the sites. Responses from the sites are obtained and sent to the fusion engine for collation.

(v) User gets the response.

It explores web directories such as YAHOO to find out searchable sites. It queries each searchable site and obtains responses from them. The responses and other information about a given site are used to assign topics to that site. Thus, each searchable site gets a wrapper containing some assigned topics, which are used for matching the topics of the users queries.

(3) Virtual Reference Desk (VRD): Virtual Reference Desk (http://www.vrd.org/) provides resources and links to experts that offer digital reference services. The site hosts searchable database of high quality 'ASK-A' service along with alphabetical and subject wise listing. Virtual Reference Desk also hosts a listserv called 'Dig-Ref' to promote and explore the growing area of digital reference services. The basic idea of VRD is that when a user asks a question and that can not be answered by a participating library then it is forwarded to the VRD network for assistance. This service include:

(i) **Collaborative Ask A Service:**A network of Ask A Services and volunteer information professionals that ensure users' questions are addressed by the most appropriate experts.

(ii) **The Learning Centre:** A web site for the K-12 community with curriculum-related websites, frequently asked questions, and other previously asked questions.

(iii) **Ask A+ Locator:** A searchable database of high quality K-12 Ask A Services.

The following are some of the Ask A Services, which are Internet based question and answer services that connect users with experts and subject expertise.

(i) Ask a Hydrologist
(ii) Ask a Linguist
(iii) Ask a Parenting Expert
(iv) Ask a Question
(v) Ask a Reporter
(vi) Ask a Scientist
(vii) Ask an Archeologist
(viii)Ask Dr Math
(ix) Ask Mr Calculus
(x) Ask the Dentist
(xi) Ask the Space Scientist

(4) 24/7 Reference: A pilot network established in the California, Los Angeles and Orange County areas to provide real time reference services directly to the library patrons over the Internet. To avail this service a librarian needs a computer with Windows 98, NT or 2000 and a direct Internet connection. This service can be used to:

(i) Guide the user's browser to the best resources on the Internet with collaborative browsing.

(ii) Communicate with users real time chat.

(iii) Send files, images, power point presentations. etc. to the patron's computer.

(iv) Conduct meetings with up to 20 participants, while sharing web pages.

(v) Network with others by transferring complex questions to a local or remote expert.

(vi) Access reports, transcripts of sessions with users, and a wide variety of usage statistics on demand.

(vii) Customise the software to integrate with user's website.

Q31. Explain an expert system, and how an expert system is useful in handling reference queries in a library and information centre?

Ans. One of the most rapidly,growing and fascinating topic in computer science, psychology, linguistics and information science is expert systems. Expert systems are of recent origin barely mentioned in literatures just a few years ago.

Expert systems belong to the broader discipline of Artificial Intelligence (Al) which has been characterised by Barr and Feigenbaum as 'the part of computer science that is concerned with designing intelligent computer systems; that is, systems that exhibit the characteristics we associate with intelligence in human behaviour—understanding language, learning, reasoning, solving problems, and so on'.

An expert system contains knowledge about a specialised area, which enables the specialist to formulate search profiles and obtain relevant solutions for various problems. The key feature of an expert system is that it involves modeling the thought processes of human experts who are familiar with the domain of a given problem.

Expert System Design: In reference service it has been observed that a large number of reference queries repeat themselves. Majority of the questions are of ready reference types and these can be answered by directing the user or through available reference sources. User may ask location of source, contact person for a particular type of service, procedure for borrowing and lending of documents, filling up of photocopying requisition form or interlibrary loan request form. etc. Providing reference service is an area, which can largely be benefited by introducing an expert system because it functions like a human expert and it does the same thing what a human expert is supposed to do. It performs question-negotiation process with the user and provides solution by analysing the question, identifying the sources that are likely to answer the question.

While designing models of such system, at the broadest level, focus or emphasis is given to four main components: actors, objects, actions, and relationship.

- **Actors:** Actors are entities that act. Actors are most often people, but in the context of a model, a machine could also be an actor. An information seeker, a computer are all categories of actors. An on-line searcher who sends messages is also an actor.
- **Objects:** Objects are things, which are acted upon. Information-seeking models include a variety of different types of objects. Best examples of objects are information sources - the most common types of objects. There are other types of objects - a reference book, an index in a reference book, a

database of reference books, a query, a record in a database, a field in a record. etc.

- **Actions:** Models of reference and search processes often describe actions. To raise a query, recommend, reformulate, look up, explain, evaluate, all are action words that appear frequently in search models. The reference process is often described in terms of the actions that are performed by the reference librarian and the user.
- **Relationships:** Finally, information seeking models are concerned with relationships. A correlation is made among the actors, objects, and actions to get the desired output in an expert system

Advantages of Using Expert System: Applying an expert system for providing reference service has a member of advantages. These include the following:

- An expert system can be designed to store complete library collections and their locations, which may be difficult for any reference librarian to remember and locate physically.
- A multi-user expert system can serve more users at a time.
- Expert system can work round the clock even when library is closed or reference librarian is on leave.
- Interactive expert system can be used by the user more frequently than to a reference librarian.
- User may ask questions from a long distance rather than approaching to reference desk.
- Expert system in one library can be linked with other libraries which may create a network of libraries thus providing much scope of availability of source to answer the question.

Q32. Describe the future of reference service.

Ans. Fast technological developments have moved, and are moving so fast that it is difficult for reference librarians to anticipate at any one time which are the cost effective formats to use, and which will be cost effective in the near future. It is very difficult to make choices between the different electronic formats, and combination of these formats, and between electronic and/or print formats,

It is very difficult to make certain predictions for the future. Predictions may be wrong sometimes because in the past fifteen years it was predicted that today's society would be a paperless society in which all of us reading newspaper on a computer screen and getting our books in on CD-ROM, etc. But the fact is that production of paper has increased and publishing of books in number has also increased.

Some prediction in the area of reference service can be made. Electronic databases, and particularly on-line databases will replace current printed reference works. For example chemical abstracts which is mostly used in research library, it is very difficult for library to maintain and create space for a huge number of printed chemical abstract.

In the future users will be less dependent on library. They may tap required information at home by means of a computer. But, at the same time cost of the on-line databases, CD-ROM and networking cost is too high for most of the user. User can get the same information at less cost from the library. Also specific and accurate information needs are great and are increasing in the present day scenario. So user may not be able to find specific information as a result they have to depend on trained reference specialist. In the light of the above more expert reference librarians are going to be needed in the future.

Digital technology has opened new ways of storing and accessing information. Whatever and in which shape the new technology is going to come in future, it will always help the reference librarian. For users the reference librarian is going to act as a hub if the library is well equipped with computer, internet and CDROM. Reference librarian and reference service will be a centre of universe of information in the future.

❑❑❑

CHAPTER 4

Internet Resources and Services

Introduction

Internet is defined as an Information super Highway, to access information over the web. The origins of the Internet can be found in the early sixties, when the U.S. Department of Defence sponsored a project to develop a telecommunications network that would survive a nuclear attack. The Internet is more than just a huge information resource. Its initial purpose was to act as a communications network and it fulfils that role well. It is the transport mechanism for electronic mail, the transfer of computer files, remote computer access and even allows for voice calls.

Search Engine refers to a huge database of internet resources such as web pages, newsgroups, programs, images, etc. It helps to locate information on World Wide Web. User can search for any information by passing query in form of keywords or phrase. It then searches for relevant information in its database and return to the user. Internet Services allows us to access huge amount of information such as text, graphics, sound and software over the internet. The Internet has established itself as the most widely-used information resource by all kinds of people for a variety of reasons. There are all kinds and types of information resources available on the Internet. Information exists on a continuum of reliability and quality. The web has become the largest available repository of multimedia information.

Q1. Write down History of the Internet.

Ans. The Internet has a glorious history. It has come across a long way to reach its current position. When traditional circuit-switched telephone networks were considered too vulnerable, DoD (Department of Defence of USA) turned to its research arm, Advanced Research projects Agency (ARPA). ARPA was created in response to the Soviet Union's launching Sputnik in 1957 and had the mission of advancing technology that might be useful to the military. This network is popularly known as ARPANET. In the late 1970s, NSF (The U.S. National Science Foundation) found the enormous impact the ARPANET was having on University research, allowing scientists across the country to share data and collaborate on research projects. However, to get on the ARPANET, a University had to have a research contact with the DoD, which many did not have. This lack of Universal access prompted NSF to set up a virtual network, CSNET, centered around a single machine at BBN that supported Dial-up lines and had connections to the ARPANET and other networks. NSF also founded some (eventually about 20) regional networks that connected to the backbone to allow users at thousands of universities, research labs, and museums to access any of the supercomputers and to communicate with one another. The complete network, including the backbone and the regional networks, was called NSFNET. It connected to the ARPANET through a link between an Interface Message Processors (IMP) and fuzzball in the Carnegie-Mellon machine room.

The number of networks, machines, and users connected to the ARPANET grew rapidly after TCP/IP became the only official protocol on 1st January 1983. When NSFNET and ARPANET were interconnected, the growth became exponential. So finally a global network was created, which connected all the types of networks around the globe, it is popularly known as the Internet.

Technically a machine is on the Internet if it runs the TCP/IP protocol stack, has an IP address and has the ability to send IP Packets to all other machines on the Internet. The mere ability to send and receive the electronic mail is not enough, since e-mail is a gateway to many networks outside the Internet. However this issue is clouded somewhat by the fact that many personal computers have the ability to call up an Internet service provider using a modem, be assigned a temporary IP address and send IP packets to other Internet hosts. It makes sense to regard such a machine being on the Internet for as long as they are connected to the service provider's router.

With tremendous growth, the old informal way of running the Internet no longer works. In January 1992, the Internet Society was set up to promote the use of the Internet and perhaps eventually taken over managing it.

Traditionally, Internet had five main applications as follows:

- E-mail
- News
- Remote Login
- File Transfer
- Research

Q2. Describe the concept of 'Internet Management".

Ans. In the second half of the past decade the Internet grew to a size that management of the Internet could no longer be provided on an ad hoc basis: a structured and standardised approach to Internet management was required. The internet has functioned as a collaborative effort among cooperating parties. The key function of this collaborative effort is to developed and evolve specifications for TCP/IP protocol that was originally developed in the DARPA research program mentioned above. In the last five or six years, this work has been undertaken on a wider basis with support from Government agencies in many countries, industry and the academic community. The Internet Activities Board (IAB) was created in 1983 to guide the evolution of the TCP/IP Protocol Suite and to provide research advice to the Internet community.

During the course of its existence, the IAB has been reorganised several times. It now has two primary components: the Internet Engineering Task Force (IETF) and the Internet Research Task Force (IRTF). The IETF is primarily responsible for further evolution of the TCP/IP protocol suite, its standardisation with the concurrence of the IAB, and the integration of other protocols into Internet operation (e.g. the Open Systems Interconnection Protocols). The Internet Research Task Force (IRTF) continues to organise and explore advanced concepts in networking under the guidance of the Internet Activities Board and with support from various government agencies.

The Internet Activities Board and Internet Engineering Task Force have a secretariat to manage its day-to-day functions. Two other functions that are critical to IAB operation are publication of documents describing the Internet and the assignment and recording of various identifiers needed for protocol operation. Throughout the development of the Internet, its protocols and other aspects of its operation have been documented first in a series of documents called Internet Experiment Notes and, later, in a series of documents called Requests for Comment (RFCs). The latter were used initially to document the protocols of the first packet switching network developed by DARPA, the ARPANET, beginning in 1969, and have become the principal archive of information about the Internet. At present, the publication function is provided by an RFC editor.

The recording of identifiers is provided by the Internet Assigned Numbers Authority (IANA) who has delegated one part of this responsibility to an Internet Registry which acts as a central repository for Internet information and which provides central allocation of network and autonomous system identifiers, in some cases to subsidiary registries located in various countries. The Internet Registry (IR) also provides central maintenance of the Domain Name System (DNS) root database which points to subsidiary distributed DNS servers replicated throughout the Internet. The DNS distributed database is used, inter alia, to associate host and network names with their Internet addresses and is critical to the operation of the higher level TCP/IP protocols including electronic mail.

There are a number of Network Information Centers (NICs) located throughout the Internet to serve its users with documentation, guidance, advice and assistance. As the Internet continues to grow internationally, the need for high quality NIC functions increases. Although the initial community of users of the Internet were drawn from the ranks of computer science and engineering, its users now comprise of a wide range of disciplines in the sciences, arts, business, military and government administration.

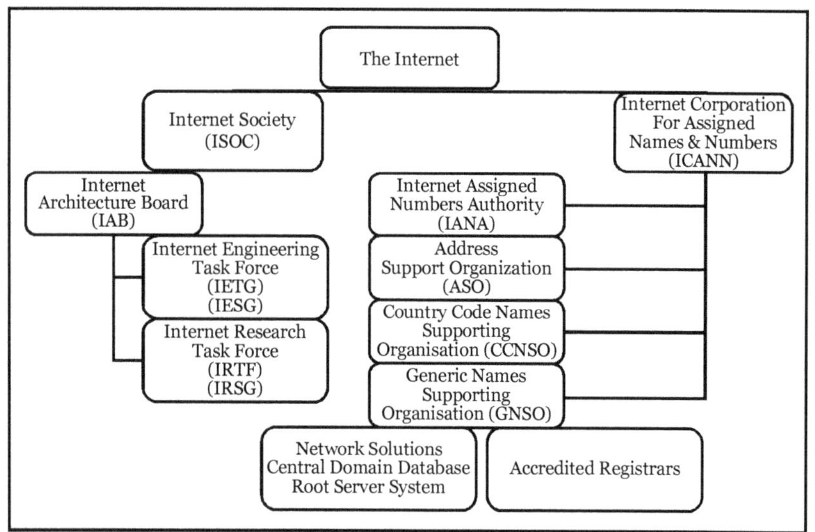

Fig. 4.1

Q3. Give the definitions of 'Internet'. Discuss growth of internet.

Ans. The Internet is the world's largest computer network that enables computers of all kinds to share services and communicate directly, as if they were part of one giant seamless global computing machine. It is a vast and sprawling network reaching into computer sites world-wide. The Internet is actually a "network of networks". The networks that comprise it are thousands of local-area networks-groups of computers including government supercomputers, campus-wide information systems, local area networks and individual workstations. Each of these different computers, connected on the Internet running on different platforms or operating systems, follows certain standards or rules of communication called protocols. The standard protocol used for Internet communication is called transmission control protocol, Internet protocol or TCP/IP. Standardised communication protocols allow similar, dissimilar, near and distant computers to communicate with one another. The Federation National Council (FNC) in 1995 referred to the Internet as a Global Information System that (1) is logically linked together by a globally unique address space based on the Internet Protocol (IP) or its subsequent extensions/follow-ones; (2) is able to support communications using Transmission Control Protocol/Internet Protocol (TCP/IP) suite or its subsequent extensions/follow-ones, and/or other IP compatible protocols; and (3) provides, uses or makes accessible, either publicly or privately, high level services layered on the communications and related infrastructure described herein. It may be seen that FNC has described the Internet as a global information system, and included in the definition is not only the underlying communications technology, but also higher-level protocols and end-user applications, the associated data structures and the means by which the information may be processed, manifested, or otherwise used. In many ways, this definition supports the characterisation of the Internet as an "information superhighway". Like the federal highway system whose underpinnings include not only concrete lanes and on/off ramps, but also a supporting infrastructure both physical and informational, including signs, maps, regulations, and such related services and products as filling stations and gasoline, and the Internet has its own layers of ingress and egress, and its own multi-tiered levels of services.

The Internet Society (ISOC) defines the Internet as a "global network of networks" enabling computers of all kinds to directly and transparently communicate and share services throughout the world using a common communication protocol. It should not be seen as merely as a collection of networks and computers. The Internet is an architecture that provides for both communications capabilities and information services. Because the Internet is an enormously valuable, enabling capability for so many people and organisations, it also constitutes a shared global resource of information, knowledge, and means of collaboration and co-operation among countless diverse communities.

Growth of Internet: The Internet which can be said to hence born thirty-five years ago as a US Defence Department Network called APPANET was initially set up with 4 hosts. In the early 80s there were only 213 registered hosts on the Internet. By 1986, the number had risen to 308 hosts connected throughout the world. By 1989, the number of networks connected had risen to five hundred. The Network Information Centre of the Defence Data Network Information Centre found 2,218 networks connected as of January 1990. By June 1991, the National Science Foundation Network Information Centre pegged it at close to four thousand. If we extrapolate based on current number the figure reached forty million people during 1996 one hundred million by 1998. Its current growth rate is 15 per cent monthly.

This high levels of connectivity has resulted in an unparalleled degree of communication, collaboration, resource sharing, and information access. The host population of the Internet has been doubling every year since 1981. What has driven this growth more than anything is the openness of the academic community. That openness shows up in the technology of the Internet, its economics and its culture. Internet has become a forum for human communication in a wide variety of disciplines ranging from computers, medicine, bio-sciences and social sciences. etc., to art, music, sports and other recreations.

Since the early 80s, when the US government began to share their network technology with the world, there has been growth on a scale that is hard to imagine. To put it into better perspective, in the early 80s there were only 213 registered hosts on the Internet. By 1986, this number had risen to 2,308 hosts.

According to the Internet Society, a non-profit society that studies and promotes the use of the Internet, 134 countries had full Internet connection and an additional 5 countries had limited access (for example, 3-mail only) in 1996. Surveys performed by the International Data Corporation and Matrix Information and Directory Services found that as of September 1997 there were between 53 and 57 million users of the Internet worldwide. By January 1999 there were about 50 million internet connections worldwide. The figure grant to 200 million users in 200 countries and territories by the year 2001. Today's telephone system is still much larger: about 3 billion people around the world now talk on almost 950 million telephone lines (about 250 million of which are actually radio-based cell phones). Also, the total numbers of host computers and users have been growing at about 33 per cent every six months since 1988 - or roughly 80 per cent per year. The telephone service, in comparison, grows an average of about 5-10 per cent per year. That means if the Internet keeps growing steadily the way it has been growing over the past few years, it will be nearly as big as today's telephone system by about 2007.

Internet 2: Internet 2 is a collaborative effort to develop advanced Internet technology and applications vital to the research and education missions of higher education. Over 140 U.S. universities, working together with partners in industry and government, are leading the Internet2 project. Internet2 is working to enable applications, such as telemedicine, digital libraries and virtual laboratories that are not possible with the technology underlying today's Internet. As a project of the University Corporation for Advanced Internet Development (UCAID), the Internet2 project is not a single separate network, but rather joins member network application and engineering development efforts together with many advanced campus, regional, and national networks. Internet2 promises to address this problem by focussing its attention on the next generation of university networks, a system that promises to be 100 times faster than today's system.

The goals of Internet2 are to create a world-class network that will support the national research community; develop a new generation of applications that push the envelope of this new leading edge network; and make the new services resulting from Internet2 available to every level of education and to the Internet community at large. Internet2 universities, working with industry, government and other research and education networking organisations are addressing the major challenges facing the next generation of university networks by:

- First and most importantly, creating and sustaining a leading edge network capability for the national research community
- Second, directing network development efforts to enable a new generation of applications to fully exploit the capabilities of broadband networks.
- Third, working to rapidly transfer new network services and applications to all levels of educational use and to the broader Internet community, both nationally and internationally.

Internet 3: Similar to the origin of the Internet, the root of the emerging Internet3 also lies with the US government and academics. These include the US government's Next Generation Internet (NGI) initiative, the National Science Foundation' (NFS) and Very High Bandwidth Network Service (VBNS). As computer and communication corporate giants such as IBM, CISCO and Intel will eventually benefit with the development of Internet3, they too are active participants in this new Internet project.

Initiated in October 1996, NGI aims to foster a partnership between academia, industry and government to develop technologies that will be essential to sustain the USA's technological leadership in computing and communications and enhance the country's economic competitiveness. The NGI by the end of the year 2002 aims to demonstrate the new Internet work with a capacity of 1 Terra-bps and over 10 advanced applications that will leverage this bandwidth. The Internet3 promises a large number of new applications on a very high-speed network.

Q4. Discuss the Internet Architecture. Also describe two popular system of communication.

Ans. A network may consist of two computers or devices with a length of wire between them, letting them communicate. At its most complex, as in the Internet, a network is a globe-spanning, heterogeneous mix of computers. The Internet connects million of computers hooked to a number of heterogeneous networks.

The Internet links millions of computers for communicating data from one computer to another. A computer linked on the Internet is known as the host computer. The term "host" means any computer that has full two-way access to other computers on the Internet. The millions of host computer are linked on the Internet for communicating with each other. The connectivity from one computer to another computer is being provided using some standard mode of linkages called Internet Protocols. A protocol can be defined as special set of rules governing connectivity for telecommunication connections. Protocols may exist at several levels and in order to communicate both end points must recognise and observe standard protocols. Peer-to-Peer and client/server are two popular systems of communication.

(1) Peer-to-Peer Communication: Peer-to-peer is a communications model in which each party has the same capabilities and either party can initiate a communication session. Other models with which it might be contrasted include the client/server model and the master/slave model. In some cases, peer-to-peer communication is implemented by giving each communication node both server and client capabilities.

On the Internet, peer-to-peer (referred to as P2P) is a type of transient Internet network that allows a group of computer users with the same networking programme to connect with each other and directly access files from one another's hard drives. Napster and Gnutella are examples of this kind of peer-to-peer software. Corporations are looking at the advantages of using P2P as a way for employees to share files without the expense involved in maintaining a centralised server and as a way for businesses to exchange information with each other directly. These are usually operated in small offices. IBM's Advanced Peer-to-Peer Networking (APPN) and Gnutellanet are the example of products that supports the peer-to-peer communication model.

(2) Client-Server Architecture: The Client-Server Architecture is based on the principle where the client computer requests for some data and the data are sent by the server computer through the network. The concept of client/server computing has particular importance on the Internet because most of the programmes are built using this design. A server is a programme that "serves" (or delivers) something, usually information, to a client programme. A server usually runs on a computer that is connected to a network. The size of that network is not important in the client/server concept - it could be a small local area network or the global Internet.

The advantage of this type of design is that a server has to store the information in one format: which could be accessed by various clients working on multiple platforms and located at different places. In the client/server model, multiple client programmes share the services of a common server programme. Both client programmes and server programmes are often part of a larger programme or application.

In the case of the Internet, the Web browser is a client programme that requests services from a Web server. The server is designed to interact with client programmes so that people using the system can determine whether the information they want is there, and if so, have it sent.

Software tools in a client-server environment work in pair. For every application in client server environment, there is a client program that is responsible for facilitating users to interact with 'server' program and explore information hosted on it. The client application works as an interface between the user and the host, collecting information about the requirement of user, translating the request into agreed language of communication between the client and the server and sending it to the relevant server computer. The server program is responsible for hosting the data and accompanied programs, receiving the request from clients, finding the information requested by client and returning it to the client. A 'server' is generally programmed to organise information stored on it, create indices and search information. The responses or data sent by the server machines are received by the client machines that decode it and convert it for appropriate display on the user's machine.

The client-server model is most suitable for packet switching as mode of communication used by the Internet. The client-server model does not need continuous communication between client and the server. Once a request from the client machine is sent to the server that contains not only the request but also the address of client machine, the client machine can use its resources for something else while it waits for response from the server. Likewise, once a request is received from a client, the server machine performs a search for resources requested by the client and sends it to the client's address. The process does not require continuous communication between client and the server. This asynchronous form of communication is not only suitable for packet switching but it also ensures that resources of client and host machines as well as communication channels are used most optimally.

Q5. Describe various methods of accessing Internet. What is the most common method of accessing Internet?

Or

Explain the term 'Digital Subscriber Line (DSL)'.

Or

Describe briefly the different methods of accessing the Internet. [June-2019, Q.No.-3.2]

Or

Write a short note on ISDN. [June-2019, Q.No.-5 (d)]

Ans. Let us see the model of centralised or cooperating utilities, such as the telephone or electricity. We can comfortably compare the Internet to one of these utilities. For example, there is a phone service in almost every part of India. A person who wants the telephone facility contacts a local area service provider (MTNL in case of Delhi). The service provider gives a "hook-up" from the residence or office to the service network. This arrangement allows you to connect to telephones almost anywhere in the world. The Internet where data moves among networks of computers works much the same way.

The connections to the Internet fall under two basic categories: dial up access and direct or dedicated access. There are two categories of dial-up access. i.e., analogue and digital. Regular telephone lines support analogue mode of data transmission that uses a continuous wave from to transmit data. Analogue connections use modems to convert digital signals to analogue signals and then analogue signals back to the digital signals. Digital transmissions such as fibre optic devices pass data along using discrete, on/off pulses. Unlike analogue connections, digital connections do not require a modem at each end of the connection.

(1) Analog Dial-up Connection: The remote client and the remote access server both connect to a common WAN infrastructure. This WAN infrastructure for analog dial-up is usually the Public Switched Telephone Network (PSTN), which is also known as the Plain Old Telephone System (POTS). The PSTN is designed to carry human voices from one phone to another as an analog signal. The analog dial-up modem in a computer converts the computer's digital information into an analog to computers as an internal card via an external connection port such as a serial or USB port.

The analog dial-up strategy is not as popular as it once was. The main advantage of analog dial-up technology is that it is a mature technology that is available in many locations where no other WAN solution exists. The main disadvantage of analog dial-up is that it is slow, transferring below 100,000 bits of data per second when compared to solutions such as cable or DSL modems that transfer more than a megabit (1,000,000 bits) of data per second. The most common reason that dial-up still exists today is that, in some geographical regions, it is the only practical low cost option to access the Internet.

Hardware Requirement: The hardware requirements common for all types of connections for user (client) and server are dealt separately. Dial-up connection to Internet specifically requires a Modem (Modulator/ Demodulator).

A MODEM is a device that enables a computer to transmit data over telephone lines. Modulator converts the discrete stream of digital 'on-off' electric pulses used by the computers into the analog wave patterns used for transmission of human voice. Demodulator recovers the digital data from the transmitted analog signal. A modem can be fixed internally into PCs or it can also be bought as external device.

A reliable and high-quality Modem is a critical requirement to ensure quality and reliability of transmitted information. The Modem should incorporate error-correction protocols and should be supported by local telecommunication facilities. It should work in asynchronous mode with a speed of 33.6 to 56 KBPS.

Software Requirements: The software requirements common for all types of connections for user (client) and server are dealt separately. Dialup connection specifically requires communication software.

Communication software is a program, which establishes contact between a computer and the Internet Service Provider (ISP) using modem. Such software have built-in functionality of automatic dialing and automatic logon procedures including dialing to the ISP, supplying User ID and Password. etc. Communication software is built into operating systems. Windows Operating System incorporates 'Hyper Terminal' as communication software. ISPs may also provide their own communication software.

(2) Digital Subscriber Line (DSL): DSL is a technology that works on the presumption that digital data does not require changes into the analogue form and back. Digital data is transmitted to your Computer directly as digital data and this allows the phone company to use a much wider bandwidth for transmitting them for you. DSL is a technology for bringing high-bandwidth information to homes and small business is over ordinary copper telephone lines. Telephone companies use the 300 Hz to 3200 Hz frequency band to transmit voice. If data have to be transmitted on these lines, they must be disguised and made to look like audio frequencies, and that's what modem do. Despite its name, DSL does not refer to a physical line but to a modem or rather a pair of modems.

Now, DSL makes use of a wider band of frequencies; it preserves the lower frequencies for voice transmission and uses high frequencies to transmit data, due to which more data can be transferred per unit time. As a consequence, the maximum transfer rate shoots up from the current 56 kbps to up to 52 Mbps. A DSL line can carry both data and voice signals and the data part of the line is continuously connected. xDSL refers to different variations of DSL such as ADSL, HDSL and RADSL. etc.

(i) **Asymmetric Digital Subscriber Line (ADSL):** ADSL is called "asymmetric" because most of its two-way or duplex bandwidth is devoted to the downstream direction, sending data to the user. Only a small portion of the bandwidth is available for upstream or user-interaction messages. However, most Internet, and especially graphics or multi-media web data need a lot of downstream bandwidth, but user requests and response are small.

(ii) **Symmetric DSL (SDSL):** This connection, used mainly by small businesses, does not allow simultaneous use of telephone at the same time, but the speed of receiving and sending data is the same.

(iii) **VDSL (Very high bit-rate DSL):** This is a fast connection, but works only over a short distance.

(iv) **HDSL (High data rate DSL):** HDSL is the earliest variation of DSL. The main characteristic of HDSL is that it is symmetrical or in other words an equal amount of bandwidth is available in both directions.

(v) **SHDSL (Single-pair High-speed Digital Subscriber Line):** SHDSL was developed as a meltdown of several symmetric DSL technologies (HDSL, SDSL, HDSL-2) producing as a result one single internationally recognised industry standard. Unlike ADSL, which is fine-tuned to the needs of a home user and can download enormous amounts of data but has limitation when large amount of data is to be uploaded. SHDSL has no problems with 'two-way' Internet traffic. With the transfer rates of up to 2.3 Mbps, this makes it a perfect high-speed solution for medium to big enterprises, branch offices, as well as high-end residential users.

(vi) **Rate Adaptive DSL (RADSL):** This is a variation of ADSL, but the modem can adjust the speed of the connection depending on the length and quality of the line.

(vii) **IDSL (ISDN Digital Subscriber Line):** IDSL provides up to 144-Kbps transfer rates in each direction and can be provisioned on any ISDN capable phone line. Unlike ADSL and other DSL technologies, IDSL can be deployed regardless of the distance the user is from the central office.

Some of the benefits of DSL connections are:

(i) **No Additional Wiring:** A DSL connection makes use of your existing telephone wiring, so you will not have to pay for expensive upgrades to your phone system.

(ii) **Cost Effective:** DSL internet is a very cost-effective method and is best in connectivity

(iii) Availability of DSL modems by the service providers.

(iv) User can use the both telephone line and internet at a same time. And it is because the voice is transferred on other frequency and digital signals are transferred on others.

(v) User can choose between different connection *speeds* and *pricing* from various providers.

Hardware Requirements: The hardware requirements common for all types of connections for user (client) and server are dealt separately later. A DSL connection to Internet specifically requires DSL modem or network terminators.

DSL modems or network terminators are digital devices that are used to connect a computer or network to a larger network via telephone wiring using DSL techniques. Modem is a misnomer in this case since there is no conversion from digital to analog. The DSL technologies use sophisticated modulation schemes to pack data onto copper wires. They are sometimes referred to as last-mile technologies because they are used only for connections from a telephone switching station to a home or office, not between switching stations. Most DSL devices connect to USB-port on desktop or notebook computer. It does not require any additional network interface card. Most DSL devices support multiple operating systems.

Software Requirements: The software requirements common for all types of connections for user (client) and server are dealt separately later. DSL connection to Internet specifically requires DSL Installation Software. However, since both telephone and ADSL service are simultaneously available from the same copper pair, a central splitter or distributed filters is required at the exchange for decoupling ADSL and telephone signals. Since the Internet connection in DSL is available virtually, the DSL connection does not require a communication package.

(3) Dedicated Leased Line: A leased circuit is a dedicated link provided between two fixed locations for exclusive use by the customer. A leased circuit may be a speech circuit, a data circuit or a telegraph circuit. Dedicated leased line can be achieved by twisted pair of telephone lines, through VSAT or radio link. Leased line charges are generally uniform for all cases and are same as applicable for point-to-point leased circuits.

Dedicated leased lines have many advantages. The major advantage is the high speed and better reliability. With a dedicated single leased line, an organisation can have many users of a local area network connected to the Internet. Being a dedicated leased line, users need not dial to connect to the Internet. All computers on a local area network using a dedicated leased line are always connected to the Internet. This type of connection is appropriate for organisations that transfer large amounts of data and have many users and workstations that must be connected to the Internet. This option requires that dedicated lines be leased through a network provider (such as Department of Telecommunication or VSNL in India) and special network hardware be installed on site, making this a complicated operation. The only disadvantage of dedicated leased line is high cost of communication and difficulties involved in its maintenance.

Hardware and Software Requirements: Besides a dedicated leased line, no other hardware or software is required except PCs and local area network along with switches or routers in the organisation for its effective usage. Dedicated connection through radio link requires radio antenna installed at the user's premises. Dedicated telephone line in India is provided by the MTNL or Department of Telecommunication. MTNL is also an Internet Service Provider.

(4) Integrated Service Digital Network (ISDN): The development of public data networks for digital communications led to the existence of different networks for different purposes. This resulted in the duplication of networks. To avoid this, interconnection of two or more compatible or incompatible networks to form an internet (network of networks) is attempted. The main aim of ISDN is to build a public network providing end-to-end digital connectivity which is capable of supporting a range of digital devices and services, both voice and non-voice, on the same basis. This allows users to send and receive data, text and image from computer systems as well as offering an enhanced telephone service. This is achieved over a single ISDN connection, so that one network can be used for all applications, providing higher speeds of transmission. Major benefits of ISDN are as follows:

(i) Single connection can support voice, data and images. An ISDN subscriber can establish two simultaneous independent calls which could be voice, data, image or combination of any two whereas only one call is possible on ordinary telephone lines.

(ii) High quality services being digital right from premises of subscribers (end to end) are available.

(iii) Eight terminals can be connected on a single line.

(iv) High-speed data transfer from PC to PC is possible – 64 Kbps against existing 9.6 Kbps (6 times faster). The call set time is very short (1-2 seconds).

(v) ISDN supports a number of supplementary services

Hardware Requirements: The ISDN telephone line is terminated on a common box called the Network Termination (NT) that is installed at the subscriber's premises. The Network Termination unit along with accessories is generally provided by the Internet Service Provider or can be procured by the subscriber. The terminal equipment has to be procured by the subscriber.

ISDN supports voice, data and image transmission over the telephone line. As such, its application is not restricted to Internet access. The hardware required for an ISDN connection would therefore depend on the applications that a user wants to run on an ISDN connection. Some of the ISDN equipment may be:

(i) ISDN feature phone: this is a simplest type of ISDN phone which has an LCD display and some additional keys
(ii) Terminal adapter
(iii) PC add-on ISDN card
(iv) Video phone
(v) G4 fax

(5) Cable Connection to the Internet: Internet can also be accessed through the cable that brings TV channels to our homes using a cable modem. Cable modem separates digital and analog signals travelling on the cable and enables a PC to send and receive data using coaxial cable on the same frequencies used by the cable TV channels. The primary advantage of cable is the large bandwidth it offers. ISDN and DSL cannot match the bandwidth and speed offered by the cable. PSTN (dial-up) offers maximum of 56 kbps, ISDN offers a maximum of 128 Kbps whereas cable starts with 64 kbps and can go upto 38 Mbps. Internet through cable is, therefore, suitable for downloading multimedia such as movies, animation. etc.

The Internet through cable uses the existing cable that already connects TV in our home. This cable is capable of carrying both video signals and data signals at the same time. Neither television nor data signals are affected by simultaneous use. Internet through cable is right solution for bandwidth intensive applications and corporate customers. Though cable has immense potentials as an access technology, it has a long way to go in terms of infrastructure, quality of service, cost factor, security. etc. Siti Cable, Ice Network Pvt. Ltd., Innomedia Technologies Pvt. Ltd., Mantra Online, BPL, Aptech Internet Ltd. and Zeenext offer Internet through cable TV in India.

Hardware Requirements: The hardware requirements common for all types of connections for user (client) and server are dealt separately later. Cable connection to Internet specifically requires a cable modem.

A cable modem is an external device that hooks up to the PC. It interacts with a Cable Modem Termination System (CMTS) installed at a central location. Cable modems use various technologies like TDMA based DOCSIS standard or more robust and modern SCDMA based TERAYON proprietary technology.

Installing cable TV also involves modification and upgradation of existing cable TV network to handle two-way data. The process involves adding signal amplifiers and coaxial cable by the local cable provider.

(6) Internet through Mobile Telephone: Internet can also be accessed through mobile telephone where the mobile functions as a high-speed modem to connect a user's mobile, PC or laptop to the Internet. Reliance India Mobile uses Code Division Multiple Access (CDMA) technology with superior voice quality and high-speed data capabilities. It offers speeds up to 144 Kbps. A data cable called 'R Connect Data Cable' is required to connect Reliance Mobile to the PC. The Data Cable is to be plugged into PC and the mobile. Software has to be installed in the PC for activating the Internet connectivity. Before start using R Connect, a user is required to subscribe to the service and activate his or her phone for R Connect.

(7) Shell V/s TCP/IP Accounts: A user requires an account with an Internet Service Provider (ISP) in order to access Internet services. The Internet account can either be a shell account or a TCP/ IP account.

Shell Account: In case of shell account, a user logs on to an intermediary computer (host) to access the Internet. The host computer that is connected to the Internet provides connectivity to the user. There may be several shell accounts on a host computer. The primary disadvantage of a shell account is that it limits access to the Internet applications running on the service provider's computer. Moreover, a user has to learn to use the operating commands on the host computer. Moreover, shell accounts support only text-based access to the Internet.

Transferring information to or from the Internet using shell account, is a two-step process. In the first step, the file is transferred from a remote machine on the Internet to the host machine and then from host machine to the personal computer of user in the second step. Shell accounts are cheaper as compared to the TCP/IP accounts. With cheaper availability of Internet connections and popularity of graphic browsers, most users do not prefer shell accounts.

TCP/IP account: The TCP/IP account facilitates a user to configure his system as a host machine. It supports graphical interface for surfing the net. TCP/IP accounts cost more than plain shell accounts.

Q6. Briefly discuss about Internet Service Providers (ISPs).

Ans. An Internet service provider (ISP) is an organisation that provides services for accessing, using, or participating in the Internet. Internet service providers may be organised in various forms, such as commercial, community-owned, non-profit, or otherwise privately owned. Internet services typically provided by ISPs include Internet access, Internet transit, domain name registration, web hosting, Usenet service, and collocation.

An internet Service Provider (ISP) gives software, specialised hardware and technical help to connect to the Internet. Many ISPs provide electronic-mail account, host customer's web pages, and offer other services as a package deal to their customers.

Choosing ISP: There is no reliable way fit for all to choose the best Internet Service Provider. Different people have different priorities: for some it is price, for others it is range of access numbers, for others it is speed. A user has to carefully examine which ISP addresses his or her priority in a better way.

Internet Service Providers (ISPs) in India: There are about 390 Internet Service Providers (ISP) in India who have been issued licence by the Department of Telecommunication to set-up their ISP and tariffs. Some of them even have their own International Gateways. About 200 ISPs are already providing service to about 2.5 million users around the country. A list of selected major ISPs along with their Web site address is given below:

- The Videsh Sanchar Nigam Ltd (VSNL)
- Mahanager Telephone Nigam Ltd.
- ERNET Society are amongst the biggest Internet Service Providers in India.

Q7. Describe the hardware and software requirement for the Internet.

Or

Explain the concept of Server-side hardware and software components.

Ans. (1) Server-side Hardware Components.

Servers: Servers are the heart of a digital library. Servers for digital library implementation need to be computationally powerful, have adequate main memory (RAM) to handle the expected work, have a large amount of secure disc storage for the database(s) and digital objects and have good communication capabilities. A digital library may need a number of specialised servers for different tasks so as to distribute the workload on to different servers. It would require one or more library server(s) to host indices and databases and one or more object server(s) to store digital objects and other multimedia objects. However, for a smaller library, many distinct activities can be performed on a single server. It is important that the server is scalable (such as Sun Enterprise Server) so that additional storage, processing power or networking capabilities can be added whenever required.

Input Devices: Image-based digital library implementation require input devices like scanners, digital cameras, video cameras and PhotoCD system. A large range of choices are available for these image capturing devices. Scanners are available in all sizes and shapes. Flatbed scanners or digital cameras mounted on book cradle are more suitable for libraries.

Storage Device: Since digital libraries require large amounts of storage, particular attention peeds to be given on the storage solution. Digital library collections that are too large to store entirely a disk use hierarchical storage mechanisms (HSM). In an HSM, the most frequently used data is kept on fast disks, while less frequently used data is kept in nearline such as an automated (robotic) tape library. An HSM can automatically migrate data from tape to disk and vice-versa, as required. intelligent storage networks and snap-servers are now available in which the physical storage devices are intelligently controlled and made available to a number of servers. Although hard disc (fixed and removable) solutions are increasingly available at an affordable cost, optical storage devices including WORM, CD-R, CD-ROM, DVD-ROM or opto-magnetic devices in standalone or networked mode, are attractive alternatives for long-term storage of digital information. Optical drives record information by writing data onto the disc with a laser beam. The media offer enormous storage capabilities. A number of RAID (Redundant Array of Inexpensive Disks) models are also available for greater security and performance. The RAID technology distributes the data across a number of disks in a way that even if one or more disks fail, the system would still function while the failed component is replaced.

(2) Server-side Software Components: A typical digital library requires a number of software packages to handle its highly diversified resources, activities and services. Different software packages are required to handle different components and activities of a digital library. For example, creating digital objects involving scanning of documents requires I document imaging software, converting material already available in digital format into PDF would require Acrobat Software Suite and organisation of digital objects with associated metadata would require a RDBMS package.

Image Capturing or Scanning Software: The process of converting a paper document into a computer-processible digital image is done using a software variably called document imaging system, electronic filing system or document management system. etc. A simple scanning software also comes with the scanners. Two important document imaging software from India are:

OmniDoc ver. 1 (Newgen Software) http://www.i~ewgensoft.com/
Data Scan (Stacks Software Put. Ltd.) http:/www.stex.corn/

Image Enhancement and Manipulation: The captured images may need manipulation to enhance their quality. Some of the image enhancement features include: filters, tonal reproduction, colour management. touch, crop, image sharpening, contrast, transparent background. etc. A few important image enhancement packages are listed below:

Adobe's Photoshop 9.0 http://www.adobe.corn/
Jasc Inc.'s Paintshop Pro 6.02 http://www.jasc.com/
Eastman Software, Inc. http://www.eastmansoftware.com/
Core1 Corporation http://www.corel.com/
Alchemy Mindworks http://www.alchemy.com/

Web Servers: Setting-up a web-based digital library requires a web server program. Many server programs are available for different platforms, each with different features and cost varying from free to very expensive. Some of the important web server programs are listed below:

Servers for Unix Systems

NCSA HTTPD http://www.ncsa.uiuc.edu/
Apache http://www.apache.org/
Jogsaw 2.1.1 http://www.w3.org/jigsaw/
Netra (for sun solaris) http://sun.com/

Servers for Windows NT

Internet Information Server (IIS) http://www.microsoft.com/iis/

Database Management Software: The database management software provide structured storage and retrieval facilities to the contents of a digital library. Digital libraries use a variety of database management system ranging from relational and extended relational database management systems to object-oriented database systems. Relational DBMS are most often used for the storage of metadata and indices with attributes that contain pointers to files in a file system. Most of the commercial RDBMS also support storage of binary large object (BLOBs). Object- oriented database systems are slowly gathering acceptance.

The relational DBMS software listed below can be accessed by using SQL (Structured Query Language):

Oracle http://www.oracle.com/
Informix http ://www.informix.com/
Sybase http://www.sybase.com/
SQL Server http://www.microsoft.com/

(3) Client-side Hardware and Software Components: Clients are the machines that reside on the user desks. Planners of the digital library, therefore, need to prescribe the minimum level of hardware and software that a user would require so as to achieve efficient and effective interaction with the digital library. Most digital libraries require an Internet-enabled multimedia PC (or Machintosh) equipped with an Internet Browser like Internet Explorer or Netscape Navigator as their clients. The client-side PCs may also require the following software packages (plug-ins) to download format-specific deliverables from a digital library:

Table 4.1: Format Specific Deliverables

Software	Used For	Web Site
Internet Explorer 5.0	Internet Browser	http://www.microsoft.com/
Netscape Nevigator 4.7	Internet Browser	http://home.netscape.com/
Acrobat Reader 4.0 (Adobe)	PDF files	http://www.adobe.com/
Microsoft Office	For display and printing of MS Word, MS Access,	http://www.microsoft.com/

	MS Excel files and Power Point presentations	
Real Player 7.0	Audio and Video	http://www.real.com/
TIFF Surfer 1.0	TIFF Images	http://www.visionshape.com/
WS_FTP Pro 6.0	File Transfer Client	http://www.ipswitch.com/

Q8. Write short notes on the followings:

(i) Internet Protocols

Ans. To exchange information, computers must understand what each other computer is saying. They use a common language. We use a common language in class, called English. That is so because we can understand what is being said. A protocol is simply a set of conventions that determines how data will be transmitted from one point to another. This also determines how to move messages and handle errors; using them allows the creation of standards separate from a particular hardware system. The data on the Internet are transmitted from one computer to another using some standard protocols. A protocol can be defined as a formal description of formats and rules two or more computers must follow to exchange that data. These can be low-level details of computer-to-computer interfaces (for example the order in which bits from a byte are sent across a wire) or high-level exchange between application programmes (for example the way in which two programmes transfer a file across a network). In simple terms, protocols are a set of technical specifications that let computers exchange information.

(ii) Transmission Control Protocol, Internet Protocol (TCP/IP)

Ans. TCP/IP stands for Transmission Control Protocol/Internet Protocol. TCP/IP is not a single protocol but is a set of communication protocols that are used to connect computers that have data to be transmitted over the Internet. Every machine on Internet transmits data. The client machine transmit queries, servers transmit answers.

A TCP connects the destination and source machines on the Internet. This enables both of them to transmit data between each other. The following are the advantages of TCP:

- The message is definitely delivered from the source to the destination
- The packets that make up the message are delivered in the same order to the destination as they are transmitted from the source.

The Internet Protocol (IP) specifies the structure of the packet. That is, the place from where the data starts and where it ends inside the packet. Also, it is this protocol which specifies the position of this packet in the set of packets that form the message so that it can be used during the time of recompilation at the destination. The packets are also called datagrams. IP also specifies the addressing scheme for the packets. Several versions of IP are released since its inception. The current version is IPv6.

When a computer (source) wants to send message/data to another computer (destination), then the source specifies the address of the destination and confirms that the message/data is to be sent. Then, IP comes into action. It splits the data into packets and specifies the addressing scheme. Once IP has done its job, TCP comes into action. It establishes a connection between the source and destination so that the packets can be transmitted between them. It is not necessary that only source sends data to destination. Once the communication starts, destination is also permitted to communicate with the source over the same connection. TCP also ensures that all the datagrams (packets) reach the destination and vice-versa. Also, it ensures that the order of receipt of packets at source/destination is the same as they are transmitted by the source/destination So, it is both TCP and IP which lead to communication between the source and destination. TCP/IP is the default standard for Internet based communication. Almost, all the network operating systems support them. That is the primary reason for Internet being a network of machines that are based on different operating systems. Needless to say, TCP/IP uses packet switching technology. The alternative is circuit switching technology in which the message/data travels along a fixed line from source to destination and the destination receives data in the same order in which it is sent from the source.

(iii) Hypertext Transfer Protocol (HTTP)

Ans. HTTP stands for Hyper Text Transfer Protocol. This is the protocol that is used to transfer web pages between web browser and web server. HTTP does a wide variety of tasks. The way the data/message is to be formatted is specified by HTTP. The way the data/message is to be transmitted is also specified by HTTP. Whenever data is transmitted between web browser and web server, both browser and server need to respond to the commands of each other. The nature of response is also defined by HTTP. When you need to go to a particular website, it is the home page which is usually loaded into your browser. So, when you type the website address/URL in the location bar of the browser and press ENTER, or click at "go", it is the HTTP which guides the web server about the web page that is to be sent to the browser in response to the URL. In the case of HTTP, both Browser and Web server will not be aware of the commands that are executed by themselves prior to the current command. This shows the statelessness of HTTP. This is one of the reasons for the existence of static websites. In the case of static websites, only web pages are transferred between the browser and the server depending on the URL entered or depending on the buttons/links clicked on the web page, but, the web pages cannot be interactive and are not dynamic. They cannot react to the user's data which is fed into a web page. Such reaction is possible in the case of dynamic web pages. Java script, Java, Cookies, Active-X, Php script, servlets and applets are used for generating dynamic web pages.

(iv) File Transfer Protocol (FTP)

Ans. FTP stands for File Transfer Protocol. This is the protocol that is used to upload/download files to/from the Internet. When files are to be exchanged between source/destination, FTP comes into action. FTP uses TCP/IP to enable the transfer of data between source/destination. Whenever a website is to be hosted, web pages are uploaded to the concerned web server. It is the FTP which enables the uploading of files.

(v) Serial Line Internet Protocol (SLIP) and Point-to-Point Protocol (PP)

Ans. SLIP stands for Serial Line Internet Protocol. This is a protocol that is used to connect to Internet through telephone lines. So, if the Internet connection is a Dial-up connection, this protocol can be used. But, SLIP is a older protocol and very few Internet service providers are using it. It was developed when the speed of connection was around 2kbps. SLIP transmits data over serial lines. That is, data is transmitted one bit at a time which is time consuming.

PPP stands for Point to Point Protocol. This is another protocol that is used to connect to Internet through telephone lines. This is the protocol that is being used by most of the ISPs (Internet Service Providers) for dial-up access to Internet. This is a protocol that works comfortably with the speeds that even exceed 64kbps. It supports error detection (That is, any error that creeps in during the transmission of the message between the source/destination can be detected) and data compression. The packets that are generated by TCP/IP are sent by PPP to a server that in turn places these packets on the Internet.

(vi) Z39.50

Ans. Access to online bibliographic resources with the rapid growth in the use of the Internet and world wide web has made it possible to access the information in ways not possible to access before hence shifting the emphasis of libraries from collecting the information to providing access to information using electronic resources. However, the major difficulty in accessing the resources is of variation in the use of software and hardware. Library professionals have to learn specific features of each system. i.e., command languages, search procedures. etc. The more electronic resources grow, the more will be the confusion as to how to access the information from diverse databases.

ANSI/NISO Z39.50 is an international standard for communication between computer systems primarily, library and information related systems for overcoming the problems of database searching with many search languages. Z39.50 is becoming increasingly important to the future development and deployment of inter-linked library systems.

In z39.50 model, the target is presumed to contain one or more databases, each of which contains a series of objects called records. Each database contains a set of access points, although not all databases need to support the same nor does every record in a particular database need to be able to be accessed by all of the access points supported for that database.

(vii) Dublin Core and Z39.85

Ans. The Dublin Core refers to a set of metadata elements that may be assigned to web pages so as to facilitate discovery of electronic resources. Originally conceived for author generated description of web resources at the OCLC/NCSA Metadata Workshop held at Dublin, Ohio in 1995, it has attracted the attention of formal resource description communities such as museums, libraries, government agencies, and commercial organisations. The Dublin Core Workshop Series has gathered experts from the library world, the networking and digital library research communities, and a variety of content specialists in a series of invitational workshops. The building of an interdisciplinary, international consensus around a core element set is the central feature of the Dublin Core. A set of 15 core elements in Dublin Core include: Title, Creator, Subject, Keywords, Description, Publisher, Contributor, Date, Resource Type, Format, Resource Identifier, Source, Language, Relation, Coverage and Rights Management. Dublin Core has now been approved as NISO standard Z39.85 (Dublin Core Metadata).

Q9. Write short note on the following:

(i) Internet Addressing

Ans. Each host computer on the Internet has its own unique address. To identify a host on the Internet, three addressing systems have been evolved: A numerical system called IP addressing, a hierarchical naming system called the Domain Name System, and an addressing system called URLs, which are used for identifying sites on the web.

- **IP address:** Each computer has a unique numerical address, such as 194.170.32.23
- **Domain name:** Each computer must have a unique name, such as www.hct.ac.ae
- **Uniform Resource Locator:** Address of file(s) to be accessible from a host computer.

(ii) IP Addresses

Ans. Every host on the Internet is assigned a unique identifier called an IP address or Internet Protocol address. The IP address is a numerical address consisting of four numbers separated by periods. An IP address looks like this: 202.54.26.82 and is read as, "202 dot 54 dot 26 dot 82."

The IP address is a set of numbers that expresses the exact physical connection between a computer and the network on the Internet. They are unique and can be equated to telephone numbers in a way: a phone number uniquely describes a user's connection to the telephone network. IP addresses work somewhat similarly but are more complex than phone numbers because there are literally millions of network connections possible and because IP addresses are intended for use by computers rather than people.

An IP address consists of a 32-bit integer that's represented by four 8-bit numbers, written in base 10, separated by periods. IP addresses are organised from left to right with the left-hand octet describing the largest network organisation and the rightmost octet describing the actual network connection. IP addresses are unique on the network and allow it to know specifically which computer is to receive which electronic packet as well as from which specific computer the electronic packet came. IP address of IIT Delhi web server is 202.54.26.82. As it may be quite difficult to remember such long IP addresses, a system to translate it in domain names has been developed. The Domain Name System (DNS) serves as directory program for IP addresses and it takes care of translating IP addresses in simpler English names. The DNS for above mentioned IP address is www.iitd.ac.in.

(iii) Domain Names

Ans. A domain name is an identification string that defines a realm of administrative autonomy, authority or control within the Internet. Domain names are used in various networking contexts and for application-specific naming and addressing purposes. In general, a domain name identifies a network domain, or it represents an Internet Protocol (IP) resource, such as a personal computer used to access the Internet, a server computer hosting a website, or the web site itself or any other service communicated via the Internet.

The domain name of a host computer looks like:

- Host computer name
- Organisation name
- Type of organisation
- Country name

IETF who designed the addressing system have planned a system, which looks like words. These words roughly map to a parallel system of numerical addresses called IP Addresses. Every computer on the Internet has both a domain name and an IP address, and when you use a domain name, the computers translate that name to the corresponding IP address.

- The server www.iitd.ac.in means
- A host computer called www
- An organisation called IITD

- An academic institution (ac stands for academic)
- Located in India (in stands for India)

Similarly, the server www.yahoo.com means a host called www, belonging to an organisation called yahoo, which is a commercial organisation (com means commercial) located in the United States (if there is no country code then it is in the United States).

In actuality, a host computer uses only numbers, turning all domain name addresses into numbers. This translation process is taken care of behind the scenes by software. The reason domain names exist in the first place is because names are more convenient for people to use and easier to remember than numbers. Domain names are used for addressing hosts rather than IP addresses.

A third level can be defined to identify a particular host server at the Internet address. In our example, 'www' is the name of the server that handles Internet requests. (A second server might be called 'www2'.) A third level of domain name is not required. For example, the fully qualified domain name could have been "totalbaseball.com" and the server assumed.

Second-level domain names must be unique on the Internet and registered with one of the ICANN-accredited registrars for the COM, NET and ORG top-level domains. Where appropriate, a top-level domain name can be geographic. (Currently, most non-U.S. domain names use a top-level domain name based on the country the server is in.) To register a U. S. geographic domain name or a domain name under a country code, contact an appropriate registrar.

More than one domain name can be mapped to the same Internet address. This allows multiple individuals, businesses, and organisations to have separate Internet identities while sharing the same Internet server.

Top-level Domain Names :- On the Internet, a Top-Level domain (TLD) identifies the most general part of the domain name in an Internet address. A TLD is either a Generic Top-Level Domain (gTLD), such as 'com' for 'commercial,' 'edu' for 'educational,' and so forth, or a Country Code Top-Level Domain (ccTLD), such as 'fr' for France or 'is' for Iceland.

A second-level domain (SLD) is the portion of a Uniform Resource Locator (URL) that identifies the specific and unique administative owner associated with an IP address. The second-level domain name includes the top-level domain name. For example, in: whatis.com, 'what is' is a second-level domain. "whatis.com" is a second-level domain name (and includes the top-level domain name of 'com'). Second-level domains can be divided into further domain levels. These sub domains sometimes represent different computer servers within different departments. More than one second-level domain name can be used for the same IP address.

The top level domain names include country names and are known as Geographic Domains and type of organisations known as Non-Geographic

Domains. The geographically based top-level domains use two-letter country designations. For example, Us is used for the United States, .ca for Canada (not California), .uk for the United Kingdom or Great Britain, and .il for Israel. Each domain has a number of hosts. A few more examples are given in the following table:

Table 4.2

Abbreviation	Meaning
au	Australia
be	Belgium
ge	Germany
jp	Japan
mx	Mexico
nz	New Zealand
uk	United kingdom

Non-Geographic Domains: There are six common top-level domain types that are non-geographical:

- .com – for commercial organisations such as netcom.com, apple.com, sun.com,etc.
- .net– for network organisations, such as internic.net
- .gov –for parts of governments within the United States, such as nasa.gov, Oklahoma.gov. etc.
- .edu– for organisations of higher education, such as harvard.edu, ucdavis.edu, mit.edu. etc.
- .mil –for nonclassified military networks, such as army.mil,etc. (The classified networks are not connected to the wider Internet).
- .org –for organisations that do not otherwise fit the commercial or educational designations.
- .int –international organisation

The lowest level in the domain name system is the host name. Host names identify a computer on the Internet. For example, in the URL www.cse.iitd.ac.in, cse is the name of computer, iitd is the host name in the ac domain.

Host Name: In some instances, there are second-level domains delegated to organisations such as K-12 schools, community colleges, private schools, libraries, museums, as well as city and country governments. Examples of second-level domains are shown here:

- CC – Community colleges
- TEC – Technical colleges
- LIB – Libraries

- K12 – Kindergarten through 12th grade schools and districts
- STATE – State Government
- MUS – Museums

(iv) Uniform Resource Locator (URL)

Ans. URL (Uniform resource locator) indicates the unique address of a file that can be plain Web pages, other text documents, graphics, or programs on the World Wide Web. This is used by Web browsers, e-mail clients and other software to identify a network resource on the Internet. URL has a specific format: protocol://hostname/location of the resource. For example, URL for the B.Lib.Sc. Programme, Faculty of Library and Information Science that appears on the IGNOU is reproduced as follows:

http://www.ignou.ac.in/ignou/aboutignou/school/soss/programmes /detail/148/2.

When this URL is broken into its three constituent parts each appears as follows:

- protocol (http://),
- host name (www.ignou.ac.in) and
- ocation(/ignou/aboutignou/school/soss/programmes/detail/14 8/2).

Q10. Write short notes on the following in the context of Internet Security:

(1) User Authentication

Ans. Authentication in a computer system uses any of three qualities to authenticate the user:

- Something the user knows, like password, PIN numbers; pass phrases, a secret handshake, etc.
- Something the user has: Identity badges, physical keys, a driver's licence, or a uniform.
- Something the user is: This is based on the physical characteristic of the user (Biometries), such as a finger print, face recognition, voice recognition, etc.

Two or more methods can be combined for more solid authentication; for example, an identity card and PIN combination.

The computer system needs a system in place to be sure that only authorised users have access to its resources. On the computer system, one of the critical areas of security is who has access to what.

There are two types of access control that can be implemented:

- **Mandatory Access Control (MAC):** MAC is an access control policy that supports a system with highly secret or sensitive information. Government agencies typically use a MAC.

- **Discretionary Access Control (DAC):** DAC is an access control policy that uses the identity of the user or group that they belong to allow authorised access. It is discretionary in that the administrator can control who has access, to what and what type of access will they have, such as create or write, read, update, or delete.

Authentication occurs when a user provides the requested information to an authentication verification authority. The traditional method of authentication is to provide a password.

To increase the level of reliability, biometric authentication can be introduced. The user is not only identified digitally, but by their physical characteristics such as fingerprint scan, iris scans or hand geometry.

(2) Firewall

Ans. A firewall is a system designed to prevent unauthorised access to or from a private network. You can implement a firewall in either hardware or software form, or a combination of both. Firewalls prevent unauthorised internet users from accessing private networks connected to the internet, especially intranets. All messages entering or leaving the intranet (the local network to which you are connected) must pass through the firewall, which examines each message and blocks those that do not meet the specified security criteria.

A firewall refers to the concept of a security interface or gateway between a closed system or network and the outside Internet that blocks or manages communications in and out of the system. Basically, a firewall, working closely with a router program, examines each network packet to determine whether to forward it towards its destination. A firewall also includes or works with a proxy server that makes network requests on behalf of workstation users.

The firewall is often installed in a specially designated computer separate from the rest of the network so that no incoming request can get directly at private network resources. A number of companies make firewall products. The firewall facilitates features such as logging and reporting, automatic alarms at given thresholds of attack, and a graphical user interface for controlling the firewall. The following are the popular firewall software programs, which can be installed:

- **Personal Computer Firewall:** Black ICE Agent, e-safe Desktop, McAfee Internet Guard Dog, Norton Internet Security and Zone Alarm.
- **Office Firewalls:** D-Link Residential Gateway, Linksys Eatherfort cable, Netgear and Sonic wall.
- **Corporate Firewall:** Check Point, CISCO Secure PIX Firewall, e-Soft-Interceptor and Sonic Wall Pro.

(3) Proxy Servers **[Dec-2019, Q.No.-5 (e)]**

Ans. Proxy servers are application level firewalls. They are also sometimes referred to as application level gateways. Unlike packet level firewalls, proxy servers do not allow any direct communication between internal and external systems. Instead they act like language interpreters between two speakers who speak different languages. The speakers carry on the conversation but never speak to each other directly. They only speak to the interpreter who translates what is communicated in one language into the other. Proxy servers function exactly this way. An interpreter tries to do a precise translation of what is being said unmindful of harmful or desirable effects the conversation may have. But, the proxy servers also examine the incoming and outgoing information to ensure that the security rules of the organisation are adhered to. In that sense, the proxy servers perform certain additional function when compared to an interpreter. A typical proxy server configuration is shown in Fig.

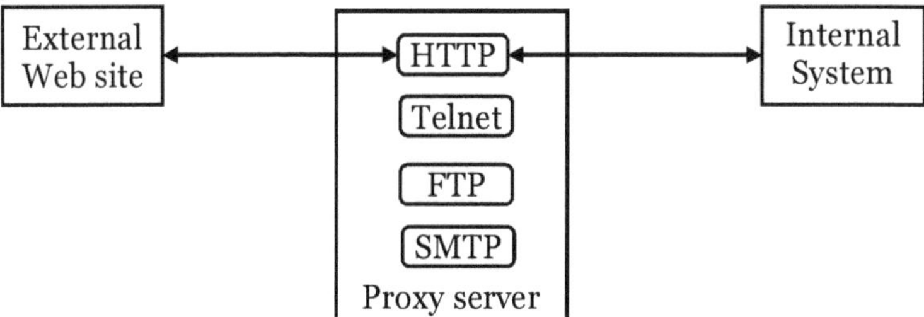

Fig. 4.2: Typical Proxy Server configuration

The proxy server shown in Fig. 12.4 supports four applications. viz. web access (HTTP), remote log in (Telnet), file transfer (FTP) and mail transfer (SMTP). A web access service connection is illustrated between an internal and an external system using hypertext transfer protocol (HTTP). Note that there is no direct connection between the internal system and the web site. The connection is via HTTP application in the proxy server. When the internal system wishes to access the web server, it sends a request to the proxy server. The proxy server, after ensuring compliance to the security rules formulates its own request to the web server. The web server replies to the proxy server and it does not even know the existence of an internal system. The proxy server examines the reply to ensure conformity to the security rules and then passes the reply on to the internal system. Thus all internal systems are protected from external systems.

(4) Data Encryption

Ans. Data encryption translates data into another form, or code, so that only people with access to a secret key (formally called a decryption key) or password can read it. Encrypted data is commonly referred to as ciphertext, while unencrypted data is called plaintext.

When the data reaches its destination, a key decodes the encrypted data into readable information. The following are the three elements associated with encryption system:

- A method of changing the data into code (algorithm);
- A hidden place to start the algorithm (key);
- Control of the key (Key management).

(5) Digital Certification

Ans. Digital certificate is an electronic credit card that establishes credentials for doing business or other transaction on the net. Digital certificates are issued by a government agency called "certification authority". This certificate contains user's name, a serial number, expiration date, a copy of the certificate holder's public key and the digital signature of the certificate-issuing authority. Digital certificates are similar to watermarks on a bank note. Digital certificates not only substantiate the authenticity of a message and its sender but also alert the recipient if the message was altered while in transit.

(6) Intrusion Detection System (IDS)

Ans. Intrusion Detection Systems are a combination of hardware and software systems that monitor and collect information and analyse it to detect attacks or intrusions. Some IDSs can automatically respond to an intrusion based on collected library of attack signatures. IDSs uses software based scanners, such as an Internet scanner; for vulnerability analysis. Intrusion detection software builds patterns of normal system usage; triggering an alarm any time when abnormal patterns occur.

(7) Virtual Private Network (VPN)

Ans. A virtual private network (VPN) is a private data network that makes use of the public telecommunication infrastructure, maintaining privacy through the use of a tunneling protocol and security procedures.

(8) Extranet

Ans. Extranet is a business-to-business intranet that allows limited, controlled, secure access between a company's intranet and designated, authenticated users from remote locations. It is a website tailored for use by your key business partners whether they are clients, suppliers or partners. It is normally available to a limited number of users who access the system using authentication method such as a username and password. It is developed to create a limited/customised link to your core computer systems for personnel who do not have direct access.

Q11. What are computer viruses and Anti-virus software? Discuss some tips to avoid viruses.

Ans. Computer Viruses: Computer virus is perverse software which causes a malicious activity. Computer virus is a relatively new phenomenon which has resulted mainly due to advancement in technology and accessibility of operating systems such as DOS. Previously, the operating system used to be secretive and hidden from the user. A user was supposed to submit his pack of PUNCHED CARDS containing a program which in turn was processed by the hardware (and propriety operating system). But with the advent of interactive computers and general purpose operating system people starlet working on machines with the idea "How to fail a computer" and hence came the concept of Computer Virus.

The term like 'Virus', 'Vaccine', 'Stoned', 'C Brain', 'Happy Birthday Joshi', 'Ping-Pong' are becoming increasingly popular. All these terms relate to the same problem. i.e., Computer Virus.

Viruses are inactive until infected applications are executed. A virus can also get activated when a computer is booted with a floppy disk that is infected by a boot sector virus. There are three main classes of virus:

- **File Infectors:** Some file infector viruses attach themselves to program files, usually selected .COM or .EXE files. Some can infect any program for which execution is requested, including .SYS, .OVL, .PRG, and .MNU files. When the program is loaded, the virus is sent as an attachment to an e-mail note.
- **System or boot-record infectors:** These viruses infect executable code found in certain system areas on a disk. They attach to the DOS boot sector on diskettes or the Master Boot Record on hard disks. A typical scenario is to receive a diskette from an innocent source that contains a boot disk virus. When the operating system is running, files on the diskette can be read without triggering the boot disk virus. However, if the diskette is left in the drive, and then the computer is turned-off or reload the operating system, the computer will look first in the A drive, find the diskette with its boot virus, load it, and make it temporarily impossible to use the hard disk.
- **Macro Viruses:** These are among the most common viruses, and they tend to do the least damage. Macro viruses infect Microsoft Word application and typically insert unwanted words or phrases.

  The best protection against a virus is to know the origin of each program or file that loaded into the computer or opened from the e-mail program. Since this is difficult, antivirus software can be bought that can screen e-mail attachments and also check all the files periodically and remove any viruses that are found.

Anti-Virus Software: Antivirus software was originally developed to detect and remove computer viruses, hence the name. Using anti-Virus software available in market. Some of these anti-virus software can be made memory resident and can be put in "AUTOEXEC.BAT" or

"CONFIG.SYS" such that they become functional soon after the computer is started. These memory resident programs try to detect the presence of offending code. In case the presence of offending code is detected the computer is halted and a warning message is flashed on the screen. Afterward the same software may be used to eliminate the detected virus from the computer. Also, certain watch dog or scan programs are available in the market. There programs regularly scan RAM and hard-disk for the presence of viruses. You must be cautions of bogus anti-viral programs that are actually viruses in disguise.

How to avoid Viruses: If you share floppies with others or download files from online services, there's no 100 per cent guarantee that you'll always be protected against viruses. To help reduce the risk of your computer being infected, follow these tips:

- Run an anti-virus programme and keep it updated often.
- Scan floppies that you suspect might be infected.
- Don't copy programmes from one computer to another. Use the original distribution diskettes to install programmes.
- Scan your system regularly with the full scanning engine.
- Avoid using floppies from unknown sources.
- Write-project your floppies by covering the notch on 5.25-inch disks or by sliding the little tab to expose the hole on 3.5-inch disks.
- Never boot your computers from unknown diskettes. If you do and you suspect there may be a virus on the diskette, shut the computer down. Boot up from a clean system diskette and check the system with an anti-virus programme.

Utilise your anti-virus programme's memory resident scanners to check all files as they are accessed, even from the Internet.

Q12. What do you mean by Search Engines?

Ans. Search engine is a tool for locating information from a collection. Search engines uses information about the information (such as metadata, catalogue) stored in the database to locate information. Sometimes they perform full text search within the document from first character to last character.

The search is done on pattern matching algorithm whether it is a database or full text. World Wide Web is a network of several information databases. In recent years, an exponential growth in these databases has made it difficult to locate a particular piece of information. Internet offers a powerful tool known as search engine to manage, filter and retrieve the information for their users.

A search engine can be defined as a tool for finding, classifying and storing information on various websites on the internet. It can help in locating information of relevance on a particular subject by using various search methods. In other words, it is an information retrieval system and assists in locating information on web.

Google and Yahoo! are Most Popular Search Engines: Search engines are also defined as online utilities that quickly search thousands of web documents for a word or phrase being searched. Although there are some subscription based search engines, most of them operate on profits from advertisements. It should be noted that no single search engine has the contents of every web page on the Internet. Instead, each search engine defines its scope in terms of contents for web pages that it would host. Moreover, some search engines index every word on every page. Others index only a part of the document. Full-text search engines generally pick up every word in the text except commonly occurring stop words such as 'a', 'an', 'the', 'is', 'and', 'or' and 'www'. Some of the search engines discriminate upper case from lower case; others store all words without reference to capitalisation. A user, therefore, gets different results from different search engines because of these reasons. Search engine are usually accessed using web clients called web browsers. Each search engine provide different search options and has its own peculiarities.

Q13. Discuss the evolution of search engines.

Ans. Internet has created revolutionary changes in this era of Information Technology. For many, it is one stop platform to find or locate any information they are interested in. Traditionally, librarians had the job to assist their users to locate the information they needed. But, now the scenario has changed a lot. Internet has in offer a variety of search tools such as search engines, search directories to locate the information on web.

A search on web is a simple process and can be conducted by simply issuing a query to the search tool. The search tool in return will look for the information in its web based information databases and retrieves those, which are relevant to the query. Searching is an iterative process, i.e. one needs to keep working on their query unless the exact information is located.

The very first tool used for searching on the Internet was Archie. The name stands for "archive" without the "v." It was created in 1990 by Alan Emtage, a student at McGill University in Montreal. Inspired with the success of Archie, the University of Nevada developed Veronica in 1993. VERONICA (Very Easy Rodent-Oriented Netwide Index to Computerised Archives) was developed at the University of Nevada to search all menu items on Gopher servers and Jughead (Jonsy's Universal Gopher Hierarchy Excavation And Display) were two other popular search programs.

Soon after launch of World Wide Web in 1993, the first robot, called World Wide Web Wanderer, was introduced by Matthew Gray to search the web. In October 1993, Artijn Koster developed an Archie-like Indexing tool for the web, called ALIWEB. It did not use a robot to collect the metadata, instead, it allowed users to submit the websites they wanted to be indexed by ALIWEB with their own descriptions and keywords. By December of 1993, three full-fledged robot-fed search engines had surfaced on the web. i.e., JumpStation, the World Wide Web Worm, and the Repository-Based Software Engineering (RBSE) spider. JumpStation gathered information about the title and header from web pages and retrieved them using a simple linear search. As the web grew, JumpStation slowed to a stop. The WWW Worm indexed titles and URLs. The JumpStation and the World Wide Web Worm did not use any ranking method to list their search results, results were listed in the order they were found. The RSBE spider did implement a ranking system.

The 'Excite' was a by-product of the project called Architext that was started in 1993 by six Stanford undergraduates. They used statistical analysis of word relationships to make searching more efficient. The Excite search software was released by mid-1993. However, the technique used by the Excite seems irrelevant because the spiders were not intelligent enough to understand what all the links meant. The EINet Galaxy Web Directory was launched in January, 1994. The EINet Galaxy became a success since it also contained Gopher and Telnet search features in addition to its web search feature.

In April 1994, David Filo and Jerry Yang created Yahoo as a collection of their favourite web pages. As their number of links grew, they had to reorganise and develop a searchable directory. The Yahoo directory provided description with each URL as an improvement to the Wanderer. Brian Pinkerton of the University of Washington launched the WebCrawler on April 20, 1994. It was the first crawler that indexed entire pages. In 1997, Excite bought out WebCrawler, and AOL began using Excite to power its NetFind. WebCrawler opened the door for many other services to follow the suit.

Three important search engines, namely Lycos, Infoseek and OpenText appeared soon after Web Crawler was launched. Lycos was the next major search engine developed at Carnegie Mellon University in July 1994. On July 20, 1994, Lycos was launched with a catalogue of 54,000 documents. In December 1995, Netscape started using Infoseek as its default search engine. AltaVista was also launched in December 1995. It brought many important features to the web searching. They were the first to allow natural language queries and advanced searching techniques.

The LookSmart directory commenced functioning in 1996. The Inktomi Corporation came about in May 1996 with its search engine called Hotbot. It was bought by Yahoo. Ask Jeeves was launched in April 1997 followed by the Northern Light.

1998 witnessed the launch of Google, the most powerful search engine till date. The Google ranks its pages based on number of inbound links to a page. Google has become so popular that major portals such as AOL and Yahoo have used Google to search their directories. In 1998, three major search engines and directories were launched, they were: MSN search, Open Directory and Direct Hit. Disney released the Go Network in 1999. Fast released its search technology in the same year, and was considered the closest competitor to Google. In 2000, the Teoma search engine was released, which uses clustering to organise sites by subject-specific popularity. In 2001, Ask Jeeves bought Teoma to replace the Direct Hit search engine.

LookSmart bought the WiseNut search engine in 2002 to power their new search product. In 2003, Google began to introduce semantic elements into its search product thereby bringing improvements in its search result, Overture purchased AllTheWeb and AltaVista. Yahoo bought Inktomi and Overture. In 2004, MSN dropped LookSmart in favour of Inktomi and Yahoo dumped Google in favour of its own search engine. Yahoo! has built a new database separate from the Inktomi database, that replaced both AltaVista and AllTheWeb in March 2004.

Q14. What are the various components of search engines?

Or

What is robot or spider? How does it work?

Ans. Search engine is a tool for locating information from a collection. Search engines uses information about the information (such as metadata, catalogue) stored in the database to locate information. Sometimes they perform full text search within the document from first character to last character. A typically search engine has the following three components:

(1) The Robot or Spider: A search engine spider, also known as a web crawler, is an Internet bot that crawls websites and stores information for the search engine to index. These programs move from one web page to another by visiting links embedded on each web page it finds and in the process builds an index to visited web pages. This process can be compared to citation searching, where a user follows a reference within a journal article to another article on the same topic. The spider is resident on a host computer and uses the HTTP. The search engine spider has one basic job and that is to crawl website content, capture information and take it back to the associated search engine. Once a bot is sent to your website it starts reading the text in the body of each web page. It also reads the HTML (source code) and discovers links to other web pages.

How it works: The basic objective of a search engine is to tell us where exactly a file or document is, that we are looking for. But before it does so, the same must be found from the hundreds of millions of Web pages that exist. To do this hunt, the search engine employs special software, called spider. These spiders build lists of the keywords found on websites. This process is called Web crawling. Web is a countless collection of documents, files and information connected together, just like a spider-web. The software designed for finding out the required information on the entire web is known as "Spider". The names and the working of search Spider on the Web are quite similar to the Web-spider.

When you enter the keywords for search, the spiders start its web-crawling. But how does any spider start its travels over the Web? Generally, the starting points are the most popular pages and the lists of heavily used servers. The spider will begin with a popular site, indexing the words on its pages and following every link found within the site. Following this pattern, the spider quickly begins to travel the web, spreading out across the most widely used potions.

(2) The Database: Robot or a spider harvest indexing information from web pages that it visited in its database or catalogue that lists URLs, titles, headers, words from title and text, first lines, abstracts, and full text. The robot performs search engine in a way that the most popular sites are found and indexed first. The resulting database, that stores millions of web pages, forms the index that is searched by the users. The size of this database determines the comprehensiveness of a search engine. Most search tools also create a separate database containing records consisting of a web page, URL, title and a summary. When a user retrieves results from a search tool, a summary record is displayed for the users.

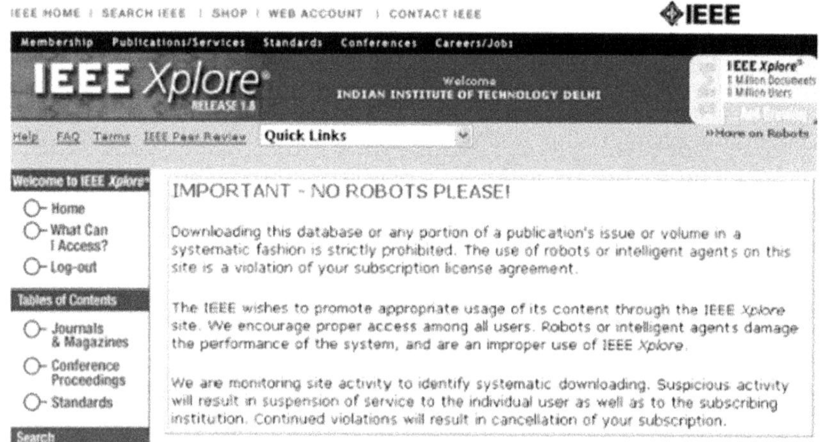

Fig. 4.3: IEEE Xplore with Instructions to Robots or Intelligent Agents Prohibiting Systematic Download of Contents from the Site

(3) The user Interface or the Agent: This is a software program that accepts queries from users and searches them through the database consisting of index of millions of pages. The agent program matches the query with the database, finds hits and ranks them in order of relevance and arranged it to present before the users.

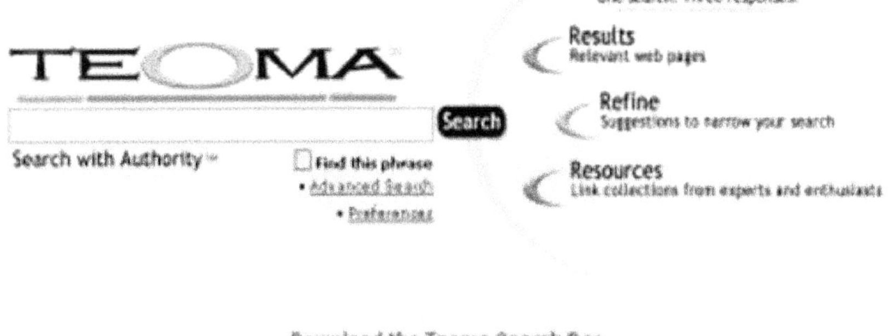

Fig. 4.4: Search Interface for TEOMA Search Engine

Q15. Explain primary search engines. Differentiate the different categories of primary search engines.

Ans. Primary search engines will generate the majority of the traffic to our web site, and as such will be the primary focus of your SEO efforts. Each primary search engine differs slightly from the others. For example, Lycos has been around much longer than Google, yet Google is the most popular search engine on the Web. Primary search engines are the most commonly used search engines. These vary to a great extent in terms of:

- **Database size:** Width and depth of websites indexed by their 'spiders'.
- **Database content:** Full-text or metadata. i.e., URL, keywords, title, description. etc.
- **Syntax used:** Word search, Boolean search, phrase search and other advanced features.
- **Ranking of results:** Paid sites, recent update, popularity. etc.

Primary search engines can also be divided into the following four categories according to the method their robots use for collecting information for their index databases:

- **Automated Robots:** The automated robots scan a large part of web wherever they are allowed.
- **Designated Robots:** The designated robots (like those used by ALIWEB or W3 catalogue) are programmed to scan only specific sites on the web rather than traverse the entire web. Sites using 'designated robots' provides users to submit their

websites to the search engine. On submission of a URL, the new URL gets added to the robot's queue of websites to be visited on its next foray out onto the web. Even if a user does not submit its site, a designated robot may pick it up from sites that provide a link to other sites.

- **Breadth-Oriented Search Engines:** Some robots concentrate more on top-level resources that tend to store larger subject-oriented index engines such as JumpStation II. A query conducted on "breadth-oriented search engines" would result in a fewer retrievals with a higher percentage of those being meta resources or subject portals.
- **Depth-Oriented Search Engines:** Depth-oriented robots (like web crawler) follow links to deeper levels. They pull out individual items located on a server's indexes and follow links to other servers. Depth-oriented robots have the tendency to retrieve duplicates or false hits also. Depth-oriented search engines have a tendency to catalogue too much information.

Q16. What do you mean by Meta Search Engines? Discuss.

Ans. Metadata in its broadest sense is data about data. The familiar library catalogue record could be described as metadata in that the catalogue record is 'data about data'. Similarly, database records from abstracting and indexing services are metadata (with a difference variation on location data). However, the term metadata is increasingly being used in the information world to specify records, which refer to digital resources available across a network. This means a metadata record refers to another piece of information capable of existing in a separate physical form from the metadata record itself. Metadata also differs from traditional catalogue data in that the location information is held within the record in such a way as to allow direct document delivery from appropriate application software, in other words the record may well contain detailed access information and the network address(s).

A meta search engine queries two or more search engines at the same time. It sends the results from the search engines back to you. Meta search engines do not have their own database or index web pages. They send their queries to search engines. The results from each search engine are combined. Duplicates (pages that are the same) are removed or merged. Pages are sometimes ranked in order of importance. Meta search engines are good for finding information quickly. They are best when keywords are used. You can use meta search engines to find out which search engines have the information you want. Meta search engines do not return all the pages found. They only return the top ten or so pages. This means you can miss good pages using a meta search engine. When you use a meta search engine, you tell it what search engines to use. Meta search engines use simple queries.

Most of these engines work on the principle of taking the highest ranking hits from the various engines they pass their requests on to, limiting that selection either by number of bits or sometimes by time elapsed in response. Results can then usually be grouped either by site, keyword, or other parameters, allowing the user to easily analyse what has appeared where and how it has been ranked. This is a very easy way of broadening coverage but minimising the effect of massive recall killing off precision: key: sites will hopefully appear in more than one system and thus be flagged up, but lesser-known sites should still appear on at least one system near the top if truly relevant. Among the most popular meta searchers are: all4one, All-inone, MetaCrawler, SavySearch, northerlight.com and cyber411. etc.

Q17. Describe the concept of 'Subject or Web Directories' as a category of search engine.

Ans. Web directories are a very common phenomenon over Internet. These are popular as they reduce the recall of search engine and increase the precision.

One can venture into the directory of any search engine and can experience increasing precision. The common example is seen searching for the term APPLE in search engines which also has a web directory. The search engine result brings the page related to APPLE as a fruit and APPLE computers. But the same search can be done using the directories of Agriculture and Computers separately. One can find now that whatever he is getting is only restricted to a particular directory. That means if the search is done in Agriculture directory the result output is only about the APPLE as ffuit not APPLE computer. It implies that if someone needs more precision in his/her search he should look for something, which searches, in a particular subject. That is what the Web Directories are doing today. They act as catalogues or guides. Directories help not only in searches but also organise the information available on WWW and provide the links. Quite a good number of Web Directories are available over the Internet.

The organisation of subjects is another issue. Mostly the web directories organise information in a hierarchical manner. The feature and organisation vary from one directory to the other.

Fig. 4.5: Web directory of Google

Web directories use hypertext links to the information resources they list. These links facilitate immediate browsing of the information resources from the directory listings.

Q18. Write short note on the followings:

(1) Hybrid Search Engine

Ans. Hybrid search engines use a combination of both crawler-based results and directory results. More and more search engines these days are moving to a hybrid-based model. Examples of hybrid search engines are:

- Yahoo (www.yahoo.com)
- Google (www.google.com)

(2) Subject Gateway or Subject Portals

Ans. Subject specific web search engines are known as subject gateways. Subject gateways are websites that compile complete information on various resources available on a particular subject. Subject gateways allow easier access to network-based resources in a given subject area. They provide a simple web-based interface for search and access to databases and indexes. They are subject-centric in the sense that they host only information related to a particular subject.

The compilation process is undertaken by information professionals and subject experts using well-established techniques to check and filter out the data and hence the information links shown by these services will in all probability be 100 per cent authentic.

The resources of high quality collected by the subject gateway experts are properly catalogued and classified using data organisation and classification schemes adopted and built on traditional and well-established principles of library science. In fact, subject gateways can be considered the Net equivalent of a library. The aim is to list and review the most important sites on the Web relevant to that subject.

The sites are usually peer-reviewed to ensure that the gateway is relevant and up-to-date. Being peer reviewed, it may avoid an important site that has recently appeared and has not yet been reviewed. Strengths include relevance, effectiveness and relatively high quality of content. Weaknesses are that they lack depth in their coverage of the subjects. Such sites are also called portals.

Q19. Enumerate the criteria of choosing a search engine.

Ans. Choosing a search engine depends on the results you're looking for, though there are some criteria that may be useful. These criteria include:

- **Browsability**— how easy is it to understand the results? Do you receive enough information from the retrieved results to make a decision about the usefulness of the results?
- **Customizability**— can you construct a sufficiently detailed search so as to eliminate or greatly reduce irrelevant results?
- **Relevance**— no matter how browsable or customisable, are the results returned relevant to your search?

For example, searching for some information on the Native American squash blossom design using WebCrawler will bring relevant results, but either OpenText or InfoSeek would be better first choices because they both give more information to help you determine relevancy.

Q20. Write a note on 'Searching Subject Directories'.

Ans. A subject directory is a service that offers a collection of links to Internet resources submitted by site creators or evaluators and organised into subject categories. Directory services use selection criteria for choosing links to include, though the selectivity varies among services.

Search directories are classified collections of documents. They are good for searching with a context. These directories are good for browsing. In subject directories, documents are pre classified by a person. Librarians' Internet Index; Google Directory; Yahoo!; dmoz are some of the examples of subject directories.

There are two basic types of directories:

- **Academic and Professional Directories:** These are often created and maintained by subject experts to support the needs of researchers. INFOMINE, from the University of California, is a good example of an academic directory.

- **Commercial Directories:** These cater to the needs of general public. Directories of Yahoo! and Google are examples of commercial directories.

Q21. Briefly discuss 'Searching Search Engines'.

Ans. World Wide Web is a network of several information databases. In recent years, an exponential growth in these databases has made it difficult to locate a particular piece of information. Internet offers a powerful tool known as search engine to manage, filter and retrieve the information for their users.

Search engines are automated tools for searching information from a collection using metadata stored in the database of search engine. In other words, it is an information retrieval system and assists in locating information on web.

Most search engines offer two types of interfaces to search their databases. i.e., basic search and advanced search. In a basic search, a user just keys-in his/her search term without sifting through pull-down menus for additional options. Full-featured search engines have options to expand or limit searches in a variety of ways. For example, in Lycos, the basic search assumes a Boolean 'or', which means that two or more terms will return results if any of the terms occur in documents indexed by Lycos. Option for 'Enhance Search' must be used to obtain more relevant and specific search results.

Basic Search: In a bibliographical information retrieval environment, searches can be divided into two main classes-known item search and unknown item search. A known item search is what is conducted when the user knows something about the item being sought. This may be any key, such as author, title, publisher, ISBN, and so on. An unknown item search is conducted when users are not aware of the existence of any document that may solve their problems. In other words, users do not know whether or not such an item exists that can meet their information requirements. There are different types of searches which are helpful to understand the entire process of search strategies.

Advanced Search or Refining your Search: Different search engines have different methods of refining queries. The best way to learn them is to read the help files on the search engine sites and practice. Options for advanced search differ from one search engine to another, but some of the common features include ability to search on more than one word, to confine the search to a specified field and to exclude words that are not required in a search by the user. A user may also search for proper names, phrases, and on words that are found within a certain proximity to other search terms. Some search engines also offer some degree of customisation of results. Several search engines allow the use of Boolean operators or signs like '+' or '_ ' to refine the search.

Boolean Operator: Logical AND, OR and NOT are known as Boolean operators. When Boolean operators are used for searching it is known as Boolean search. The operators are used for combining more than one word with certain conditions. These kind of searching also known as combinatorial search.

(1) Operator 'AND': This operator will retrieve all the documents which contains all the keywords occurring at both ends of the AND operator.

Syntax: <Search Term A>AND<Search Term B>

Example: Library AND Information

Output:

(i) The above query will retrieve only those documents which contains both the terms Library and Documentation

(ii) The precision in search is more. The number of documents retrieved will be less hence less is the recall value.

(2) Operator 'OR': This operator will retrieve all the documents which contains all the keywords occurring at both ends of the OR operator.

Syntax: OR

Example: Library OR Information

Output:

(i) The above query will retrieve all documents which contains both the terms Library and Documentation

(ii) The recall in search is more. The number of documents retrieved will be more but the precision in retrieved documents will be less.

(3) Operator 'NOT' or' AND NOT': These operators increase the precision of the search result. The query can be made more specific by using these operators. Using the capitalised AND NOT operator preceding a search term eliminates documents that contain that term. **Syntax** <Words to be searched>AND NOT <Words not to be searched

Example: If user is looking for information on Drivers and do not want documents that include information relating to the Screw Drivers the query could be "Driver" AND NOT Screw.

Phrase Searching: The ability to query on phrases is very important in a search engine. A phrase is a group of words that must appear next to each other in a specified order. Phrase searches are especially useful when searching the famous sayings or proper names. Most search engines support this feature. It can be used when the search terms appear in an exact order. To indicate a phrase, surround it in double quotation marks. For example the following searches can be made as phrases:

- "Web-based library services"
- "Bar code-based circulation services"

- "Mohan Das Karamchand Gandhi"

Phrase searching is one of best search features that can be used to increase the chance of retrieving relevant results.

Proximity Searching: Proximity Search This is another kind of Combinatorial search where the proximity of two words is checked. The term proximity means 'nearness of words'. Proximity is given in terms of number of words by which two words should be separated. There are two kinds of proximities:

- Near Proximity
- Exact Proximity

Parentheses: Most search engines permit the use of parentheses to group related terms. This is particularly useful for clustering synonyms or for searching specific terms together before other terms are searched. Parentheses may be used in combination with other search techniques. The example below indicates how to use this feature: (Library Computerisation or Library 'near' Automation) and India

Truncation Search: Truncation means concatenation of words. In other words, if the root string of the words is searched it brings all the derivatives derived out of the given root string. Truncation is of three types based on truncation techniques:

(1) Left Truncation: When the root string is concatenated from the left side, it is known as left truncation. For example, if the left truncation is implemented for the root string ISM, it will bring all the words which ends with the string ISM, like

- BRAHAMINISM
- COMMUNISM
- SUPHISM

(2) Right Truncation: When the root string is concatenated from the right side it is known as right truncation. For example, right truncation is used with the root string CLASS, it will bring all the words which starts with the root string CLASS, like

- CLASS
- CLASSIFICATION
- CLASSIFICATIONIST
- CLASSIFIER

Case Sensitive Search: One of the major features of search tools is their support to search words based on their case. In other words, search tools can differentiate between Upper and lower cases. For example, DUKE and duke will bring different search results based on the case. In an ordinary/plain search, search tool performs searching irrespective of their cases. However, if case sensitive search is invoked, search tool brings exact search string based on the case of search string.

Field Searching: Web pages are made up of different parts or 'fields'. Several search engines can limit a search to a specific area of a web page. This technique helps to increase the relevance of search results. The help section of search engines that support field searching would describe which fields can be searched. The actual field names may differ among search engines. The following fields are commonly supported:

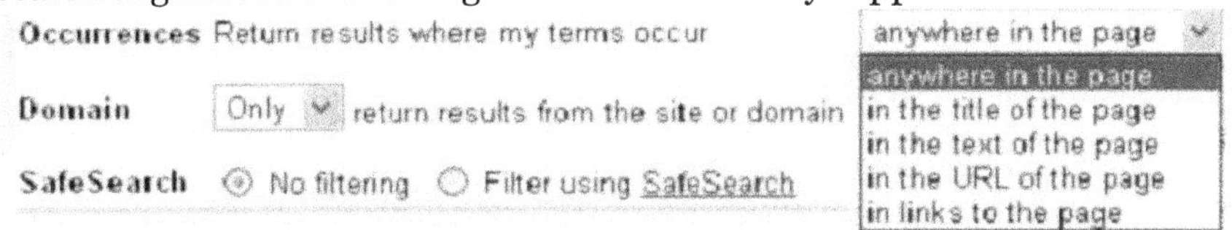

Fig. 4.6: Pull-down Menu in Advanced Google Search for Limiting Search to Specific Field in Document

Title Search: Finds pages that contain the given term in the page title (which appears in the title bar of most browsers).

Table 4.3

Command	Supported By	Examples
title:	Alta Vista, All The Web	title: automation
in title:/	Google	in title: automation
allintitle:	Google	allintitle:automation

URL Search: Looks for words that are parts of the URL (web address). For example: url: niscair, would look for URL having niscair in it.

Table 4.4

Command	Supported By	Examples
url.all:	All The Web	url.all:niscair
Allinurl:/inural:	Google	allinurl:niscair inurl:niscair

ink Search: Used for finding all the web pages that point to the given url.

Table 4.5

Command	Supported By	Examples
link:	Alta Vista, Google,	link:www. iitd.ac.in
	Northern Light	
linkdomain:	Inktomi, MSN	linkdomain:www.iitd.ac.in

Site Search: A user can restrict his or her query search within a domain. This can be helpful in obtaining highly relevant results from a specific site.

Table 4.6

Command	**Supported By**	**Examples**
host:	Alta Vista	Indest host:www.iitd.ac.in
site:	Excite, Google	Indest site:www.iitd.ac.in
domain:	Inktomi (HotBot)	Indest site: www.iitd.ac.in

File Types Search: Some search engines allow the user to restrict his or her search to a specified file format.

Table 4.7

Command	Supported By	Examples
Filetype	Google	Filet ype:pdf

Definition Search: This command allows searching for definition for a word or phrase.

Table 4.8

Command	Supported By	Examples
define:	Google	Define: search engine

Concept Searching: Unlike keyword search systems, concept-based search systems try to determine what a user means. In the best circumstances, a concept-based search returns hits on documents that are 'about' the subject/ theme that is being explored, even if the words in the document do not precisely match the query.

There are various methods of building up an algorithm for concept searching, some of them are highly complex, relying on sophisticated linguistic and artificial intelligence theories. Excite, for example, uses a numerical approach. Excite's software interprets meaning by calculating the frequency with which certain important words appear. When several words or phrases that are tagged to signal a particular concept appear close to each other in a text, the search engine concludes, by statistical analysis that the piece is 'about' a certain subject.

For example, the word heart, when used in the medical/ health context, is likely to appear with such words as coronary, artery, lung, stroke, cholesterol, pump, blood, attack and arteriosclerosis. If the word heart appears in a document with others words such as flowers, candy, love, passion and valentine, a very different context is established, and a concept-oriented search engine returns hits on the subject of romance. Concept-based searching is not supported by all search engines.

Natural Language Searching: The natural language searching feature allows a user to search in the same language as it is spoken. Suppose a user wants to know who was Jawaharlal Nehru. His/her query would be: "Who was Jawaharlal Nehru?". The search engine that supports this technique retrieves relevant web pages that would answer this question.

Q22. Explain the concept of 'Search Results'.

Ans. Search engines usually give us a list of best matches to least likely matches in descending order. The software has been designed to rank the sites in likely order of relevance. It does this by assigning a number to each word in a Web site title, address, and perhaps to all the words in a document. It's then a matter of matching numbers to our key words. Some programmes are more sophisticated than others.

Even if the search engine we are using does not allow limiting factors, such as Boolean logic, we will generally get the sites that are closest to our request first. This helps; however, we still may have to go through several dozen-site listings, depending on how specific our original key words were.

(1) Result Lists: Generally, we will receive a list of 10 to 15 sites. At the bottom of the list will be an option to click for more hits. The software may have a limit to how many sites it retrieves. It might give us the first 100 sites it found that matched our key words. There may still be other sites we would be interested in, however, they did not get listed. Some search engines allow us to change the amount of sites listed.

As search engines allow for specific requests that let us fine-tune our research, they will become more valuable. Many people use search engines but sift through countless lists of irrelevant sites. If we don't find one useful site in the first 50 listed, chances are that the search request we put in is not going to give us the results we are looking for. We should start all over again.

(2) Result Description: Result Descriptions: Some search engines offer descriptions of sites to help us determine whether the link is worth following. Others will include the first few paragraphs of a document. We might be able to choose the level of description we get with a listing. Many search engines simply give us a listing with little explanation.

The following table lists major search engines, directories, and archives with brief follow-on help for using them well. There have been major changes in most of the search engines in the past few months. To take full advantage of them, be sure to read their help files regularly. There is a great deal of information available on the web that the major search engines cannot find.

Table 4.9

Name	URL	Comment
Altavista	http://www.altavista.com	250+million pages and six million articles from 50,000 Usenet newsgroups. Full text search of pages. Good for academic research.
Excite	http://www.excite.com	130+ million pages

		and directories. Full text search.
Hotbot	http:www.hotbot.com	110+ million pages, WWW, Usenet newsgroups, most keywords on pages indexed.
Infoseek	http://www.infoseek.com	100+ million pages, web sites, but also images, newsgroups, faqs, news, companies, phone numbers and email addresses, current news and Directories.
Lycos	http://www.lycos.com	Directory, reviews of the best Web sites, browse-able by category and rated on a scale of 1-50.
Northern Light	http://www.northernlight.com	Search web sites, articles or a special collection (over 1 million articles from books, magazines, journals, newspapers etc). Sorts results by relevance, and removes duplicate links.
Webcrawler	http://www.webcrawler.com	Search web sites, usenet, gopher, ftp. Searches only titles, keywords and URL's.
Yahoo	http://www.yahoo.com	Directory, useful for browsing, general searching and locating popular sites. 14 broad categories (such as computers/internet, news and media, regional, society and culture).

(3) Relevance Ranking: Once a user finishes his search, the search engine retrieves results and displays the hits. How a search engine organises its findings varies greatly from search engine to search engine.

Most of the search engines return results with confidence or relevancy rankings. In other words, they list the hits according to how closely they think the results match the query. In spite of ranking methods used and advanced search facilities offered, users find thousands of websites as a result of their searches, many of them seem completely irrelevant.

Most search engines use frequency of keywords on a web page as a primary way of determining whether a document is relevant or not. A search engine will analyse how often keywords appear in relation to other words in a web page. Those with a higher frequency are often deemed more relevant than the others. Some search engines consider both the frequency and the positioning of keywords to determine its relevancy, considering that if keywords appear early in the document, or in the headers, it is likely that the document is more relevant. For example, one method is to rank hits according to how many times keywords appear and in which fields they appear (i.e., in headers, titles or in plain text). Links given by other websites is a popular method used for ranking of websites considering the fact that there are several other users that find the site useful and important.

As far as the user is concerned, relevance ranking is critical, and becomes more so as the sheer volume of information on the web grows. The user neither has patience nor time to go through scores of hits to determine which hyperlinks he/she should actually explore. A user would naturally prefer a search engine that provides more relevant sites in its first few results.

Q23. Define the Meta Tags.

Ans. We might be aware of, and perhaps may have used, search engines such as Google to look for web pages on a topic of interest. The META Tag comes in useful if you want your web page to be easily locatable by search engines. When you enter a search string, the search engine shows web pages containing that string, provided the web page has used those in META tag appropriately. The search engine interacts with the META tag of the HTML page in order to find the required string. Information inside a Meta element should be such as to describe the document. Consider the following example (Figure 2.10).

```
<HTML>
 <HEAD>
  <TITLE>IGNOU</TITLE>
  <META NAME = "author" CONTENT = "IGNOU">
  <META NAME = "description" CONTENT = "This website shows
you the different courses offered by
  IGNOU">
  <META NAME = "keywords" CONTENT = "Website, different
courses offered IGNOU, mca, bca">
  </HEAD>
  <BODY>
```

<P>

The meta attributes of this document identify the author and courses offered.

</P>

</BODY>

</HTML>

Different search engines look at meta tags in different ways. Some rely heavily on meta tags, others do not use them at all. Google, currently the most popular search engine, does not index the keywords in meta tags. The 'title' and the 'description' meta tags are considered important for websites, since several major search engines use them in their indices. Use of relevant keywords in title on different pages is important for the website. Unless the author of the web document specifies the keywords for his/her document, it is up to the search engine to determine them. Essentially, this means that search engines pull out and index words that appear to be significant. Since search engines are software programs, not rational human beings, they work according to the rules established by their designers for what words are usually important in a broad range of documents. The title of a page, for example, usually gives useful information about the subject of the page. Words that are mentioned at the beginning of a document are given more weightage by most search engines. The same goes for words that are repeated several times throughout the document.

Q24. Describe the evaluation of search engines.

Ans. As the Internet provides unlimited amounts of information that can be accessed with low effort and cost, search engine represents powerful tool that assists the Internet users in their interaction with the online environment (Liaw & Huang, 2006). A search engine is an information retrieval system with a set of programs with search tools used to perform searches (Liaw & Huang, 2003), designed, developed, and used for finding information from the web (Katz, 2010) using different strategies. Search engines perform the basic retrieval task including the acceptance of a query, a comparison with a database and the production of retrieved digital information such as text, audio, video, data and simulations (Rieger, 2009; Rowley, 1998). A search engine tool is a utility available in the Internet in which the user inputs specific name, subject, and/or key words for the purpose of retrieving a list of web links that match the user's query terms (Vaughan, 1999). The search engine facilitates the users to apply their criteria to a database to build a set of matches. The examples include Google, Yahoo!, AltaVista, Webcrawler, Lycos, Excite, Infoseek, Excite, HotBot, Bing, Ask, AOL, and other portal sites. Usually the search engine indexes with automatic software and the catalog is built manually with human input. Search engines gather web pages that form the universe from which the users retrieve information by issuing queries and the required information is retrieved by using information retrieval algorithms (Gordon & Pathak, 1999). Usually the search engines provide search services on the web based on directory services and query based (Liaw & Huang, 2003). The directory services (e.g. yahoo) provide a hierarchical organisation of resources developed by human cataloguers (Callery & Tracy-Proulx, 1997); the query based services (e.g., Excite) provide broad coverage of the Internet through intensive automation of query retrieval process (Jenkins et al., 1998). Users usually search for information trying to maximise the accuracy of search outcome with minimum effort exerted to acquire it (Bettman, 1979). It is important to focus on how end users interact with and evaluate their experience in using the search engines (Leroy et al., 2007). A framework for evaluating search engines is provided by Sutcliffe & Ennis (1998) consisting of four steps:

- Problem identification
- Need articulation
- Query formulation and
- Results evaluation.

During problem identification, a user realises the need to retrieve information; in the 'need articulation' stage the user consult external sources for the required information or formulate the terms (from the user's own domain knowledge) to search; during query formulation the user combines the terms in query suitable for a search engine; and finally during results evaluation stage the required information is compared with the retrieved information.

Though the user's interactions with search engines are often brief, users will form an opinion of the search engine and tools used (Spink et al., 2001) and these impressions form "mental models" resulting from the user's interactions with search engines (Johnson & Crudge, 2007). These mental models facilitate the users in evaluating the search engines and represent the user's evaluative view which can be used to understand the user-based criteria for evaluation. Some of the user-based/user-centered criteria are effectiveness, efficiency, interaction/usability, and overall satisfaction and/or success (Su, 2003a; Spink, 2002; Johnson et al., 2001). Effectiveness refers to the impact of users' interactions with search engines and usability refers to the capabilities of the search engine. In general, the criteria are diminishing the effort and cost of search and improving the decision-making process in using the search results (Haubl & Trifts, 2000). In particular, the following criteria are used for evaluating search engines:

- Value of the search results - major features (options that make the site unique, informative, and any value addition to the search results) - quality of retrieved items (proving current and authoritative information) (Jones & Timm, 2008) convenience of various search tools.

- Ability of search engines to locate information on the Internet.
- The usability of search tools (interface design -availability of basic and advanced search features with
- Instructions for effective searches - overall ease of use) (Su, 2003b; Vaughan, 1999) - most frequently applied measure effectiveness (number and precision or relevance of returned results) (Ziff-Davis, 1995)
- Search engines' capacity to retrieve the information that matches user's informational needs (Pan et al., 2007) comprehensiveness of the Web engines by number of documents indexed (Venditto, 1996)
- Search capability options, how the results were displayed (readability), update frequency of information (Courtois et al., 1995)
- Brows ability (ease of understanding results) -navigation (easy-to-use format for finding and viewing the information) (Jones & Timm, 2008)
- Customizability (ability to construct a search to weed out irrelevant results)
- Name (the name of the site), on-screen help, speed (response time/timeliness), database coverage, number of links, accessibility and others.

Q25. Discuss the criteria for evaluation of search engines for three different components.

Ans. Joe Barker, University of California has identified the following criteria for evaluation of search engines for the three different components:

(1) Database of Web Documents: Database of web documents Size of database:

(i) How many documents does the search engine claim it has?

(ii) How much of the total web are you able to search?

Currency or Up-to-date:

(i) Search engine databases consist of copies of web pages and other documents that were made when their crawlers or spiders last visited each site. How often is the database refreshed to find new pages?

(ii) How often do their crawlers update the copies of the web pages you are searching?

Indexing:

(i) Are there any provisions for use of controlled vocabulary?

(ii) Does it use a stop word list? How extensive it is? Is it documented as to what it identifies as a stop word?

Coverage:

(i) Types of resources indexed in the database of the search engine (ftp, www, newsgroup, etc)

(ii) Are there any special criteria for inclusion?

Completeness of Text:

(i) Is the database really "full" text, or only parts of the pages?

(ii) Is every word indexed?

Types of documents offered:

(i) All search engines offer web pages.

(ii) Do they also have extensive PDF, Word, Excel, PowerPoint, and other formats like WordPerfect?

(iii) Are they full-text searchable?

Speed and Consistency:

(i) How fast is it?

(ii) How consistent is it? Do you get different results at different times?

(2) Capabilities of a Search Engine

(i) All search engines let you enter some keywords and search on them. What happens inside?

(ii) Can you limit in ways that will increase your chances of finding what you are looking for?

Basic Search options and limitations:

(i) Automatic default of AND assumed between words?

(ii) Accepts " " to create phrases?

(iii) Is there an easy way to allow for synonyms and equivalent terms (OR searching)? Can you OR phrases or just single words?

Advanced Search options and limitations:

(i) Can you require your search terms in specific fields, such as the document title? Can you require some words in certain fields and others anywhere?

(ii) Can you restrict to documents only from a certain domain (org, edu, gov. etc.)? Limit to more than one or only one?

(iii) Can you limit by type of document (pdf or excel. etc.)? More than one?

(iv) Can you limit by language?

(v) How reliably and easily can you limit to date last updated?

General limitations and features:

(i) What do you have to do make it search on common or stop words?

(ii) Maximum limit on search terms or on search complexity?

(iii) Ability to search within previous results?
(iv) Can you count on consistent results from search to search and from day to day?
(v) Can you customise the search or display?
(vi) Is there a "family" filter? Does it work well? Is it easy to turn on or off?

(3) Results Display

(i) All search engines return a list of results it "thinks" are what you are looking for.
(ii) How well does it "think like you expect it think"?

Ranking:

(i) Are they ranked by popularity or relevancy or both?
(ii) Do pages with your words juxtaposed (like a phrase) rank highest?
(iii) Do you get pages with only some of your words, perhaps in addition to pages with them all?

Display:

(i) Are your keywords highlighted in context, showing excerpts from the web pages which caused the match?
(ii) Some other excerpt from the page?

Collapse pages from the same site:

(i) If it shows only one or a few pages from a site, does it show the one(s) with your terms?
(ii) How easy is it to see all from the site?
(iii) Can this be changed and saved as your preferred search method?

Q26. Briefly discuss various primary search engines.

Ans. A primary search engine is the type we think of most often when search engines come to mind. Some important primary search engines are as follows:

(1) Google (http://www.google.com/): Each of the major search engines differs in some small way. Google, is the king of search engines, in part because of the accuracy with which it can pull the results from a search query. Sure, Google offers all kinds of extras like e-mail, a personalised home page, and even productivity applications, but those value-added services are not what made Google popular. Google has become the pre-eminent web search engine for many, since it was launched in 1999. It has made its mark with its relevance ranking based on link analysis, cached pages, and aggressive growth. Since its beta release, it has had phrase searching. In June 2000 it announced a database of over 560 million pages, which grew to over 600 million by the end of 2000 and then to 1.5 billion by December 2001. The 2+ billion visits reported on their home page as of April 2002, includes indexed pages, unindexed URLs, and other file formats. By November 2002, they moved their claim up to 3 billion, and in July 2004 it went to 4.26 billion. The biggest strength of Google is the size of its database and link based relevance ranking.

Its database, besides web pages, includes additional file types such as PDF, .ps, .doc, .xls, .txt, .ppt, .rtf, .asp, .wpd and more. The Google also has a database of images, Usenet News group, paid advertisements that are usually shown on the right side under 'Sponsored Links' and web-based news sites.

Google supports Boolean searching, proximity searching, field searching, limit to file type, language and domain, character searching, numbers and number range searching. Results are sorted by relevance that is determined by links from other pages with a weightage given to authoritative sites. Pages are also clustered by site. Only two pages per site are displayed, with the second indented. The display includes the title, URL, a brief extract showing the text near the search terms, the file size, and for many hits a link to a cached copy of the page. This cached copy is from Google's index and may be older than the version currently available on the web. The cached copy will display highlighted search terms. If more than one search term is used, each has a different colour highlighting. The default output is 10 hits per screen, but the searcher can also choose 20, 30, 50, or 100 hits at a time on the preferences page.

(2) MSN Search (http://search.msn.com/): MSN's search capabilities aren't quite as mature as those of Yahoo! Or Google. As a result, MSN has not yet developed the in-depth link analysis capabilities of these other primary search engines. Instead, MSN relies heavily on web site content for ranking purpose. However, this may benefit new web sites that are trying to get listed in search engines.

The link-ranking capabilities of Google and Yahoo! Can preclude new websites from being listed for a period after they have been created. This is because (especially where Google is concerned) the quality of the link may be considered during ranking. New links are often ignored until they have been in place for a while.

Because MSN relies heavily on page content, a web site that is tagged properly and contains a good ratio of keywords will be more likely to be listed- and listed sooner- by the MSN search engine. Therefore, though it's not the most popular of search engines. MSN, is one of the primaries, and being listed there sooner rather than later will help increase our site traffic.

(3) Teoma (http://teoma.com/): Teoma (from Scottish Gaelic *teòma* "expert") was an Internet search engine founded in April 2000 by Professor Apostolos Gerasoulis and his colleagues at Rutgers University in New Jersey. The Teoma search engine was officially launched in April

2001. Ask Jeeves, Inc acquired Teoma on September 18, 2001. It lacks full Boolean and other advanced search features, but it has more recently expanded and improved its search features and added an advanced search. While Teoma results can show up in three separate sections, it has only one database of indexed web pages. It may also include paid ad results (from Google's AdWords database) under the heading of 'Sponsored Links'. No additional databases or portal features are directly available. Ask Jeeves switched to Teoma instead of Direct Hit in Jan. 2002 for the search engine results. Teoma supports Boolean searching, proximity searching, field searching and searches restricted to field in a limited way.

(4) WiseNut (http://wisenut.com/): WiseNut was a crawler-based search engine that officially launched on September 5, 2001. Like Teoma, WiseNut automatically clustered search results, a technology called *WiseGuide.*

Despite being referred to as a "Google killer" and having a good start, WiseNut never managed to become a major search engine. It lacked Boolean search in the standard search and other advanced search features. The company was based in San Francisco, California. WiseNut does have one partner site, Korea WiseNut. It supports proximity searching and search limits to languages. By default, sites are sorted in order of perceived relevance. There is no option for sorting alphabetically, by site, or by date. Results display title, 1 or 2 lines as it is, number of links to other matches from the same site and the URL. WiseNut clusters results by site, but aids the searcher by giving the number of other matches from the same site. Above the search results, WiseNut displays the query, total number of results, the WiseGuide categories, and then the first 10 results.

WiseNut offers a personalisation capability that allows users to control display of the number of records with or without summary, turn site clustering on or off, choose encoding scheme and turn WiseGuide categories on or off.

(5) Fast Search and Transfer (http://www.fastsearch.com/): Fast Search & Transfer (FAST) created the search engine and database for All the Web and Lycos. The web search unit of FAST was bought by Overture in February 2003. Launched in1999, Fast Search and Transfer, offered their Fast search engine at www.alltheweb.com. The first major expansion came in January 2000 with the appearance of their database on the Lycos site. Starting at 80 million URLs, Fast grew to 200 million by August 1999 and 300 million in January 2000. They passed 2 billion in June 2002. The search engine plans to index all the public, indexable web.

The FAST Search interface consists merely of a navigation bar and a search entry box and a number of links at the page bottom. There is very little in the way of advertising on any of the site's pages. The Advanced

Search interface is different only in so far as it provides additional options for the searcher.

(6) Alta Vista (http://www.altavista.com/): AltaVista, a business of Overture Services, Inc., is a leading provider of search services and technology. AltaVista, which means "a view from above", was launched in1995 when scientists at Digital Equipment Corporation's Research lab in Palo Alto, CA, devised a way to store every word of every HTML page on the Internet in a fast, searchable index. This led to AltaVista's development as the first searchable, full-text database on the World Wide Web. Other notable AltaVista inventions include the first-ever multilingual search capability on the Internet and the first search technology to support Chinese, Japanese and Korean languages.

The Alta Vista was the first Internet search engine to launch image, audio and video search capabilities. It was the first search engine that offered advanced search features and capabilities like multimedia search, translation, language recognition and specialty search. The Alta Vista allows users to perform simple or complex searches and has speedy retrieval times and well-developed robot technology. If no connector is used in the search, the default is 'or.' Truncation is possible. A user can limit his/her search to a field, URL, title and links. The link search retrieves pages where at least one link represented on that page matches the search query. Advanced searching is also available by using Boolean operators and adjacency symbols. The search engine supports proximity operators and parentheses for nesting.

Web pages are evaluated for relevance. i.e., its ranking system is not as effective as that of other search engines because it indexes any and all references to a search term, no matter how far off it may be from the query's intent. Its search engine does not allow truncation as other search engines do, which means that searches are performed only on the exact phrase. i.e., plurals and other forms of words are left out. However, if a document is found in the search, a user can be sure that his/her search terms are somewhere in it. Alta Vista also provides dates in its results list. Although a user can refine his/her search by using the Power Search option, Alta Vista does not have as much on-screen help as other search engines. Alta Vista allows a user to bookmark results, making future site visits much easier.

(7) Go.com (http://www.go.com/): Formerly InfoSeek, Go.com is owned by the Walt Disney Internet Group (WDIG) and powered by the Google search engine. It is a free directory and keyword searchable service. A user can browse the directory for various topics and subtopics or look for specific information through its search interface. Go.com indexes over 1 million web pages. It also indexes Usenet newsgroups, FTP and Gopher sites, e-mail addresses, and Frequently Asked Questions lists. Search features are similar to Google Advanced Search and include

Boolean search with AND, OR and NOT. It supports phrase searching and proximity searching. Results are ranked by relevancy and include that ranking, a link to the site of the information, the URL of the site, the size of the document, some description of the document, and a link to similar pages. A user can bookmark results, making return visits to the sites much easier.

(8) Lycos (http://www.lycos.com/): Back in December of 1995, Lycos claimed to have indexed 92 per cent of the web. Now, it claims to be the only complete guide to the Internet. Lycos graduated from being simply a keyword searchable index to adding a directory, which goes by the name of A2Z. Lycos also provides a service called Point, which provides reviews and ratings of the top 5 per cent of all the Internet sites they index. Lycos searches every word in a website. The advanced search features include Boolean searches through a pull-down menu. i.e., any of the word, all of the word and none of the word. Searches can be restricted to desired locations in web pages. i.e., title, description, body or the URL. A search can also be restricted to a language. A user can also choose the level of relevancy of the search. Display options range from showing 10-40 results per page in either standard, summary or detailed form. Standard display includes a link to the document, the relevancy ranking, an outline, an abstract, the URL, and the size of the document.

(9) Excite (http://www.excite.com/): This search engine offers two ways of searching: concept or keyword. Many times there are no significant differences between the results of two types of searches. There is no Boolean searching, so trying to find specific information on a topic can be frustrating. The Excite offers a user to choose for a directory search (like Yahoo!) or a keyword search. The entire database is checked and updated weekly by spiders that are sent out on specific missions: One is sent to the What's New sites to compile a database of new URLs. Another is then sent out to bring back the page contents to the Excite database.

Q27. Describe various important web directories.

Ans. Some important web directories are as follows:

(1) Yahoo! (http://www.yahoo.com/): Yahoo! is an American web services provider headquartered in Sunnyvale, California, and owned by Verizon Media. Yahoo! is one of the best known and most popular Internet portals. Originally just a subject directory, it is now a search engine, directory and portal. A search on Yahoo! provides search results that include a few categories from the directory and Inside Yahoo!, followed by sponsored links (ads), and then the bulk of the results based on an Inktomi database. Yahoo is also backed-up with an Image database, Yellow Pages, Products and a News database. Yahoo supports Boolean searching, proximity searching, field searching, limits to language, domain, date, filetype, country and adult content. However, some advanced features such as truncation is not supported.

Results are sorted by a relevance algorithm. Pages are also clustered by site. Only one page per site is displayed. Others are available via "More pages from this site link" after the cached link at the end of the record. Yahoo! provides results in six categories. The first lists of results under web are from the search engine with the page title, a keyword in context extract (or directory description or meta description), the URL, file size, cache link, and a possibly "a More pages from this site link". The second tab is a link to their image database. The Yahoo! directory results are available under the Directory heading. The Yellow Pages tab goes to a Yellow Pages search form. The News tab goes to the Yahoo! News database while the Products tab, goes to the Yahoo! Shopping search.

(2) LookSmart (http://www.looksmart.com/): LookSmart is one of the larger and better-known directories. It is used by AltaVista, AltaVista Australia, Anzwers, MSN Search, and Go2Net. LookSmart has over 2.3 million unique URLs according to the company with 250,000 categories and 200 editors. In addition to the LookSmart database, Direct Hit results are also available via a "Top 10 Most Visited" link. If no hits are found in LookSmart, results from AltaVista are shown, and these may include RealNames results as well. LookSmart Live is a service more than a database that offers personalised email responses to questions. Some prominent search services that use the LookSmart directory include AltaVista, Anzwers, MSN Search, Netscape, Excite, and Go2Net. LookSmart supports Boolean searching and automatic truncation. It does not support phrase searching, proximity operators, limits to field search. etc.

The sites appear to be sorted randomly, but they may be ordered by relevance. If a LookSmart search fails to find any hits in LookSmart directory, the search is automatically passed on to AltaVista. While this can be handy, it is rarely as effective as a well-structured search run directly on AltaVista. LookSmart first displays categories that contain matches. Then sites are displayed with their title hyperlinked to the URL, a two-line description, and a linked connection to the category in which the site is listed. After the sites, results from AltaVista are displayed.

(3) D MOZ Open Directory Project (http://dmoz.org/): The Open Directory Project, formerly known as NewHoo, is owned by Netscape but is run by volunteer editors. Entries in the Directory are all selected by the editorial team of over 30,800 editors. Many entries come from submissions. Open Directory has over 2,152,000 unique entries divided into over 314,000 categories and subcategories. The Open Directory as seen at http://dmoz.org/is only one database. Partners using the Open Directory include AltaVista, Netscape, Lycos, HotBot, and others. D MOZ Open directory supports Boolean searching and truncation, It does not support proximity searching, phrase searching and field searching.

Categories in DMOZ Open Directory are presented first if they match or sometimes if they contain records that match. Then sites are listed, presumably in order by some relevance score, but the method of ranking is not described. Open Directory first displays up to five categories. Then sites are displayed with their titles hyperlinked to the respective URLs, a brief description, a linked connection to the category in which the site is listed, and a number in parentheses.

(4) Galaxy (http://www.galaxy.com/): The Galaxy is another hierarchical, topically organised search engine. Each topic has its own page in the Galaxy, and each page is organised into many lists. For example, the Topic Lists page provides links to other Galaxy pages containing specific information about the search topic. Search results consist of a series of indexes from which to choose. One can search on the full word or on the acronym on the Galaxy. Boolean 'and', 'or' and 'not' can be used to refine the search process. The advanced search in Galaxy provides for restricting the search to title, description, body or other locations in a page. A user can also restrict his or her search on a domain name. Galaxy provides for phrase searching and a user can define search depth to medium, shallow, deepest and surface.

The Galaxy has a link called "You can add information to this page!". Clicking on it brings up a form which can be used to add references to an existing page, or send comments to Galaxy staff. Each index provides its own results, which are scored according to the frequency with which specified keywords are found.

Q28. Describe briefly some important meta search engines.

Ans. Some important meta search engines are as follows:

(1) Web Crawler (http://www.webcrawler.com/): A web crawler (also known as a web spider or web robot) is a program or automated script which browses the World Wide Web in a methodical, automated manner. This process is called Web crawling or spidering. Many legitimate sites, in particular search engines, use spidering as a means of providing up-to-date data. Web crawlers are mainly used to create a copy of all the visited pages for later processing by a search engine, that will index the downloaded pages to provide fast searches. Crawlers can also be used for automating maintenance tasks on a Web site, such as checking links or validating HTML code.

Also, crawlers can be used to gather specific types of information from Web pages, such as harvesting e-mail addresses (usually for spam).

(2) HotBot (http://www.hotbot.com/): ***HotBot*** is a VPN provider and a former search engine. Originally, it just used the Inktomi database and then added Direct Hit and the Open Directory. In December 2002, it was re-launched as a multiple search engine with Inktomi, Fast, Google and Teoma. HotBot also uses other primary search engines to conduct searches. HotBot offers the choice of three search engine databases, namely HotBot (which is actually a Yahoo!/Inktomi database), Google and Ask Jeeves (the Teoma database). A user can switch between these databases with a simple click of button. Sponsored links on the top come from Overture while the side ones may come from other advertisers. While HotBot (Inktomi) includes some PDF, MS Word, PowerPoint, and Excel files, there is no limit for searching them. HotBot supports Boolean searching, proximity searching, field searching, limits to language, file types, page content, domain name, region, date. etc. Results are sorted by relevance. However, only a limited number of results per domain are displayed, often two to four. The display includes the relevance score, title, URL, a brief extract, and date. HotBot displays 10 records at a time, by default. However, users can request display of 10, 25, 50, 75, or 100 records at a time. More search engines should give such options.

(3) MetaCrawler (http://www.metacrawler.com/): MetaCrawler is a search engine. It is a registered trademark of InfoSpace and was created by Aaron Collins. MetaCrawler is a search service that has no internal databases. It simply acts as a front end for 9 different search engines: OpenText, WebCrawler, Inktomi, Alta Vista, InfoSeek, Yahoo, Lycos, Excite and Galaxy. MetaCrawler sends the query from a user to the search engines, then puts them into a uniform format for display. The search screen offers a number of options. There is the usual search line but beneath it are 3 search options: search as a phrase, search all these words, search any of these words. Below these search options are options to limit by regions of the world, by type of site, by the maximum amount of time you want to wait for results and by the minimum score. The results display the title of the document, selected text or an abstract (depending on the search engine), the relevancy ranking, the URL, and the search engine from which the information came.

(4) Ask Jeeves (http://www.askjeeves.com): Ask Jeeves initially gained fame in 1998 and 1999 as being the 'natural language' search engine that facilitates search by asking questions and responds with what seemed to be the right answer to everything. In reality, technology was not what made Ask Jeeves perform so well. Behind the scenes, the company at one point had about 100 editors who monitored search logs. They then went out onto the web and located what seemed to be the best sites to match the most popular queries. Today, Ask Jeeves instead depends on crawler-based technology to provide results to its users. These results come from the Teoma search engine that it owns.

(5) SavvySearch (http://www.search.com/): SavvySearch is a search tool that provides a common interface for searching a variety of search engines. A user may enter his/her search on the query line and it sends the query to multiple search engines. It ranks search engines by a number of factors, including how appropriate they might be and how fast is the response time. The search results are integrated and duplicate results are removed. To perform a search, a user needs to enter the search words, choose 'and', 'or', or 'adjacency' operators from the query options, choose the number of results to be returned from each search engine, choose the display format, opt for integrating the results and click at 'Search'. Since it is searching more than one search engine, a user may have to wait longer than when he/she is using a single search engine. The normal display provides most of the standard display for the specific search engine providing the results. SavvySearch lists the name of the search engine providing the results. SavvySearch is currently available in 18 different languages.

Q29. What are the important subject portals or subject gateways? Briefly explain.

Ans. One of the most interesting, logical developments has been the rise of specialist index or gateway. These are directories of Internet resources in particular subject areas, compiled and organised by specialists and information professionals in their respective fields, which typically represent the best of sites available in the field concerned. Some of the important subject portals or subject gateways are given below:

(1) LibrarySpot.com (http://www.libraryspot.com/): LibrarySpot.com, published by StartSpot Mediaworks, Inc., is an award-winning 24-hour virtual library resource center for educators and students, librarians and their patrons, families, businesses and anyone exploring the Web for valuable research information. LibrarySpot.com aims at breaking through the information overload of the web and bring the best library and reference sites together. Sites featured on LibrarySpot.com are hand-selected and reviewed by an editorial team for their exceptional quality, content and utility. Published by StartSpot Mediaworks, Inc. in the Northwestern University/Evanston Research Park, LibrarySpot is the first in a family of vertical information portals designed to make finding the best topical information on the Internet a quick, easy and enjoyable experience. The LibrarySpot.com has received more than 30 awards and honours. Most recently, Forbes.com selected LibrarySpot.com as a 'Forbes Favourite' site, the best in the reference category, and PC Magazine named it one of the top 100 websites. LibrarySpot.com has been featured on CNN, Good Morning America, CNBC and in many other media outlets.

(2) Librarians' Index to the Internet (LII) (http://lii.org/): The Librarians' Index to the Internet is a searchable subject directory of some 10,000 web sites. Free e-mail subscription to the LII New This Week (http://www.lii.org/search/ntw) incorporates most recent resources added to the LII. It has close to 12,000 subscribers in 85 countries. ILL also offers co-branding service to the libraries that are members of the Library of California. The site provides both browsing and searching interfaces.

(3) Argus Clearing House (http://www.clearinghouse.net/): The Argus Clearinghouse provides a central access point for value-added topical guides which identify, describe, and evaluate Internet-based information resources. The Argus Clearinghouse is a non-profit venture run by a small group of dedicated individuals. It is intended to be a resource that brings together finding aids for students, researchers, educators, and others interested in locating authoritative information on the Internet.

(4) Vlib: The Virtual Library (http://www.vlib.org/): The Virtual Library is the oldest catalogue of the web, started by Tim Berners-Lee, the creator of html and the web itself. Unlike commercial catalogues, it is run by a loose confederation of volunteers, who compile pages of key links for particular areas in which they are expert; even though it isn't the biggest index of the web. The Virtual Library pages are widely recognised as being amongst the highest-quality guides to particular sections of the web. Individual indexes live on hundreds of different servers around the world. A set of catalogue pages linking these pages is maintained at http://vlib.org. Mirrors of the catalogue are kept at East Anglia (UK), Geneva (Switzerland) and Argentina. Each maintainer is responsible for the content of their own pages, as long as they follow certain guidelines. The central affairs of the VL are now coordinated by a newly-elected Council.

(5) Academic Info (http://www.academicinfo.com/): Academic Info, online since 1998, began as an independent Internet subject directory owned by Michael Madin and maintained with the assistance of a quality group of subject specialists. In the spring of 2000 Michael left the University of Washington Gallagher Law Library to focus solely on Academic Info. In 2002 Academic Info became a registered non-profit organisation of the State of Washington. Academic Info is now ad-free and relies on donations to remain online. Academic Info aims to be the premier educational gateway to online high school, college and research level Internet resources. The primary focus of the site is academic, with its intended audience at the upper high school level or above. A priority is adding digital collections from libraries, museums, and academic organisations and sites offering unique online content. The current focus is on English language resources but selectively sites in other languages will be considered.

(6) BUBL (http://bubl.ac.uk/): BUBL LINK is the catalogue of selected Internet resources covering all academic subject areas and catalogued according to DDC (Dewey Decimal Classification). All items are selected, evaluated, catalogued and described. Links are checked and fixed each month. LINK stands for Libraries of Networked Knowledge. BUBL 5:15 provides an alternative interface to this catalogue, based on subject terms rather than DDC. The aim is to guarantee at least 5 relevant resources for every subject included, and a maximum of 15 resources for most subjects, hence the name 5:15. Big subject areas are broken down into smaller categories. However, the upper limit of 15 is not rigidly applied, so there may be up to 35 items for some subjects. The subject terms used in BUBL LINK/5:15 were originally based on LCSH (Library of Congress Subject Headings) but have been heavily customised and expanded to suit the content of the service. The aim is to make it very easy to locate Internet information about a large number of subjects. The BUBL LINK catalogue currently holds over 11,000 resources. This is far smaller than the databases held by major search engines, but it can provide a more effective route to information for many subjects, across all disciplines.

(7) BIOME (http://biome.ac.uk/): BIOME is a collection of gateways, which provide access to evaluated, quality Internet resources in the health and life sciences, aimed at students, researchers, academics and practitioners. A core team of information specialists and subject experts based at the University of Nottingham Greenfield Medical Library creates BIOME. The Internet resources are selected for their quality and relevance to a particular target audience. They are then reviewed and resource descriptions created, which are stored, generally with the associated metadata, and generally in a structured database. The consequence of this effort is to improve the recall and especially the precision, of Internet searches for a particular group of users. BIOME is a hub within the Resource Discovery Network (RDN) (http://www.rdn.ac.uk), and is funded by the Joint Information Systems Committee (JISC) (http://www.jisc.ac.uk/). There are five dedicated subject services (gateways) within BIOME, each covering a specific area within the health and life sciences. These gateways are AgriFor, VetGate, OMNI, Natural Selection and Bio Research.

(8) Edinburgh Engineering Virtual Library (EEVL) (http://www.eevl.ac.uk): Edinburgh Engineering Virtual Library (EEVL) is an award-winning free service, which provides quick and reliable access to the best engineering, mathematics, and computing information available on the Internet. It is created and run by a team of information specialists from a number of universities and institutions in the UK for students, staff and researchers in higher and further education, as well as anyone else working, studying or looking for information in Engineering, Mathematics and Computing. EEVL provides a central access point to networked engineering, mathematics and computing information. Resources being added to the catalogues are selected, catalogued, classified and subject indexed by experts to ensure that only current, high-quality and useful resources are included. They include e-journals, databases, training materials, professional societies, university and college departments, research projects, bibliographic databases, software, information services and recruitment agencies.

EEVL, in addition to Internet Resource Catalogues, provides targeted engineering search engines - to UK engineering sites, to engineering e-journals, engineering newsgroups, and to specialised information services, such as the Recent Advances in Manufacturing (RAM) bibliographic database, and the Offshore Engineering Information Service. MathGate at EEVL is involved in the Secondary Homepages Project for UK Mathematics Departments. EEVL's scope is limited to the three subjects, and is therefore more focussed than the big search engines. Searching EEVL will retrieve high quality resources, but because EEVL's resources are handpicked, the number of sources covered in it is not comparable to the number of Internet search engines.

(9) Social Science Information Gateway (SOSIG) (http://sosig.ac.uk/): The Social Science Information Gateway (SOSIG) is a freely available Internet service which aims to provide a trusted source of selected, high quality Internet information for students, academics, researchers and practitioners in the social sciences, business and law. It is part of the UK Resource Discovery Network. The SOSIG Internet Catalogue is an online database of high quality Internet resources. It offers users the chance to read descriptions of resources available over the Internet and to access those resources directly. The catalogue points to thousands of resources, and each one has been selected and described by a librarian or academician. The catalogue is browsable or searchable by subject area. Social Science Search Engine is a database of over 50,000 Social Science web pages. Whereas subject experts have selected the resources found in the SOSIG Internet Catalogue, those in the Social Science Search Engine have been collected by software called a 'harvester' (similar mechanisms may be referred to as 'robots' or 'web crawlers'). All the pages collected stem from the main Internet catalogue and this provides the equivalent of a social science search engine.

Q30. Define the term 'World Wide Web'. Explain the importance of the Web.

Or

What is world wide web? Discuss, its features and working.

[June-2018, Q.No.-4.1]

Ans. The World Wide Web (WWW), commonly known as the Web, is an information system where documents and other web resources are identified by Uniform Resource Locators (URLs, such as https://www.gullybaba.com/), which may be interlinked by hypertext, and are accessible over the Internet. The resources of the WWW are transferred via the Hypertext Transfer Protocol (HTTP) and may be accessed by users by a software application called a web browser and are published by a software application called a web server. English scientist Tim Berners-Lee first developed the World Wide Web in 1989 while working at CERN, European Particle Physics Laboratory in Switzerland, and has since become the most powerful, and popular, resource discovery tool on the Internet.

Importance of the Web: The World Wide Web is important for libraries because it provides an extremely powerful method of organising, and providing access to, information. It can provide one interface to a large variety of network information resources and systems. With the Web and its browsers libraries can:

- Electronically publish anything that they now publish on paper.
- Provide access to in-house hypertext documents or to hypertext documents available out on the Internet.
- Create electronic orientation services with floor maps and descriptions of services.
- Provide access to Internet tools such TELNET, gopher, FTP, and WAIS through a single interface.
- Create interfaces to in-house databases or bibliographies.
- Collect information from patrons through the forms feature.

With all its power, the Web is the most serious step yet towards creating electronic libraries. It provides a mechanism to present a wide variety of information resources to library users-and all Internet users-in a simple, efficient and effective manner.

(1) The Web is a hypertext system: In contrast to the hierarchical menu system used by earlier Internal tools such as Gopher, etc, the Web is a hypertext system, in which users move from one document to related documents through embedded links, such as a word or a phrase that, when selected, calls up another document on that topic. Instead of moving from menu to menu, as in Gopher, users of the Web can jump directly from document to document by clinking on hypertext links.

(2) The Web is a multimedia system: Before graphical Web browsers (e.g., Mosaic and Netscape, etc), most of the information available on the Internet was in the form of ASCII text - simple text devoid of any elements common to the printed page, such as large titles, italics, pictures, and other graphical content. With the advent of graphical browsers, however, the Web has become a multimedia system, combining many different types of media into one document. Specifically, web documents can contain:

(a) Normal text

(b) Features such as large fonts, bold, italics, indents

(c) Images such as pictures, graphics, fancy logos, illustrations

(d) Audio content such as sounds, music, commentary, voice messages

(e) Video content such as movie clips, animations, or computer generated simulations.

(3) The Web is a distributed system: Normally, the documents in a hypertext system reside in one place, such as on a hard drive or a CD-ROM. Documents on the Web, by contrast, can be located not only on a local machine, but also on any machine on the network whether next door, across a city, or around the world. From the perspective of the user, one set of related documents may appear to reside in one location, but in reality, the successive pages they read may have been requested from anywhere in the world. In this way, the Web is a distributed hypertext system because the Web documents are distributed throughout the network.

(4) The Web incorporates other Internet tools: The Web can provide links to other types of Internet tools, such as WAIS, Gopher, FTP and TELNET. One Web page on a particular topic, for example, can point to other relevant information resources on the network, regardless of whether that information is available on a gopher, through TELNET, or at an FTP site. In this way, the Web and its browsers become a method to seamlessly provide access to information available through many different Internet tools.

(5) The Web provides an interface to other database systems. A particularly powerful features of the Web is that it can act as an interfaces to database systems connected to the Internet (e.g., WAIS, Z39.50 and library databases). Three elements are needed to create this interface. First, a Web browser which is used to collect information from the user through the forms processing feature - a method of creating interactive boxes on a Web page into which users can type information, or select among alternatives. Second, a database system of some sort, like a library catalogue. And third, a control gateway interface (CGI) that sits between the Web browser and database. It takes the information gathered from the Web browser and passes it on to the database. Once the request is processed, the CGI passes the results back to the Web browser in a format that it can display.

Q31. Write short note on the followings.

(1) Client- Server Architecture

Ans. Like most Internet tools, the Web adheres to the client-server model in which two separate software programmes-really, two complementary halves of one system work together to perform some specific task. The software on the user's computer is the client, while the software on the remote computer is the server. In the case of the Web, the task is to explore hypertext documents and examine information resources. The Web client does the job of asking for, and displaying electronic documents, and the Web server does the job of storing and sending electronic documents to the client.

(2) Hypertext Transfer Protocol (HTTP):

Ans. In order to communicate through the network, clients and servers need a common language, and the common language within the Web is Hypertext Transfer Protocol, or HTTP. It is a fairly simple protocol, like the Gopher protocol, in which a document and its elements (e.g., text and images) are transferred through separate, brief network connections. Once all the needed parts of a document arrive, the connection is broken and there is no more interaction with the server until the next request is made.

(3) Hypertext Links: Uniform Resource Locators (URL):

Ans. What about the links themselves? Links are based on a standard called a Uniform Resource Locator (URL). URLs contain all of the information needed for the client to find and retrieve a HTML document. An example of a URL is: http://www.zodiac.ca/htdocs/home.html

It has four parts:

- The protocol used to connect to the remote server. In this example, the protocol is HTTP, the protocol used to connect to Web servers. The protocol could also be Gopher, FTP, or TELNET, indicating that the link is to one of these Internet tools,
- The Internet address of the server where the document resides. In this case, the address is www.zodiac.ca'
- The directory on the server where the document is located, called the document path. In this case, the path is/htdocs
- The filename of the document itself. In the example, it is home.html, where the html extension indicates that the document is marked up with HTML.

Q32. What do you understand by Web Servers?

Ans. Web architecture contains two classes of computers: servers, which store information and clients which access it. Together, these are the two ends of the Web, each with its own supporting software. Server software runs exclusively on server machines, handling the storage and transmission of documents. In contrast, client software such as Netscape Internet Explorer. etc. runs on the end-users' computers accessing, translating and displaying documents. The two ends communicate through the Internet using a protocol known as Hypertext Transfer Protocol (HTTP).

A web server is a software package that processes HTML documents for viewing by Web browsers. The server enables users on other sites to access documents that you have chosen to make available to them.

Web servers can be run from any hardware platform. There are servers that are specifically designed for Macintosh computers, PCs, Silicon Graphics, and various other platforms, including the Amiga. The most important software is the web server itself. Just as it can be run under a number of hardware platforms, it can also run under several operating systems, including MS Windows, Windows NT, Unix, and VAX's VMS.

The web server is responsible for document storage and retrieval. It sends the document requested (or an error message) back to the requesting client. The client interprets and presents the document. The client is responsible for document presentation. The language that web clients and servers use to communicate with each other is called the Hypertext Transfer Protocol (HTTP). All web clients and servers must be able to speak HTTP in order to send and receive hypermedia documents. For this reason, web servers are often called HTTP servers, or HTTP Daemons (HTTPD).

There are many different web servers, running on many platforms. In this example you are using a browser (Netscape, or Mosaic, or some other browser) and you click on a reference to Webmaster Magazine Online. The browser is able to figure out that what you really want (in web terminology) is the object the web knows as http://www.cio.com/WebMaster/wmhome.html-the Web address (or URL) for WebMaster Magazine Online. WWW documents transmitted between client and server are written in a text-formatting language, called Hypertext Markup Language (HTML) that describes the structure and character formatting data of documents. The key to remember is that HTML is a language, neither an application nor a software package. It is simply a data-set of text and instructions that requires additional client software to be used.

Q33. Describe the concept of 'Web browser'. Also, discuss some important web browser or web clients available to surf the Internet.

Ans. A web browser is the software programme you use to access the World Wide Web, the graphical portion of the Internet. The first browser, called NCSA Mosaic, was developed at the National Center for Supercomputing Applications in the early '90s. The easy-to-use point-and-click interface helped popularise the Web, although few then could imagine the explosive growth that would soon occur. The two hottest graphical browsers battling for the top spot are Microsoft Internet Explorer and Netscape Navigator. Both are fast and both have integrated audio and video. Microsoft Internet Explorer can be downloaded at no charge. All of Netscape's products that are available via download, including Netscape Navigator, are free to anyone who qualifies as an educational user.

A web browser is a client programme that uses the Hypertext Transfer Protocol (HTTP) to make requests of Web servers throughout the Internet on behalf of the browser user. The software that enables you to go from one resource to another by following hyperlinks is known as a web browser. The basic capabilities of a browser are to retrieve documents from the web, jump to links specified in the retrieved document, and save and print the retrieved documents.

There are several web browsers or web clients available to surf the internet. Some of the important ones are:

(1) Mosaic Version 2.1.1 (http://archive.ncsa.uiuc.edu/SDG/Software/WinMosaic/HomePage.html): At one time first and foremost among web clients was the Mosaic graphical interface. It was developed in 1993 by the National Centre for Supercomputing Applications (NCSA) at the University of Illinois. Before Mosaic, all interfaces to the web were simple textbased, line-by-line interfaces. They were hypertext, but not graphical or multimedia. When the Windows version of Mosaic became available to Internet users for free, suddenly the web became the hottest information system on the Network because it was so much more powerful.

(2) Netscape Navigator 7.1 (http://www.netscape.com/): The Netscape Navigator was developed by the same people who created Mosaic at NCSA. The Netscape 7 browser has a tabbed user interface that allows easy switching from one open web page to another. A user can create bookmarks that open a specific set of tabs. Another convenient feature is one-click search. Highlight a word (but not a link) in the browser window and right-click on it, and start a search for it from any search engine. The new version of Netscape has also implemented the 'Sidebar' pane that runs down the left edge of the screen. Internet Explorer does the same thing (click on Favourites or History and a thin left-hand window opens). Netscape's Sidebar provides tabbed access to addresses, bookmarks, news, history, and a variety of other useful things. The Netscape has a mail client and address book that is quite adequate. The biggest difference between Netscape 7 and Internet Explorer is integration. Because Microsoft presumes ownership of your desktop, it has less need to pack as many applications into its web browser. Netscape, on the other hand, ties together e-mail, browsing, and instant messaging in one application. For example, both AOL's instant messaging client and ICQ are integrated into the browser. Microsoft's Messenger client is not fully integrated. In Netscape 7, the integration feels smooth and natural.

(3) Internet Explorer 6.0 (http://www.microsoft.com/windows/ie/): Microsoft Internet Explorer 6 (IE6) is the sixth major revision of Internet Explorer, a web browser developed by Microsoft for Windows operating systems. It was released on August 27, 2001, shortly after the completion of Windows XP. It can also be downloaded from their website free of cost. Over 75 per cent of Internet users use the Internet Explorer. It is the default browser shipped with Windows XP and Windows Server 2003, and was also made available for Windows NT

4.0, Windows 98, Windows 2000, and Windows Me. It also includes a free copy of the Advanced Searchbar, which is an Internet Explorer toolbar that allows users to quickly access and search over 60 search engines and is jam packed with features including blocking of pop-up windows.

(4) Avant Browser v9.02 (http://www.avantbrowser.com/): Avant Browser is an ultra-fast web browser. Its user-friendly interface brings a new level of clarity and efficiency to your browsing experience, and frequent upgrades have steadily improved its reliability. This browser add-on, runs on top of Internet Explorer. An integrated pop-up stopper and Flash animation filter protect users from unwanted distractions. Avant Browser supports tabbed-multi-window browsing. i.e., the tabbed interface lets a user open several sites inside one browser and makes navigation easier. The built-in Google search engine lets a user search right from the browser's taskbar. It is fully Internet Explorer compatible and supports all Internet Explorer functions, including cookies, ActiveX Controls, Java Script, Real player and Macromedia Flash.

(5) Enigma Browser (http://www.suttondesigns.com/): The Enigma Browser is a free browser based on Internet Explorer. Unlike Internet Explorer, however, it has automated and built-in ad-blocking abilities, with its default settings set to block adverts, detected malware, adware, system monitors and trackers. Furthermore, it does not send user data to sites requesting it unless the user explicitly gives permission for that data collection.

The interface for Enigma Browser is fairly user-friendly, and its use of large icons for the top "ribbon" of the window makes it simple to find a control or command. The program has a number of features that are not found in most default browsers. For instance, it has a translation tool and multi-language dictionaries built into it, a quick search bar, and a management system for cache as well as cookies. The user should take note, however, that given its use of Internet Explorer as a foundation, the program will require that Internet Explorer (specifically, IE5) be installed in the computer first before it can itself be installed. This is due to its requirement of several IE files for a full installation (it simply reuses those files for itself). The program is also compatible with Windows operating system versions Vista, XP, 9x, ME, NT and 2000.

(6) Crazy Browser v1.05 (http://www.crazybrowser.com): Crazy Browser facilitates browsing multiple websites at once. It blocks advertisements. Users have the option to turn off multimedia and browse the web in text mode. Users can search on a number of search engines that come with the program. It incorporates Smart Pop-up Filter. It supports tabbed-multi-window browsing.

(7) Automatic Search Browser (http://www.4comtech.com/): Automatic Search is a search-themed web browser that automatically finds related links, subjects, and topics associated with the current website being viewed. It features an integrated search engine utilising the popular engines (Dmoz, Google, Yahoo, All the web, MSN, Lycos, Hotbot. etc.) and allows users to quickly switch among the search results using tabs. Users can also save and access their favourite websites easily by using toolbar buttons.

(8) Mozilla v1.7.2 (http://www.mozilla.org): Mozilla, developed by the Mozilla.org open-source community, is a cross-platform product with support for Windows, Linux, and Macintosh 8/9/X. It incorporates a filter to stop pop-up advertisements. It supports tabbed multi-window browsing that lets a user open new pages easily instead of forcing a user to open a new window and then click back to see the previous screen while the new window loads. Mozilla offers a tab to the new window and loads that page in the background, letting you stay focussed on the work at hand. Another welcome advance is the ability to turn off pop-up ads and animated GIFs. Besides the browser, Mozilla includes an instant-messaging application, an e-mail client, web-composer software, and some nifty cookie-management and antispam features.

(9) Opera (http://www.opera.com/): Opera browser is designed for Windows with built-in pop-up stopper to stop unwanted pop-up pages. It supports tabbed multi-window browsing. It has integrated Google search engine that lets a user search right from the browser's taskbar. It has a built-in mail client. Opera is extremely well designed with minimum resource use in terms of hard disc and memory requirement. Opera is fully customisable and it has page magnification capability, and graphics handling which make Opera an alternative to Internet Explorer or Netscape.

(10) EasyBrowser v2.0 (http://www.vrameen.com/): EasyBrowse is a free Internet browser that works on all Windows platforms (95 and above). The new version includes the Pop-up disabler option to a standard list of features including plug-ins, direct linking to 11 search engines, plug-in checker, large browsing window, favourites and a history list.

(11) NeoPlanet Browser (http://www.neoplanet.com/): NeoPlanet was a Trident-shell graphical web browser initially released in 1987 by New York based Bigfoot International, Inc. and later maintained and developed by its subsidiary NeoPlanet, Inc. it was one of the first browsers to be fully skinnable.

Neoplanet was a "plug-out" extension for Internet Explorer which created an integrated branded environment for the user. Within the environment, users could web browse, email, and chat. Much simpler to use than basic browsers, Neoplanet was a portal-like browser created for non-techie users. Unlike web portals which lost control of the users every time they surfed to a new site, chatted, or emailed, Neoplanet's environment followed the users wherever they went on the Internet.

(12) Lynx (http://www.browser.lynx.org/): Lynx is a text-based, full screen interface to the web. Arrow keys, tabs, and the cursor are used to move around and select items instead of a mouse. Lynx interface is not multimedia, and so pictures, icons, maps and other graphical elements cannot be viewed.

Q34. What do you understand by Plug-ins or Helper Programs?

Ans. A web author can incorporate text files (formatted or unformatted), images, video clippings, audio files, graphics, animations, and other types of actions in a web page. The browser cannot handle all these files and formats and thus requires additional software programs to execute them.

Initially, the Netscape browser allowed users to download, install, and define supplementary programs that played sound or motion video or performed other functions. These were called helper applications. However, these applications run as a separate application and require that a second window be opened. A plug-in application is recognised automatically by the browser and its function is integrated into the main HTML file that is being presented.

Plug-ins or helper applications are external software programs that allow web users to view or hear multimedia presentations, regardless of platform. Plug-ins can easily be installed and used as part of web browser. Plug-ins or helper applications extend and enhance the capabilities of web browsers such as, Netscape and Internet Explorer, and are needed to handle many of the newer hypermedia such as, streaming audio, vector graphics, three-dimensional multimedia and virtual worlds. Browsers hand over data to appropriate helper applications such as, RealAudio, Adobe Acrobat, QuickTime, Shockwave and others.

Native Helper Programs: Native helper programs are integrated into the browser itself, just like some word processors include internal spell check programs. In practice, the browser identifies an element, and then calls up a native helper program to execute an action. For example, when a browser identifies a file stored in the JPEG format (a type of compressed image), it calls up an internal program that can translate JPEG files. The internal program then processes and displays the image inside the browser's viewing area. Netscape has a native helper program that can handle JPEG files this way. Browsers that do not have the same capacity must use external helper programs to read images.

External Helper Programs: External helper programs address the fact that there are too many file formats for one browser to handle alone. Instead of one massive omnilingual program that can read every type of file the WWW carries, browsers incorporate smaller external helper programs to accomplish the same end. These specialised programs are separate from the browser and perform functions identical to native helper programs, except that the actions are executed outside of the browser. For example, when a browser identifies a sound file stored in .WAV format, it calls up an external program that can translate .WAV files. The browser passes the .WAV file to the external helper program, which then processes and plays it.

There are two main differences between native and external helper programs. The first difference is that external helper programs run independently of the browser. This means that once files are passed from the browser to the external helper program, the browser is free to resume navigating the WWW. In contrast, native helper programs tie up the browser until the native program completes its action and is closed. The second difference concerns how the two types of helper programs are acquired. Native helper programs are included within the browser itself. However, external helper programs must be acquired independently by the end-user. The end-user then has to configure the browser to point to the external program, telling it when to use it (e.g., to view a particular file format) and where it is located within the computer's storage. Most often this is done through setting the Preferences area of the browser's Options.

Q35. Briefly explain how to use web browser and web browser's toolbar buttons.

Ans. A user should know how to use and move around the web with the web browser. It can really make using the web much easier. Although the specific features might differ from browser to browser, there are a few things that are common to virtually every web browser.

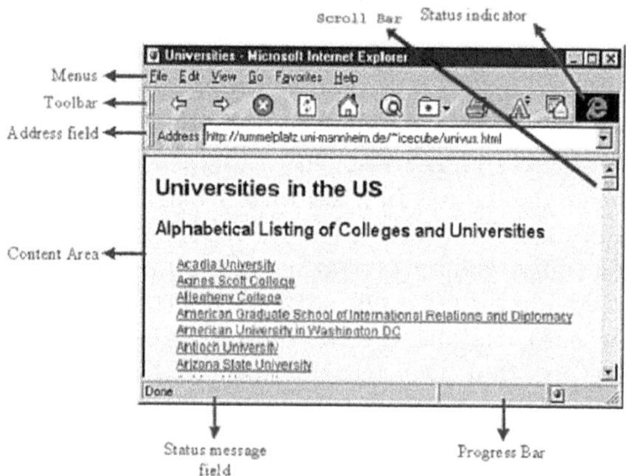

Fig. 4.7

Menu Bar: Located along the top of the browser window, the menu bar offers a selection of things you can do with a web page, such as saving it to your hard drive or increasing the size of the text on a page. Many of the choices are the same as the buttons on the toolbar.

File: 'File' menu has options like new, open, edit, save, save as, page set-up, print, print preview, send, import and export, properties, work offline and close. Several of these options are common to other packages that students would have used. This Unit would deal with save and print menus.

Saving and Printing Web Pages: A user can save web pages on to the computer or on a disk and print out a hard copy of a page.

Saving a Web Page: A user can save a web page on to computer's hard drive or on to a floppy disk. Follow the following steps in order to save a web page:

Saving a page on to the hard drive (C:)

Open the page in the browser.

Click on the 'File' menu

Select 'Save As' from the file menu.

A dialogue box will open. A user may choose the disc or folder where s/he wants to save the file, name of the file and its format.

Click on the 'Save' button in the dialogue box.

Printing a Web Page: The first thing to ascertain when printing a web page is the size of the page. A web page may actually run into several pages. The browser would assume that a user wants to print all the contents of the document. Follow the steps given below to print only a portion of the page:

Open the desired page in the browser.

Click on the 'File' menu.

Select 'Print Preview'.

In the print preview screen, use the 'next page' button to advance till you find out total number of pages.

Observe pages that contain the material required to be printed (The page numbers are displayed in the bottom, left corner of the screen).

Click on the 'Close' button in the print preview dialog box.

Either select 'Print' from the 'File' menu, or hit the 'Print' button in the toolbar.

The print dialogue box will open.

Enter the first page and the last page of the section of the document to be printed.

Press 'OK'.

View: 'View' menu has the following options:

Toolbar: When checked, the Toolbar is displayed. If not, it is hidden from view.

Status Bar: When checked, the Status Bar at the bottom of the window is displayed. If not, it is hidden from view.

Explorer Bar: Explorer bar has options such as, Search, Favourite, Media, History and Folders. Most of these options are already covered under toolbar.

Go to: Back, Forward and Home (same as in the toolbar).

Stop (Loading): Stops or interrupts the loading of the current document. (Same as Stop Button).

Refresh: Refreshes the document by reloading from local memory. (Same as Refresh Button).

Text Size: Changes size of fonts to smallest, smaller, medium, larger and largest.

Encoding: By default encoding is set to western European. Most web pages contain information that tells the browser what language encoding (the language and character set) to use. If the page does not include that information, and select the Auto-select feature, Internet Explorer would usually determine the appropriate language encoding.

Source: Views the HTML codes for the current document.

Full Screen: Hides menu bar, tool bar, address box, status bar. etc. Shows the content area on the entire screen.

Options: Customises Internet Explorer for your PC.

Favourites: Favourites menu has the following options:

Add to Favourites: Adds the document that is being viewed to the Favourites list.

Organise Favourites: Opens the Favourites window. Allows users to rearrange their collection, delete entries, add category headers, rename items. etc.

Favourites Items: Each of the Favourite items appears in this Favourites list. Select any Favourites from the menu to go to that document. Folders will allow opening of secondary menu with additional items.

Tools: 'Tools' menu has the following options:

Mail and News: Menu options allow a user to opt for the mail program of his/her choice.

Synchronise: Allows a user to update web pages from the desktop to server.

Windows Update: Latest news about the Windows operating system. Messenger: Invokes Hotmail or default messenger.

Show Related Links: Opens a side bar with links related to document that is being currently viewed.

Internet Options: Opens the window that allows a user to customise and configure the Internet Explorer.

Help: A user can take help of the 'Help' menu as and when required. If the user has a question or a problem, or if he/she wants to learn more about the capabilities of Internet Explorer, s/he is to click on the help menu and select 'Contents and Index' which will allow the user to search through the topics of the Help menu and select appropriate help.

Toolbar: A browser's toolbar consists of buttons that are shortcuts for menu commands.They make browsing faster and easier.

Fig. 4.8: Toolbar

The 'Back' and 'Forward' Buttons

Fig. 4.9

Once a couple of web pages are loaded, 'Back' button gets activated. With a click on this button, the web browser will return the user to the last web page viewed. The 'Forward' button (when activated) takes a user to the next web page viewed.

Stop: The 'Stop' button is active (red) only when a new page is in the process of opening. While the page is opening (downloading), a user can choose to stop the download by clicking on the stop button. A user may like to stop downloading for a number of reasons, for example, the file being downloaded might be taking much more time than expected or the size of the document being downloaded is very large and is likely to take a long time to load. The 'Stop' button, like the Status Indicator, also indicates that browser is in the process of downloading information. A download is in progress when the 'Stop' button is red.

Fig. 4.10

Refresh: Refresh button loads a fresh copy of the web page being displayed currently. Web pages get stored in the Internet temporary files when a user visits a website. When a user revisits a page that he/she has visited earlier, the browser displays the file stored in cache of the PC, rather than the current page on the web to save on download time. Browser's 'Reload' button re-downloads the newest copy of the current web document.

Fig. 4.11

Home: A click at the 'Home' button returns the user to the home page defined in the browser. A user can designate any web page as his/her home page.

Fig. 4.12

Search: In case of Internet Explorer, a click at the 'Search' button will take a user to the MSN Search in the left pane. The Internet Explorer with its Search Assistant, gets more useful search results by specifying the type of information being searched beforehand (such as, an address, web page, company, or map). Other browsers may display a choice of popular Internet search engines in the left pane. When a link is clicked, the page appears in the right pane, so that a user does not lose the sight of his/her search results.

Fig. 4.13

Favourites: Favourites (referred to as 'Bookmarks' in Netscape) provide a convenient way to keep track of commonly visited, or interesting web pages. At any time, a user can use the Favourites menu to show a list of current favourite sites and jump to a page immediately by selecting it from the menu. Favourites allow a user to save a URL of a site that he/she has visited earlier. It displays a list of the sites that a user has saved as Favourites. A click on any item in the list will trigger a visit to the selected site. A user can create, move, rename, or delete folders or files from options.

Fig. 4.14

To view existing Favourites, click on the button 'Favourite' in the Internet Explorer toolbar, or bring up the Favourites menu by clicking on Favourites in the main toolbar (at the top of the screen).

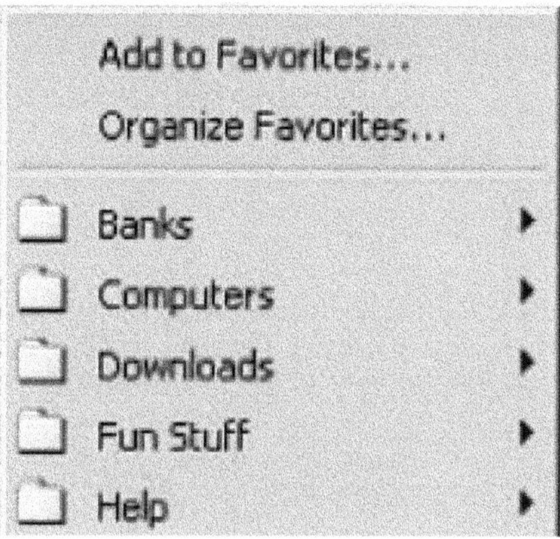

Fig. 4.15

To add a Favourite site in Internet Explorer, visit the web page to be added, so that it is displayed in the browser window, and its URL is displayed in the Address field. From the Favourites menu, choose the following:

To Add to Favourites....

Edit the name of the Favourite in the Name field (if required)

To place the new Favourite in a particular folder, click at 'Add to Favourite' button. This will display a list of available folders. Select one by clicking it once.

Click OK.

To Create a New Favourite Folder, follow the following steps:

Choose Organise Favourites... from the Favourites menu.

In the Organise Favourites window, press the 'create new' button.

The new folder will appear in the list of folders. Type a name for it (e.g. search engines, digital libraries, e-Books. etc.). Press the Enter key to confirm the name of the folder.

Click the Close button.

To Jump to a Favourite

Select the Favourite directly from the Favourites menu.

Organising Favourites into Folders: When a site is added to the Favourites using Add Favourite, the Internet Explorer places it at the end of the list of Favourites. As the number of Favourites grows large, specific Favourites are harder to locate. To help overcome this problem, the Internet Explorer allows users to group bookmarks together into hierarchical folders, similar to the folders used to store files on the computer's hard disk.

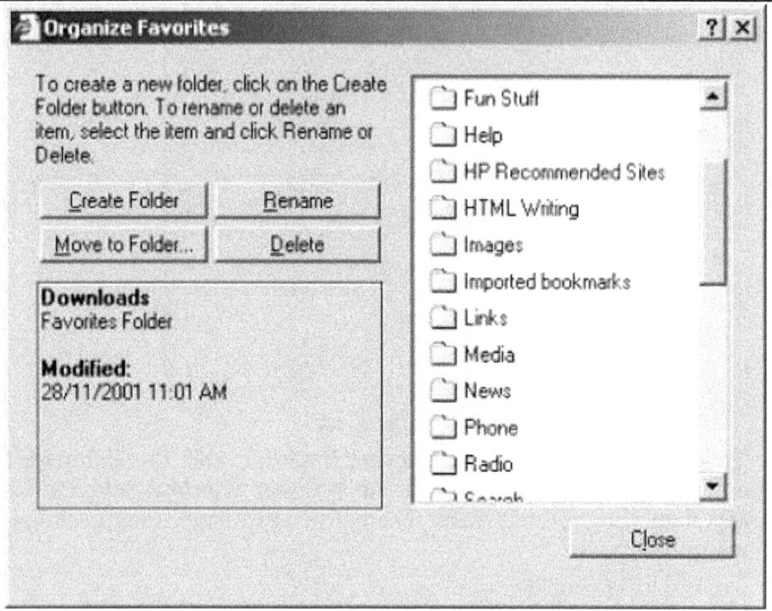

Fig. 4.16: Organising Favourite Web page

To Edit the Name or URL of a Favourite Manually

Bring up the Favourites window by choosing Organise Favourites... from the Favourites menu.

Select a particular Favourite by clicking on it. To edit the name of the Favourite, press the Rename button, and edit the Favourite name.

Edit the URL associated with the favourite by clicking on the Favourite with the right mouse button, and choose Properties from the pop-up menu.

Select the Internet Shortcut or Web Document tab and edit the URL in the URL field.

Click the OK button. Click Close to close the Organise Favourites... window.

To Sort the Favourites in a Particular Folder

Open the Favourites menu;

Right-click the Favourites menu to display its context menu;

Select Sort by Name (close to the bottom of the context menu). This will alphabetically sort this menu.

This method can be repeated on any sub-folder by right-clicking the pop-up menu of any sub-folder.

Print: Prints the page that is being viewed. This is one way to save information from the Internet and read it at leisure.

Fig. 4.17

History: This button will open the history folder containing all the links to pages that have been previously visited while browsing the Internet. The Internet Explorer History list makes it easy to find and return to websites and pages that were visited in the past.

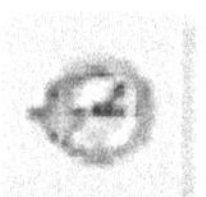

Fig. 4.18

Mail: This button opens into a drop down menu from which a user can select to read or send email. Users can also open up their newsgroups from this menu. It connects users to Microsoft Outlook.

Fig. 4.19

Edit: This button will get enabled on the toolbar only on Windows system web editor (such as, Microsoft Front page or Microsoft Word or Notepad installed on the computer. The edit will launch one of the above-mentioned software and open the document that is being viewed currently.

Fig. 4.20

The Location (URL) Box: Most web browsers have an address window where a user can key-in the URL that he/she wants to visit. The URL window displays the Internet address of the website that is being viewed currently along with specific directory and filename of the current document. The location or the URL can be edited directly and a click at 'go' will take the user to the new location.

Address http://www.ignou.ac.in

Fig. 4.21

Q36. What do you mean by Mark-up Languages?

Ans. The most common method of creating a web documents is with Markup Languages. Most of these are created by adding a set of formatting code to ASCII text to show fonts, justifications, links. etc. on the web. A markup language is a language that uses tags to indicate a change in presentation style or a change in content type. A mark-up language describes explicitly. In sum, HTML describes explicitly the parts of the hypertext multimedia document, and the web client uses this information to construct the document on the user's screen.

Three basic concepts are fundamental to understanding of all mark-up languages, when described in SGML terms. These are

- Mark-up entity
- A mark-up element and its associated attributes
- A document type.

Q37. Explain the SGML, and XML.

Or

Write a short note on XML. [Dec-2018, Q.No.-5 (d)]

Ans. Standard Generalised Mark-up Language (SGML): SGML (Standard Generalised Markup Language) is the first known standard for how to specify a document markup language or tag set. SGML is based somewhat on earlier generalised markup languages developed at IBM, including General Markup Language (GML) and ISIL. SGML is not in itself a document language, but a description of how to specify one. It is a Document type definition (DTP).

SGML is based on the idea that documents have structural and other semantic elements that can be described without reference to how such elements should be displayed. The actual display of such a document may vary, depending on the output medium and style preferences. Some advantages of documents based on SGML are:

- They can be created by thinking in terms of document structure rather than appearance characteristics (which may change over time).
- They will be more portable because an SGML compiler can interpret any document by reference to its document type definition (DTD).
- Documents originally intended for the print medium can easily be re-adapted for other media, such as the computer display screen.

An SGML document consists of the following three distinct parts:

- **Declaration:** it gives fundamental information like language of document and code set being used (i.e., English/ASCII)
- **DTD:** Details of codes and rules restricting their use.

- **Instance:** The text being published, marked up with the codes described in the DTD.

SGML concerns itself with the structural features of a document while the appearance and display features are left to the ultimate presentation system to determine how those features appear on display or print. Resultantly, when documents move from system to system, or portions of one document are used in another, they do not need to be recoded. Because of its powerful and flexible structuring capabilities, as well as its capability to capture and organise information about the publications, SGML-coded documents can be used effectively to search information contents of documents based on the structure and content of the information. Many SGML depositories are considered as 'text databases'. Since they enable a publisher to organise the published information in different ways for different contexts.

Extensive Mark-up Language (XML): XML (Extensible Markup Language) is a flexible way to create common information formats and share both the format and the data on the World Wide Web, intranets, and elsewhere. For example, computer makers might agree on a standard or common way to describe the information about a computer product (processor speed, memory size, and so forth) and then describe the product information format with XML. Such a standard way of describing data would enable a user to send an intelligent agent (a programme) to each computer maker's web site, gather data, and then make a valid comparison. Any individual or group of individuals or companies that wants to share information in a consistent way can use XML.

XML, a formal recommendation from the World Wide Web Consortium (W3C), is similar to the language of today's web pages, the Hypertext Markup Language (HTML). Both XML and HTML contain markup symbols to describe the contents of a page or file. HTML, however, describes the content of a web page (mainly text and graphic images) only in terms of how it is to be displayed and interacted with. For example, the letter "p" placed within markup tags starts a new paragraph. XML describes the content in terms of what data is being described. For example, the word "phonenum" placed within markup tags could indicate that the data that followed was a phone number. This means that an XML file can be processed purely as data by a programme or it can be stored with similar data on another computer or, like an HTML file, that it can be displayed. For example, depending on how the application in the receiving computer wanted to handle the phone number, it could be stored, displayed, or dialed.

XML is "extensible" because, unlike HTML, the markup symbols are unlimited and self-defining. XML is actually a simpler and easier-to-use subset of the Standard Generalised Markup Language (SGML), the standard for how to create a document structure. It is expected that

HTML and XML will be used together in many web applications. XML markup, for example, may appear within an HTML page.

Early applications of XML include Microsoft's Channel Definition Format (CDF), which describes a channel, a portion of a web site that has been downloaded to your hard disk and is then updated periodically as information changes. A specific CDF file contains data that specifies an initial web page and how frequently it is updated. Another early application is ChartWare, which uses XML as a way to describe medical charts so that they can be shared by doctors. Applications related to banking, e-commerce ordering, personal preference profiles, purchase orders, litigation documents, part lists, and many others are anticipated.

Q38. Write notes on the followings:

(1) Hypertext Markup Language (HTML)

Ans. HTML stands for HyperText Markup Language. It is a language, which is used to develop web pages. It is a collection of several tags to describe visuals of a webpage. The goal of HTML is to provide a display format to the given set of data so that it can be read on a web browser. HTML was originally designed by Sir Tim Berners-Lee in 1991 at CERN Lab. HTML is an offshoot of SGML.

HTML is the building block of a website. It allows multimedia objects to be embedded in the webpage including audio, video, text and graphics. The language consists of tags. A tag is an element (known as HTML element), which has certain properties. These properties are applied on the data embedded in between tags. It is an individual component of an HTML document. Hence, HTML documents are collection of tags. These tags may simply contain data or can co-exist with other tags establishing parent child relation. A tag has certain attributes, which are applied, on the contained data or on the child tags (or elements).

The number of tags used in HTML is fixed hence the language uses closed vocabulary. The structure of a web page is as follows:

```
<!DOCTYPE HTML PUBLIC"-//W3C//DTD HTML 4.01//EN"
"http://www.w3.org/TR/html4/strict.dtd">
<HTML>
 <HEAD>
  <TITLE> My first HTML document</TITLE>
 </HEAD>
 <BODY>
  <P>Hello world!
 </BODY>
</HTML>
```

An HTML document has two parts,

- Head, and
- Body

'HEAD', contains elements (tags) for TITLE of the document. The 'TITLE' element stores information about the title of the document.

<TITLE>Website of Indira Gandhi National Open University </TITLE>

There is another element used in 'HEAD' section, i.e., 'META' element. 'META' element stores information about the document such as author, copyright, location, relation, keywords and so on.

<META name="Author" content="Sneha Tripathi">

In the META tag first attribute or the property is defined under the NAME attribute and its value is given under CONTENT. In the above example Author is an attribute and value of author is 'Sneha Tripathi'.

These attributes are the attributes of the document, which is being described. Sometimes an attribute may use closed vocabulary or a scheme. In such cases META element also specifies the SCHEME used.

<META scheme="ISBN" name="identifier" content="0-8230-2355-9">

The second part of an HTML document is BODY element. The body of a document contains the document's content. The BODY element contains all the tags or elements, which are used to display the data over a web browser. It includes a variety of tags such as:

<H1>...</H1>
<H2>...</H2>
<H3>...</H3>
<H4>...</H5>
<TABLE>...</TABLE>
<P></P>
<B></B>
<I></I>

Each element inside BODY tag can have various attributes, which is defined in HTML Standard Specification. The current version of HTML specification is 4.01. The next version of HTML, which is due, is HTML 5.0.

(2) Dynamic HTML:

Ans. The Dynamic HTML is a collective term for a combination of new Hypertext Markup Language (HTML) tags and options, that will let you create web pages more animated and more responsive to user interaction than previous versions of HTML. Much of dynamic HTML is specified in HTML 4.0. Simple examples of dynamic HTML pages would include (1) having the colour of a text heading change when a user passes a mouse over it or (2) allowing a user to "drag and drop" an image to another place on a web page. Dynamic HTML can allow web documents to look and act like desktop applications or multimedia productions.

The features that constitute dynamic HTML are included in Netscape Communications' latest Web browser, Navigator 4.0 (part of Netscape's Communicator suite), and by Microsoft's browser, Internet Explorer 4.0. While HTML 4.0 is supported by both Netscape and Microsoft browsers, some additional capabilities are supported by only one of the browsers. The biggest obstacle to the use of dynamic HTML is that, since many users are still using older browsers, a web site must create two versions of each site and serve the pages appropriate to each user's browser version.

Q39. What is Virtual Reality Modelling Language (VRML)? Write their uses.

Ans. VRML stands for Virtual Reality Modelling language and is pronounced 'vermil'. It is a standard for delivering 3D picture on the net, just like HTML is a standard for web pages. VRML is a subset of the Open Inventor standard developed by SGI for their graphics workstation. To view a VRML file, you need a VRML viewer or browser, which can be a plug-in for a web browser you already have. Among viewers that you can download for the Windows platforms are blaxxun's CC Pro, Platinum's Cosmo Player, webFX, WorldView, and Fountain. Whurlwind and Voyager are two viewers for the Mac. Virtual reality refers to an immersive environment, an environment that you feel you are inside of. You can attain this immersive feeling with computers using 3D graphics and audio. Sounds in a virtual world can be specialised so that they sound louder when you are closer to them.

When virtual reality happens on the Internet, new possibilities arise for distributed, networked virtual environments. In HTML, inline images let you include graphics from anywhere on the web on to your web page. In VRML, you can have inline parts of a virtual world, so that a chair in a VRML world can come from a URL on a server in France, while the garden comes from a server in Japan, and the soundtrack is from a URL on a server in England. In addition, hyperlinks from an object in a VRML world can lead to another URL on the web, which could be another VRML world, an HTML page, or any other URL!

Uses of VRML: There are many applications for VRML, varying in focus from VRML's open 3D file format, to its networking capabilities, to its multimedia nature. Here are some applications for which people are currently using VRML.

- Computer-aided design (CAD)
- Scientific simulations
- Games
- Data visualisation
- Distributed, multi-user environments
- Social computing
- User interfaces to information

- Financial applications
- Product marketing and advertising
- Education
- Entertainment

Q40. Write short note on internet applications.

Ans. The Internet has many important applications. Of the various services available via the Internet, the three most important are e-mail, web browsing, and peer-to-peer services.

Individuals, companies, and institutions use the Internet in different ways. Business houses use the Internet to provide product information, online support service. etc. Companies carry out online trading, including advertising, selling, buying, distributing products, and providing after-sales services. Institutions use the Internet for audio and video conferencing and other forms of communication that allow people to telecommute or work from a distance.

The use of Internet services has resulted in increase in communication among companies, co-workers, and individuals. Media and entertainment companies use the Internet to broadcast audio and video, including live radio and television programmes; to offer online chat, online news and weather information. Scientists and scholars use the Internet to communicate with colleagues, to perform research, to distribute lecture notes and course materials to students, and to publish papers and articles. Individuals use the Internet for communication, entertainment, finding information, and to buy and sell goods and services.

Q41. What are the various Internet-based communication services? Discuss briefly.

Or

Write a short note on List Serv and News Groups.

[June-2018, Q.No.-5(e)]

Ans. Various internet-based communication services are as follows:

(1) Electronic Mail (E-mail): Electronic mail, or email, is the transmission of text-based messages among networked computers. Email is one of the earliest and most basic messaging resources on the Internet and in many ways it still acts as the lowest common denominator for computer communications.

Features

(i) It is faster and more secure than conventional mail.

(ii) It requires less physical effort to edit and send a letter of communication.

(iii) Once the hardware, software, and Internet connection are in place, email on the Internet is free, even if messages is to be sent to the other side of the world.

(iv) Unlike communication by telephone, email does not require the attention of both parties at the same time.

Need of Email

Email has become an important and integral part for the people who are living away or who has someone far away. For different persons the reasons are different towards using email. In general the reasons are:

(i) An email ensures faster/easier delivery of messages as long as email address is correct.

(ii) It provides time-stamped proof of an interaction. Also, many email services (such as Gmail) collate the conversation on the same subject into single threads.

(iii) It is more secure and inexpensive compared to other modes of communication.

(iv) It is easy to archive for future recall. Most of the email services provide search facility through emails.

(v) An email can be edited and rephrased as much as it is desired before sending to the recipient(s).

(vi) It is easy to send the same piece of information to several people simultaneously such as circulation of memos, agendas, and minutes, or disseminate educational material.

(2) E-mail Client: An email client is a program that lives on your computer and lets you send or receive emails. Typical examples include Outlook and Windows Live Mail.

The client usually consists of a combination of a simple text editor, address book, filing cabinet and communications module. The text editor allows for the creation of the message itself, and usually includes simple spell checking and formatting facilities.

The e-mail clients also facilitate files, documents or pictures to be attached to the message. The address book allows the users to store commonly used e-mail addresses in an easy to get format, reducing the chance of addressing errors. The filing cabinet allows for the storage of e-mail messages, both sent and received, and usually provide some form of search function, allowing easy retrieval of a desired message.

(3) Mail Server: A mail server is an application that receives e-mail from e-mail clients or other mail servers. It is the workhorse of the e-mail system. A mail server usually consists of a storage area, a set of user definable rules, a list of users and a series of communication modules. The storage area is where mail is stored for local users, and where messages that are in transit to another destination are temporarily stored. It usually takes the form of a simple database of information. A person, sometimes called a Postmaster, maintains the mail server and the list of user accounts that it supports.

(4) Chat or Instant Messengers: The Internet provides facility for a real time (on-line) communicating with one to one or one to many computers. This is popularly known as chat. On the Internet, chatting is talking to other people who are using the Internet at the same time you are. Usually, this "talking" is the exchange of typed-in messages requiring one site as the repository for the messages (or "chat site") and a group of users who take part from anywhere on the Internet. In some cases, a private chat can be arranged between two parties who meet initially in a group chat. Chats can be ongoing or scheduled for a particular time and duration. Most chats are focussed on a particular topic of interest and some involve guest experts or famous people who "talk" to anyone joining the chat. Transcripts of a chat can also be archived for later reference.

Chats are also conducted on online services (especially America Online), by bulletin board services, and by Web sites. Several Web sites, notably Talk City, exist solely for the purpose of conducting chats. Some chat sites such as Worlds Chat allow participants to assume the role or appearance of an avatar in a simulated or virtual reality environment. One to one chat is commonly used to communicate with friends, relatives or co-workers. A chat can also be conducted using sound or sound and video, assuming you have the bandwidth access and the appropriate programming.

Instant messaging (sometimes called IM or IMing) is the ability to easily see whether a chosen friend or co-worker is connected to the Internet and, if they are, to exchange messages with them. Instant messaging differs from ordinary e-mail in the immediacy of the message exchange and also makes a continued exchange simpler than sending e-mail back and forth. Most exchanges are text-only. However, some services allow attachments.

(5) Conferencing: One of the most existing feature of the Internet is to communicate, talk, and see the groups of people in different locations around the world, without the expense of travel. Conferencing can take many forms, such as web chat, audio conferencing, video conferencing, multimedia conferencing, screen-sharing. etc. The conferencing programmes, such as the popular CU-SeeMe, allow workgroups to use the Internet to see each others' faces in small windows on the computer screen and to hear their voices through computer speakers. We can use the desktop video and audio simultaneously, use the audio alone, or just use the screen-sharing capability without either audio or video.

(6) Audio Conferencing or Internet Telephony: Telephony is normally associated with the transmission of voice between distant parties using a handheld device containing both a speaker or transmitter and a receiver. However, we believe that telephony does connote voice or spoken and heard information predominately. It is a temporarily dedicated point-to-point (rather than a broadcast) connection. With the transmission of digital signals over the Internet, it is now possible to have the following services.

(i) The ability to make a normal voice phone call (whether or not the person called is immediately available; that is, the phone will ring at the location of the person called)

(ii) The ability to send fax transmissions at very low cost (at local call prices) through a gateway point on the Internet in major cities.

(iii) The ability to leave voice mail at a called number.

Some companies that make products that provide or plan to provide or plan to provide these capabilities include: IDT Corporation (Net2Phone), Netspeak, NetXchange, Rockwell International, Vocal Tec. And Voxspeak.

(7) Video Conferencing: Videoconferencing is one of the most exciting areas of development in telecommunications, with applications ranging from business to government to education to home and family. Videoconferencing involves sending video signals as well as audio and computer data signals. Conferencing can be done one-to-one, one-to-many (called multicast), and many-to-many (called multipoint). While video conferencing we are able to talk as well as see the people sitting miles away as if all are discussing in one room facing each other. One of the most popular applications is transmission on news from various locations by the TV news channels. It also has enormous potential for enhancing communications for small and mid-sized companies, as well as distance learning. However, because at the very minimum you need an ISDN connection for acceptable video quality, entry barriers are still high. As a result, desktop conferencing is not yet widely implemented for business and educational use. As bandwidth increases, we expect to see desktop videoconferencing blossom. The PictureTel and Vtel are two of the largest companies that sell videoconferencing equipment.

(8) NetMeeting: NetMeeting delivers a complete Internet conferencing solution for all Windows users with multi-point data conferencing, text chat, whiteboard, and file transfer, as well as point-to-point audio and video.

NetMeeting can be used for common collaborative activities such as, virtual meetings. It can also be used for customer service applications, telecommuting, distance learning, and technical support. The product is based on ITU (International Telecommunication Union) standards; so, it is compatible with other products based on the same standards. Some of NetMeeting's built-in features are listed below:

(i) Place calls to anyone using the Internet or an Intranet

(ii) Talking to someone over the Internet or an Intranet

(iii) Seeing the person being called
(iv) Working with others in an application
(v) Using the whiteboard to sketch in an online meeting
(vi) Checking Speed Dial list to see contacts that are logged on
(vii) Sending typed messages in Chat
(viii)Sending files to everyone in a meeting

Using the directory, one can find someone to communicate with and call them. Communication can be established using text chat, video or audio provided both the parties have the necessary hardware support.

Files, such as, documents or pictures, can be exchanged. One of the problems with net meeting is the break-up in audio that sometimes it becomes inaudible when using it on the Internet, though it works fine over a high-speed company network.

(9) NetShow: NetShow is basically a low-bandwidth alternative to video conferencing. It provides live multicast audio, file transfer and on-demand streamed audio, illustrated audio, and video. It is also a development platform on which software developers can create addon products. According to Microsoft, NetShow takes advantage of important Internet and network communication technologies to minimise traffic while providing useful tools for multi-user collaboration. NetShow also uses streaming technology (as discussed above), which allows users to see or hear information as it arrives, rather than wait for it to be completely transferred.

(10) Listserv: E-mail also provides a platform for sharing information quickly, and on a large scale by using listservs. Listservs are electronic groups that typically centre around broad topics such as, Digital Libraries or Reference Service. etc. Listservers of IFLA with the name IFLA-l, Digilib-l, LIBJOBS-l are good example of this. Every e-mail message sent to the listserv is distributed to all members of that Listserv, which are potentially hundreds or thousands of people. It does not cost anything to subscribe to a Listserv, but simply requires that the user sends an e-mail message to the appropriate address with the message: subscribe (listserv) Firstname Lastname. Each Listserv has one address where a user sends requests to subscribe, un-subscribe, search the archives. etc., and another address to send actual questions or responses to the readers of the list. Apart from organising discussions, job announcements and conference announcements are popular usage of Listservs.

(11) News Groups: Another Internet service similar to Listserv is a News Groups. News Groups are like an International bulletin board. Each group is a forum for a different subject, where a subscriber can post his/her questions or answers. There are thousands of groups covering just about every area of interest. The difference between Listserv and News Group is that when a user joins a group, the mail is no longer automatically deposited into his/her mailbox. Instead a user is expected to go to the newsgroup himself/herself to read it. Some listservs can also be accessed as a newsgroup. A good analogy to a newsgroup is a bulletin board. i.e., one can go to it, as opposed to having mail delivered to his/her desk. The mails from newsgroup do not get cluttered and they can be easily regulated as to how often messages are read. A drawback of a newsgroup lies in the fact that a user must remember to go out to the newsgroup to look for information.

There are hundreds of newsgroup communities. They centre around topics such as, computing, news, recreation, social, and 'alternative' topics. Each newsgroup's name begins with a code that identifies the type of newsgroup that is. For instance:

(i) **comp.human-factors** is a newsgroup dealing with the human factors of computing.

(ii) **soc.college.teaching-asst** is a social newsgroup for college teaching assistants.

(iii) **alt.fan.jimmy-buffett** is an alternative newsgroup for fans of Jimmy Buffet.

(iv) **clari.biz.market.otc** a business newsgroup for counter stock market exchange.

There are newsgroups dealing with virtually every topic under the sun (and new groups appear every day). The only problem one might encounter is that it is left up to the service provider to determine which newsgroups will be made available on the new system.

(12) Usenet: Usenet is a collection of more than 8,000 newsgroups, or discussion groups, on every conceivable subject. For example, some newsgroups are self-help groups for victims of cancer or sexual abuse, and others give the latest in gossip about show business personalities. Anyone can contribute a message, called an article, to a Usenet newsgroup or post a reply, known as a follow-up post, to an existing article. With the aid of a newsreader (a programme designed to access Usenet newsgroups), you can read an entire threat-all the replies to an interesting article.

The system is intended for exchange of information in an informal way. Anyone can post new messages to the group and reply to other messages. News groups are arranged in a loose hierarchical order covering about 5,000 subjects. About half of these are related to computing, the rest are for recreational subjects, professional discussion and trivia. To use Usenet you need a news viewer and access to an NNTP server. Most Internet service providers have such a server, as do most large academic institutions.

Q42. Discuss the services that can be used for establishing connection to servers on remote locations.

Ans. The services that can be used for establishing connection to servers on remote locations include the following:

(1) Remote Login/Telnet: Remote Login is the ability of a computer user in one location to establish an on-line connection with another computer elsewhere. Once a connection is established with a remote computer, users can use that remote system as if their computer were a hard-wired terminal of that system. Within the TCP/IP protocol suite, this facility is called "Telnet". Utilising Telnet, an Internet user can establish connections with a multitude of bibliographic databases (primarily library catalogues), campus information systems of various universities, full-text databases, data files (e.g., statistics, oceanographic data, meteorological data, geographic data. etc.), and other on-line services. Many of these systems are available for any Internet user to access and use without an account.

Telnet is the service of the Internet that allows you to access remote computers outside your area. Many computers on the Internet are set up to allow Telnet access. Some require login names and passwords, but many do not have any restrictions. Telnet is a powerful Internet application that enables librarians to access other libraries' online catalogs worldwide. Accessing other libraries' catalogues can help you verify information for acquisitions, inter-library loan, and copy cataloguing. Some systems, such as CARL's UnCover (database.carl.org), enable you to search magazine article indexed online. The original idea behind Telnet was to let researchers from different institutions share resources with one another. Telnet allows remote login to host computers, and commonly is used to connect to electronic catalogues and databases at near and distant libraries. Hytelnet is a tool that helps you access the various sites through Telnet. The World Wide Web lets you access sites through Telnet and use FTP to retrieve documents you find.

Telnet, like most other services, is based on the client/server model. The client programme, running on your machine, initiates the connection with a server programme, running on a remote machine. Keystrokes are passed from your terminal directly to the remote computer just as though they were being typed at a terminal on the remote computer. Output from the remote computer is sent back and displayed on your terminal.

(2) File Transfer Protocol (FTP): File transfer is one of the most frequently used Internet applications, enabling you to copy files from over a thousand different archives around the world. You can think of these archives as libraries-electronic libraries housing digitised information. Although information in traditional paper-based libraries is stored in books and magazines, the file is the unit of storage in electronic libraries. These files hold such things as text, images, sound, and executable programmes.

FTP or File Transfer Protocol is used to transfer files between computers on the network. There are two types of FTP connections, anonymous and non-anonymous. Some sites enforce a strict FTP authorisation that prohibits you from accessing files until you obtain a login name and password for their computer. Many other sites, the ones you will most often be connecting to, allow anonymous FTP, which provides unrestricted access to public files. Anonymous FTP access means that you don't have to be a registered user to connect to the remote host. You connect to an anonymous FTP server, then you would use anonymous as your login name and your e-mail address as a password. Non-anonymous, you will need a private login name and password. There are also two types of file transfers. ASCII and binary. ASCII is for text transfers only. Binary transfers are for transferring anything else. If in doubt, use binary (bin).

In order to provide a reasonable level of performance and to avoid overloading their system, FTP sites install user limits for anonymous FTP. When one site is busy, one or more archive sites around the world are usually available that can provide the same files. These archives are referred to as mirror sites.

The following procedure can be used for downloading a file from a remote server:

(i) The remote computer's Internet address (either the domain name address or the IP address)

(ii) The pathname that tells you the path of directories you must follow to get from the root directory to the directory where the file resides; and

(iii) The file name itself.

Q43. Briefly discuss Gopher and WWW as information resources.

Ans. Gopher: Gopher is an Internet system developed at the University of Minnesota (land of the Golden Gophers), which allows a site to create an invisible tunnel from itself to other sites. Gopher was originally developed in April of 1991 by a team of experts including Bob Alberti, Farhad Anklesaria, Paul Lindner, Mark McCahill, and Daniel Torry at the University's Microcomputer and Workstation Networks Center. The originators define Gopher as "a software following a simple protocol for burrowing (as a gopher does) through a TCP/IP Internet. The protocol and software follows a client-server model." Once on a gopher, you can work through a menu system to connect to other gophers that exist in North America and throughout the world. When ultimately connected to another gopher, the menu looks the same as the home, or initial gopher. There is no prompt to logon. Instead, all of the resources available on the remote gopher appear to reside at the point where you began your search.

The Internet Gopher is a simple protocol for building distributed information systems and organising access to Internet Resources. It uses a series of menus to organise and automate access to information and other on-line system wherever they reside on the Internet. The Internet Gopher client software presents users with a virtual information matrix (gopher space) that they can navigate by either browsing a hierarchical arrangement of items, or search by submitting queries. For browsing in gopherspace, the gopher client software presents the user with a list of items from which the user selects an item of interest. User can read or access an item without having to worry about domain names, IP addresses. etc. For example if you want to access the on line library catalogues at the University of California, rather than looking up the address and telnetting to it, you find an entry in a menu and select it. The gopher then "goes for" it. You may be even able to arrange inter-library loans if library permits it through on-line catalogue. Alternatively a user can select an item where a query can be put. User is prompted for what works to search for and a full text search is done by the server.

The resources on a gopher system vary from site to site. Generally gophers include full text documents (such as speeches, reference books, news items, subject bibliographies, campus publications. etc.), campus or institutional information for that location (class schedules, campus events, lists of campus organisations, job postings), access to library resources and databases, and access to systems other than itself. The resources are found by working through the menu system. Some gopher sites even allow the user to retrieve documents found at that site in a very easy manner. Even if your Internet connection is not a gopher site itself, it is possible to telnet to any number of gophers and use that gopher to tunnel to other gophers.

WWW as Information Resource: The web has established itself as the most widely used information resource by all kinds of people for variety of reasons. There are all kinds and types of information resources available on the web. Electronic resources on the Internet manifest themselves in numerous flavours and categories, although most of them emulate the traditional publishing while others are revolutionary in their design and approach. While the present trend to imitate and emulate the traditional models of scholarly communication may continue for some time, eventually the capabilities added by the new media would be used in more innovative ways. The information resources available via the web includes electronic journals, courseware, tutorials, manuals, patents, preprints, news, software, technical reports, theses and dissertations, bibliographic databases, images, audio, video, equipment/product catalogues, scientific data sets, library catalogues, museums and archives, virtual libraries, electronic books, online bookselling and print-on-demand, reference sources including dictionaries, encyclopaedias, biographies, abbreviations, thesauri, subject headings, handbooks, maps, organisations and people including employment and career sources, funding/grants sources, libraries/information centres, organisations, research institutes, companies, societies, people, experts, scientists, directories and subject portals.

Q44. Write short notes on the followings:

(1) Archie

Ans. Archie is a software tool for locating files on anonymous FTP sites. Archie is an indexing spider that visits each anonymous FTP site, reads all the directory and file names and then indexes them in one large index. A user can then query Archie which checks the query against the index. Currently, it indexes about 12,000 servers and over 2 million files. The Archie service is accessible through an interactive elnet ession, e-mail queries and command line and X-Window clients.

Finding a file on the Internet by simply browsing through the directories of hundreds of FTP sites is physically impossible. Herein lies the purpose for learning how to use Archie. Archie servers provide a search mechanism for locating files. Anyone who has access to the Internet can search the indexes. Search results tell you which FTP server stores a particular file or directory and what the pathname is for locating it. Although each Archie server is a separate entity, they all perform the same service and even index close to the same FTP sites.

A query can be put to Archie to find filenames which contain a certain search string or whose description contains a certain word. It returns the actual filenames that meet the search criteria, and the name of servers containing those files. Then you can retrieve the desired file using FTP.

(2) Veronica

Ans. Veronica and Jug head are named after the Archie of comic book fame. Veronica attempts to index the world of Gopher servers, much like Archie attempts to build a comprehensive index of all anonymous FTP servers. A central server periodically scans the complete menu hierarchies of Gopher servers appearing on an ever expanded list. The resulting index is provided by the Veronica server and can be accessed by Gopher servers.

Veronica usually is a menu item on a Gopher or World Web server. There might be several Veronica sites available on a given Gopher or WWW server. This variety enables a user to select a not-too-busy Veronica server. After the user selects a Veronica, Gopher asks the user for their search words. A successful search formed the Veronica returns a new menu of Gopher items satisfying the conditions of the search.

The search engine supports sophisticated search strings specifically to target the desired information. The Veronica search engine permits limited Boolean and substring searches. Boolean searches enable the user to include land, or, and not, along with a hierarchy of parentheses, to control the search. Thus, if the search were the following, all references including both smoking and drinking would be included. Veronica is one of the most useful Internet information-hunting tools around.

Unfortunately, because it's also the one that has the fewest servers, reaching a Veronica server can be very difficult.

(3) Wide Area Information Server (WAIS)

Ans. WAIS (pronounced WAYS) stands for wide area information servers. Real-time connections are used to connect to other WAIS servers and to search their indexes. In combination with the World Wide Web, WAIS can be used as a back-end search engine. WAIS relies on indexed data collections, or libraries. These libraries are the collections that consist mostly of informational material. If molecular biology is your meat and drink, for example, several journals on the subject are available online through WAIS libraries. These data collections generally have been indexed and made available by volunteers at academic sites. Commercial WAIS libraries, such as the Dow Jones Information Service, also are available. WAIS was developed by Thinking Machines in collaboration with Apple Computer. Dow Jones, and KPMG Peat Marwickl had developed a generalised retrieval system for accessing data around the world. i.e., to provide a common interface to a multitude of Internet databases. WAIS works in two parts.

- The server side, which indexes WWW sites periodically and maintains this index for access by WAIS and WWW clients.
- The client side, which includes WAIS clients and WWW clients.

Q45. Discuss the use of Internet supports traditional library activities.

Ans. One of the most significant achievement in the information and communication sector is the introduction of advanced communication network, i.e., the internet, the technology connecting a computer with millions of computers in the network. The internet today has become one of the most important mode of communication and its services are being exploited by people in every walk of life such as business, education, defence, medicine. etc. in the field of library and information science, the Internet has become one of the most popular and talked about subject.

Various uses of internet for supporting traditional library activities are as follows:

(1) Aquisition and Collection Development: Internet has made simple and speedy purchase of information sources/documents like books, journais and electronic publications. A number of commercial databases are available for the librarians to exploit viz the CAB abstracts, Agricola, Medline, Agris, Biological Abstracts, Compendex. etc. of Dialog and BRS Information Technology

Most of the publishers and booksellers have their web sites on the internet and place their regular catalogue and leaflets of new publications. Some of the publishers of primary journals like American Chemical Society, IEEE (USA), Elsevier Science publishers are providing their journals online. The IDRC, Canada is providing books on research and development that can be ordered online through the URL http://www.idrc.ca/bookhque. IDRC also publishes its best reports online which are available at web site http://www.idrc.ca. CAB Publishing has recently launched a series of subject specific online communities catering to the needs of librarians and researchers, each community will feature a comprehensive abstract databases with 25 years archive.

Examples of some of the useful set of links available through the internet for acquisition are:

(i) Association of learned and professional society publishers http://www.alsp.org. uk/member.html

(ii) Ingentia journals, provides access to bibliographical information from more than 550 journals from Academic Press, Royal Geographical Society, White House Press and Harwood Academic. etc. and can be searched without restriction http://www.ingentia.com

(iii) ARL Directory of Electronics Journals produced by Association of Research Libraries gives Information on electronic journals and newsletters along with details of the subscription.

(iv) Britannica Online offers the world's first online encyclopaedia. The libraries can provide access to the readers by paying some registration fee. The Britannica Online has advantage of accessing articles not yet in print, and Britannica Book of the Year http://www.eb.com/

(v) Amazon.com books web site provides access to greater selection of books with over one million title which is searchable by keywords, author, title or subject. The site also has provision for purchase, via Netscape's secure commerce server or over the phone. http://www. amazon.com

The library and information professionals can easily browse through the current publications available on various web sites in their area of interest, confirm the prices. etc. and place orders online. Any discrepancy in the invoices or bills, edition of books, printing. etc., can be clarified within minutes through e-mail and much of the paper work is reduced. It is estimated that within the next 5-6 years the internet will become the mechanism for distribution of three fourth of the specialised journals and also the major medium for transfer of research information.

The librarians will thus need to change their attitude towards collection development, as the technology advances in future, it will encourage access to document rather than ownership. In future, virtual libraries may replace traditional libraries which means there would be purchase of access to information rather than the source. This trend will generate many questions about values of libraries.

(2) Technical Processing of Books: The Internet can be used to access latest authoritative tools related to classification and cataloguing to render help in better and faster processing of documents. Links to tools like Library of Congress Classification Schedule, LC Subject Headings, MARC Documentation, OCLC User Documentation, other thesauri and subject dictionaries available on the web can render required help to the staff members involved in technical processing of books. Also, the library can provide a monthly/weekly list of books acquired by the library through the library website.

(3) Journals Ordering and Management: Most publishers maintain their websites with subscription information about their journals that can help the staff involved in journal selection, ordering and management. Several websites maintain meta resources with links to journals from various publishers. The library can provide a complete list of journals subscribed by it as well as weekly list of issues of journals received by it. List of complete journals holding of the library on the website would also enhance the usage. Link to union catalogue of journals subscribed by a group of libraries would help in resource sharing.

(4) Reference Service: The number of reference sources available on the web has increased exponentially during past decade. The libraries can develop subject portals that would provide links to important reference sources through the Library website. Meta sites like Xrefer provides a basket full of reference sources with a single search interface to help the users to retrieve information in a quick and efficient way.

Q46. Enumerate the traditional library services modified in the Internet era.

Ans. The traditional library services modified in the internet era are as follows:

(1) OPAC to WebPAC: When remote access to the library catalogue meant a telnet connection, users had little incentive to visit the library Web page.

As Web PACs matured to the point where the interface was reasonably functional, many libraries phased out their dumb terminal OPACs. The library Web site then became a more logical gateway to the catalogue and other Web-based library resources. An informative home page introduces users to helpful information about the library, its collections, and services. This order of access is a good opportunity to distinguish between the catalogue and other electronic indexes and databases. Web PAC is welcome with open arms because: the Web interface is familiar and graphics aid navigation. The user can click complex subject, or other, headings, less typing is good, there are no UNIX, VMS or other weird commands, it's easy to check periodical holdings in a new browser window without losing search results.

WebPAC: It offers the libraries the opportunities to have access to various resources of other libraries on the web.

(i) It allows users to interact with documents stored on computers all over the world.
(ii) Makes easier to access catalogue data in the form of bibliographic records.
(iii) Sometime has the ability to search the OPACs of other libraries.
(iv) Powerful tool that links all the electronic resources for easy access.
(v) Make the catalogue from providing information to providing access to large banks of actual information.
(vi) It becomes another search engine.
(vii) Referred as 'Web Cats' and as well a type of 'Information Gateway'.
(viii)Some require a login ID, user name and or password.
(ix) Some include information on the screens such as login ID, user name or pass word in boxes and users can see when they access the catalogue.

(2) CD-ROM to Web-based Indexes and Databases: The CD-ROM becomes widely available in the late 1980's was determined as a medium of highest storage and longevity. Due to its advantages, all the library resources were made available through CD-ROM as it has decreased the cost. The libraries nowadays are witnessing another migration to web-based bibliographic databases from bibliographic databases on CD-ROM. The web-based interface provides fast access to users by using hyperlink and other facilities in the web document from the full-text publisher websites. The CD-ROM version of the bibliographic databases has been migrated to the web-based version and due to which the resources are open for remote users.

(3) From Manual Reference Service to Digital Reference Service: The key areas of the digital library include reference service and imparting training to the library users. Now the librarians use the digital reference format instead of waiting for the reference desk. The reference librarian also delivers reference services that require deep intellectual understanding which can be delivered through electronically mediated reference services which are available through libraries for other information centers.

The digital reference service provides internet base question and answer services which can be called as ask-an-expert or ask a librarian service which connects individual to specialise person of that particular subject, who are also known as volunteers or mentors, time information specialist and are affiliated to various libraries virtual reference desk.

(4) From Manual Reference Service to Real Time Digital Reference Service: Library Chat Rooms: Many libraries are experimenting with Internet chat technology as an innovative method for offering real time digital reference service, using chat software, live interactive communication software, call counter management software, web contact software, interactive customer assistance system, such as LivePerson, AOL Instant Messenger, Conference Room and Google Talk. etc. While digital reference service is asynchronous method of information delivery, the Internet chat providing the benefit of synchronous communication between a user and a reference librarian (or mentor). Interactive reference services facilitate a user to talk to a real, live reference librarian at any time of day or night from anywhere in the world. Unlike with email reference, the librarian can perform a reference interview of a sort by seeking clarifications from the user. The librarian can conduct Internet searches and push websites onto the patron's browser, and can receive immediate feedback from the patron as to whether his or her question has been answered to his satisfaction. Several institutions in US including Cornell University, Internet Public Library, Michigan State University, North Carolina University are offering Internet chat-based service.

(5) From Manual Document Delivery to Electronic Delivery Services: Systems which employ electronic technology for receipt of request and supply of documents are known as Electronic Document Delivery Systems (EDDS). "British Library Direct (now BLDSS)" and "British Library Direct Plus" are some of the examples of EDDS. Online Dictionary of Library and Information Science defines Electronic Document Delivery Service as "The transfer of information traditionally recorded in a physical medium (print, videotape, sound recording. etc.) to the user electronically via e-mail or World Wide Web. The libraries employ digital technology to deliver the information contained in the documents and files placed on reserve and requested via inter-library loan."

EDDS provides immediate access to the needed information. In such systems, the request may be received by telephone, e-mail, Fax or online ordering. The document is sent electronically via e-mail, Fax or document delivery software like Ariel. EDDS can provide instant access to material needed. Apart from speed, it is the convenience in accessing information which makes EDDS the preferred method over traditional document delivery methods.

ADONIS, a full-text CD-ROM storage and retrieval system is initiated and developed by a consortium of biomedical publishers. It can be considered as one of the earliest examples of electronic document delivery systems. ADONIS started as a trial project. Ten international publishers, concerned about the widespread photocopying of their material, developed an optical disc system to create journal archives for the sale of single article on demand. In ADONIS, the journals were scanned as soon as they were published. The machine-readable images were stored on CD-ROM, which were shipped to participating libraries and document delivery centres along with cumulated indexes for searching the articles.

ADONIS also supplied two sets of software, one for article retrieval management and other for generating statistics of usage. ADONIS provided on-screen page browsing as well as printing facility. Libraries receiving CD-ROM disks, searched the articles on their personal computers with compatible CD-ROM drive. The required article could be sent to the user by mail or by fax. The printing was automatically monitored on site in the libraries and quarterly reports were generated and sent to ADONIS for per article billing. After two years of trial period, ADONIS was launched commercially in 1991, providing full-text articles of 850 biomedical journals from over 70 publishers to the subscribing libraries. The annual subscription fee was about 16,000 U.S. dollars. ADONIS stopped this CD-ROM product in the year 1997. The availability of full-text e-journals on the Internet, offering wide range of options, like online searching, viewing and pay-per-article basis, led to the closure of this product.

Some of the important Electronic document delivery services include:

Uncover	http://uncweb.carl.org/uncover/subtitle.html
Articles in Physics	http://ojps.aip.org/
Bioline Publications	http://bioline.bdt.org.br/journals
Chemport	http://www.chemport.org/
ScienceDirect	http://www.scienceDirect.com/
OCLC	www.oclc.org/
Northern Light	www.northernlight.com/

Q47. What are the internet-based new library services? Briefly discuss.

Or

Describe different Internet-based new library services.

[Dec-2017, Q.No.-4.2]

Or

Enumerate the different categories of Internet-based library services. Explain Internet-based new library services.

[June-2019, Q.No.-4.2]

Or

Write a short note on web-based user education.

[Dec-2018, Q.No.-5 (e)]

Ans. The internet-based new library services are as follows:

(1) Virtual Library Tours: Websites of libraries provide virtual library guide to the physical facilities including collections, services and infrastructure available in the library. The combination of the following three web-based interfaces are used to facilitate the virtual library tours.

(2) Library Maps and Floor Plans: Most library websites provide library layouts and floor plans to guide users to physical location of facilities and services along with links to relevant information. Client-side image maps are used to make various parts of floor plans as clickable image maps. An example can be seen at the Home Page of the Central Library, IIT Delhi at: http://www.iitd.ac.in/acad/library/layout.htm.

(3) Library Websites: The starting point in development of the Internet based library service is the development of the library's website. The web has opened up enormous possibilities for the development and delivery of services to the library users. A well designed site can go a long way in facilitating library users to access library resources and services at their own convenient time and place. The world wide web is now so widely used that most libraries are trying to use it to improve communications. Librarians now use the web to channel information both to remote and on-site users. Earlier the library websites used to be static providing only factual information about the library with some links to external resources. They have now evolved over the years as more dynamic, interactive and service oriented web portals. The foremost task in developing a website for the library is to understand the user needs and design it around these needs. Service oriented sites were first initiated with the conversion of the library OPACS into web OPACs. This further got extended with the online provision of databases and full text digitised contents, both licenced and ones that are in house developed ones. The present day library websites that we come across are very dynamic and interactive with features like virtual referencing, online chats, etc.

(4) Subject Gateways or Library Portals: Subject gateways are also known as: subject-based information gateways (SBIGs); subject based gateways; subject index gateways, virtual libraries; clearinghouse; subject trees; pathfinders; quality –controlled subject gateways. etc.

Subject gateways is nothing but the facility that allows easier access to networked-based resources in a definite subject area. The simplest type of subject gateways are sets of web pages containing lists of links to resources. "Subject gateways" as a term was popularised in the UK Electronic Libraries Programme (e-lib).

According to Dempsey, L; Gardner, T and D. Michale, UKOLN, University of Bath, UK) "Subject gateways are Internet services which supports systematic resource discovery. They provide links to resources(documents, objects, sites or serivces) predominantly accessible via the Internet. The service is based on resource description. Browsing access to the resource via a subject structure is an important feature".

According to (Emma Place, ILRT, University of Bristol, UK) "Subject gateways are Internet- based services designed to help users locate high quality information that is available on the Internet. They are typically, data bases of detailed metadata (or catalogue) records which describes Internet resources and offer a hyperlink to the resources."

Subject Gateways offer user an alternative to the generalised approach of the commercial global automatic "vacuum cleaner" type of search engines, as infoseek; altavista. etc. Subject gateways are characterised by two key factors:

(i) They are selective, pointing only to Internet resources that meet with quality selection criteria.
(ii) They are built by subject and information specialists- often librarians.
(iii) Generally limited to specific subjects
(iv) Scope-policy declaring what subjects they are indexing
(v) Defined target group-, e.g. academics, researchers. etc.
(vi) Manually created records- rich resource description containing relevant information
(v) Distributed cataloguing – a scattered group of subject specialists contribute to the databases

(5) Web-based User Education: Web guides and teaching tools are found everywhere on the web because they are easily updated, accessed and printed on demand. The web based user education provides a high degree of interactivity and flexibility to the users. The library websites can use web-based user education for imparting training to users in the following area:

(i) Basic library skills along with glossary of library terms
(ii) Using Library OPAC/Web OPAC, locating books, magazines and other library materials
(iii) Instructions for searching CD-ROM and web based databases and other electronic resources
(iv) Instructions on subject search training, using Boolean operators and searching internet resources through search engines.

(6) Frequently Asked Questions (FAQ): Most library websites have Frequently Asked Questions (FAQ) along with their answers. Some libraries have database-driven FAQs along with search interface. These FAQs are generally on the services and facilities that the library provides. These FAQs generally do not include reference questions.

(7) Library Calendar: The library calendar lists events or show information for forthcoming events. Library calendars can have improved look and functionality with JavaScript or special software.

(8) Web Forms: Library websites have some web forms for suggestions and comments on the library services. Different types of web forms are available on web that may be an Indent form for acquiring some publications, interlibrary loan request form for document delivery, Ask-a-Librarian forms, on line reservation form or user survey form. etc.

(9) Bulletin Boards, Threaded Discussion Forums and Listervs: Most of the libraries are using bulletin boards, threaded discussion forums and listservs to help promote and evolve web-based library services. A Bulletin board is an electronic communications forum that hosts posted messages and articles connected to a common subject or theme or interest. It allows users to call in and either leaves or retrieves messages. The messages may be directed to all users of the bulletin board or only to particular users. But all messages can be read by all users. Several libraries are using bulletin boards for their web-based library services. The bulletin board system is also used as an interactive interface to invite suggestions on activities and services of a library. It can also be used as an interface to distribute library services.

A Discussion Forum gives you an opportunity to participate in virtual conversations at any time and any location. Threaded discussions refer to online postings on a specific topic. All messages for a given topic or thread are grouped together for the convenience of users. Discussion forums are basically modified bulletin boards, which have added feature of dividing messages into logical groupings called thread. Threads enable a person to focus on a particular topic and see input from many individuals making comments on the topic.

A Listserv is a method of communicating with a group of people via email. We can send one email message to the "reflector" email address, and the software sends the email to all of the group's subscribers. Several libraries host listservs for the users for providing them a platform to discuss and share their views on books that they have read, or discuss specific books/authors and so on.

Q48. Define Internet information resources. Explain the nature of e-Resources.

Ans. The traditional sources of information in any branch of knowledge are the written, words and, therefore, information sources in a given discipline were (and even t I now) referred to as "literature" that included all definitive sources of information including journals, encyclopaedias, handbooks, textbooks, monographs in series, progress reports, annual reviews, conference proceedings, dissertations and data books. However, with the growth of other forms of dissemination of information especially on electronic media, the term "information sources" was increasingly used in preference to 'Literature".

Internet information resources can be defined as resources (including documents and non-documents) in electronic format that provide information or an indicator to the information and are accessible over the Internet.

Nature of e-Resources: The different types of electronic resources are identified and explained as follows:

- **Primary Sources of Information:** These include electronic conferences, electronic journals, electronic pre-prints and e-prints, electronic theses and dissertations, patents, standards, technical reports, project reports including status reports of current ongoing projects, news, software courseware, tutorials, manuals and the like.

- **Databases, Data sets and other Collections**: These include abstracting and indexing databases; digital collections comprising images, audio, video; scientific data sets comprising numeric, properties, structural databases; library catalogues; virtual libraries; museums and archives. etc.
- **Electronic Books:** Such as NetLibrary (http://www.netlibrary.com/); Ebrary (http://www.ebrary.com/). etc. Generally online book selling and print-on demand features also facilitated. For instance NetLibrary has entered into print-on-demand marketplace. Similarly, Amazon.com (termed as the largest library – though not a library in true sense of the word) facilitates online book selling (http://www.amazon.com/)
- **Reference Sources:** such as dictionaries; encyclopaedias; biographies; handbooks; thesauri and the like.
- **Organisations and People:** Information about organisations and people ranging from funding agencies to libraries; information centres; research institutes; and experts; directories of people of varied nature (scientists; archeologists. etc.)
- **Meta Resources:** Resources that facilitate easier access to network based resources in a defined subject area and a plethora of such resources under various names available on the Internet, such as subject gateways; virtual libraries; clearing house; pathfinders and the like.

Q49. Mention the publishers of e-Resources on the Internet. Explain with examples.

Ans. The publishers of electronic information resources include traditional players offering electronic versions of their printed resources as well as several new enterprises offering new products and services that are "born digital". The market also has several subscription agents in their new role as electronic aggregators. Institutions of higher-learning, specially distant and continuing education departments, are actively supporting and contributing to the development and implementation of computer-assisted instructions and multimedia interactive educational courseware. The publishers of Internet information resources include:

- **Traditional Commercial Publishers:** Most well-known commercial publishers of printed resources such as Elsevier Science, Kluwer Academic Press, Academic Press, Springer Verlag, Wiley InterScience, Sage Publications. etc. offer electronic versions of their printed resources through their web sites or through special interfaces and web-based services developed for this purpose.

- **Scholarly Societies/Bodies:** Scholarly societies such as SIAM, ACM, IEEE/IEE. etc. are making electronic versions of their publications available online through their web sites. Some of the scholarly societies have developed their own technology for web publishing and hosting (e.g. American Computing Machinery and American Institute of Physics), while others hire technology and hosting services from other electronic publishers. IEEE/IEE provides their web-based resources through Information Handling Services (IHS), while the American Society of Civil Engineers (ASCE) ust:s Online Journal Publishing Services (OJPS) from the American Institute of Physics for hosting its web resources.
- **Institution of Higher Learning:** Several academic and research institutions host their specialised collections like courseware, theses and dissertations; and also offer subject gateways and portals. etc.
- **Electronic Aggregators:** Electronic aggregators are intermediary services that aggregate electronic journals and other resources from different publishers and offer them to their clients through a single interface or search system. Aggregators can be compared with the online vendors like DIALOG and STN. While online vendors offer databases from different developers through a single search interface, aggregators provide full-text access to electronic journals and other resources through their search and browse interfaces. Examples of aggregators are: JSTOR; OCLC; Lexis-Nexis and the like.
- **Others:** Collections and meta resources compiled by various groups and individuals are flourishing on the Internet. Several meta resources are dedicated to providing access to electronic resources that are offered free of charges on the Internet. Examples of such meta resources include: Librarians' Index to the Internet (http://lii.org/); Vlib:The Virtual Library (http://www.vlib.org/); Internet Public Library (http://www.ipl.org/) and others.

Q50. Write a note on subscription of e-Resources.

Ans. Journals are made available through the web at varying price models. Some of the prevalent pricing models are:

- **Electronic Subscription is linked to the Print Subscription:** The electronic subscription to journals in Gst of the cases is linked to their printed counterparts. i.e. it may be offered free with print subscription (e.g. publications of American Society for Physics) or priced at a fixed per cent over the print subscription (e.g. IEEE's ASPP package).

- **Electronic Subscription with Campus Licences:** Electronic publisher facilitates campus-wide unlimited access to subscribed journals on payment of a fixed amount of platform fee. Example: Elsevier Science (Science Direct).
- **Electronic Subscriptions are Bundled:** Several electronic publishers offer access to the entire range of their electronic journals and other publications bundled into one. For example, IEEE 1 IEE . . Electronic Library (IEL) and ACM Digital Library offer access to their entire site on subscription. Access to individual journals or a subset is not permissible. Similarly, Academic Press offer all journals available on their site (Academic's Project IDEAL) for 10 per cent more than the print subscription to library consortia.
- **Pay-per-look:** Publishers and aggregators have started experimenting with models wherein a user can search a database online for a modest usage fee, identify articles on interest, and then call up such articles in full-text on a per-look basis.
- **Consortium Licensing:** Consortia provide union strength to negotiate with electronic publishers for the best possible price and rights. Most publishers already have well-defined policies and offers for libraries subscribing as consortia. The consortia licensing is widely used the world over by the libraries. It is slowly picking-up in India as well.

Q51. Enumerate some general information resource, which are important for the library and information science professionals.

Ans. Some general information resource, which are important for the library and information science professionals are as follows:

(1) Internet Library for Librarians (http://www.itcompany.com/inforetriever/): Internet Library for Librarians has been one of the most popular information resource sites for librarians since 1994. It is an information portal specifically designed for librarians to locate Internet resources related to their profession. It has received many awards, including SUNLINK Link of the Week, Digital Librarian Award from Argus Clearinghouse, the Best Library and Reference Site from LibrarySpot, and Five Stars from Anbar Cool Sites, et al. It has been recommended by many professional magazines. Internet Library for Librarians is featured on hundreds of websites and recommended by hundreds of libraries and library related organisations, including the Library of Congress and OCLC.

Internet Library for Librarians provides links to more than 4,000 resources. All the resources are recommended, selected, and reviewed by librarians. Each entry has a full description of the goals and/or scope of the resource, as well as the contact information if provided. Internet Library for Librarians is a handy and useful tool for both novices and experienced library staff.

(2) Librarians' Index to the Internet (www.lii.org/): A searchable, annotated subject directory of more than 11,000 Internet resources selected and evaluated by librarians for their usefulness to users of public libraries. lii.org is used by both librarians and the general public as a reliable and efficient guide to Internet resources.

(3) BUB Information Service (http://bubl.ac.uk/): BUBL Link (http://bubl.ac.uk/link/): It provides free user-friendly access to selected Internet resources covering all subject areas, with a special focus on library and information science. It has a large subject directory with British focus covering many academic and other topics.

(4) WWW Virtual Library (www.vlib.org): Virtual library facilitates access to many excellent resources. It is basically, a rich collection of subject guides on many subjects. However, sites are not annotated or evaluated.

(5) CIT-Online Resources for the Solo Librarian (http://www.unc.edu/cit/guides): It provides a collection of handy links for information professionals working in isolated or specialised libraries, or in other settings with limited access to a wide variety of on-site reference resources and other tools of the library profession. The site includes a great collection on: useful tools and services; book information and reviews; book sources (new, used and out-of-print); reference desks and virtual libraries; professional reading; professional organisations; librarian's marketplace. etc.

(6) Infomine (http://infomine.ucr.edu/): A collection of over 121,465 academically valuable resources, cooperatively compiled by universities and college-level, academic librarians of the University of California campuses.

(7) Academic Info (www.academicinfo.net): AcademicInfo is an online education resource center with a plethora of online degrees, online courses and distance learning information from a selection of online accredited schools.

(8) The Internet Public Library Reference Center (www.ipl.org): A virtual reference library created in an attempt to replicate a library without walls on the Internet. Internet Public Library (IPL) is similar to using a reference room, with links to many resources by type and/or by subject.

(9) J-Gate (http://j-gate.informindia.co.in): J-Gate is an electronic gateway to global e-journal literature. Launched in 2001 by Informatics India Limited, J-Gate provides seamless access to millions of journal articles available online offered by 12,331 Publishers. It presently has a massive database of journal literature, indexed from 55,468 e-journals with links to full text at publisher sites. J-Gate also plans to support online subscription to journals, electronic document delivery, archiving and other related services.

(10) Other Sites: Other general sites for reference are given below:

(i) General Search Sites

Google: http://www.google.com/
MetaCrawler: http://www.metacrawler.com/
HotBot: http://www.hotbot.com/
Alta Vista: http://www.altavista.digital.com
Yahoo!: http://www.yahoo.com/

(ii) People's E-mail Addresses/Web Pages: Search for Someone's E-mail Address, the following sources could be tried.

Yahoo! People Search: http://people.yahoo.com/
Internet @ddress Finder: http://www.iaf.net/
The White NetPages:http://www.aldea.com/whitepages/white.html
WhoWhere? E-mail Addresses: http://www.whowhere.com/
Bigfoot.com: http://www.bigfoot.com/

(iii) Search for Someone's Telephone Number: The following site is useful to search for someone's telephone number.

Switchboard: http://www.switchboard.com/
AOL International Directories:
http://www.aol.com/netfind/international.html

(iv) College and University Web Pages

To search for College and University Web Pages, the following site may be tapped

SearchEdu.com: http://searchedu.com/

Academic Institutions Webpages – Christina DeMello's List of Colleges and Universities:

http://www.mit.edu:8001/people/cdemello/univ-full.html

(v) Search for Listserv Lists, Web Forums, and News Groups: Locating peers is possible through Online Discussion Groups or usenet newsgroups or usenet on the www which is supported by browsers line Netscape Navigator and Internet Explorer. Although some academic disciplines prefer Newsgroups over Listserv-type email groups as their scholarly forum, Newsgroups tend to be popular. The best tool for locating newsgroups at present is 'Google Groups'.

For finding mailing lists

Tile.Net/Listserv: http://www.tile.net/listserv/ is the best tool.

Others are:

Liszt Directory of Email and Discussion Groups: http://www.liszt.com/

Impulse Research Corp.'s E-Mail Discussion Groups/Lists: http://webcom.com/ impulse/list.html

Forum One's Forum Finder: http://www.ForumOne.com/

Stephanie da Silva's Publicly Accessible Mailing Lists: http://paml.alastra.com/

DejaNews Research Service: http://www.dejanews.com/home_ps.shtml

(vi) Maps: Map Meta List: The Perry-Castañeda Library Map Collection:

http://www.lib.utexas.edu/Libs/PCL/Map_collection/Map_collection.html

MapQuest: http://www.mapquest.com/

U. S. Census Map s: http://tiger.census.gov/cgi-bin/mapbrowse-tbl

Weather Maps: http://www.provide.net/weather.html

Maps of India: http://www.natmo.org

Q52. Explain the information resources by source type.

Ans. There are several types of resources available such as:

(1) Electronic Journals and Newsletters: A journal, which is produced in an electronic format, is the electronic equivalent of a paper-based journal. Journals can be accessed over the Internet, which are appearing with increasing frequency and timeliness. Now an increasing number of journals are produced entirely in electronic format. Most of these journals are full-text journals. Such resources facilitate quick and easy access to current as well as back volumes. Besides, one does not need to go on browsing through all the articles, to pick up only papers of interest. There are number of sites that provide access to e-journal resources in Science Technology and Medicine (STM), Social Sciences and Humanities. Examples include:

(i) Science Technology and Medicine (STM)

Elsevier Science (http://www.elsevier.com/) or (http://www.sciencedirect.com)

Elsevier Science has become the undisputed market leader in the publication and dissemination of literature covering the broad spectrum of scientific endeavors. It plays an important role in advancing the technologies necessary to create a seamless electronic information delivery environment. The access to full-text data is fee-based. It provides access to over 1,800 scientific, technical and medical peer-reviewed journals; search to over 4 million articles and 59 million abstracts from scientific articles; and links to articles from over 120 other publishers, online access to multimedia features not otherwise available in print journals is also facilitated. In 2002 Science Direct launched a new commercial service for academic libraries, adding a new licence for users to gain electronic access to both Elsevier Science and Academic Press journals on Science Direct. Science Direct EChoice enables access via a single convenient platform, and a single licence agreement. Flexible access for Science Direct guest users - that is, users not associated with a Science Direct account - are permitted to browse and read abstracts from all of the Science Direct journals for free. They can also set up free table of contents e-mail alerts and create personal journals.

Springer Science Online (http://www.springer.de/)

Springer publishes annually over 4,000 new books and approximately 700 journals, most of which are available in electronic form.

Blackwell Scientific Journals

(http://www.blacksci.co.uk/uk/journals.htm)

Publishes over 600 prestigious journals. Nearly all Blackwell Publishing journals are available online as well as in the print edition.

(ii) Social Sciences: World Wide Web Virtual Library - Social Sciences (http://vlib.org/SocialScience.html). It includes over 100 journals on various areas of Social Sciences. The index lists journals in alphabetical order and search can be initiated by clicking on the letter to jump to the appropriate section. Besides, directories of all types of WWW e-Journals and other online indexes of print or electronic journals are also part of this site. A snapshot of the home page World Wide Web Virtual Library showing various subject categories for which resources are available is reproduced below. On clicking on the concerned link it shows a pool of resources in the area. Sites of journals included in the Social Sciences World Wide Web Virtual Library as such cannot be reproduced, since it is a long list, which you will be able to explore by yourself on navigating this site.

Register of Leading Social sciences E-Journals (http://www.clas.ufl.edu/users/gthursby/socsci/ejournal.html)

Keeps track of on-line serials of significance to researchers in Social Sciences and Humanities. This site is part of the Social Sciences Virtual Library, which was established at the Australian National University.

ECONbase-Elsevier Science

(http://www.elsevier.com/homepage/sae/econworld/menu.htm) Or (http://www.elsevier.nl/): This site acts as an access point to 79 economics journals. Currently, the resource-base provides access to 60,000+ online papers. Online access to full-text articles in ECONbase is available to those readers whose library is - either registered with ScienceDirect web editions or subscribes to Science Direct Digital Collections. In all cases, access is restricted to those journals to which the library holds a current subscription. Except for online access to full-text, there are no restrictions on access to information within ECONbase.

Available functionality includes: browsing tables of content, searching titles, authors, abstracts, keywords in a database of 67 journals. Besides this, provision is also made available for author and keyword indexes for each individual journal, viewing abstracts for all 67 ECONbase journals, selected full-text of a limited number of journals and a free sample copy of each journal.

PSYCLINE (http://www.psycline.org/journals/psycline.html)

The website was started in 1995 by Dr. Armin Günther a psychologist, from Germany, under its former name Links to Psychological Journals and has won a high reputation as one of the most comprehensive and up-to-date index of psychology and social science journals on the web. It provides access to over 1,500 journals in the area of Psychology and Social Sciences with free table of contents and abstracts.

(iii) Humanities: Technical Documentation from HW Wilson - Humanities Index/Abstracts with Full-Text Journal List (http://www.hwwilson.com/Databases/humani.htm)

It is a good source for tracking journals in the Humanities area. Humanities Index/Abstracts with Full Text over 550 journals, excluding name changes. This number represents active, ceased, dropped journal titles.

Social Sciences and Humanities Electronic Journal -UCSD Libraries (http:// libraries.ucsd.edu/sage/ejournals/social_sciences_and_humanities.html) It is another source that provides access to a large number of e-journals in the area of Humanities and Arts.

CARL UNCOVER (http://www.ingenta.com/): CARL is a computerised network of library services developed by the Colourado Alliance of Research Libraries (CARL). CARL UnCover is the Alliance's index to journals and magazines. Access to CARL UnCover is now available through the web at Ingenta. Ingenta has been working to integrate the two databases in order to provide you with a more comprehensive and easy-to-use service. The integrated service offers free searching and browsing of more than 27,000 publications with 11,000 titles that were not available in UnCover. In addition, a number of new services have been introduced. Searching Ingenta is free but Article delivery service is charged. One can arrange to have articles faxed, delivered, or sent electronically (HTML or PDF format) directly. One has to provide his personal credit card number and the articles will be charged to that account.

Project Muse (http://muse.jhu.edu/): Project MUSE is a joint venture of Johns Hopkins University Press and Milton S. Eisenhower Library. It offers access to journal titles in the field of literature and criticism, history, the visual and performing arts, cultural studies, education, political science, gender studies, economics. The number of journals covered is 250 from about 40 publishers. At present, its subscriptions are available only to institutions.

ISI Web of Science (http://wos.mimas.ac.uk/): ISI Web of Science service is a massive resource base covering all the three main divisions of human knowledge. i.e., Science and Technology, Social Sciences and Humanities. The basic databases covered under Web of Science and made available are:

Science Citation Index Expanded with Cited References and Author Abstracts (1981-)

Social Sciences Citation Index Expanded with Cited References and Author Abstracts (1981-)

Arts and Humanities Citation Index with Cited References (1981-)

(2) Directories of All Types of WWW E-Journals World Wide Web Virtual Library (http://vlib.org/)

It is the oldest catalogue of resources on the web. It was started by none other than the creator of WWW, Tim Berners-Lee in 1991. It covers all the branches of knowledge ranging from arts to social sciences, sciences, engineering, and technology. It is an excellent source for starting the search for e- journals.

Directories of Electronic Journals (http://gort.ucsd.edu/ejourn/jdir.html): This site provides a keyword searchable database and extensive links to other resource facilities, supported by the University of California at San Diego.

New Jour (http://gort.ucsd.edu/newjour/): It is an archive for a major list of electronic journals and newsletters available on the Internet.

Scholarly Journals Distributed via the World Wide Web (U. Houston, USA) (http://info.lib.uh.edu/wj/webjour.html): It is a directory organised alphabetically that provides links to established web-based scholarly journals that offer access to English language article files for free.

(3) Online Indexes of Print or Electronic Journals: Social Sciences World Wide Web Virtual Library also includes other online indexes of print or electronic journals for reference purposes. Examples include the following:

Anthropological Index Online (http://lucy.ukc.ac.uk/cgi-bin/uncgi/Search_AI/search_bib_ai/anthind)

An index to current periodicals in the Museum of Mankind Library (incorporating the former Royal Anthropological Institute library). Currently it is available for the years from 1970 onwards. The index is searchable by year, subject area, author, title, or journal.

(4) Table of Contents (TOC): In order to keep abreast of new developments in a particular topic or issue, one of the means or services that people use is current contents listings of the journals. With the advent of e-publishing and Internet, these current contents of journals have become current in real time situations. Not many journals have full-text available on the web, Hence, many academic publishers have designed web pages for each of their journals, wherein they list the current contents of the latest issues of the journal, sometimes with abstracts. So, a regular scan of relevant journal web pages can help to keep up-to-date with new articles as they appear. Almost all the journals available in e-format provide access to table of contents for free.

This is a very useful resource for librarians for Current Awareness Service. These resources help users to stay up-to-date in their research. Also, all such resources are an excellent aid in saving research time. Examples include:

(i) STM: 'Contents Direct' Service by Elsevier (http://www.contentsdirect.elsevier.com/): the service covers over 800 journals. 'Uncover' service provided by CARL agency having TOC of over 16,000 journals. ISI's TOC Alerting Service (journal tracker) (http://alerting.isinet.com/jt_home.html). It provides a choice of about 8,000 journals from which you are allowed to choose 25 titles. You are provided with the complete bibliographical details besides the author abstracts.

(ii) Social Sciences: Academic Press Journals (http://www.apnet.com/journals): Now part of Elsevier Science provides links to the latest Table of Contents, and subscription information for all 174 Academic Press journals in the area of social and behavioural sciences.

(iii) Humanities

Current Contents/ Arts and Humanities (http://www.isinet.com/isi/products/cc/editions/ccah/): ISI Current Contents/Arts and Humanities provides access to complete bibliographic information from articles, editorials, meeting abstracts, commentaries, and all other significant items in recently published editions of over 1,120 of the world's leading arts and humanities journals and books from a broad range of categories. The source besides facilitating regular features of such service has provision for combining comprehensive coverage with numerous access points, exclusive search capabilities; optional coverage of past research; and saves research time by providing one source for a variety of research information - including author abstracts, author addresses, and more information per bibliographic record than in other resources.

Current Contents Search

(http://library.dialog.com/bluesheets/html/bl0440.html)

A weekly service that reproduces the tables of contents from current issues of leading journals in the arts and humanities, social sciences, and sciences.

(5) Preprints and Working Papers: The term 'preprint' most often refers to a manuscript that has not yet been published, but may have been reviewed and accepted, submitted for publication, or intended for publication and being circulated for comments. A preprint accessible over the web may also be referred to as an 'e-print'. Many e-prints are electronic versions of research papers that have been submitted for dissemination and review among peers; for publication in journals; or prior to presentation at conferences. Preprints also cover papers that authors have submitted for journal publication, but for which no publication decision has been reached, or even papers electronically posted for peer consideration and comment before submission for publication. In fact, preprints can also be documents that have not been submitted to any journal. Some preprint servers may define preprints as any electronic work circulated by the author outside of the traditional publishing environment.

The Internet is increasingly being used by academics to publish the full-text of conference papers, draft papers or work-in-progress, and other similar material, often to facilitate peer review process. Examples include the following:

(i) STM

ePrint Network (http://www.osti.gov/eprints/index.html)

Searchable gateway to eprint servers that deal with scientific and technical disciplines of concern to DOE. The ePRINT Network provides access to electronic preprints available from diverse sites. Developed by the U.S. Department of Energy (DOE) Office of Scientific and Technical Information (OSTI), the Network is a "one-stop shopping" site for eprints in science and technology.

Directory of Mathematics Preprint and e-Print Server (American Mathematical Society) (http://www.ams.org/global-preprints)

PubMed Central (http://www.pubmedcentral.nih.gov/)

PubMed Central is a digital archive of life sciences journal literature, developed and managed by the National Center for Biotechnology Information (NCBI) at the U.S. National Library of Medicine (NLM). It contains data from diverse sources stored in a common format in a single repository. It allows fast searching, manipulation and cross linking of the complete collection. PubMed Central provides the following two services: GenBank, the genetic sequence data repository, and PubMed, the database of citations and abstracts to biomedical and other life science journal literature. GenBank, along with the powerful search facilities has helped molecular biologists make rapid advances in their field. PubMed (which encompasses Medline) helps, to locate relevant articles and, in many cases, link directly to a publisher's site for the full-text. GenBank has proven the advantages of collecting DNA sequences in a central repository with a common format.

(ii) Social Sciences

WoPEc (http://netec.mcc.ac.uk/WoPEc.html)

It is an effort at international level to collect together and make available working papers in the area of economics from academics. WoPEc is part of a larger project called NetEC, an international academic project for networking interactions in economics. It provides access to thousands of working papers from hundreds of series and contains over 100,000 documents in electronic format: 76,311 working papers; 100,286 journal articles and 3,900 registered authors. These are downloadable but not necessarily free.

(iii) Humanities: CH Working Papers

http://www.chass.utoronto.ca/epc/chwp/: CH Working Papers (or Computing in the Humanities Working Papers) provides access to refereed articles of an interdisciplinary nature on computer-assisted research. They serve the needs of the researcher at an intermediary stage at which questions of computer methodology in relation to the main discipline are of interest to the scholar before the computer disappears into the background.

(6) Discussion Lists or Forums/Usenet Newsgroups: Discussion lists, Usenet newsgroups, mailing lists are used almost in the same connotation. The fact is that the Internet is interactive and offers new channels for scholarly discourse and new sources of information based on archives of this discourse. One can choose to communicate with people or simply to observe other's communications.

Discussion lists are also sometimes called mailing lists or listservs. These are e-mail based lists available to a group of users who are interested in a particular topic in a specified subject area. Software is used to enable e-mail users to subscribe to (join) a list, who can then post messages to the whole group, participate in discussions, receive all the messages which are posted. Joining the forum is called 'subscribing' while leaving the forum is called 'signing off'.

A major network resource that serves the purpose of current awareness, Usenet newsgroups are a worldwide distributed system of bulletin boards, which are arranged hierarchically into topic areas. These are similar to discussion lists in that different users can discuss a particular area of interest, but users do not have to subscribe, and anyone can view the messages, provided they have access to the software required. Usenet newsgroups and discussion lists are differentiated by their means of accessing the information. However, there are similarities such as the ways in which the newsgroups and discussion lists are commonly used. There are three such ways: (i) users may wish to post a query or a reply, (ii) they may lurk in a newsgroup or list, that is reading the messages and follow the discussion but without posting a message; (iii) or they may want to browse an earlier discussion using an archive. Discussion lists or Usenet newsgroups provide an important platform to keep up-to-date with current developments; seek solutions to the problems you pose; and know about new Net resources. Of course, there are some drawbacks also - such as receiving irrelevant mails or what you call junk mails. etc. There are a large number of scholarly discussion groups available and some possess archives of all the messages posted to them, which can be often searched by keyword.

Examples include the following:

(i) STM

Gentalk - Subscription to: listserv@usa.net

Provides a forum for discussion of genetic problems, lab protocols, current issues dealing with genetics and genetic engineering in general.

(ii) Social Sciences

Mailbase (http://www.mailbase.ac.uk/lists.html)

Provides access to over 2,000 electronic discussion lists for the UK higher education and research community. The site provides education descriptions, message archives and subscription information for numerous mailing lists relevant to education. The site also includes information about how to join any of these lists.

The SOSIG Mailing List (http://www.mailbase.ac.uk/lists/sosig/)

It has over 400 members from the worldwide social science community and distributes messages about among other things, new Internet sites and services for social scientists.

(iii) Humanities

HUMBUL-Humanities Bulletin Board

(http://users.ox.ac.uk/~humbul)

Gateway site, maintained by Chris Stephens at Oxford University, is the best Internet resource in the humanities, and also with a conference diary. Search or browse by clicking on 19 broad categories in the arts and humanities. A good starting point to identify quality web resources in this area.

Humanist Discussion Group

(http://www.princeton.edu/~mccarty/humanist/ humanist.html)

Exclusively for people working and interested in Humanities related discussions.

(7) Directories of Newsgroups and Mailing Lists

Deja.com (formerly Deja News) (http://www.deja.com)

Provides access to a vast number of discussion forums and Usenet groups, including archives of previous postings. The new Deja.com now also aims to serve as an Internet consumer guide, with ratings of products.

Deja Tracker informs you by e-mail about new postings in your favourite newsgroups.

ForumOne (http://www.forumone.com) Speciality search engine; helps you locate messages posted on over 270,000 web discussion forums.

Liszt (http://www.liszt.com) Searchable database of over 90,000 mailing lists/discussion groups.

Usenet Groups (ftp://rtfm.mit.edu/pub/usenet-by-hierarchy/) A directory to Usenet groups by hierarchy.

(8) Software Archives: There are thousands of software packages both shareware, which allows free trial use, and freeware for all purposes and all makes of computer via the Internet. The Internet offers access to numerous software archives that are held at a number of sites on the Internet. Examples include the following:

(i) STM

HENSA-The Higher Education National Software Archives (http://www.hensa.ac.uk/)

Software is mostly in public domain and shareware covering a wide range of applications but especially networking. The archive of microcomputer software is at Lancaster, and the Unix archive at Kent.

(ii) Social Sciences

Software and Datasets for Sociology and Demography (http://www.stat.washington.edu/raftery/Research/Soc/soc_software.html)

There are several software and datasets available from this site

(iii) Humanities

Text Analysis Info Page (http://www.textanalysis.info/)

Text Analysis Info is a website that provides information on text analysis and especially software for the analysis of human communication content. This is mostly text, but not limited and quite a few programs can handle audio and/or video data. The first version started in April 1999, has become quite popular site now. There is a whole lot of information and there are links to various resources available at this site ranging from conferences, workshops and forums; mailing lists; news to text archives; books and regressive imagery dictionary and of course, to software (classification of text; analysis software; definitions and terms; transcribing software (audio/video); language: linguistics information retrieval and much more).

(9) Data Archives: A data archive is a permanent, electronic collection of datasets with accompanying metadata such that users of the data can acquire, understand, and use the data. Data archives are resource centres for analysts who use data for research and teaching. Data archiving is a method of conserving very expensive resources and ensuring that their research potential is fully exploited. Archives ensure that when technology changes, the data in their holdings are technically transformed to remain readable in the new environment. Their functions usually include: being more than a long-term backup, being more than an index or catalogue with pointers to datasets stored elsewhere, ensuring that data are preserved against technological obsolescence and physical damage, cataloguing their technical and substantive properties for information and retrieval, supplying them in an appropriate form to secondary users. Data archives have been established in most European countries and in the United States. They are actively used for testing hypotheses and for other scholarly purposes. Examples include the following:

(i) STM:

National Space Science Data Center (http://nssdc.gsfc.nasa.gov/)

The National Space Science Data Center (NSSDC), USA archives and provides access to a wide variety of astrophysics, space physics, solar physics, lunar and planetary data from NASA space flight missions, in addition to selected other data and some models and software. NSSDC provides online information bases about NASA and non-NASA data as well as the spacecraft and experiments that have or will provide public access data. NSSDC also provides information and support related to data management standards and technologies and much more.

(ii) Social Sciences: There is large number of data archives available on the Internet in the area of social sciences. Some of these are indicated below:

Social Science Hub (http://www.sshub.com/index.html)

Social Science Hub covers resources for Anthropology, Sociology and Archeology and other associated disciplines. Provides links to data archives, websites, newsgroups, news, research tools and publications

Guide to Primary Social Science Research Data and Related Resources Available on the Internet (http://www.chass.utoronto.ca/datalib/other/)

It is a guide to data libraries, data archives, and related institutions about which information is available through the Internet, as well as to primary research data and related resources available for access or acquisition. Literature is also available on data management. The guide includes quantitative (numeric) data, as well as textual resources. It is a major resource guide to provide links to directories of data archives and data libraries; individual data archives, data libraries, and related institutions, besides other useful resources in social sciences.

(iii) Humanities

JSTOR (www.jstor.org)

Provides full-texts of articles relating to ecology, economics, education, finance, history, mathematic, political science, and population studies. Resources are listed by subject and by title also.

Arts and Humanities Data Services (http://www.ahds.ac.uk/)

The Arts and Humanities Data Services (AHDS) is a UK national service funded by the Joint Information Systems Committee and the Arts and Humanities Research Board. AHDS helps you to create, deposit, preserve or discover and use digital collections in the arts and humanities. It provides access to the work of the AHDS, their training events, publications, and wide-ranging collections.

(10) Subject Databases: Databases are a collection of records each of which contains details of a different data item, whether numeric, textual or image-based, and which are usually available in a searchable format. Examples of database resources available on Internet include the following:

(i) STM

PubMed (http://www.ncbi.nlm.nih.gov/PubMed/)

PubMed is one of the several versions of MEDLINE made available via the Internet. The database provides access to nine million citations held in original MEDLINE database plus pre- MEDLINE basic data which has not yet been added to MEDLINE). Besides, the site also provides access to other related databases.

PubMed, a service of the National Library of Medicine, provides access to over 12 million MEDLINE citations back to the mid-1960's and additional life science journals. PubMed includes links to many sites providing full text articles and other related resources.

(ii) Social Sciences

UNESCO Social Science Database - DARE: Directory of Social Sciences Institutions, Specialists, Periodicals (http://www.unesco.org/most/dare.htm)

The DARE database offers over 11,000 worldwide references to social science research and training institutes; social sciences specialists; social science documentation and information services; social science periodicals. The database also contains special references to peace, human rights and international law research institutes.

ERIC- Educational Resources Information Center (http://www.eric.ed.gov/)

The ERIC database is the world's largest source of education information. The database contains more than one million abstracts of education-related documents and journal articles. You can access the ERIC database on the Internet or through commercial vendors and public networks. You can also access ERIC abstracts in the print publications Resources in Education and Current Index to Journals in Education.

(iii) Humanities

The OCLC FirstSearch service connects a world of library users to a universe of information. FirstSearch gives library users instant online access to more than 70 databases, including the namely, OCLC databases:

OCLC WorldCat, OCLC FirstSearch Electronic Collections Online, OCLC ArticleFirst, OCLC PAIS International, OCLC PapersFirst, OCLC ProceedingsFirst, and OCLC Union Lists of Periodicals. Best of all, library holdings are displayed up front, so users can easily identify items in their own library's collection. OCLC FirstSearch is a comprehensive and complete reference service with a rich collection of databases and with links to the World Wide Web, over 10 million online full-text articles, full-image articles from over 4,000 electronic journals, library holdings, and interlibrary loan. It supports research in a wide range of subject areas with well-known bibliographic and full-text databases in addition to ready-reference tools such as directories, almanacs and encyclopaedias.

(11) Campus Wide Information Systems (CWIS): Campus-Wide Information System is an information system intended to present an integrated view of the institution to the members of its community, as well as to alumnae, prospective students and others with an interest. Generally within the menu hierarchy, a broad array of local and Internet resources are made available. The CWIS is a growing resource always 'under construction'.

Campus Wide Information Systems are becoming an important resource base on the Internet for worldwide university campuses that are available online. Such resources provide an in-depth information about the desired campus — whether about academics, resources, course curriculum, library catalogues, databases and other library resources, campus accommodation, tuition fee, scholarships and the like. Besides the individual university campus-wide information systems, most of the universities have web pages for each department that provide contact details of the respective faculty and staff. There are a number of sites that aim to help you find web pages for particular University and also particular department of a university. Generally, the information that is included at such sites comprises the following:

- Information about student organisations and campus services
- Library catalogues and other databases
- Research opportunities
- University newsletters and journals
- Technical reports and preprints
- Administrative or academic department policies
- Schedules of lectures, plays or movies on campus
- Athletic event schedules
- Directory information
- Faculty research interests and publications
- Course offerings and syllabi

There are several advantages for the academic institutions in joining the system. These include the following:

- Making your department or organisation more visible

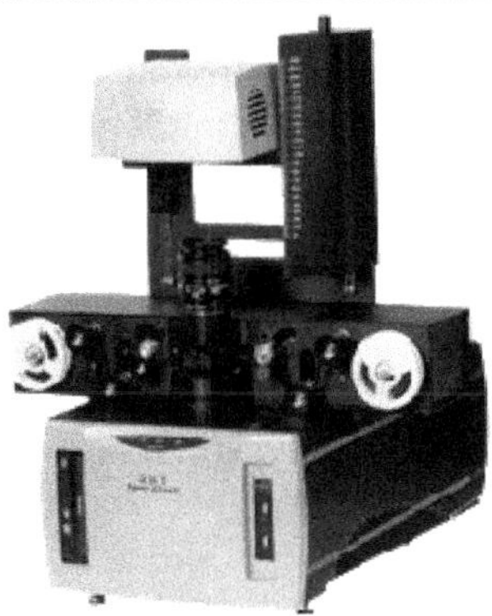

Fig. 2.13

(vii) Video Frame Grabber or Video Digitiser: Video digitisers are circuit boards placed inside a computer and attached to a standard video camera. Anything that is filmed by the video camera is digitised by the video digitiser

(viii) Handheld Scanners: Handheld scanners use the same basic technology as a flatbed scanner, but rely on the user to move them instead of a motorised belt. This type of scanner typically does not provide good image quality. However, it can be useful for quickly capturing text.

(2) Scanning Software: Scanning software comes with the scanner and helps to create image files in formats such as TIFF, JPG, GIF, etc. In addition to this, image editing software is also used which helps to work on the image after it has been scanned.

The scanning software is used for scanning the image and capturing it in the computer. This software is provided by the manufacturer of the product to the buyers. These drivers translate the instructions into commands, which the scanner understands.

Image Editing Applications: Image editing applications are used once the process of scanning the image is over and the image is available in the computer for further manipulation. Most image editing software offer features like image editing, sharpening, filter, cropping, colour adjustments, forms conversion, resizing. etc. Most image editing software can also be used for capturing the images.

Q27. What do you mean by digitisation of audio and video?

Ans. The songs or speeches that we generally listen from tape recorders or radio are in an analogue form. The analogue sound tracks can be digitised by attaching an audio player to a system through an audio capture card so as to record the sound to the system. The audio files can be saved as wav, mp3, midi. etc. MP3 format is highly compact and the sound quality is better in comparison to other formats. Audio files can be further processed using noise reduction software.

Another example of CWIS is that of Massachusetts Institute of Technology (http:// web.mit.edu). Broadly, the site provides you pointers to access detailed information regarding the following:

Spotlights

News–latest news, research, Open Courseware

Academics–admissions, schools, courses, libraries

Research–labs, centers, and programs

Administration–offices and programs, giving to MIT

Resources–for alumni, faculty, staff, and students

Campus–life groups, activities, jobs available

Events–calendar campus events and activities

About MIT–facts, map, virtual tour, evolving campus

Search–Anything you are interested in

(ii) Social Sciences: The following are some of the important websites on CWIS giving information about social science departments:

Campus Wide Information Systems (CWIS) Using WWW (http://www.hcc.hawaii.edu/hccinfo/cwis.html)

Economics Departments, Institutes and Research Centers (EDIRC) in the World (http://ideas.uqam.ca/EDIRC/index.html)

(iii) Humanities: The following are some of the important websites on CWIS giving information on the humanities departments:

University of Massachusetts–English Department (http://www.umass.edu/english/links.html)

Division of the Humanities, University of Chicago (http://humanities.uchicago.edu/humanities/)

UCSC Humanities Division (http://humwww.ucsc.edu/)

(12) Technical Reports: Technical reports constitute an important information source for academics and researchers and for governmental agencies. Academics and researchers, particularly in STM disciplines often try to get access to technical/ research reports in the areas of their interest. Their importance lies in the following aspects:

They provide additional material, which is usually not available in published literature.

They provide details of interim/progress reports or completed R&D projects.

They provide more details than papers in journals or conferences.

They provide more nascent information than what is available in published literature.

(13) Library Catalogues: The library catalogue lists all of the material available in the library with information on where to find it, whether it is available and how long you may borrow it for. Reservations can be placed on material that is currently on loan to another person. You can find the following materials on the library catalogue:

- Books
- Periodicals (e.g. journals, magazines, newspapers, reports and official publications)
- Pamphlets and Official Documents
- Theses
- Audiovisual material
- Microfiche and microforms
- Electronic resources

The Library of Congress Online Catalogue (http://catalog.loc.gov/): The Library of Congress Online Catalogue is a database of records representing the vast collection of materials held by the Library. In addition to these records, the Online Catalogue provides cross-references, notes, and circulation status, as well as information about Library materials still in the acquisitions stage.

The Library of Congress Online Catalogue contains approximately 12 million records representing books, serials, computer files, manuscripts, cartographic materials, music, sound recordings, and visual materials. The Catalogue also displays searching aids for users, such as cross-references and scope notes. The catalogue records reside in a single integrated database; they are not separated according to type of material, language of material, date of cataloging, or processing/circulation status. As an integrated database, the Online Catalogue includes 3.2 million catalogue records from an earlier database. These catalogue records, primarily for books and serials cataloged between 1898 and 1980, are being edited to comply with current cataloging standards and to reflect contemporary language and usage.

Questia (http://www.questia.com/)

Believed to be one of the world's largest online library. The documents are arranged subject wise basis.

(13) Patents: According to U.S. Patent and Trademark Office publication "A patent for an invention is a grant of a property right by the Government to the inventor...The right conferred by the patent grant is...the right to exclude others from making, using, or selling the invention. What is granted is not the right to make, use, or sell, but the right to exclude others from making, using, or selling the invention."

There are also resources that give general information regarding patents, such as how to file a patent. etc. For example General Information Concerning Patents (http:// www.uspto.gov/web/offices/pac/doc/general/index.html) is one such source.

(14) Document Delivery: Document Delivery Service is an important component of the Library's interlibrary loan activity by which users' are facilitated not only to obtain information about the location of a document but the document itself. The Document Delivery Service or DDS is usually a fee-based service provided to faculty, staff and students, as well as to business, industry and individual researchers, etc., by various universities, and other information providers/organisations. Document Delivery staff generally locates, photocopies, and sends directly to the customers office or home a variety of documents owned either by the library or has access to resources wherein the same are being accessed and sent through traditional post or electronically. There are a number of such services available on the Internet, most of which are fee based. Examples include the following:

British Library Document Supply Centre (BLDSC) (http://www.bl.uk/services/ document.html)

British Library Document Supply Centre is a single largest source for all your document needs. BLDSC is the leading document provider in the world. A rapid and comprehensive document supply and interlibrary loan service from BLDSC's extensive collections and its library network to researchers and scholars in all kinds of libraries and organisations is being entertained by this centre. You can register for a range of services available for UK and overseas customers. If you want to order a copy of a particular journal article or conference paper straightaway, the Articles Direct service is probably what you are looking for. Inside web provides options for searching for relevant journal articles and conference papers as well as ordering them over the web. Facilities for several other services for more specialists copying of library materials are also included at this site.

ISI Document Delivery (http://www.isinet.com/documentdelivery/)

A document delivery service provides access to full-text items from virtually any publication within or outside of the ISI database. This flexible, fast, and convenient service provides wide coverage, reliable customer support, fast and varied delivery options, and efficient management tools. The system offers the following:

One-stop shopping — with comprehensive coverage that includes documents from research journals, conference proceedings and papers, book chapters, technical reports, government reports, annual reports, standards, and monographs.

Helps to researchers to get the information they need fast - processing orders for documents in the ISI collection within 24 hours of receipt, and providing delivery options that include fax (30-minute delivery upon request), courier, or traditional mail service.

Provides easy tracking of orders and accounts - via a professional customer support staff that helps verify order status and confirm order pricing and payment balance.

Eases record keeping by eliminating hidden costs: all materials have a standard processing fee, a variable copyright fee, and are copyright cleared.

(15) Reference Sources: A vast number of reference sources such as dictionaries, directories and other reference sources are freely accessible on the Internet. Reference sources have been categorised in two groups as listed below based on the nature of their coverage.

Specific Reference Resources

Humanities Reference Sources

(http://www.library.siue.edu/lib/info/refhum.html)

General Reference Resources

Web of On-line Dictionaries: (http://www.yourdictionary.com/)

Links to on-line dictionaries in languages from Aklon to Zulu, as well as multilingual dictionaries and other language tools.

Dictionary.com: (http://www.dictionary.reference.com)

Dictionary.com is produced by Lexico Publishing Group (http://www.lexico.com/), a leading provider of language reference products and services on the Internet. This site provides links to various dictionaries, thereby facilitating search to various dictionaries at one place. In order to use the dictionary, you need to simply type a word in the blue search box that appears at the top of every page and then click the option 'Look it up' button. This will perform a search for the word in the several dictionaries hosted on this site (list of all dictionaries covered herein appears in the homepage of this site). If you don't know how to spell the word, just guess, you will get a list of suggestions if you are wrong.

Thesaurus.com: (http://www.thesaurus.com)

Thesaurus.com is also produced by Lexico Publishing Group. In order to use the thesaurus, simply type a word in the gold search box that you will find on the web page when you access this site and click the option 'Look it up' button. A list of synonyms and antonyms will be returned. The thesaurus that appears on this site is Roget's Interactive Thesaurus.

Encyclopaedia.com: (http://www.encyclopaedia.com)

Encyclopaedia.com is the Internet's premiere free encyclopaedia that provides users with more than 57,000 frequently updated articles from the Columbia Encyclopaedia, Sixth Edition. Each article is enhanced with links to newspaper and magazine articles as well as pictures and maps – all provided by eLibrary. This eLibrary is a comprehensive digital archive for information seekers of all ages where one can search across 13 million documents from full-text newspaper and magazine articles, television and radio transcripts, international newswires, classic books, maps, photographs, as well as major works of literature, art and reference books. One can find both current and historical events within the diverse eLibrary archive.

(16) Other Resources: Apart from the type of resources explained above, there are several other types of Internet resources which are grouped here as other resources.

Data Centres: Data Centres are primarily sites comprising databanks that provide actual statistical data related to specific subjects. These sources are of utmost importance in areas where statistical data is key input. Examples include the following:

The Humanities and Social Sciences Data Center (http://www.scc.rutgers.edu/datacenter/humanities/about.htm)

This data centre at Alexander Library is a unique resource for Rutgers faculty, students, and other scholars. The Data Center facilitates access to the Rutgers University Libraries' Government, ICPSR (Inter-University Consortium for Political and Social Research). The Center serves as a clearinghouse for existing or newly created data collections located elsewhere.

The Data Center's holdings provide access to a number of full-text databases, such as the Packard Humanities Institute database, the Thesaurus Linguae Graecae, the Oxford English Dictionary, CETEDOC, and Letteratura Italiana Zanichelli. It also offers a convenient point of access to full-text Web-based databases, for which it provides supplementary documentation and tutorials. Some of these databases are the African American Poetry Database, the English Poetry Database, ARTFL, and the Dartmouth Dante Project.

Research Resources/ Research Projects: Research projects are an integral component of a resource-base in any subject area. Research resources/research projects provide a good starting point for researchers and academicians in any subject area to navigate what is broadly available and locate sources in their area of research. Such resources also provide links to tools that help in research work in the requisite subject area of interest.

Examples include:

Education-Line (http://www.leeds.ac.uk/educol/)

Education-Line (http://www.leeds.ac.uk/educol/)

Virtual and Remote Experimental Laboratories: A shared virtual learning environment is a resource-based approach to the provision of learning materials. It addresses some of the pressures on higher education caused by the changing student population. Students will be able to access on-line learning resources and keep in touch with course mates from their home computers.

Discursive learning labs are very good for social sciences, languages, and humanities subjects. In the languages they are an effective way for students to practice their writing, speaking and listening skills among a peer group. They enable remote students to take part in the group discussion and arguments that are central to the humanities and social sciences. In fact, the collaboration tools that underlie discursive learning labs provide an excellent way for remote students to keep in touch with course-mates. Discussion boards should be adopted as a central component of a shared virtual learning environment. However, it may be indicated that remote laboratories without manipulation are effectively just video conferencing suites. For example:

Web-Lab Information Page (http://weblab.badm.sc.edu/web-lab-information/web-lab-information.htm)

Directories: Directories are search services, which involve human input in identifying relevant resources and allocating them to particular subject category or theme. Tools are usually searchable and browsable via the directory. Resources are not evaluated in terms of quality prior to their inclusion in the directory. There is galore of such search services available in Social Sciences via Internet. All types of directories are available be it specialists, e-mail directory, institution or the like. Examples include the following:

DARE: Directory in Social Sciences - Institutions, Specialists, and Periodicals (http://database.unesco.org/dare)

DRIS - Research Information Systems Worldwide
(http://www.niwi.knaw.nl/en/oi/dris/toon)

Online Documents: Traditional textbooks are not commonly made freely available over the Internet. However, some academics have created their own online textbooks and these are often of a very high quality, with comprehensive coverage and excellent interactivity. Examples include:

The Web Center for Social Research Methods
(http://www.socialresearchmethods.net/kb/index.htm)

Online Multimedia Projects and Exhibits: The multimedia projects and exhibits have special significance as a resource for humanities area. Multimedia basically means combination of audio, visuals, text, graphics, 3 D visuals. etc. all on a single platform. Hence, facilitating the virtual display of the product/resource and the like. Examples include of such multimedia resources include the following:

Alive TV (http://www.ktca.org/alive/season12.html)

The Electronic Academic Village
(http://jefferson.village.virginia.edu/home.html)

Others: Besides the above-indicated type of resources, there are several other resources as well. New resources are being added to the Internet on continuous basis. Hence, any list is liable to date.

It may However, be re-iterated that within different types, the sources fulfil more than one condition for being categorised under different types, Therefore, overlap of resources under different types is un-avoidable.

Q53. Discuss the searching techniques from where to start for accessing information on the internet.

Ans. With billions of websites online today, there is **a lot** of information on the Internet. **Search engines** make this information easier to find. Let's look at the basics of using a search engine, as well as some techniques we can use to get **better search results**.

(1) There are many different search engines we can use, but some of the most popular include **Google**, Yahoo!, and Bing. To perform a search, we'll need to navigate to a search engine in our web browser, type one or more **keywords**—also known as **search terms**—then press may look for something, which is stored in specialised searchable databases.

(2) Subject-based gateway services and virtual libraries would probably be the best starting point from where we can reach to the enormous number of guides. Using a gateway or a virtual library as a starting point can save us a lot of time and effort because we need not sift through thousands of outdated and useless sites. Facilities like Argus Clearinghouse can act as a great source to begin with.

(3) After we run a search, we'll see a list of **relevant websites** that match our search terms. These are commonly known as **search results**. If we see a site that looks interesting, you can click a link to open it. If the site doesn't have what we need, we can simply return to the results page to look for more options.

(4) If you don't find what we're looking for on the first try, don't worry! Search engines are good at finding things online, but they're not perfect. We'll often need to **try different search terms** to find what you're looking for. For instance, if we are looking for 'Breast Cancer in Women', we may look for a broader term 'cancer'.

(5) If such approach does not prove useful, then one should move to general subject directories or catalogues, although they tend to be larger but less selective in terms of site quality.

(6) If still nothing useful is found, then the next option should be the search engine. These yield comprehensive search results, though these could be less specific.

(7) The final option would be to opt for a meta search engine, and still if nothing worthwhile is found, it may be time to presume that no relevant item is available on the Internet on that specific query, which is of course very rare.

(8) In such situations when we have exhausted options, we may want to ask someone through a discussion group.

Q54. What are the methods to keep up-to-date with new internet resources? Discuss some resources that can help us in this regard.

Ans. The Internet is getting bulkier day by day. New resources are being added to the Internet every now and then. The Internet can be useful for maintaining current awareness within a particular subject field. It is important to keep a track of new sites that are added in the concerned area of specialisation. The following are some such sites that can help you in keeping up-to-date with new resources. Similarly we can bookmark or preserve URL of a source in a file for future use, which we think, is appropriate. There are some sources on the internet, which keeps us posted about new resources. Example are as follows:

(1) Scout Report Fdr Social Science (http://wwwscout.cs.wisc.edu/)

The Scout Report is one of the Internet's longest-running weekly publications. offering a selection of new and newly discovered online resources of interest to researchers, educators, and anyone else with an interest in high-quality online material. A very useful regularly updated source of information for new resources covering all types of resources like full-text papers; table of contents for new journals; forthcoming conferences: statistics and much more. The Report is available both on the web site, and in e-mail form via mailing list subscriptions. Past issues of the Scout Report, as well as past issues of the discontinued subject-specific Reports, are available from this site as back issues pages.

(2) WWW Social Sciences Newsletter (http://www.clas.ufl.edu/users/gthursby/ socsci/news.htm)

This online newsletter (ISSN 1323-9376) is a part of the Social Sciences WWW Virtual Library and is provided as a service to the World-Wide Web community. To receive the listings of new or improved WWW sites in the form of e-mail, you may subscribe to such a service by sending an e-mail message to majordomo@clas.ufl.edu with the following information in the body of the message subscribe socsci-news "Firstname Lastname" e-mail address.

(3) Internet Resources Newsletter (http://www.hw.ac.uWlibWWW/irn/ irn.htm1)

The free, monthly newsletter for academics, students, engineers, scientists and social scientists. Possibly the most useful round-up of new resources for academic users. The Internet Resources Newsletter is edited by: Roddy Macleod, Catherine Ure & Catherine Ferguson, Heriot Watt University Library, includes new additions to the Internet in various subject areas.

(4) Netsurfer Digest (http://www.netsurf.com/nsd/)

Netsurfer is now charging money for full access to their content. However some stuff is still free. For subscription to such a service full details about the new subscription system can be found at: SUBSCRIPTION INFO: http:// www.netsurf.com/subs~letter.htm

(5) BUBL LINK Updates (http://bubl.ac.uk/link/updates/current.html)

Selected Internet resources covering all academic subject areas. One could select appropriate subject area such as social sciences and find out new resources.

(6) Infomine: scholarly Internet resource collections (http://infomine.ucr.edu/)

Click on what's New next to each subject category to view new additions to the directory. You can also join an Alert Service, to receive e-mail information of new sites as they are added to the directory. New Resource Alert Service lists new resources. The e-mail notification service can keep you informed of new resources as they are added to I-NFOMINE. You can initially choose (and later modify) one or more general subject areas of INFOMINE to receive alerts as well as the frequency with which they are received.

(7) Academic Info - What's New (http://www.academicinfo.net/new.html)

Sign Up mailto: madin@academicinfo.net to receive their monthly announcement list.

Q55. What is the need of evaluation in internet resources?

Ans. A library selects documents for its collection after careful evaluation and adds them to its collection in their proper context. The process of selective acquisition adds value to information resources available in a library that, in turn, helps library users to harvest the information that they need. Internet resources cannot be treated differently from those in printed media considering the fact that most of the Internet information resources do not go through the process of filtration prevalent in the printed world. The web is merely a new medium that acts as an effective system for delivering electronic information. Librarians have been traditionally selecting, evaluating, describing and providing intelligent access to information resources for decades; they are, therefore, best suited to do this job. The need for evaluation of Internet-based information resources can be justified on the following grounds:

- Authenticity of information published on the web need to be established;
- The author of published information may not be an authority or an expert in the area
- The information on the Internet may be outdated
- Reliability of information on the network may not have been established;
- The information needs to be presented for a given audience. The librarian needs to establish its relevance for the targeted audience.

Q56. Explain Quality assessment.

Ans. As assessment of quality is primarily dependent upon two core factors, namely,

- the needs of the individual, and

- nature of the source being evaluated.

Besides, extensive usage of a particular resource will also give you a fair indication about quality of the material. However, in general, to know the quality of a source one should look for the following aspects:

- Currency and maintenance of the resource – how frequently the resource is updated;
- Scope and purpose of the source - what is the coverage and intended readership or audience of the source;
- Creator/producer of the source – whether it is produced by a reputed organisation/ individual/NGO and the like; and
- Presentation, ease of usage and help in using related resources.

Q57. Briefly discuss the evaluation tools on the net.

Ans. From a librarian standpoint, we need to use the same critical evaluative skills in looking for information on the Internet that we would do for a book, a paper, index, a musical score, or on an online commercial database. The content of the Internet is only more diverse because of the potential of interaction with more media. With the growth of information on the Internet and the development of more sophisticated searching tools, there is now more possibility of finding information and answers to real questions. But, within the morass of networked data are both valuable nuggets and an incredible amount of junk.

How should users today approach searching on the net and critically evaluating the data they find? You need a systematic approach to evaluating the tools you will use for searching and what they will cause you to receive or keep you from receiving. At the same time you also need a systematic approach to evaluating the document or result that you receive as a result of your search. As information professionals we are in the best position to determine and expand the relevance of existing criteria to new and future formats.

Learning how to determine the relevance and authority of a given resource for your research or for providing relevant information to users is one of the core skills of the research process. There are a number of sites that direct and assist you in evaluating quality of Internet resources, such as the following:

Internet Detective (http://sosig.ac.uk/desire/internet-detective.html)

This is a very useful and entertaining inter-active tutorial for evaluating the quality of Internet resources.

Searchability: Guides to Specialised Search Engines
(http://www.searchability.com)

A good descriptive guide to specialised search engines, and to search directories of search engines, evaluating their subject coverage and effectiveness.

Search IQ (http://www.searchiq.com)

Provides access to a very large number of search engines and directories, and combines this with independent search-engine reviews and rankings, to help you identify the right search tool for the job - and those with the highest IQ! Also offers tips to improve your searching techniques, with tutorials and guides.

Others

- **Intermediary Tools:** Bschool.com, (http://www.bschool.com/): Originally, the Marr-Kirkwood business school rating guide. A review guide that describes the resource and puts its stamp of approval by the number of stars.

  Yahoo! (http://www.yahoo.com) is one of the tools that helps you identify like resources so that you can compare them.

- **Popular Search Engines:** In a number of cases it makes more sense to search a popular search engine to go directly to material on your specific term than it does to browse through directories or review tools.

  With these tools you are searching using the value of description rather than that of evaluation. Most search engines today have some sort of associated portal. Danny Sullivan's Search engine Watch (http://www.searchenginewatch.com/) and Greg Notess' Search Engine Showdown (http://www.notess.com/search) are two current tools for keeping abreast of search engine developments. There is no good advice as to which one search engine is the best. They keep changing constantly.

- **Search Engine Partners:** Search engine partners such as Ask Jeeves (http://www.ask.com/) (question answering resource) Teoma (http://www.teoma.com/) (subject specific popularity). Each adds a value depending upon its niche.

- **Directory Partners:** Check to see if your search engine has licenced one of these or is creating its own. Inktomi (http://www.inktomi.com/) - purchased by Yahoo in 2003; Look Smart. (http:// www.looksmart.com/)

  Sites are springing up that purport to provide 'evaluations' of Internet resources. The next thing that is needed is to evaluate their track record to determine the value of their evaluations. While there are criteria in each case, the implementation of the evaluations is frequently subjective or biased. It may be worth mentioning here that this is really no different than what we have lived within the print environment, except that now it is digital.

- **General Guides and Directories:** Such as WWW Virtual Library (http://vlib.org/); Yahoo! –(http://www.yahoo.com/)

- Such as WWW Virtual Library (http://vlib.org/); Yahoo! – (http://www.yahoo.com/) Among the general guides there are a number of sites that purport to be the site you should start with:

  About.Com (http://www.yahoo.com/);

  Webfile (http://www.thebighub.com/);

  Search Engine Colossus

  (http://www.searchenginecolossus.com/)

  You might want to compare in terms of value, to you the level of specificity in Yahoo and the WWW Virtual Library and the newer general directories versus the set of categories in the various directories of the search engines.
- Specialised Guides: Examples include:

  A Business Researcher's Interests (http://www.brint.com/);

  StreetEYE Supersites

  (http://www.streeteye.com/index/index.html);

  Bschool.com (http://www.bschool.com/);

  OneLook Dictionary (http://www.onelook.com/)
- More traditional library resources (fee-based and generally worth the cost):

  Examples include:

  EBSCOhost (http://www.ebscohost.com/);

  First Search (http://firstsearch.oclc.com/);

  Proquest (http://www.proquest.com/);

  Thomson Gale (http://www.gale.com/)

Q58. Mention the types of evaluation criteria for information resources.

Or

Discuss the generic criteria for evaluation of an Internet resource. [Dec-2018, Q.No.-4.2]

Ans. In the research process you would usually encounter many types of resources including books, articles and websites. But not everything you find on your topic is suitable. How do you evaluate its authority and appropriateness for your research? It is necessary to understand the current state of the Internet to determine how you best identify the quality of an Internet resource in this volatile, continually changing environment.

The two types of evaluation criteria are:

(1) Generic Criteria for Evaluation: To evaluate an Internet resource, you need to think critically, even suspiciously, by asking a series of questions that will help you decide how much of the resources displayed by a website are to be trusted.

The techniques that you will be employing for the process begins with looking at your search results from a search engine or other source, followed by investigating the content of page, and extends beyond the page to what others may say about the page or its author(s) credentials and other quality factors.

(i) URL Appropriateness: Before you leave the list of search results, glean all you can from the URLs of each page. Then choose the pages most likely to be reliable and authentic.

What can the URL tell you? It can help you in several ways such as whether the URL is appropriate. You can check:

- Is it somebody's personal page?
- Is the server a commercial ISP or other provider mostly of web page hosting like aol.com What type of domain does it come from ?
- URLs can also reveal bias, such as microsoftsucks.com.
- Who 'published' the page? Is it published by an entity that makes sense?

Personal pages are not necessarily bad, but you need to verify the author's (credentials) very carefully. For personal pages, there is no publisher or domain owner vouching for the information in the page. In general, perhaps a site hosted on a free server might not have the same credibility as one from a .gov or .edu site. Use Whois Domain Lookup (http://www.networksolutions.com/cgi-bin/whois/whois) to know who owns the domain. In general, the publisher is the agency or person operating the server computer from which the document is issued. The server is usually named in first portion of the URL (between http:// and the first/). For instance, you can coolly look for health information from any of the agencies of the National Institute of Health on sites with nih somewhere in the domain name.

(ii) Responsibility/Author: The first thing that you should look for on this aspect, is:

- Who is responsible for the work to decipher authority or author or creator
- What are the author's credentials on this subject?
- Does the purported background or education look like one who is qualified to write on this topic?

Look for the name of the author, or the name of the organisation, institution, agency, or whatever is responsible for the page. An e-mail contact is not enough. If there is no personal author, look for an agency or organisation that claims responsibility for the page. An e-mail address with no additional information about the author is not sufficient for assessing the author's credentials. If you cannot find this, locate the publisher by truncating back the URL. You should hold the author to the same degree of credentials, authority, and documentation that you would expect from something published in a reputable print resource such as a book, journal article, good newspaper.

There should be an 'about us' page, with contact information and credentials. Any site that omits this information is of questionable authority.

(iii) Purpose: Why was the page put on the web? (to: inform, give facts, give data, explain, persuade, sell, entice, share, disclose?)

What is the tone of the page (ironic, satire, and the like)

Is the page merely an opinion or it has some quality basis (from research point of view)?

Is the page a rant, an extreme view, possibly distorted or exaggerated?

These are some of the reasons to think of. The web is a public place, open to all. You need to be aware of the entire range of human possibilities of intentions behind web pages. Anyone can put anything on the web for pennies in just a few minutes. Your task is to distinguish between the reliable and questionable. Many web pages are opinion pieces offered in a vast public forum.

(4) Documentation: If you cannot find strong, relevant credentials, look very closely at documentation of sources.

Are sources documented with footnotes or links?

Who do they link to?

Who links to them?

Do the links work?

Does it include copyright information?

In scholarly/research work, the credibility of most writings is proven through footnote documentation or other means of revealing the sources of information. Saying what the author believes without supporting documentation is not much better than just expressing an opinion or a point of view.

Check the external links to see what kind of places they lead to. Are some of them questionable? Do an AltaVista field search (link::"whatever the URL is")to find out who links to them. Links that don't work or are to other weak or fringe pages do not help strengthen the credibility of the page. Look at the bottom of such articles for copyright information or permissions to reproduce. If you find a legitimate article from a reputable journal or other publication, it should be accompanied by the copyright statement and/or permission to reprint. If it is not, be suspicious.

(5) Recognition by Others: Try to determine whether the site has been recognised as exemplary, either in reviews or by others linking to it.

Who links to the page?

Is the page listed in one or more reputable directories or pages?

What do others say about the author or responsible authoring body?

Find out how many links are there, what kinds of sites link to it, what do they say, are any of them directories and the like. Sometimes a page is linked to only by other parts of its own site (not much of a recommendation). Sometimes a page is linked to by its fan club, and by detractors. Read both points of view. If a page or its site is in a bonafide directory, think about whether there is much critical evaluation of the links in the directory.

Good directories include a tiny fraction of the web, and inclusion in a directory is therefore noteworthy. If the viewpoint about author or creator is radical or controversial, expect to find detractors. Think critically about all points of view. Figure out the comparability with related sources from the links that it includes or is being linked to.

(7) Information: The information component needs to be viewed from three angles:

- Content
- Currency
- Coverage

In terms of the content, one needs to ascertain the stability of information

Can I rely on it staying there?

Coverage – should focus on the scope and objectives of the content vis-à-vis the user requirements.

Currency – should generally be viewed in terms of the following:

Is the page dated?

Is it current enough?

When was the last update?

Look for the date last updated - usually given at the bottom of a web page. Check the date on all the pages on the site. Do not rely on a date given in Internet Explorer's File Properties or Netscape's View Page Info displays. These dates can be automatically kept current and are useless in critical evaluation.

However, the requirement of currency depends on your needs. For some topics you want current information, while for others, you may want information put on the web near the time it became known.

(8) Personal Discretion: Personal discretion would be based on common sense. Just because a major search engine may suggest the site, it doesn't mean it's accurate. Use the same kind of 'internal filter' you use when reading print material like newspaper and magazine articles and junk mail.

Ask yourself if the web is truly the best place to find resources for the research you are doing.

Is this as good as resources that I could find if I used the library, or some of the web based indexes available through the library, or other print resources?

What is your requirement or your user's requirement for the quality of reliability of your information?

Specific Criteria for Evaluation: The various evaluation parameters or criteria have been broadly categorised under four categories as shown below:

(i) Content Criteria: The information content is a primary consideration when evaluating Internet resources.

The content of resources can be evaluated by considering the following criteria:

(a) Validity: Consider the following under this parameter/ criteria

Do the resources fulfil the stated purpose? (Find out the scope and missing information, if any)

Does the information appear to be well researched? (Whether sources of information such as references and bibliography are included?)

Is there any mention of the resource being available in another format?

What was the incentive of the information provider for making the information available? (Just for vanity, or other purposes)

Is the information genuine at least by what it appears to be? Does the URL support the claim of authorship? Does the resource point to other sources, which could be contacted for confirmation?

(b) Authority: Here, mainly authority and reputation of the source will be deciphered. Whether the resource is well documented or not. Where is it hosted? Who and how reputable is the information provider? (Credentials of the author/creator in terms of his reputation or is he frequently cited author, subject expert?, etc.)

(c) Substantiveness: Does the resource contains more than contact details? Is the information full-text? Is it merely advertising? Do we get some value added information such as an annotated bibliography or things like that?

(d) Accuracy: Is the information accurate with regard to content, grammar and typographical errors.

(e) Comprehensiveness: The extent of details the resource has is another important parameter of evaluation. The things one can look for this is whether the title is informative; an abstract is given; some sort of opening mission statement of the purpose of the resource is given; or keywords that indicate the information content are included. Besides, you need to see whether everything you expect to find in the site is there.

(f) Uniqueness: This parameter or criterion addresses the uniqueness or otherwise of information available on the site, This can be broadly judged by the nature of the material whether it is primary material; or any original work available at the site; or material having any relation to other works or whether is site inward focussed which means it is not just a list of links to external sites but much more than that.

(g) Overall Format: Yet another important aspect is how well the information is composed and organised. Good composition with respect to following of basic rules of grammar, spelling and literary composition for the text and related aspects. Good organisation of information refers to good structure; logical and consistent arrangement of information within a resource that is user friendly; segmentation of information for easy consumption and registering; clarity in the content description; well framed meaningful headings. etc.

(ii) Form Criteria: This category of evaluation parameters or criteria is primarily user-specific concerned mainly with evaluation of the medium. Therefore, form criteria should be applied by looking at and evaluating the medium, design and presentation of the resource. Different people see Internet resources in different forms due to heterogeneous systems. As such, these criteria focus on user-friendly aspects that shall facilitate the user's navigational activity and on ease of use. The form of resources can be evaluated by considering the following criteria:

(a) Ease of Navigation: This refers as to how easy it is to navigate the resource. Whether the links, graphics are clearly identifiable and easily navigable; do print options have convenient layout, and so on. For instance, whether index is available or can be generated automatically. Besides, how effective and efficient search facility is provided.

(b) User Support: Does the site provide for adequate essential instructions; online help; online documentation and other requisite online customer support?

(c) Standards: Whether use of recognised standards such as those of metadata have been used; multimedia formats like MIME used; standard language such as HTML with requisite extensions that all browsers recognise has been used, and so on.

(d) Technology: Appropriate use of technology is another criterion in finding quality of information. Here, one could observe whether appropriate interactivity is available.

(e) Aesthetics: As the term indicates, here one could view as to whether due consideration has been given to the appearance of the site. Good design principles have been followed; look and feel of the site is aesthetically sound; sound balance between colour schemes used, graphics, links and the like.

(iii) Process Criteria: These criteria are mainly concerned with aspects of system evaluation. The resources on the Internet are volatile and likely to change over time and the integrity of Internet resources is dependent on three driving forces - original information provider, the website manager, and the underlying technology. The process criteria need to be applied by considering the processes and systems, which exist to support the information resource. The information, the interface and the system supporting the resource should all be reliable. The processes associated with resources can be evaluated by considering the following criteria:

(a) Information Veracity: Information veracity is basically the work of the information provider. Here, the relevant evaluative questions can be:

Is the information current and up to date?

How durable is the nature of the information?

Is there adequate maintenance of the information content? and so on.

(b) Site Uprightness: The work of the website manager should address issues like regular updation of the site, removing all dead links, referring to corresponding links if an existing URL is dysfunctional and things like that. He should effectively administer and maintain the site so that durability and ongoing maintenance and stability of the resource is ensured.

(c) System Integrity: System integrity being the work of the system administrator, he should focus on issues as to whether technical performance of the resource is acceptable; stability of the system is ensured and necessary measures to maintain the integrity of the system are taken, for instance whether the site is mirrored, and the like.

(iv) Other Key Indicators: The other key indicators that are crucial for critical evaluation of resources include the following:

(a) Resource Suitability: Suitability in terms of –Scope – whether the resource covers the right stuff in right proportion that the user is interested in.

- **Audience:** Intended audience for this source. For instance, to find resources listing the latest research trends in social sciences of interest to medical professionals, you may want to avoid the SOSIG (Social Sciences Gateway on the Net) which will bring up information on this for social science researchers rather than for medical practitioners.
- **Timeliness:** Avoid using undated websites. Always check the date when source was published or the date last updated if it is a website Library catalogues and periodical indexes always indicate the publication date in the bibliographic citation.

Scholarly versus Popular: A scholarly journal is generally one that is published by and for experts and all articles are peer-reviewed that ensures quality of resource. Scholarly sources would usually include: bibliography and footnotes; author's name and academic credentials.

Popular magazines range from highly respected publications such as Scientific American and The Atlantic Monthly, to general interest newsmagazines like Newsweek and US News and World Report. Articles in these publications are usually written by staff writers or freelance journalists and are geared towards general audience. While most magazines adhere to editorial standards, articles do not go through a peer-review process and rarely contain bibliographic citations.

Try to conduct your searches in journal indexes and try narrowing your search by limiting to refereed publications. This will retrieve only scholarly journals matching your search terms. If you do your searches in Web of Science, Current Contents, you will retrieve only scholarly articles since only academic journals are indexed in these databases.

(b) Authority: The author (s) academic credentials are crucial in deciphering the worth of the resource. This aspect has already been discussed earlier. There are reference sources available that list biographical information about authors and scholars.

(c) Other Indicators: Other indicators for quality evaluation include the following:

- **Documentation:** A bibliography, along with footnotes, indicate that the author has consulted other sources and it serves to authenticate the information that he or she is presenting. In websites, expect links or footnotes documenting sources, and referring to additional resources and other viewpoints.
- **Objectivity:** Information content of a resource should be factual, unbiased and written objectively. It should not be a propaganda, non-encouraging advertisements in the website sponsored by a company that advocates a certain philosophy. There are resources such as magazines for libraries. etc. that can be consulted which indicate whether a publication is known to be conservative or progressive, or is affiliated with a particular advocacy group.
- **Primary Versus Secondary Research**: In determining the appropriateness of a resource, it may be helpful to determine whether it is primary research or secondary research. Primary research presents original research methods or findings for the first time. Examples include: journal article, report, or other publication or a newspaper account written by a journalist.

A secondary research does not present new research but rather provides a compilation or evaluation of previously presented material. Examples include: an encyclopaedia entry and entries in most other reference books and textbooks.

(d) Reference Sources: Many reference sources provide evaluative description about various sources such as the following:

- **Book Reviews:** A book review can appear in a journal, magazine or newspaper, which provides a descriptive, evaluative discussion of a recently published book. Reading how others have evaluated a book may help you decide whether to use that book in your research or not. There are a number of indexes you can consult that provide references to book reviews: Book Review Digest (1905-current) available also Online for 1983- current; Book Review Index (1965-)
- **Journal Indexes:** You may also find reviews of books in many journal indexes in a given subject area by searching on the title and/or author of the book.
- **Citation Indexes:** To see the impact a particular source has had on scholarship, you may want to consult a citation index. A citation index lists when and where a work has been cited. The citation indexes are all available in the following database: Web of Science: http://www.webofscience.com; Science Citation Index (1945-present); Social Sciences Citation Index (1970-present); Arts & Humanities Citation Index (1975-present) The citation indexes are available in print, CD's and also online.

(e) Links: The links to and from quality resources to the given site depicts the quality of the resource.

Question Papers

Information Communication Technologies: Applications: MLII-104

December, 2017

Note: Attempt all questions. All questions carry equal marks. Illustrate your answers with suitable examples and diagrams, wherever necessary. Write relevant question number before writing the answer.

Q1.1. Define data structure. Discuss its importance in database design. Explain different types of data structures.

Ans. Refer to Chapter-1, Q.No.- 6, Q.No.-9

Q1.2. Define 'File Organisation' and mention its difference with access method. Explain different access methods.

Ans. Refer to Chapter-1, Q.No.- 8

Q2.1. Describe the procedural model of library house keeping operations. Illustrate the model with reference to analysis of activities for book ordering.

Ans. Refer to Chapter-2, Q.No.- 1, Q.No.-3

Q2.2. Explain the concept of digitisation and name two digital library software available free on Internet. Discuss planning and implementation of digitisation in a library.

Ans. Refer to Chapter-2, Q.No.-18, Q.No.-29, Q.No.-30

Q3.1. Define 'Information and Referral services'. Discuss these services in the context of academic and special libraries. Enumerate different types of table of contents service and describe any three of them.

Ans. Information and Referral Services: Information and Referral Services (IRS) is a generic umbrella service. It is a broad term denoting many similar services. Alerting Services, Bibliographic Services, Reference and Referral Services (that is, excepting document delivery) may be grouped under IRS.

They are aimed at turning potential users into actual users of a library. Or, in converting existing dormant users into active users. In a public library, IRS may take the form of Community Information and Referral Service.

In academic and special libraries, IRS may take the form of Current Awareness Service, Selective Dissemination of Information, Electronic Clipping Service. etc. CAS, SDI, ECS – all these services have one thing in common: Current and recent information is the focus. As they are alerting in nature they are together called Alerting Services. An Alerting Service alerts an individual about some contemporary and current literature or information of relevance to him. Currency and relevancy are important issues. Alerting Services notify, inform, announce, signal, create awareness of, or forewarn the user about nascent, current information as it is generated and released for public consumption.

Such information items need not necessarily be available readily in the library but accessible or otherwise procurable. At times, alerting services also concern themselves with future events, book releases, publications in progress. etc. Alerting services are offered to most customers throughout their membership as a continuous service.

Q3.2. What is a digital reference service? Enumerate their categories depending upon the mode of receiving question and delivering information. Explain their advantages and disadvantages.

Ans. Refer to Chapter-3, Q.No.-28

Q4.1. Define 'Search Engine' and describe briefly its different categories.

Ans. Refer to Chapter-4, Q.No.-12

Different categories of search engines are:

(1) Primary Search Engines [Refer to Chapter-4, Q.No.-15]

(2) Meta Search Engines [Refer to Chapter-4, Q.No.-16]

(3)Subject or Web Directories [Refer to Chapter-4, Q.No.-17]

(4) Hybrid Search Engines [Refer to Chapter-4, Q.No.-18(1)]

(5) Subject Gateways or Subject Portals [Refer to Chapter-4, Q.No.-18(2)]

Q4.2. Describe different Internet-based new library services.

Ans. Refer to Chapter-4, Q.No.-47

Q5.0. write short note on the followings:

(a) Approaches to database

Ans. Refer to Chapter-1, Q.No.-1

(b) Distributed database and its advantages

Ans. Refer to Chapter 1, Q.No.-20

(c) RFID and its usage

Ans. Refer to Chapter-2, Q.No.-1

(d) E-Print archives

Ans. Refer to Chapter-2, Q.No.-29

(e) Document delivery service of NISCAIR

Ans. Refer to Chapter-3, Q.No.-23

❑❑❑

Information Communication Technologies: Applications: MLII-104

June, 2018

Note: Attempt all questions. All questions carry equal marks. Illustrate your answers with suitable examples and diagrams, wherever necessary. Write relevant question number before writing the answer.

Q1.1. What is Relational Database Management System (RDBMS)? Describe the criteria for a database management system (DBMS) to be relational (RDBMS). Explain the characteristics of a 'Relation.

Ans. Refer to Chapter-1, Q.No.-17

Q1.2. What do you understand by information retrieval? Describe the major characteristics that differentiate it from data retrieval. Describe the steps involved in carrying out effective and efficient searches for retrieval of information.

Ans. Refer to Chapter-1, Q.No.-24, Q.No.-26

Q2.1. What is an Open Source Software (OSS)? Discuss the advantages of using OSS for library management. Describe the features of KOHA.

Ans. Refer to Chapter-2, Q.No.-17, 15

Q2.2. Define 'Digitisation and discuss its benefits. Describe the criteria used for selection of materials for digitisation.

Ans. Refer to Chapter-2, Q.No.-18 and Q.No.-19

Q3.1. What do you understand by Electronic Clipping Service (ECS) ? Is it a form of SDI service? Describe the operation of ECS with particular reference to the services provided by DIALOG: Alert services and ISI: Alert Services.

Ans. Refer to Chapter-3, Q.No.-7

Q3.2. What is meant by full text bibliographic databases ? Enumerate any five sources to procure such databases and explain any three of them.

Ans. Refer to Chapter-3, Q.No.-9 and Q.No.-11

Q4.1. What is World Wide Web ? Discuss, its features and working.

Ans. Refer to Chapter-4, Q.No.-30

Q4.2. What is meant by Internet information resources? Describe different categories of e-resources and also the different agencies who publish them. Give examples.

Ans. Refer to Chapter-4, Q.No.-48, 49, 51

Q5.0 Write short note on the followings:

(a) Different levels of database architecture

Ans. Refer to Chapter-1, Q.No.-5

(b) Barcode system

Ans. Barcode is a system of encoding characters by means of a series of parallel bars. This method uses a number of bars (lines) of varying thickness and spacing between them to indicate the desired information. An optical barcode reader can read such bars and convert them into electrical pulses to be processed by a computer. In a barcode-based circulation system accession number of a document is converted into bar-coded form and pasted on the book itself after taking print out of the same. Similarly, bar-coded form of member ID is placed on the member card. A handheld barcode reader is required to translate the barcodes into useful information. These barcodes then acts as pointers to the respective databases. Such a method saves data entry work and eliminates human error in input stage. RFID based circulation is meant for the self-issue and self-return facility in an automated environment. An RFID system comprises three components: a tag, a reader and an antenna. The tag is paper-thin chip, which stores vital bibliographic data. The tag is generally fixed on the inside cover of the corresponding document. RFID reader and antenna are often integrated into patron self-checkout machines or inventory readers. The reader powers the antenna to generate Radio Frequency field to decode information stored on the chip. RFID reader sends information to the central server, which in turn communicates with the library automation software. RFID, apart from self-issue facility, also supports stock verification, theft detection, and identification of misplaced books and inventory counts.

(c) OPAC

Ans. Refer to Chapter-2, Q.No.-13

(d) Modes of document delivery service.

Ans. Refer to Chapter-3, Q.No.-20

(e) List Serv and News Groups

Ans. Refer to Chapter-4, Q.No.-41

❑❑❑

Information Communication Technologies: Applications: MLII-104

December, 2018

Note: Attempt all questions. All questions carry equal marks. Illustrate your answers with suitable examples and diagrams, wherever necessary. Write relevant question number before writing the answer.

Q1.1. Discuss databases from the point of view of library and information science. Discuss its different types by giving examples.

Ans. Refer to Chapter-1, Q.No.-4, 3

Q1.2. Describe the steps involved in developing an effective search strategy. Explain the different methods of searching a database.

Ans. Refer to Chapter-1, Q.No.-25, 26

Q2.1. Describe the functions of computerised serial control module along with its advantages.

Ans. Refer to Chapter-2, Q.No.-1

Q2.2. Enumerate library automation packages of Indian origin. Describe any two of these.

Ans. Refer to Chapter-2, Q. No.- 15

Q3.1. News Filtering Service is an important category of CAS. Discuss the different sources of such services.

Ans. Refer to Chapter-3, Q. No.- 2

Q3.2. Explain the modes of document delivery service. Describe the steps involved in it.

Ans. Refer to Chapter-3, Q.No.-20 and Q.No.-22

Q4.1. Explain the working of a search engine. Enumerate its different categories.

Ans. Refer to Chapter-4, Q.No.-12

Different categories of search engines are:

(1) Primary Search Engines [Refer to Chapter-4, Q.No.-15]

(2) Meta Search Engines [Refer to Chapter-4, Q.No.-16]

(3)Subject or Web Directories [Refer to Chapter-4, Q.No.-17]

(4) Hybrid Search Engines [Refer to Chapter-4, Q.No.-18(1)]

(5) Subject Gateways or Subject Portals [Refer to Chapter-4, Q.No.-18(2)]

Q4.2. Discuss the generic criteria for evaluation of an Internet resource.

Ans. Refer to Chapter-4, Q.No.-58

Q5. Write short note on the followings:

(a) Architecture of a DBMS

Ans. Refer to Chapter-1, Q.No.-14

(b) Organising digital image

Ans. Refer to Chapter-2, Q.No.-28

(c) Copyright and licensing issues in Bibliographic full text services

Ans. Refer to Chapter-3, Q.No.-18

(d) XML

Ans. Refer to Chapter-4, Q.No.-37

(e) Web-based user education

Ans. Refer to Chapter-4, Q.No.- 47

❑❑❑

Information Communication Technologies: Applications: MLII-104

June, 2019

Note: Attempt all questions. All questions carry equal marks. Illustrate your answers with suitable examples and diagrams, wherever necessary. Write relevant question number before writing the answer.

Q1.1. What is a DBMS? Discuss its need and purpose. Describe its evolution in terms of generations.

Ans. Refer to Chapter-1, Q.No.-10, Q.No.-12

Q1.2. What are data models? Enumerate their various types, describing any two of them.

Ans. Refer to Chapter-1, Q.No.-16

Q2.1. Discuss the activities of an automated circulation system.

Ans. Refer to Chapter-2, Q.No.-10

Q2.2. Explain the criteria for evaluation of a library automation software.

Ans. Refer to Chapter-2, Q.No.-16

Q3.1. Discuss the modes of providing digital reference service.

Ans. Refer to Chapter-3, Q.No.-28

Q3.2. Describe briefly the different methods of accessing the Internet.

Ans. Refer to Chapter-4, Q.No.-5

Q4.1. Explain the different categories of search engines.

Ans. Different categories of search engines are:

(1) Primary Search Engines [Refer to Chapter-4, Q.No.-15]

(2) Meta Search Engines [Refer to Chapter-4, Q.No.-16]

(3)Subject or Web Directories [Refer to Chapter-4, Q.No.-17]

(4) Hybrid Search Engines [Refer to Chapter-4, Q.No.-18(1)]

(5) Subject Gateways or Subject Portals [Refer to Chapter-4, Q.No.-18(2)]

Q4.2. Enumerate the different categories of Internet-based library services. Explain Internet-based new library services.

Ans. Refer to Chapter-4, Q.No.-47

Q5.0. Write short note on the followings:

(a) Normalisation of Relations

Ans. Refer to Chapter-1, Q.No.-18

(b) AI and Expert Systems

Ans. Refer to Chapter-1, Q.No.-22

(c) NewGenLib Software

Ans. Refer to Chapter-2, Q.No.-15

(d) ISDN

Ans. Refer to Chapter-4, Q.No.-5

(e) Electronic Document Delivery Service

Ans. Refer to Chapter-3, Q.No.-21

❑❑❑

Information Communication Technologies: Applications: MLII-104

December, 2019

Note: Attempt all questions. All questions carry equal marks. Illustrate your answers with suitable examples and diagrams, wherever necessary. Write relevant question number before writing the answer.

Q1. What do you understand by 'File Organisation' and 'Access Methods'? Discuss different access methods applied to file organisation.

Ans. Refer to Chapter-1, Q.No.-8

Or

Discuss the functional requirements that a library automation software package should satisfy.

Ans. Refer to Chapter-2, Q.No.-13

Q2. Define digitisation and explain its need. Discuss the steps involved in its planning and implementation.

Ans. Refer to Chapter-2, Q.No.-19, 30

Or

Discuss the functions of a computerised serial control module stating its advantages.

Ans. Refer to Chapter-2, Q.No.-1

Q3. Explain the importance of news alerting service for different user groups. Describe different sources for news-based services in Internet Environment.

Ans. Refer to Chapter-3, Q.No.-2

Or

Explain the various modes of document delivery service. Discuss copyright issues involved in it and services of copyright facilitators.

Ans. Refer to Chapter-3, Q.No.-20, 25

Q4. What are protocols? Describe TCP/IP and HTTP protocols and their working.

Ans. Refer to Chapter-4, Q.No.-8

Or

What do you understand by Internet Security? Enumerate

the mechanisms used in this regard. Explain any two.

Ans. The security of computer and data transmitted on Internet is recognised as having a major threat. In fact, threat to security is the biggest hurdle to expansion of e-commerce on the Internet. Internet security is recognised as methods used by an organisation to protect its institutional network from intrusion. A system administrator has to ensure that intruders or hackers do not reach and manipulate data kept on the servers. The best way to keep an intruder from entering the network is to provide a security wall between the intruder and the institutional network. Most often, an intruder enters the network through a software programme (such as a virus, Trojan horse or a worm) or through a direct connection. Methods such as firewalls, data encryption and user authentication are used to check a hacker from entering the network.

Now, Refer to Chapter-4, Q.No.-10

Q5. Write short notes on any three of the following (in about 300 words each):

(a) Normalisation of relations

Ans. Refer to Chapter-1, Q.No.-18

(b) Memory hierarchy

Ans. Refer to Chapter-1, Q.No.-7 (a)

(c) Digital reference service

Ans. Refer to Chapter-3, Q.No.-28

(d) Copyright issues in DDS

Ans. Refer to Chapter-3, Q.No.-18

(e) Proxy servers

Ans. Refer to Chapter-4, Q.No.-10 (3)

❑❑❑

Wondering who is Gullybaba?

© Gullybaba is a combination of two significant words '**Gully**' & '**Baba**'. The word 'Gully' comes from the ancient game played in Rural India–**Tip cat.** In Hindi, we call it **Gully Danda** (गुल्ली डंडा) which is a great **symbol of Focus & Fitness.**

The word 'Baba' stands for **Respect & Honour**. And these are the fundamental parameters for achieving success. **Focus & Fitness** are required to help one go a long way in life. This is all about achieving excellence in education and giving respect & honour to everyone, and thus, the name 'Gullybaba'.

To know more about why name GullyBaba visit: **GullyBaba.com/why-name-gullybaba.html**

NOTES

NOTES

www.ingramcontent.com/pod-product-compliance
Ingram Content Group UK Ltd.
Pitfield, Milton Keynes, MK11 3LW, UK
UKHW021709190726
13853UKWH00001B/472